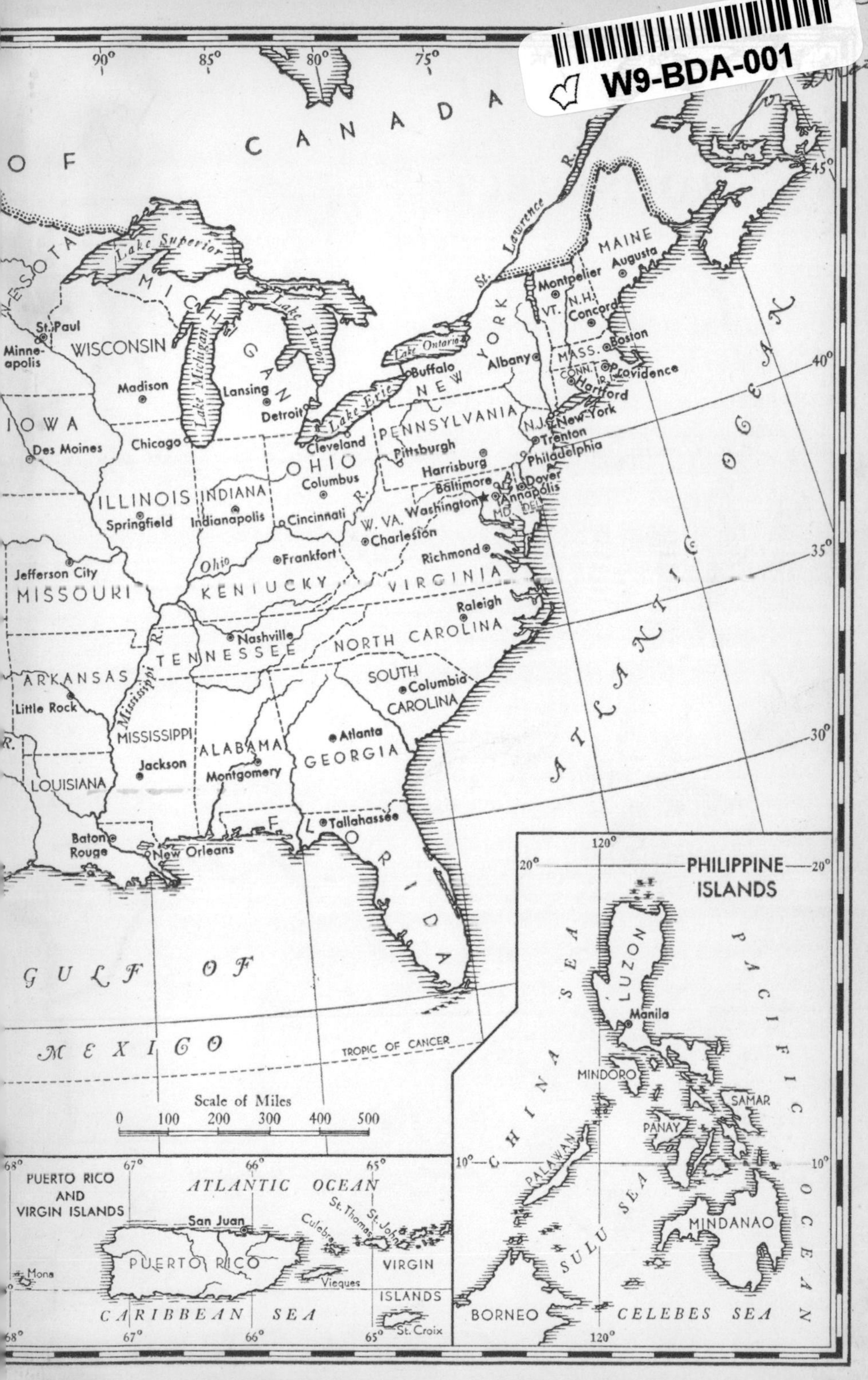
W9-BDA-001
CANADA
St. Lawrence R.
Lake Superior
Lake Michigan
Lake Huron
Lake Ontario
Lake Erie
MICHIGAN
WISCONSIN
St. Paul
Minneapolis
Madison
Lansing
Detroit
IOWA
Des Moines
Chicago
ILLINOIS
Springfield
INDIANA
Indianapolis
OHIO
Columbus
Cleveland
Cincinnati
NEW YORK
Buffalo
Albany
PENNSYLVANIA
Pittsburgh
Harrisburg
Philadelphia
MAINE
Augusta
VT.
Montpelier
N.H.
Concord
MASS.
Boston
CONN.
R.I.
Providence
Hartford
New York
N.J.
Trenton
Dover
Baltimore
Annapolis
Washington
MD.
DEL.
W. VA.
Charleston
Richmond
VIRGINIA
KENTUCKY
Frankfort
Ohio
Jefferson City
MISSOURI
Mississippi R.
TENNESSEE
Nashville
NORTH CAROLINA
Raleigh
SOUTH CAROLINA
Columbia
ARKANSAS
Little Rock
MISSISSIPPI
Jackson
ALABAMA
Montgomery
GEORGIA
Atlanta
LOUISIANA
Baton Rouge
New Orleans
FLORIDA
Tallahassee
ATLANTIC OCEAN
GULF OF MEXICO
TROPIC OF CANCER
Scale of Miles
0 100 200 300 400 500
PHILIPPINE ISLANDS
LUZON
Manila
MINDORO
SAMAR
PANAY
PALAWAN
MINDANAO
CHINA SEA
SULU SEA
PACIFIC OCEAN
BORNEO
CELEBES SEA
PUERTO RICO AND VIRGIN ISLANDS
ATLANTIC OCEAN
San Juan
PUERTO RICO
Mona
Culebra
St. Thomas
St. John
Vieques
VIRGIN ISLANDS
St. Croix
CARIBBEAN SEA

ROOSEVELT TO ROOSEVELT

Roosevelt to Roosevelt

THE UNITED STATES IN THE TWENTIETH CENTURY

BY

DWIGHT LOWELL DUMOND

Associate Professor of History,
University of Michigan

NEW YORK
HENRY HOLT AND COMPANY

PRINTED IN THE
UNITED STATES OF AMERICA

PREFACE

The author makes no apologies in presenting this book for the use of college students, being perfectly aware of the difficulties inherent in an attempt to interpret the events of one's own generation. The progress of research will change much of what is here written down. Errors of fact no doubt will be discovered. The views of other men will not coincide with all the interpretations. The author hopes, however, that it will prove useful for the study of Recent United States History.

Students should read widely along the lines of their own particular interests. The many stimulating interpretations listed in the bibliography will furnish additional data for their consideration and preclude the possibility of a uniform pattern of thought—a result greatly to be desired.

D. L. D.

Ann Arbor, Michigan
September, 1936.

CONTENTS

CHAPTER I

THE HERITAGE OF TWENTIETH-CENTURY AMERICANS

The South

The turn of the century opened a new era in the history of the United States. The westward movement was complete. The spirit of imperialism had been satiated, finally, by the acquisition of our island possessions in the Caribbean and the Pacific. Boundary disputes with Canada and Mexico, the interminable search for a satisfactory land policy, herding of Indians into reservations, the fratricidal contest over human bondage—all these problems of national expansion had been disposed of, however unsatisfactory the disposition might have been in many respects. The people of the United States were a nation, smugly satisfied with their achievements, glorying in their strength and, for the most part, tragically unaware of the unsolved problems created by the blunderings of past generations.

The veterans of the Union armies of the Civil War had finally come into their own and were wielding a power in the nation far beyond their numerical strength. They were enjoying the reward of earlier sacrifice at the expense of the public treasury, and the glory that was theirs shone too brightly for most people to see the stark realities of a great national tragedy. We had freed the slaves, given them civil equality with the whites, and saved the Union from dismemberment; but the superficial attempt to elevate the Negro in the South to social and political equality with the whites had been abandoned amid a wreckage of social disorganization and economic chaos. The twentieth-century South was free from the odious sin of slavery only to bear the curse of social and racial cleavages with their hideous consequences of lynchings, political demagogues, and blind party allegiance. Reconstruction did not end in 1876. It did not, in fact, begin until the nineties.

The Old South had excelled in facilities for higher education. It had made exceptional progress in establishing a common school system under the handicap of sparsity of population. The war wiped out endowments, dispersed faculties, impoverished state and local governments. Carpet-bag rule added the threat of mixed schools, and a generation of whites grew up with precious little formal education, combining ignorance, poverty and indifference in resistance to human progress. The great contributions of men like Curry and Aycock and of Washington to the establishment of correct social attitudes and of the Peabody and Slater funds in training a corps of teachers can not be ignored; but years passed and the new century was well under way before the task of building a dual school system was begun in earnest. Poverty still casts a blight over wide areas. Illiteracy and near illiteracy remain to plague us in the solution of new social problems.

The Old South also had a fixed relationship between the two races. Its merits and deficiencies are fairly well established but not germane to our present problems. It may be that a slow transition from the status of slavery to that of freedom could have been arranged had reason rather than emotion prevailed; but emancipation did not come as the consequence of natural evolution or of social planning. It was violent, forced, and without regard to the creation of new and difficult problems. The shock of the social upheaval produced by this forced rearrangement of status, both of groups and individuals, continued to reverberate for generations. It carried over into the new century with a horrible record of lynchings and forced a new approach to an old problem. Interracial committees finally replaced Klan Conclaves with the promise of a new and happier day.

The Civil War had disrupted the plantation system, dispossessed many old families of their estates and put at an end the system of forced labor in agriculture. New owners of large land holdings replaced the old. Forced labor gave way to the crop rental system. The expensive factorage system by which slave owners had financed their operations was diffused into a new crop *lien* system. The country merchant replaced the merchant prince of exporting centers; but the laborer in the cotton fields continued to pay his annual tribute to one crop culture, a vicious credit system, and absentee landlords. His standard of living scarcely equalled that of the former slave. His very existence required the combined labors of his entire family.

The emancipation philosophy that every man was entitled to the products of his own labor fared little better with the march of time than the great delusion of "forty acres and a mule." Child labor was a sorry substitute for the pre-war promise of a better day. It fastened its ugly tentacles deep in the soil of the great agricultural states of the South and West and, under the protecting mantle of agrarian individualism, spread to the new industrial units of the Piedmont Crescent. There it remained to take its annual toll of stunted bodies and blighted souls, a direct challenge to twentieth-century America's scale of human values.

The Old South had enjoyed the benefits of a vigorous two party rivalry. Blessed with an economic system which encouraged participation in public affairs either as a profession or as an avocation, that section had furnished the nation with a succession of distinguished statesmen. Thomas Jefferson, James Monroe, John Taylor, and Spencer Roane of Virginia, John Calhoun of South Carolina, Henry Clay of Kentucky, Andrew Jackson of Tennessee, Alexander Stephens, Howell Cobb and Robert Toombs of Georgia, and Jefferson Davis of Mississippi, are names to conjure with in that long space of agrarian control in national affairs. Staunch defenders, for the most part, of their own section's peculiar institutions, they also furnished intellectual leadership for parties and political coalitions national in scope. If there were questions of national interest which gave them national and international prominence, it is also true that they reached that high estate by the rough road of the local hustings. Each state had its own peculiar social and economic problems aligning men one against another into parties for control of state and local governments. There was a healthy interest in public affairs which sent men of ability to governorships and the state legislatures. The Civil War period changed the entire pattern of political organization. Seward and others had hoped to seize the opportunity offered by the disruption of the Whig party after 1852 to extend the Republican party organization throughout the South. It was a golden opportunity for abolitionists to reach into the southern states with their antislavery agitation. Fear of that was at least a contributory factor to the South's stroke for independence. The first steps in the reorganization of state governments under Lincoln's and Johnson's proclamations gave promise of continuing the two party system along the lines of former cleavages in the white population as modified by events of the war period. It was then that Congressional leaders of the Republican party, through ignorance of the human elements involved or ineptitude, threw precedents to the winds and sought to extend and perpetuate their control of the South, and through it, of the nation by enfranchising the former slaves and corralling them into the fold. Honest fear in the North that the Negro could be protected in his new civil liberties in no other way was an important factor in the decision. Slowly at first and then more rapidly as the Klan and Union League swung into action, the southern whites withdrew from the Republican party, closed their ranks and thereafter scorned everything and everybody tainted with Republicanism. There were threats, at times serious, to the Solid South thus created; but the century closed with that section, as Congressional Reconstruction left it, cursed with blind allegiance to a one party system and a perfect breeding ground for political demagoguery of every sort. Political preferment fell to those who questioned not or, questioning, remained discreetly silent. Deprived of their natural allies in the great agricultural states of the Middle West, who just as blindly voted for the opposing party on the basis of ancient prejudices, southern agrarians had to be content within a minority party and seldom sat at the council table of the nation.

Neither was the nation's loss the Negro's gain. One device after another was perfected in most of the southern states to thwart the plain intentions of the Fifteenth Amendment and the enforcing act. They had no choice if even a semblance of honest government was to be maintained. The Supreme Court (*United States* v. *Cruikshank*) decided that neither the Amendment nor the enforcing act contained a positive grant of the franchise; that federal courts could not intervene unless disfranchisement arose by action of a state and then only if the disfranchising action were based on race, color, or previous conditions of servitude. Deprived of recourse except in state courts, faced with the administration of literacy tests by hostile election judges, poll tax hurdles and long lists of disqualifying crimes, and unwilling to endanger personal connections by impolitic action, the natural leaders of the Negro race abandoned the thankless task of arousing their people from lethargy and despair. Individuals voted occasionally in urban communities, seldom in the rural districts and for the most part only when dragged into the political picture by the importunities of unscrupulous whites engaged in factional strife. The hierarchy of politicians in the national Republican party continued to maintain skeleton organizations even in the Black Belt as a convenience in the distribution of patronage, and because Black and Tan delegations to national conventions were always an asset to those in control of the party machinery.

The West

The Civil War era likewise left its scar upon the Great Valley and the West. Three distinct reversals of traditional governmental policies vitally affected that region. It was and, for the most part, remained an agricultural area. The contest between an agrarian economy and an industrial economy is as old as civilization. The two systems and the political philosophies they produce scarcely can be reconciled. The agrarian interests of the South and West had largely controlled the legislative and executive departments of the national government before the Civil War. They had suffered some defeats in the early years of the republic but had recovered and were in command of the situation when the slavery controversy disrupted their party in 1860. The war had not progressed very far when Congress came under the control of the old Whig element of the Republican party, which revived, as war measures, its pet tariff and banking policies. Tariff walls erected for the protection of new war industries remained and were increased and extended until the country became, if not a closed market, certainly a very privileged one for all classes of manufacturing enterprise. The farmers of the great plains, unlike those of the Ohio Valley, became producers of staple crops. They learned by experience the nature of the cotton planter's grievances. Wheat was not as sensitive to world price fluctuations as cotton, but an exportable surplus—and there always has been one—destroyed the efficacy of tariffs and depressed prices in the domestic market to world price levels.

The banking act of 1862 had its inception in the desire to facilitate the sale of government bonds. It established a national banking system, designed to promote commerce and industry, but with little to offer agrarians in the way of easy, long term credits or flexible currency. Congress followed with the 1865 act taxing notes emissions of state banks out of existence. State banks did not recover from the blow thus dealt until the widespread use of personal checks gave them a new lease on life. Meanwhile, the agrarians, whose money income depended upon the prices received for what they produced, suffered from a contracting per capita volume of currency. They had assumed heavy obligations during the period of war inflation, only to find those same obligations increased relative to their ability to pay. Finally, in the sphere of fiscal policies, the war time Congresses had authorized the issue of fiat money to the amount of nearly $500,000,000. The question of its retirement in the post-war period was not a mere academic one. Retirement meant further price deflation and the West opposed it. Forced, therefore, to sell in the world market and buy in a closed market, to adjust his financial necessities to a new banking system and to yield to the usurious interest rates of eastern money lenders, the western farmer had little cause to rejoice over the changed government policies. Nevertheless, voting the Republican ticket became a habit. The great anti slavery impulse had come out of the Ohio Valley. A Republican Congress had passed a free homestead law in 1862. Thus was the original strength of the party in that section created. It survived by tradition.

Free homesteads, the long-cherished hope of frontiersmen, were not an unmixed blessing. The liberal land donation policy which made possible free homesteads, also bequeathed imperial tracts to the railroad promoters and eased the path of the land speculator and exploiter of natural resources. State and local governments made their contribution, in cash and accumulated debts to railroad building, and in zealous encouragement to prospective immigrants. Expansion and exploitation were unrestrained. Hundreds of millions of dollars of public funds were poured, directly or indirectly, into the building of the railroads, without a single safeguard for the public interest. The government did not even receive a minority share in their ownership, much less insist upon a previous recognition of the principle of regulation or control. Unscrupulous promoters levied ruinous tribute upon communities the railroads were built to serve. They corrupted legislatures and courts. They wrecked the financial structure of their own enterprises in the mad, competitive struggle for private gain.

Equal lack of foresight prevailed in the disposition of the great national forest areas. Settlers had long been notoriously destructive of timber resources in their haste to bring the soil under cultivation, and little concern was felt when the timber barons undertook to exploit remaining areas on an industrial basis for profit. The devastation was complete in the upper Mississippi Valley and Great Lakes region by the turn of the century. Millions of acres of marginal and submarginal agricultural land had been abandoned to forest fires, soil erosion and the jetsam population of the lumber camps—wreckage left behind by an impulsive people, heedless of their children's heritage.

More far-reaching in its ultimate consequences perhaps than any other public policy was the startling rapidity with which the public lands were transferred to private ownership during this period. The Homestead Act of 1862, the encouragement of foreign immigration and the post-war depression combined to promote the final and most extensive phase of the westward movement. Four and one-half million acres of land had been entered under the Homestead Act within three years after the close of the war, and more than nineteen million acres before 1880. Foreign immigration mounted steadily until a total of fourteen million people came into the country between Lincoln's election and the Spanish-American War. Eleven new western states were admitted to the union during the same period, leaving New Mexico, Arizona, Oklahoma, and Alaska the only remaining continental territories.

Industrial East

How many millions of people, weary of the restraints and inequalities of older sections or revolting against the numerous tyrannies of Europe, had found a haven in the boundless West will never be known. We shall never be able, probably, to assign to each of the impelling motives in migration of people its relative importance. Certain it is, however, that the lure of the West offered an amazingly simple solution to many of life's problems. It carried the nation through periods of unemployment and economic distress. It drained away from the industrial East both the incompetents and the natural leaders of labor. It made possible an uncritical development of industrial life because the solution of social problems thus created did not keep pace with material and technical progress. Discontented laborers escaped to the frontier and their places were filled by immigrants. Thus industry paid neither the cost of rearing its labor nor of supporting its derelicts. Little wonder, therefore, that industry, wealth and population should have shown such phenomenal growth in the period following the Civil War. No government ever dispensed its wealth of natural resources more liberally, no people ever exploited them more recklessly, and no nation ever received a more generous gift of mature men and women for industrial exploitation.

The population of the United States more than doubled during this period, reaching a total of approximately seventy-six million by 1900. The increase was not all in the West. In fact, the combined population of seven of the new states is still less than that of Indiana. It was a period of rapid industrial development and urban growth. After the eighteen seventies immigrants, for the most part, came from the Latin and Slavic nations of Europe and furnished the labor for factories, transportation and mining enterprises. They were joined by millions of native men and women, and the cities grew apace. Together they constituted the human resources for industrial exploitation.

Those who had raised their voices in defense of human bondage as well as some who inveighed against it, notably Wendell Phillips, had hurled severe indictments against the *Northern* industrial system. The Southern slaveholder could not discharge his laborers when the cotton crop failed or could not be sold at a profit and then take them back again when profitable operations could be resumed. Nor could he turn them out to starve when injury, sickness, old age made them unfit for productive labor. The maintenance of his laborers at all times and under all conditions was a fixed charge against the owner. That was not true in the Northern industrial system. Child labor, sweatshops, hazardous and unhealthy working conditions, a competitive labor market, constantly recurring and sudden periods of unemployment, long hours, and distress in sickness and old age combined to form an unsavory social pattern. These were the things from which men had fled to the frontier. They continued throughout the nineteenth century because the moral force of the nation was exhausted in the contest over bond slavery, because the acquisitive instinct was so universally predominant after the war, and because such a large proportion of the laboring class was of foreign origin. It was not until the twentieth century that there appeared in the nation a group of men who, in social consciousness, moral enthusiasm or intelligence were comparable to those who initiated and carried through the crusade against slavery. Laboring men were unable to organize effectively or, having organized, to accomplish much in the way of reform for a variety of reasons. Individual independence was still a prominent characteristic of American life. The most aggressive and capable among them were able to rise from the ranks into supervisory or managerial positions. A diversity of racial origins, languages and living standards militated against group solidarity. Lacking intelligent leadership, influenced by foreign radicalism and faced by employer-controlled governmental agencies, they struck out blindly against intolerable conditions in a riot of mob violence, death and destruction.

Decades came and went and we became the greatest industrial nation in the world without a single achievement in the direction of economic security for the laboring classes or machinery for the elimination of industrial conflicts. Corporations had their technical laboratories and their expensive research departments designed to maintain and increase profits; but not even a sense of social responsibility, much less established formulas for adjusting their businesses to human relationships. Labor succeeded in forming craft organizations, a part of which were loosely joined in the American Federation of Labor; but it became progressively more representative of labor's aristocracy. Non-technical laborers, especially the Negroes, the agricultural laborers and the servant groups remained unorganized and unrepresented. Nor did organized labor display any inclination or ability to assume responsibilities commensurate with the rights and privileges it sought to establish. Warfare continued year after year and was viewed by society as the inescapable growing pains of an industrial system. There was no general acceptance of the theory that strikes were but surface indications of underlying maladjustments in the economic and social system. Society was content, therefore, to see each violent outbreak adjusted as quickly as possible or summarily suppressed, seeking only to keep the total inconvenience and property loss at a minimum.

In the realm of government it is pertinent to remember that our chief concern from the time of founding of the Republic had been to protect minorities against the unrestrained will of majorities. John Adams and the Federalists generally had arranged an elaborate system of checks and balances in the federal system. The Jeffersonians had preached the doctrine of decentralization on the theory that the happiness of the greatest number could best be secured by retaining wide powers in local and state governments. Calhoun, cognizant of the power of a permanent majority to control the judicial as well as the legislative and administrative branches of the government, had devised a scheme for placing restraining powers in the hands of minorities for whose benefit limitations had been imposed. The Federalists were willing to trust their fortunes to the judgment of the Supreme Court. The Civil War closed the half century between these contending political philosophies. It left us with the written Constitution as a fundamental law and the Supreme Court as the final judge of the powers of Congress and the several state legislatures. The ultimate recourse of a majority checked by the Court remained, as always, in constitutional amendments. The power of amendment, however, was not exercised again for nearly a half century.

Meanwhile, the Fourteenth Amendment turned out to be something quite different than was intended at the time of its adoption. Instead of being a safeguard for the rights of the Negro it became, by virtue of successive Supreme Court decisions, a charter of liberties for a new creature of the law: corporations. The point is that this amendment to the fundamental law did not transfer powers from the state governments to the Congress of the United States. It circumscribed and narrowed the powers of the state legislatures without adding to the powers of Congress, thus creating a broad immunity to corporations from regulation by either agency. The federal government having no police powers could not go beyond the regulation of interstate commerce in its effort to remedy abuses in production. The states retained the power to charter corporations engaged in interstate commerce and certain states were willing to enact extremely lax corporation laws for the sake of revenue. On the other hand, the states could not interfere with interstate commerce, nor go beyond definite limits in regulating corporate practices because of the "due process" clause of the Fourteenth Amendment. Thus it was that when society became conscious of its responsibilities for protecting human rights in our new industrial society, it found property rights firmly entrenched behind a clause written into the fundamental law to protect the rescued victims of an earlier exploitation. The amendment could not have been adopted had not southern states been compelled to ratify it in order to regain representation in Congress; and it is safe to assume that the agrarian West and South would never have approved it had the purpose of its framers been known and the Negro question been absent. The men who framed the amendment purposely concealed their objective. The revelation of how and why it was done was not made by Roscoe Conkling until 1882. The Supreme Court did not accept all of its implications as a basis for reinterpretation of the Fourteenth Amendment until 1889. The full effects of the change did not appear until the twentieth century.

Many things, therefore, contributed to the unprecedented industrial development of the country during this period: (1) the expansion of agriculture into the region west of the Mississippi, affording a rich market for all kinds of artifacts; (2) the rich reservoir of previously untouched natural resources suddenly brought into use by technical improvements and scientific discoveries; (3) a super-abundance of labor provided by unrestricted immigration and the release of agricultural laborers by improved farm machinery; (4) freedom from restrictive legislation due to the prevailing doctrine of *laissez faire* and the protecting mantle of the Constitution as interpreted by a friendly judiciary.

This combination of forces was destined to present twentieth-century America with a magnificent accumulation of material wealth and an appalling array of social and economic perplexities. Agriculture expanded more rapidly than our ability to provide adequate means for consumption and was forced to rely upon foreign markets which were neither stable nor permanent. Immigrants flowed in faster than the nation could assimilate them, until business men and agrarians alike mistrusted the safety of our Anglo-Saxon traditions. Technical progress opened new fields of employment, but likewise lessened the necessity for human labor, destroyed the ancient skills and shortened the life span of productive endeavor. *Laissez faire* brought us to the low estate of an industrial feudalism which in some respects was less compatible with the liberties of men than the landed feudalism of the Middle Ages. Industrial expansion created a surplus of manufactured goods for sale in world markets at a time when there was a surfeit of agricultural products for export and a firmly established system of protective tariffs. It drew men and women from the soil into great metropolitan districts, increasing the hazards of economic depressions, and created such a multitude of material comforts that the accumulation of wealth became a major objective in life. It increased production to the point where the literacy and intelligence of the masses was essential to the functioning of our economic system.

Parties and Public Policies

Many forces in operation during this period tended to produce a marked change in the administration of public affairs. That the government has never been as faithfully administered in all departments as honorable men desire is a simple historical fact. We are prone to forget, however, that the term "the people" is an historical fiction. Society is made up of individuals with diverse interests, ideas and ideals. They group themselves into political parties seeking control of the agencies of government in order to direct its policies along the lines of their own peculiar philosophies; or they form organizations for the purpose of influencing governmental policies through pressure politics and propaganda. Retention of wide powers in local and state governments tends to minimize the clash of such rival groups. Centralization of powers in the federal government tends to increase it, and centralization went on at a terrific rate after the close of the Civil War. Pressure groups likewise increased in number and influence, notably the Grange, the Grand Army of the Republic and the American Federation of Labor. This combination of circumstances made it increasingly difficult for political parties to write their platforms and choose their candidates. They cultivated the art of ambiguity, wrote platforms of meaningless generalities, spoke the sort of platitudes that sounded well in country stores and barber shops, and chose candidates who had never been identified with public questions in such a way as to make enemies. They raised false issues to confuse the voter and act as a smoke screen for the deficiencies of their candidates and the corruption of their administration. The strength and stability of the government builded upon the affection of the people and a widespread appreciation of the justice and righteousness of its acts was slowly undermined. Hatreds engendered by the Civil War created a blind party allegiance which lived on in families for generations. Political parties paid tribute to it by drafting men for public office whose sole qualification was an honorable record of service in the army of their section. The power of accumulated wealth increased until it could influence legislatures; the United States Senate was spoken of as a millionaires club; and extra-legal or *liaison* officials known as "bosses" came into being. The free lance newspaper editor who knew no superior all but disappeared, abandoning public opinion to the mercies of unintelligent and, ofttimes, intellectually dishonest editorial hack writers. Official corruption, spreading through all branches of the public service, was condoned by many, regarded with helpless alarm by others, and utterly disregarded by the public at large. Individuals who betrayed the public trust were seldom punished. Parties suffered no more than temporary embarrassment. Nothing was done to strike at the roots of a system which was destined to threaten the very existence of popular government itself. The mere misappropriation of public funds, bad as it was, belongs to the history of that period and is of little concern to us here; but the forces which alter civilizations are very subtle and very deep. The roots of impulses which give character to national life reach back through many generations. The fact that men should seek high official positions fifty years ago for no other purpose than to be able to sell the prestige thus gained for private gain and do so without fear of condemnation and disgrace—is evidence of a diseased body politic pregnant with meaning to the twentieth century.

The incompetence of Congress to deal with social and economic questions on any other basis than that of political expediency was clearly demonstrated. Reconstruction legislation took its character from the desire to insure Republican electoral votes from the southern states and congressional interference was terminated only because of the growing displeasure of northern voters. It was politics which reduced the House of Representatives to an inferior position in the government and which forestalled the adoption of an adequate civil service system. But overshadowing all else was the brazen fashion in which Congress built up an elaborate system of Civil War pensions, whereby thousands who had no honest claim for support against the government and thousands more who had no need for it received their monthly government dole. Pension agents infested the land and ageing veterans became choice meal tickets for thousands of young women who were destined to constitute a formidable list of pensioners after most veterans had answered the final roll call. Patriotism was thus tainted with materialism and an unwise precedent established for future generations. It would have required a courageous Congress, indeed, to have restricted financial aid to those suffering from service disabilities; but Congress had no desire to be courageous. War veterans and their families represented such a considerable group as to hold the balance of power in all closely contested elections. The Republican party could hardly have won a presidential election during the period against a hostile G. A. R. Pensions for veterans, their widows and dependents carried on the war tradition after waving the bloody shirt lost its appeal. Moreover liberal pensions relieved that party of the embarrassing treasury surpluses accruing from high tariff rates. Tariffs represented everything but a scientific adjustment of the cost of production at home and abroad. They probably did little to protect the American workingman's standard of living because immigration always provided a surplus of cheap, competitive labor; but they were defended on that ground. They did, however, afford the manufacturer a wide margin of profit and the Republican party made high tariffs its own special province. The Democratic party ceased to be a unit for free trade and repudiated Cleveland when he advocated lower tariff rates and a correction of pension abuses. The tariff and pensions, therefore, supplemented each other as a source of profit to two powerful groups. Never before had the government so openly taken money from the consumer for the benefit of favored classes in society. It presaged the day when the taxing power was to be used frankly for the purpose of redistributing wealth as a new form of social control.

The large industrialists were not the only privileged group which directed governmental policies through the agency of the Republican party, with enough support from Bourbon Democrats to offset agrarian defections in the West. The financiers—bankers, brokers, commission men—were their faithful allies. They stood for "sound money," meaning a circulating medium which retained a fixed value in terms of gold irrespective of how much havoc it wrought by a fluctuating purchasing power. Specifically, they supported the gold standard as opposed to bimetallism and for the retirement of all fiat money. They were not as consistently successful in their battles with the agrarian West, but had little cause for complaint. They prevented the issuance of more greenbacks at the expense of retaining permanently as a part of the currency $346,681,000 of those already in circulation. They passed the Resumption Act in 1875 establishing the value of greenbacks at a parity with gold. They established the national banking system, with government bonds as the basis for bank note issues and drove the bank notes of state banks out of circulation. They prevented the restoration of free coinage of silver, but not the limited purchase of silver, for coinage by the treasury department. They did nothing, and prevented anything from being done, to establish a flexible or adequate currency system, to provide agricultural credits at manageable rates, or to safeguard prices and values against periods of ruinous deflation.

Associated with these two groups were the railway builders and promoters. Sharing abundantly in the reckless generosity of the government, they resisted every effort at regulation or control. Billions in watered stock were added needlessly to the capital structure of the railway systems necessitating exorbitant rates to the public and seriously handicapping the roads later in their struggle with automotive competition. Roads were built into regions for no other reason than the profits of construction. Parallel lines were built between distant terminals, and the losses occurring from competitive rates on through traffic balanced by discrimination against helpless shippers, mostly farmers, from intermediate points. These and other abuses indicate the extent to which railroads were built and operated for decades purely as private enterprises for profit. Money extorted from the public was used to corrupt their state and national governments in resistance to regulation. They suffered a temporary reverse with the enactment of the state Granger laws in the seventies, but recovered their independence when the Supreme Court, in 1886, reversed its former principle and limited the state legislatures to control of intrastate commerce. They suffered an apparent defeat with the enactment by Congress in 1887 of the Interstate Commerce Act, but again the Supreme Court came to their rescue, and the century came to a close without a really worth-while accomplishment in the direction of railroad regulation. The questions of determining valuations as a basis for rate fixing, of top-heavy financial structures, of speculative banker control, of consolidations in the interest of economy and public service, and of possible government ownership, were passed on for a later generation to ponder over at a time when new economic developments tremendously complicated the whole question of transportation. Finance, manufacturing and transportation, closely knit together by economic forces and controlled by interlocking directorates, creating billions of intangible wealth based upon nothing more secure than probable earning power, exploiting the nation's natural resources, building the nation's highways, controlling its circulating medium and dictating its fiscal policies; all in the interest of private gain and to the end of a vast concentration of accumulated wealth more powerful than political parties, more powerful in its indirect influences than Congress—that was the great American achievement of the late nineteenth century. America's achievement was the achievement of the Republican party by its own admission. Thus did the party's philosophy and interests change. It had risen to power as the party of protest. In its inception, it was the party of youth and idealism. It ventured greatly, even war, in its crusade against property rights, established privilege and class, then serenely secure in the strength of the Democratic party and the majesty of the fundamental law. It had championed the cause of human rights in the name of the "higher law," threatening Courts and Constitution alike. Three decades later the situation was completely reversed, and the party both represented and defended accumulated wealth, established privilege, government by precedent rather than impulse, the sacredness of the Constitution and the infallibility of Supreme Court decisions.

Opposition to this composite edifice of economic and political power did not come from the Democratic party as such. That party had its Tildens, its Clevelands, and its Gormans, conservative by instinct and association. Bourbons were in control, for the most part, in the southern states and the party was, even more than the Republicans, a congeries of contradictions. The only opposition which succeeded in organizing and seriously threatening the capitalistic control of the government came from the agrarian West and it also represented a propertied interest. Populism did not offer much except the substitution of the principles of an agrarian economy in the formulation of governmental policies for those of an industrial economy. It would certainly have utilized its power to aid the farmers as the industrialists had used theirs to aid business and manufacturing. It would have lowered the tariff rates, brought the railroads under strict supervision or public ownership, revised the currency and banking systems and, perhaps, instituted governmental interference in business to the end of eliminating monopolies, etc. That would have constituted a real revolution in our economic life, and might have restored agriculture to its previous high estate; but it would not necessarily have led to the solution of the many social and economic problems peculiar to our industrial civilization. The Populists had no program for that and their individualism and decentralizing philosophy would certainly have restrained them from investing the central government with the power to carry through such reform measures. The West's great contribution in these closing years of the nineteenth century arose from its frontier characteristics more than from its agrarianism. Men had been moving into new regions beyond the limits of established authority continuously for more than a century. They had never hesitated to establish their own governments in such cases, drawing upon the experiences of the older sections and upon their inherent creative abilities, applying both to the task of meeting the exigencies of their new environment. Territorial organization and state making had followed in due time. This constant process of state making had been the rich reservoir from which flowed new ideas, democratizing tendencies and leveling influences into the expanding structure of American life. Much that had been initiated had been discarded by the test of time. Much, also, had become an established part of our national system. True to precedent, this last great experience of American state-making made its contribution to creative political thought. It did not come in time to alter materially the course of nineteenth-century development; but it did give to twentieth-century America most of its leading statesmen and much of its new governmental machinery. We shall see its influence in the careers of men like Borah, Walsh, Norris, Clark, and Johnson, and through such innovations as woman's suffrage, the popular election of United States Senators, the Initiative and Referendum, and Preferential Primaries.

It must be remembered, however, that this last concerted effort of the agrarians to wrest control of the federal government from the industrialists was so narrow in vision as to be almost naïve. Its tragedy lay in its utter futility. America was already industrialized and was becoming more so. The agrarians did not see the inadequacy of their program for shaping the destiny of an industrial people, nor did the industrialists quite realize the importance of restoring agricultural prosperity. It remained for our generation to seek, perhaps in vain, for the correct formula—not for reconciling the two philosophies, for they can not be reconciled—by which the two economic systems can be maintained under the same government to their mutual benefit.

Entirely aside from this contest which resulted in a submerged agricultural population was the effort to free a rapidly changing social and economic state from a static social philosophy. Surviving inhibitions of agrarianism complicated the task in many ways. The test of any civilization is the degree to which it applies intelligence to the solution of problems created by its own development. Answers to its problems are not given, nor do they spring spontaneously from the brain of any man. The wisdom of the ages is not thus concentrated. The rapidly developing industrialism created an unbalanced economic system and hopelessly deranged the equitable adjustment between the rights of property and the rights of man; but it also paved the way for the corrections of its evils by making possible a degree of widespread literacy and intelligence never before known to mankind.

The richest inheritance of twentieth-century America was the foundation of its school system, combined with academic freedom and the freedom of the press. Industry and science produced wealth, and only a wealthy people could have established an educational system extending from the kindergarten through the universities available to every child. Joseph Pulitzer could reach the minds and hearts of millions with his forthright denunciation of injustice and corruption, and his defense of the lives and fortunes of the masses against privilege, demagoguery and plutocracy because the press was free and the people literate. Thorstein Veblen's merciless criticism of the unsocial consequences of the accumulation of wealth became a vital, moving force because young men and women sat at his feet and learned the way to a better life. Countless thousands entered the universities and colleges during these three decades to drink deeply of the humanities and learn something of new social and economic theories. Every civilization produces its men and women to whom life offers no other value so incomparably rich as constructive service. This one produced its Henry George and Thorstein Veblen, its William James, its Robert G. Ingersoll, its Henry D. Lloyd, its Jane Addams and many others whose historic stature looms large in this period of transition from an agricultural to an industrial civilization.

Finally, in the closing years of the century, the United States acquired by conquest vast island possessions in the Caribbean and the Far East. Thus was still another perplexing problem created. All previous acquisition of territory had been contiguous to the United States and relatively uninhabited except for infiltrations of our own people. It had been comparatively easy to extend the federal authority over such new territory, survey it, throw it open to settlement and establish territorial governments looking to ultimate statehood. These new possessions, however, were far distant and already inhabited by foreign peoples. A new system of territorial government had to be evolved, provoking many questions of Constitutional law. The determination of their final status involved foreign policy, national defense and trade.

CHAPTER II

SURVIVALS AND SYMBOLS

Population

It is difficult to realize now the extent to which people in the United States were moving about at the turn of the century. Foreign immigration was at its peak. Young men and women were deserting the rural sections for the more attractive life of the new metropolitan districts. Negroes were abandoning the inhospitable surroundings of the rural South for the more secure haven of northern cities. Rural folk were still seeking better soil and more elbow room in the West. A spirit of restlessness, born of insecurity and the inherent desire to better one's economic situation, pervaded the land.

Considerable more than twenty million Europeans had come to this country during the nineteenth century. Economic opportunity had been the lodestar of this restless mass of humanity. Freedom from religious and political oppression and, to some degree, from military service had contributed heavily to the movement in pre-Civil War days; but it was America as the land of opportunity that figured most prominently in our advertisements and their response in the last three decades. Western states, railroads, steamship lines and industrialists joined forces in selling America abroad. Then, there came a day of repentance and a demand for selection, for restriction, ultimately for exclusion. It originated with the labor unions. Organized labor, composed of American-born artisans, early recognized the advantage accruing to capital from the plentiful supply of foreign immigrants. They were a handicap to labor organizations, a threat to American standards of living, and a dual menace at times of industrial strife. Immigrants were used as strike breakers, and alien radicals welcomed every incident of industrial unrest as an opportunity for violent agitation. Thus their presence rendered ineffective labor's only weapon and cost it the valuable support of public opinion.

Radical agitation reversed the attitude of industrialists. They had recruited labor abroad for the process of industrial expansion. Latins and Slavs had built the railroads, laid the pipe lines, operated the stone quarries and mines, and furnished the constantly increasing percentage of unskilled labor required for mass production. Not all of them, however, were strong and docile. Many were intelligent, radical refugees from the espionage systems of European autocracies. They brought the beneficent ideas of European liberalism, much that was extremely radical, and a desperation born of despair. Socialism and anarchy were equally abhorrent to the dominant class in America. They were synonymous terms to most people, and evoked abject fear for the safety of American institutions. Conservative opinion, therefore, began to demand some restrictive measures to exclude the *undesirable* radicals.

A third source of dissent was the new social consciousness. For decades, immigrants had come from Northern Europe and settled in agricultural areas. Industrial expansion and the exhaustion of free lands drew an increasing number from Southern Europe to our own industrial centers. They lived in their own sections of the cities, preserving their racial customs and morals, establishing their own economy, and finding it unnecessary to speak the English language. Pauperism, crime, and immorality—old evils, but new problems—were charged to the account of racial origins. The idea that an unbalanced economic system might be partially responsible received little attention.

All of these objections were accentuated in the case of Orientals. It was against them that legislation was directed first. Chinese laborers were excluded for ten years by Congressional action in 1882. The act was renewed in 1892, extended in perpetuity in 1902 and made applicable to Chinese in Hawaii and the Philippines. Contract labor was excluded after 1885. Control of immigration was assumed by the federal government in 1891. An act of Congress providing for a literacy test was vetoed by Cleveland in 1897. Waves of immigrants continued to roll in, reaching an annual volume of more than one million in 1905 and a grand total for the twentieth century of more than 13,000,000 before our entry into the World War. All of these early attempts to place some restriction on immigration aimed to set up selective machinery for the exclusion of undesirables: paupers, criminals, mentally deficient, prostitutes, etc. It was not until many years later that anything was done to reduce the numbers of immigrants by assigning quotas to each country.

Less spectacular than this addition of foreign millions to our urban populations, but equally significant, was the first trek of Negroes from the rural South. The disintegration of the Black Belt—the most historic section of the country—had begun. The reason for it can not be stated with finality. The abuses of the tenant system—crop *liens*, one crop tillage, falsified accounts—and myriad other links in the chain of economic slavery no doubt were a factor. The increasing difficulty of wresting a living from exhausted lands, or of restoring their fertility without cash resources; the desire to escape from a pattern of rural life in which competing economic groups of the white race wielded their power ruthlessly to preserve racial inequality; the alluring legends of urban freedom; the certain benefits of an independent racial economy; the influence of educational opportunities—all these, and other influences, no doubt, contributed to the movement. In any case, the urban Negro population increased 489,000 in the South and 193,000 elsewhere during the first decade. At the same time, the Negro rural population in the South increased only 336,000 and decreased 27,000 elsewhere. Foreign immigration kept them out of the North until the World War. The sharp decline in immigration at that time, coupled with the withdrawal of many men from industrial pursuits for military service and the pressure for increased production, accelerated the migration and turned it northward.

During the second decade of the century, Negro urban population increased 397,000 in the South, while the rural population decreased 233,000. It increased 479,000 in the North during the same period.

The repercussions from this second great shifting of population almost defy description. The threatened depletion of the South's agricultural laborers became an actuality in many sections. Productive cotton plantations became abandoned lands. The aged, the infirm and the children were left behind, increasing the percentage of population in unproductive ages with far-reaching effects upon taxation and relief. Those who migrated, because they began at the bottom of the industrial ladder, crowded into the least desirable residential sections of the cities; but, flowing into the cities faster than the whites could or would make way for them, they overflowed the segregated districts, precipitating race riots and innumerable court battles. They were excluded from labor unions, and served as strike-breakers. They competed with whites under a dual wage standard, profiting by depressions and being thrown back upon relief when recovery began. But, year after year, the Negro press of the North, particularly the *Chicago Defender*, urged them to hasten to the section of economic equality and, in the new environment, they steadily increased their contribution to the composite civilization that was America: Bert Williams, of Ziegfeld Follies, said by W. C. Fields to have been the funniest and saddest man in the world, star of *Under the Bamboo Tree;* Charles Gilpin, star of Eugene O'Neill's *The Emperor Jones* and recipient of the Spingarn Medal; Paul Robeson affectionately known among his people as King of Harlem, graduate of Rutgers University, member of Phi Beta Kappa and forever associated in the minds of those who love artistry with the production of *Porgy* and *Show Boat;* Jules Bledsoe, internationally known singer and actor in *In Abraham's Bosom;* Frank Wilson, who rose from the status of a Harlem mail carrier to enduring fame as a foremost actor in *Porgy;* and Richard B. Harrison, the "Lawd" in Marc Connelly's *The*

Green Pastures. They also entered the field of productive literature: Paul Lawrence Dunbar, known to most people for his *Ships that Pass in the Night* and *Lyrics of Lowly Life,* but with an established reputation in the fields of short stories, classic English poems and dialect verse; William E. B. Du Bois, poet, novelist, historian and essayist, successor to Booker T. Washington as the outstanding leader of his race and author of *The Souls of Black Folk, Dark Princess* and *The Quest of the Silver Fleece;* William Stanley Braithwaite, prominent poet and critic, contributor to the Boston *Evening Transcript, The Forum, Century* and the *Atlantic,* author of *Lyrics of Life and Love* and *The House of Falling Leaves;* James Weldon Johnson, sometime Secretary of the National Association for the Advancement of Colored People, author of the anthems "Lift Ev'ry Voice and Sing" and "The Young Warrior"; and a younger generation of poets including Claude McKay, Countee Cullen, and Jean Toomer.

The South was the scene, also, of the most pronounced population shift from rural to industrial life—this in the Piedmont Crescent. Textile manufacturing in the Piedmont began in the late eighties and early nineties. The existence of a tremendous reservoir of cheap labor, rather than proximity to raw materials, was responsible. The first factories were established by intrepid Southerners as community enterprises. They were followed by branch factories of northern companies and, later, by large investments of foreign capital, particularly in the rayon industry. The labor for these enterprises was drawn from the hinterland—simple upland folk and mountain people. It does not show heavily in population statistics by states; and, because water power and then electric power made decentralization possible, it does not show in the growth of large cities. Nevertheless, it was one of the most important developments at the turn of the century, pregnant with meaning for future generations.

Nowhere else in the country did the attitudes and inhibitions of an agricultural philosophy carry over so completely or survive so tenaciously in the new industrial system. Paternalism and patronage, honest attitudes in the first generation, instruments of exploitation in the second; child labor, regrettable perhaps though not wholly bad under parental control in simple rural life, but an atrocious robbery of body and soul in a factory system; individualism, the strength of a sturdy yeomanry, but a fatal weakness in an industrial laborer—these were agricultural and frontier survivals. Society reveled at the prospect of increased wealth and an opportunity for honest work for a ne'er-do-well segment of population. It was slow in developing a critical attitude toward the new industrial process. The prevailing racial cleavage served to distract attention from economic grievances. Fear of radical influences upon the Negro population and prevailing resentment against outside interference, both survivals of Reconstruction days, militated against organized labor movements. All of these things were destined to exert a mighty influence in the history of the nation within a generation.

The shifting fortunes of country towns and villages can not be gleaned from statistical tables. They had served, for more than a century, as the shopping and amusement centers for surrounding farming populations. Here were located the hardware and dry-goods stores, the barber shops and drug stores, the blacksmith shops, the post offices, the banks, the elevators, the railway stations and the express offices. Here, too, were the doctors and lawyers, the circuit preachers, the secondary schools, the newspapers, the justice courts, the taverns and barrooms. Hamlets, villages and county seats alike, they served as the hubs about which rural economy revolved. They not only served a rural population, but were rural themselves. A large proportion of their population consisted of retired farmers. Few of them were wealthy, although many, deceived by increasing land values, thought they were. Tenantry increased, the value of farm mortgages soared and all the evils of absentee ownership appeared as more and more moved into the towns.

The children of these retired farmers, their ranks swelled by their more countrified cousins, turned eagerly toward the cities, again leaving behind the less capable and the aged. It is safe to say that almost every family in the small towns and rural sections of the North and Midwest contributed at least one member to city population during the first two decades of the century. Automobiles and good roads hurried the social and economic transformation begun by electric and steam railways. Business decayed and all but disappeared from the majority of the small towns. Blacksmith shops and rural churches alike lost their patronage, and the little red schoolhouse, most colorful of American institutions, became little more than a memory. Improved roads and consolidated schools added their burden of bonded indebtedness to a drooping rural economy. County seats and larger industrial centers grew in wealth and importance, serving larger areas, and exercising a city influence upon those areas in the same way that the rural areas had formerly influenced the small towns.

In view of these facts, it is not strange that the urban population of the country should have increased from 40 per cent to more than 65 per cent of the whole in thirty years; that the percentage of our foreign born in the populations of states like Massachusetts, Rhode Island, Connecticut, New York and New Jersey should have steadily increased; that persons of voting age should constitute a larger percentage of the population in urban than in rural areas; and that the combined population of Massachusetts, New York, New Jersey, Illinois and Michigan should have increased from 19,200,000 to 33,351,000 in thirty years as compared to an increase from 8,388,000 to 10,678,000 in the strictly agricultural states of Wisconsin, Iowa, Nebraska, Kansas and Mississippi. Cities not only grew in size, but overflowed their boundaries so that today comparisons must be made between metropolitan districts to be of any value.

This rapid urbanization, already in progress in 1900, presented some interesting developments and many vexatious problems. The relatively rapid transportation provided by street railways permitted unlimited expansion of metropolitan districts. Residential suburbs established their own governments, utility services and schools, resisted consolidation, and thus aggravated the evils of extravagance, corruption and crime. Fortunes were made in real estate. Bonded indebtedness for streets, lights, water-works, garbage disposal plants, municipal buildings and schools was lightly assumed. An outmoded county government system superimposed on an expanded town government, both political in character, produced mediocrity at best and more often appalling corruption in the discharge of public affairs.

The individual citizens, making the transition from rural to urban economy, were forced to adjust themselves to intensified nervous strains, new food habits, new forms of relaxation and amusement. They were forced to adjust themselves entirely to a money-making and money-spending basis, modified by the insecurity of employment. Apartments, with their bathrooms, improved heating and lighting systems, and close proximity to one's neighbors, were not always a fair exchange for the gardens and flowers and fresh air of yesterdays. Some people made the change easily and gracefully; others faltered before the glittering allurements of vice and crime; still others suffered varying degrees of discomfort from the inevitable derangement of bodily functions and mental habits. The birth rate declined. Cities came to have a much higher percentage of voting population than rural sections. Women deserted the home for remunerative labor in the shops and factories. Family income rather than that of the husband and father came to determine the standard of living; and, eventually, 11,000,000 women were working, 15,000,000 men were idle, and millions of young people approached maturity without prospect of honest labor.

It was different with the unfortunates: the immigrants, the Negro, the native rural whites who should have remained close to the soil. These were the low income groups. They contributed most heavily to the sweatshop systems, to child labor and to female employment. 206 out of every 1,000 women over sixteen were gainfully employed in 1900, including 769,-

000 married women. By 1910 it had increased to 243 of every 1,000, and to 1,891,000 married women. Percentages varied only slightly thereafter, but the total number of women employed in 1930 was 10,500,000 and of married women slightly more than 3,000,000. The greatest gains were in domestic service, manufacturing and clerical occupations. In domestic service and manufacturing, immigrant and Negro women predominated. Living conditions for these low income groups were deplorable. Slums and tenement houses, unbalanced diets, lack of sunshine, fresh air and recreation facilities, inadequate medical attention and impure water supplies contributed to a death rate among women and children as appalling as that on the early frontier.

Technology

Never before in the history of man did such a bewildering array of technical inventions alter human life so completely within the span of a single generation. There were 8,000 automobiles and 144 miles of paved highway in the United States in 1900. The speed limit was fixed by law at 15 miles an hour in Connecticut, and one was required to publicly advertise his intention of going upon the highway with an automobile one week in advance in the state of Tennessee. Thirty years later there were 25,000,000 automobiles, 750,000 miles of hard-surfaced roads, and speeds ranging upward to 80 miles an hour with safety. Curves had been eliminated from the main highways, obstructions to vision removed, dangerous crossings and embankments protected, and many grade crossings eliminated. A trip of twenty-five miles in one day by horse and buggy had been unusual. Passenger automobiles are now driven more than three hundred billion miles annually. The vast automobile manufacturing plants and distributing agencies, garages and service stations, tourist camps, highway markets and paying-guest homes suggest something of the economic change. Social changes represented by the closer contact between cities and rural areas, and between citizens of widely separated regions through tourist travel; by the effect of increased mobility upon education and crime, and the amusements and recreations of the people can hardly be estimated.

There were no radios or airplane travelling in 1900, although the former was in process of development and the latter already an accomplished fact. The first permanent radio broadcasting station, KDKA, was established by the Westinghouse Electric and Manufacturing Company in 1920. Its first program announced the election returns of that year. In 1921, the company opened stations WBZ at Newark, New Jersey, and KYW at Chicago. Thereafter, the opening of new stations proceeded rapidly and the radio has, within two decades, influenced the lives of the people in a great diversity of ways. The objectives of the broadcasting companies were the development of good will and markets for radio equipment, until the American Telephone and Telegraph Company operating station WEAF hit upon the idea of toll broadcasting in 1924. The public desire for entertainment soon altered programs from sales talks to music, drama, etc. The Red and Blue Networks were organized in 1926. The operation of broadcasting stations became a major industry, selling time to commercial broadcasters who, in their effort to please the masses, introduced cheap entertainment, jazz, inferior monologues, and drama.

Lessons in accounting were broadcast by WJZ as early as 1923. The Smithsonian Institution began weekly scientific talks in 1924. Lectures on Greek and Roman Classics were broadcast by New York University in 1925. Courses in Philosophy, Psychology and Physics were soon added, and other universities took up the work with ever-expanding curricula. A Public School of the Air was established in Atlanta, Georgia, in 1926. The Standard Oil Company supplied an educational program for the schools in 1928. The Columbia Broadcasting System started the American School of the Air in February, 1930, with programs including history dramas, literature, art, travelogues, foreign news and music. Walter Damrosch began educational music concerts for the schools on Friday mornings of each week. These and dozens of other programs of superior quality carried the finest music, drama and public lectures into the farthest corners of the world and most remote sections of our own country. They emancipated our rural and mountain people from the blighting influence of ignorant and incompetent leadership. The radio's use in transportation, especially in the air and marine service, in industry and business, and in government and politics is almost without limit.

Radio broadcasting brought its problems. Commercial advertisers were reluctant to sponsor educational programs because of the limited audiences. The pressure to popularize university broadcasts was great. The University of California lost its radio time to *True Story Magazine*. The air was filled with programs deemed unfit and actually detrimental to children. All of which created a new problem of public policy and led to the demand by prominent educators like Robert G. Sproul, President of the University of California, and Professor Grace Abbott of the University of Chicago that entire wave channels be withdrawn from commercial use and turned over to educational institutions; or that all radio broadcasting be government owned and operated. Opposed to these demands was the ever present fear of political influence, bureaucratic control, and the much greater obstacle to cultural programs of getting the people to listen to them. The news of the day, sports of all kinds, farm programs, and religious services did not encounter these same difficulties. The World Series games were broadcast, beginning in 1922. The National Farm and Home Hour, presented by the United States Department of Agriculture, became one of the most popular programs of the air, and the inspiring talks of Drs. S. Parkes Cadman, Harry Emerson Fosdick and Daniel Poling were brought to the homes of all who cared to listen.

The motion picture made its appearance in 1895. Thomas A. Edison was primarily responsible for its development with his original peep show machine. Thomas Armat added a projector to produce the vitascope. The first successful showing of a picture was that of *The Great Train Robbery* in 1903.

Several theaters were opened in the eastern cities in 1905 on the basis of a five cent admission charge. Biograph Studios engaged the services of D. W. Griffith in that year, and presented Mary Pickford in 1909 in *The New York Hat.* She was quickly followed on the screen by other stars including Mabel Normand, Norma Talmadge, Anita Stewart, and others. Adolph Zukor turned the attention of actors from the legitimate stage to pictures with his production of *Queen Elizabeth* made famous by Sarah Bernhardt. Serials became popular in 1913. Slowly the nickelodeon gave way before the films until, in 1930, the motion picture houses of the country were able to seat one-tenth of the population at one time and an estimated one hundred million people paid admissions each week. Sound pictures were introduced in 1927 as a result of long and patient research by the Bell Telephone laboratories and the General Electric Company. They have become tremendously popular both as an agency for amusement and for education in the schools and churches. The influence of motion pictures upon habits of dress, diction, etc., is not easily determined; but their combined utility in the field of advertising, of scientific research and education is enormously large.

Equally significant as the automobile, radio and motion picture, though less spectacular in effect, have been a veritable host of other inventions and discoveries which altered our personal habits and institutional characteristics: the tin can for preserving fruits and vegetables; electric cookers, sweepers, washing machines, refrigerators, and ironers; X-rays, infra-red rays and ultra-violet rays; calories, vitamins and irradiation of foods; the many biologicals used in controlling contagious diseases.

Urbanization and technical progress combined steadily to broaden the horizon of life's activities for young men and women after the turn of the century. It is pertinent to remember that not every one who moved to the city entered into the factories. As a city grows, it builds its own diversified economy, including institutions and services non-existent except in dense populations. This, in turn, multiplies manyfold the special fields of productive enterprise open to young people and creates new requirements of specialized training, opportunity for the development of special talents and a sharper division into groups and classes on the basis of intelligence and inherent ability. This process became so rapid and continuous after the turn of the century that life's possibilities were vastly different for each maturing generation. It steadily lengthened the period of education, increased the percentage of people, both men and women, gainfully employed, and enlarged their productive capacity. It altered our norms of conduct and our social philosophy, creating a really serious crisis in the lives of millions who found difficulty in making the adjustment. That was particularly true where parental authority, religious sanctions, and the rights of private property were involved.

Life's basic pattern changed as completely for women as it did for young people. The feminist movement had begun before the Civil War. By the turn of the century, women were enjoying the franchise in several states, equal educational opportunities and some privileges in business and public life. Nothing had been done, however, to relieve them of the inevitable drudgery of rearing large families. The gains of the nineteenth century, therefore, were relatively small and limited to a small portion of their sex. Since then household electrical appliances have done more to emancipate women than all the generations of agitation by militant suffragettes. Add to their benefits those of new methods in the care of children, the eradication of many children's diseases, and the assumption by the schools of responsibilities formerly resting upon mothers, and it is not difficult to realize that women were living in a new and happier world. Leisure time became a reality. Women's clubs of all kinds sprang up like mushrooms. The joy of homemaking replaced the drudgery of housekeeping, and even the tyranny of servants could be dispensed with by those who were financially able to employ them.

Youth was given recognition. The universal longing of parents to give their children advantages they, themselves, had never enjoyed assumed a new importance. America became child conscious. Not only did parents make untold sacrifices to provide their children with a college education, but society spent enormous sums for new school plants and equipment, children's playgrounds and parks. Each new advantage brought corresponding responsibilities for child welfare. Rearing children in the isolation of a rural homestead had been simplicity itself compared to rearing them in the new economic age. Parental control was no longer sufficient. Only society through government agencies could cope with the new environment, and so there emerged an ever-increasing demand for rigid censorship of the movies, radio and magazines, for the regulation of milk and food supplies, for the suppression of gambling and prostitution, and for the prohibition of the sale of alcoholic beverages. This urge for reform legislation did not arise entirely from the circumstances of the new environment. It was, in part, a revival of the great reform and benevolent movements of pre-Civil War days, which had been submerged by that conflict. It was, also, the result of a new interest in childhood. It can not be separated from the new attitude toward child delinquency, the crusade against child labor or the establishment of public health, nursing and children's aid societies. It was a severe blow to a nation which had, for thirty years, shown a progressive interest in its children to be told by the White House Conference of 1930 that more than one-fifth of the 47,608,000 were suffering from blindness, deafness, tuberculosis, heart disease. or were crippled or mentally deficient.

Institutions

It was inevitable, of course, that such a dynamic civilization should modify severely ancient institutions like the family, the schools, the church, and the government.

Life's activities ceased to revolve about the home as rural isolation was broken down. Commercialized amusements such as motion pictures, and increasing facilities for outdoor recreation in public playgrounds, parks and golf courses demanded more of the time of more and more people. Large scale commercial canning, meat packing and baking, laundry and cleaning services, and the wearing of custom-made clothing by every one relieved the home of its function as a unit of production. Youth's new freedom not only lessened the restraints of parental control, but robbed the night of its terrors and increased the day's activities by many hours. Seldom, indeed, are all the members of a modern family together except at meal-time, and frequently not even then. Children ceased to be cherished as an economic asset whose labor in youth supplemented the family income and whose contributions would alleviate the privations of old age. Parents became companions of their children and something more than a burden in maturity. The size of families came to be regulated to conform with the ability of the parents to properly rear and educate them rather than by accident and God's providence. Young people married at an earlier age; divorces increased; families decreased in size; but the rearing of children became more of a conscious privilege and responsibility. Family relationships are anything but uniform even in the same community, and they vary greatly between city, village and rural environments; but what has been said above indicates discernible trends during the past three decades.

The influences of an earlier day and the new economic order are both readily discernible in the modern school system. Free public schools for all children, with no distinctions of wealth or social position, have always been one of the most unique and cherished of our social institutions. From kindergarten to university, no barriers have ever existed for any child except the tests of ability provided within the system itself. Our school system, moreover, has always been decentralized and largely under local control. Both of these fundamental characteristics survived the tests of a new order; but industrialism and urbanization forced important modifications in other equally fundamental features. Reduction in child labor, new cultural standards and the demands for a more intelligent citizenship increased school enrollment rapidly. The number of students in institutions of higher learning increased from 284,000 in 1900 to 1,178,000 in 1930, in secondary schools from 630,000 to 4,740,000, and the total school population to twenty-nine and one-half million. The curriculum also changed to meet more adequately the needs of a diverse civilization. In 1890, most high school pupils were studying Latin, geometry, algebra, and history. By 1900, physical geography, physiology, English literature and civil government had been added. During the next decade, German was added, only to be discarded during the hysteria of the World War. Zoology and botany were introduced, but lost favor after a few years. Physical geography almost disappeared before 1920. The percentage of pupils studying algebra, geometry, physics and chemistry declined sharply after the beginning of the second decade. English literature and rhetoric assumed a leading position as required subjects, and enormous gains were made by general science, community civics, home economics, manual arts, music, art, bookkeeping and typewriting. These changes were largely due to the influence of the educational philosopher John Dewey, whose *School and Society* (1899) popularized the theory of experimentation in educational processes to the end of properly equipping the child as a useful member of society.

Not only did enrollment increase and curricula change, but the organization and administration of the several units of the school system were radically revised. The rural school of one room, one teacher and eight grades predominated at the turn of the century. Certification of teachers was under the control of county examining boards. Village and city schools retained the eight elementary grades, with four year secondary schools over which the colleges and universities exercised strong indirect influence. All of this rapidly changed. Consolidated schools replaced the old type rural school. Junior high schools were introduced. Senior high schools ceased to serve primarily as college preparatory schools. The junior college and normal schools took over the work of the first two years of university training, with strong indications that the junior college and senior high school would ultimately become a single unit, the four-year college disappear, and the university be devoted increasingly to preparation for graduate work and research. The field of education, also, was extended by the establishment of nursery schools, extension departments, and adult education classes.

Finally, there was the unique development of a dual school system in the southern states. The South was confronted with the twofold problem of restoring the shattered school system for the whites and formulating a policy with respect to Negro education. After the close of Congressional Reconstruction, the idea of destroying race prejudice by forced association of Negro and white children in mixed schools was repudiated. The principle of a dual system was generally agreed upon, and slightly more than $100,000,000 had been spent for Negro education by southern states before 1900. That represented real progress in view of the handicaps to be overcome: widespread poverty and prevailing prejudices against mass education, particularly of the Negro. The most serious threat was an attempt to base school appropriations for each system on the ratio of taxes paid by each race. The greatest problems were to secure adequately trained Negro teachers and overcome the reluctance of Negro parents to educate their children.

The work of Samuel C. Armstrong at Hampton Institute and of his pupil, Booker T. Washington, at Tuskegee Institute, did much to build up correct attitudes among the Negro race toward both education and labor, to break down prejudice against Negro education among the whites, and to promote mutual understanding and cooperation between the two races to the end of sectional betterment. The George Peabody Fund (1867) and the John F. Slater Fund (1883) were so administered as to promote the training of Negro teachers and the appropriation of public funds for the establishment of elementary schools for both races. By 1927 more than 300 accredited high schools had been established by these foundations. Building slowly upon the basic achievements of these pioneering efforts, great things were accomplished after the turn of the century. The Anna T. Jeans Fund (1908), the donations from the General Education Board (1902), the Caroline Phelps Stokes Fund (1913), and the Julius Rosenwald Fund (1914) made posssible the establishment of adequate supervision, fellowships and scholarships for teachers' training and research, comprehensive surveys and the erection of modern school buildings in every rural community.

There are still many discouraging aspects of the situation, principally inadequate enforcement of attendance laws, the lingering apathy of the Negroes themselves and the inequality of public expenditures in the lower South; but the trend is unmistakable and the accomplishment of three decades far from negligible. Low property valuations, low density of population, a high percentage of children, the gravitation of the better teachers to regions of higher salaries, and the predominantly rural nature of the section must always be considered in making comparisons between the South and other sections of the country.

No institution could expand so rapidly and adjust its functional structure so quickly to the changing needs of society without encountering difficulties. It was difficult to secure an adequately trained corps of teachers and keep them from being drawn away from the profession by more lucrative returns in other fields of employment. Local control too often introduced personal prejudices and politics into the schools at the expense of efficiency. The burden of increased taxes to meet bonded indebtedness and current expenses aroused severe criticism of each new addition to the curriculum. It was often difficult to reconcile the demands of the universities and the needs of the community. The promotion of extra-curricular activities, play and recreation, the new training for social life, and the teaching of new natural and social scientific principles too frequently clashed with the political, religious and economic prejudices of parents, produced tension in family circles and brought a storm of protest down upon the heads of the teachers. One might go on to fill a volume with the symptoms of progress. The annual expenditures for public elementary and secondary schools increased from a paltry $215,000,000 in 1900 to more than $2,000,000,000 in 1930. The value of school property increased from less than one billion dollars to more than seven billion dollars in the same period. The number of people who doubt the wisdom of educating the masses gradually lessened. Many were fretful over the huge outlay of public funds and, at times of economic depression, lost no opportunity to bring about a retrenchment, but the faith of the people, generally, has deepened in the one institution which, more than any other, has served to teach men how to live happily and harmoniously together and thus given solidarity to the nation. That such material prosperity as the nation came to enjoy could never have been possible with an illiterate people has become an accepted truth.

The church yielded less, perhaps, to the pressure of changing conditions than either the family or the schools. Nevertheless its social attitudes and its influence in the lives of its members depend largely upon the degree of cultural and economic isolation of the people. Many aspects of religious institutions were swept away beyond recovery with the breakdown of rural isolation. At the turn of the century, liberalism in large urban communities and in institutions of higher learning was heresy elsewhere. People in the small towns and country still went to church, zealously supported church enterprises, reveled in the spirit of denominational rivalry and believed explicitly in the orthodox faith. Every community had its several denominational church groups, served by resident or circuit preachers who, as a rule, were more dogmatic than intelligent.

Slowly but surely, the church lost its vise-like grip upon the more essential customs of the people. Marriage and divorce came to be regarded as far too important to be controlled by religious sanctions. The clergy, along with teachers, lost much of their commanding position as authorities on all matters, temporal as well as spiritual. Small, struggling churches were abandoned, denominational rivalry lost its appeal, and community churches made their appearance. Less emphasis was placed upon individual salvation and religious dogma, more upon social reform and economic justice. The camp-meeting and mid-winter revival disappeared almost entirely from large sections of the country. Billy Sunday marched through the land in the early years of the century, lambasting sinners and successfully appealing to hundreds of thousands to hit the sawdust trail; but in the last years of his life audiences were amazingly small and his picturesque language had lost its flavor. Family worship and familiarity with the Bible were rare in the new generation and religious inhibitions no longer controlled sex relations, birth control, marriage and divorce. There was no uniformity in these matters between denominations, of course, and even within single denominations there came to be fundamentalists, modernists and cynics. Naturally, in an age when science became a household word and anything called scientific was accepted without question, increasing numbers of churchmen tried to reconcile science and Christianity. Naturally, too, those who clung to the fundamentals of orthodoxy resisted to the point of open conflict within the church and to heresy hunts without. The brunt of the battle fell upon the public schools, colleges and universities and upon that portion of the population which regarded Sunday as a day for recreation in sports and movie houses.

About fifty per cent of the people belonged to a church at the turn of the century and about the same proportion do today. It is pretty generally agreed that an increasing number render only lip service to their professed faith and regard the obligation of membership lightly. On the other hand, many who do not care to affiliate with church organizations contribute liberally to their support, attend religious services and utilize the services of ordained ministers for marriage and burial ceremonies in much the same way as those of a public notary transacting legal business. The churches have more women members than men, and a higher percentage of the population in the cities than in rural communities. Of the 212 independent denominations, more than half have only a few thousand members.

Corporations

One of the most revolutionary changes of the period, a change which began before the turn of the century but increased progressively thereafter, was the development of large scale operations in manufacturing, in finance and in distribution. Volumes have been written about combinations, corporations, trusts and holding companies, but the whole story has not yet been told. Stability and security from the uncertainties of unrestricted competition were largely responsible. The desire for greater profits by increasing efficiency and establishing monopolies; the desire to create wealth through stock issues against future earning power; the influence of banking interests which got to gambling with the people's money in investment trusts; and the demands of the public for new fields of investment—all these entered into the mergers of independent companies, stores and banks, and the creation of holding companies.

The movement began near the end of the nineteenth century. It was, therefore, a survival about which nothing had been done—a development which was to evoke more public discussion, consume more of the energies of men in public life and arouse more bitterness than any other subject in the next three decades. This was true for three principal reasons: (1) consolidation did not lead to economic stability; (2) the profit motive predominated with little regard to social responsibilities; and (3) the concentration of wealth and economic control gave to a few men extraordinary power over the lives of the people and the government itself.

The history of this mobilization of property interests is too complicated to be described adequately by illustration. It is best to designate the nature of what was accomplished in every field of production and distribution. Until near the close of the nineteenth century business was conducted under the competitive system, with each of the units owned and operated by one man or a small group of men. The small neighborhood retail store, the small local bank, were characteristic of the several units. Capital and management were combined in the same hands and there was close contact between the employer and the employee. Then began the process of integration. Improved communication broadened the markets of the producer. Mechanization made possible large scale production. A surplus of fluid capital became available for huge financing operations and facilitated the sale of stock to the public.

Soon after the Civil War, intrepid manufacturers began to add coal and iron mines, railroad and steamship lines and innumerable factory units all along the line of production to their holdings. Only occasionally did such tremendous corporations remain under the ownership and control of the men who created them. The Ford and Mellon corporations are such exceptions. More often monopolies were created by bringing competitive industries under the same management through trusts or holding companies. The banking interests who financed and arranged for consolidations received enormous commissions in the form of common or preferred stock which they disposed of as rapidly as possible to the investing public through the medium of the stock exchanges. The owners of the constituent companies received fabulous amounts of stock in the new companies in exchange for their properties. The total amount of stock issued, most of which was eventually purchased by thousands of small investors, invariably exceeded the actual value of the physical property involved. It had no par value and sold for whatever it would bring on the stock exchange, which was whatever the investing public thought it was worth on the basis of probable dividends or for resale at a profit. The stock sold to the public did not always carry voting power, that stock being retained by the small group who manipulated the organization. The same procedure was followed in the organization of banking trusts and retail chain stores.

The social and economic implications of this whole development are startling. Management was thus separated from ownership. The thousands of owners had no direct interest in the manufacturing process, being concerned only with the size of their dividend checks and the stable or increased resale value of their holdings. The savings of people who would never venture to purchase stock directly were inevitably drawn into the system as directors of insurance companies, banks and trust companies invested the funds under their control in stocks and bonds. A greater cleavage exists between the employee and the manager than was ever possible between employees and owner control. Thus management became independent of ownership and the needs of labor, ruthless in its dealings with smaller competitors, reckless in its handling of the people's savings—in short, economic freedom and rugged individualism were severely modified. Every individual in the nation, whether or not he owned stock or was employed by these huge corporations, came directly under their influence through his use of public utility services, his purchase of the necessities of life, his quest for amusements and the disposition of his savings.

Centralized control of the newspapers, the motion pictures and the radio increased the control of a relatively few people over public opinion. Mass impression became as significant a term as mass production and had vastly greater implications. It is one thing for millions of people to wear the same kind of clothes and drive the same make of automobile, but quite another thing altogether for them to read the same newspaper, see the same picture shows and hear the same radio programs. It is something else, again, if the men who control these powerful agencies permit them to be used for purposes of propaganda and for the promotion of selfish interests, or deny their use to those whose opinions and ideas are distasteful to their own social philosophy. Would interests which were powerful enough to exclude the writings of abolitionists from the mails also have been able to keep their voices off the air? If the showing of a single film, *The Birth of a Nation*, was responsible, as we think it was, for the subsequent revival of racial hatreds, what vast possibilities for social change rest in the control of such an instrument?

The fact is that the creation of large corporations for the control of manufacturing, of banking and credit, of the press, of radio, of motion pictures, of public utilities and services, gradually gave to their directorships the character of positions of great public trust and responsibility. In so far as events of the period showed them to have been used for selfish rather than for social purposes, we shall see demands arising for governmental ownership and control.

Government

The governmental system of the country, both state and national, was essentially the same in 1900 as it had been at the close of the Civil War. The Supreme Court had recovered much of the prestige that it had lost during the war period, and was about to enter upon the most stormy period of its existence. The social and economic trends of the period created many problems in government and led to many legislative experiments. Time after time, the people were to find difficulty in regulating their affairs within the limits of a written constitution and the delegation of powers belonging to the federal government. Due process, equal protection of the laws, the obligations of contracts and interstate commerce proved to be havens of refuge for minority property interests and a source of unending labor for the Justices of the Supreme Court.

In its outward appearances, the government changed but little during the first three decades of the twentieth century. One amendment was adopted giving the franchise to women and another providing for the popular election of United States Senators. A law prohibiting the manufacture and sale of intoxicating liquors was written into the Constitution and afterwards removed. Otherwise there was no change in the fundamental law. Nevertheless, the functions and powers of the several departments of the federal government no less than those of the state governments increased tremendously.

The most interesting innovations involved the division of power between the federal and state governments: the reserved rights of the states and the limitations placed upon the power of Congress by the Constitution as interpreted by the Supreme Court. The people of the United States, finding it impossible to cope with modern social and economic conditions through the agencies of forty-eight independent state governments, were yet reluctant to surrender local autonomy by conferring larger powers upon the central government by constitutional amendment. It was not the difficulty of amendment but the faith in state rights and fear of a federal bureaucracy surviving from an earlier day that was responsible. They chose rather to test the limits of the Constitution under liberal interpretation and then to rely upon previously unexplored fields of experimentation.

The concentration of wealth and income within a relatively small section of the country placed them beyond the reach of most state governments and made the tax on individual and corporate incomes the particular province of the federal government. It took the place, practically speaking, of the public domain as a rich resource from which the federal government could make grants in aid to the several states. The power of Congress to tax and spend for the general welfare had never been questioned. The practice of making unconditional grants to the states for education and internal improvements was based on ample precedent extending back to the early nineteenth century. The device of making conditional grants in aid to the states from the federal treasury followed as a natural sequence. Congress, in 1911, inaugurated the policy of requiring the states to match its subsidies with an equal amount of money. Later, it began to set up boards and commissions to approve and exercise supervision over the projects for which appropriations were made in the fields of agricultural and vocational education, highway construction, conservation, etc. Much of the legislation of the Roosevelt recovery program was based on these precedents, especially the public works and social security acts. How far Congress may be allowed to go in this direction depends upon the willingness of the several states to surrender their special prerogatives in return for financial assistance and upon the degree of regulation the Supreme Court will allow the federal government to exercise by compulsion. The whole experiment was somewhat shaken by the Court's invalidation of the AAA (*Hoosac Mills Corporation* v. *United States*). In any case, it represents one method by which the legislative branch of the government has sought to overcome the handicap of a decentralized governmental system in a nation whose economic and social institutions demand an ever-increasing uniformity of regulation.

The second innovation along new lines was stimulated by the desire to preserve the sovereignty of the states. The pleas for state rights so eloquently advanced by one party or the other throughout American history are more than a fetish of professional politicians. There can be no question that adherence to the principle has promoted domestic tranquillity, served the peculiar interests of widely separated sections and fostered a rich variety of social institutions. The submergence of the state governments within a highly centralized system would deprive the nation of their use as experimental laboratories. Yet, in large measure, that was the trend at the turn of the century. The remedy lay in closer cooperation between governors and state legislatures within natural sectional areas to the end of uniform state legislation and administration. The need for cooperative action in handling the liquor traffic, automobile traffic and the suppression of crime are cases in point. Out of those very problems came the urge for action. President Roosevelt called the first Governor's Conference at Washington in 1908 and such conferences were held with increasing frequency thereafter. A legislator's association was organized in 1925. The organization, however, which ultimately gave indications of taking the lead was the American Bar Association which organized committees for drafting uniform legislation to be passed upon by the Association and then presented to state legislatures for adoption. The success of the scheme is still problematical in view of the general inefficiency and provincial viewpoints of most state officials.

Returning to the expansion of federal power during the period, we find that much of it arose out of control of interstate commerce. It began with the revolutionary Interstate Commerce Act of 1887, designed to regulate the railroads. Subsequent changes to strengthen the government's control were made by the Hepburn Act (1906) and the Esch-Cummins Act (1920). In 1912, Congress passed an Interstate Commerce Act for the control of wireless communication; in 1926, the Air Commerce Act for the control of aviation; and in 1927, the Radio Control Act for the control of radio. All of these measures established commissions modeled after the Interstate Commerce Commission of 1887. In 1914, Congress created the Federal Reserve Board, the Tariff Commission and the Federal Trade Commission; in 1920, the Federal Power Commission and the Federal Farm Board. The host of boards and commissions established under the recovery acts of Roosevelt's Administration beginning in 1933 will be mentioned later.

The attempt of Congress to expand federal authority by using the taxing power to destroy was curbed by the Supreme Court in the case of *Bailey* v. *Drexel Furniture Company* (1922). This act placed a prohibitive tax upon the products of child labor and was based upon the precedent established in 1865 when Congress drove state bank notes out of circulation by a ten per cent tax on all such issues.

Finally, the powers and duties of the federal enforcement agencies were increasingly taxed by legislation designed to drive out of existence certain social evils: the white slave traffic, stolen automobiles, narcotics and liquor. By 1930, such cases were occupying most of the time of the federal courts. The evasion of income taxes by those engaged in these professions enabled the treasury department to lend its assistance and the combination gave the federal government, indirectly, important police powers in the breaking up of numerous rackets and criminal syndicates. Demands for more effective control of trusts, public utilities, stock and security exchanges, and banking increased as centralization of control was established in these several fields. Each will be discussed at length.

The nature of the demands for federal service in the new machine age are clearly shown by the history of rural postal service. The breaking down of rural isolation, carried swiftly along by the automobiles, the radio and improved highways, was first begun by the telephone. Its development and influence are too familiar to need repetition except to say that between 1900 and 1930 the number of telephones increased from 1,355,000 to 20,201,000. In 1896, however, the federal government took an important step in this direction by inaugurating rural free delivery mail service. The mileage of these routes increased steadily from 29,000 in 1900 to 1,354,000 in 1930. This service multiplied contacts with the outside world, increased the circulation of newspapers, and made possible the development of the great mail order houses such as Sears and Roebuck and Montgomery Ward which depend largely upon a rural patronage. Not more than 800 cities had free delivery service in 1900. By 1930, the service had been extended to nearly 3000 cities.

Other demands for service in the collection of information and its distribution to business men, manufacturers, consumers and the public at large were met by the creation of the Department of Commerce, the Public Health Service in the Treasury Department, and the Bureau of Home Economics and Food and Drug Administration in the Department of Agriculture.

State governments no less than the federal government responded to the demands of the new age by extending the scope of their services and the exercise of police powers. The rapid extension of the school system required funds for operation which could be provided only by the state. State legislation was necessary to permit consolidation of school districts. State normal schools and universities required ever larger appropriations to train the teachers and accommodate the thousands of young people who were no longer satisfied with a high school education. State superintendents of schools and state certification supplanted the old township boards and county teachers' examinations. State old age pensions and mother's pensions replaced the old county poor farms. New facilities were provided for handling the mentally ill and criminally insane. The use of new serums in combating contagious diseases required the distribution of numerous biologicals. The growth of corporations, particularly of great utility holding companies, called for state utility commissions and legislation to regulate stock sales. The automobile rendered obsolete the former dirt and gravel roads, required the construction of new highways and the hard surfacing of all. New interest in recreation led to the building of state parks, the conservation of game and protection of forest areas. Commercialized amusements failed to function in conformity with modern moral standards without regulation. The ease with which automobiles could be stolen and transported long distances, the dangers to public safety from irresponsible drivers and the increased mobility of criminals resulted in state automobile license systems for cars and drivers and the establishment of state constabularies. State tax commissions, budget commissions, law drafting bureaus, welfare departments and public employment agencies were created. The courts failed to administer properly the new workmen's compensation laws and state industrial relations boards came into existence. There was legislation for the regulation of chain stores, small loan companies, farmers' cooperatives, the practice of law, medicine and dentistry, hotels, restaurants and barber shops.

Much of this new legislation came at the insistence of organized labor. Mechanization increased the productive capacity of labor but the laboring man had no control over the unit of production, and lived in an atmosphere of insecurity. His inability to secure a guaranteed return from his labor sufficient to provide what once were luxuries but now were necessities led to his dependence upon the state for them. Every new free social service added to the real income of the laboring man. It enabled him to get indirectly by taxation what he was unable to gain directly in wages. Some of the new control legislation was enacted to appease the reform groups who capitalize upon the supreme faith of the American people in their ability to effect changes in the habits and customs of the people by compulsion. Some of the new services were created to satisfy politically powerful minority groups. Most of them, however, were the inevitable result of the inability of local government agencies to function in the new social and economic order.

Yet there was remarkably little progress toward eliminating obsolete units of government. Township and small county organizations, with their host of minor officials, contribute little in the way of efficiency and much in the nature of extravagance and annoyance. They continue to exist because our entire political spoils system depends upon them. They constitute the most serious obstacles to the efficiency of taxation and crime control and to civil service reform. The power of all state legislatures was restricted by taking away from them the election of United States Senators. The powers of many of them were curbed by the adoption of elaborate state constitutions and the Initiative and Referendum. Responsibility was transferred from legislatures to governors by the adoption of state budgets and the creation of state administrative boards. Bicameral city councils disappeared. Mayors were replaced by city managers. An increasing number of cities adopted the civil service reform.

CHAPTER III

RESURGENCE OF JEFFERSONIAN LIBERALISM

Sources of Discontent

The years between the close of the Spanish American War and our entry into the World War may well be designated the flowering period of reform. A widespread revolt against the prevailing philosophy of government and its relation to human rights and property was already brewing when Roosevelt stepped upon the stage of national politics. It was, in the first instance, a demand that the individual be accorded a larger, more effective share in the processes of government from the nomination of candidates for office to the enactment of one's favorite ideas into law. It was, also, a demand for more honesty and efficiency in government service, and for more consideration of the public interest at the expense of accumulated wealth both in the selection of public officials and in the discharge of their duties. The Liberal Republican movement of 1872 centered around civil service reform. The Pendleton Act of 1883 had established a United States Civil Service Commission and had placed on the classified list certain employees of the Treasury and Post Office Departments. Presidents Harrison and Cleveland both had made some additions to the service; but, at the turn of the century, public officials were the political sub-lieutenants of their party's chief officer to whom, as President of the United States, they also were responsible for honest public service. The question was to remain as troublesome in 1936 as it had been in 1872. Meanwhile, much emphasis was being placed upon the need for purifying elections by the use of secret ballots and voting machines; for extending the franchise;

and for making public opinion a potent force in public affairs. These reforms, which required action by the states, were accomplished in the early years of the century.

The second source of discontent with the way politicians were running the country was the agrarian West. The great agricultural states had made their bid for control of the national government under the banner of William Jennings Bryan in 1896 and had lost; but Bryan had not faltered in his crusade to educate the country to a realization of the actual grievances of his section. That ringing challenge of 1896 could not so easily be thrust aside:

"We say to you that you have made the definition of a business man too limited in its application. The man who is employed for wages is as much a business man as his employer. The attorney in a country town is as much a business man as the corporation counsel in a great metropolis. The merchant at the crossroads store is as much a business man as the merchant of New York. The farmer who goes forth in the morning and toils all day—who begins in the spring and toils all summer—and who, by the application of brain and muscle to the natural resources of the country, creates wealth, is as much a business man as the man who goes upon the board of trade and bets on the price of wheat. You come to us and tell us that the great cities are in favor of the gold standard. We reply that the great cities rest upon our broad and fertile prairies. Burn down your cities and leave our farms, and your cities will spring up again as if by magic; but destroy our farms, and the grass will grow in the streets of every city in the country."

Bryan was destined to be the candidate of his party in 1900 and again in 1908, and four years later to place his mantle upon the shoulders of one, who, still unidentified with unpopular causes, was to lead the forces of reform to victory in an era of unprecedented progressive legislation. The reform of banking, currency and credit, and of the tariff system could only be accomplished by the Congress of the United States. These things were delayed until the forces of reform were politically strong enough to get control of the federal government. That was to come, however, only as the result of a revolt within the Republican Party.

These states of the upper Mississippi Valley and Great Lakes region were Republican by tradition. There is no escaping the fact that "gentlemen" voted the Republican ticket here just as they voted the Democratic ticket in the southern states. In no other way can the survival of the two old parties, each embracing industrial and agrarian groups, be explained. Republicans followed their progressive leaders in the enactment of state reform legislation, returned them to Congress in spite of their violent disagreements with the party leadership, but would not follow them in support of Democratic presidential candidates. La Follette bolted his party in the campaign of 1924 and polled five million votes; but he carried only his own state. Norris, whose career represents the most resplendent non-partizanship of the century, was returned to Congress over his own protests in 1928, but could not carry his state for the Democratic candidate, Alfred E. Smith. William E. Borah of Idaho often opposed his party's policies in Congress but never opposed its candidate in presidential elections. This situation accentuated the cleavage between the two sections of the Republican party. Year after year, the gulf between the agrarian West and the industrial East widened. Year after year, the position of the western Republicans became more difficult. They disagreed generally with the economic fundamentalism of their party and particularly with its refusal to alter government policies which were enriching the industrialists at the expense of the farmers. They carried their disagreement to the point of open insurgency in Congress during Taft's Administration, and secured the legislation they had so long desired when Wilson entered the White House.

The political reformers and the western agrarians were not alone in their demand for a new concept of government. Not all of the abuses of the new industrial system had appeared at the turn of the century, but the trend was plainly visible.

The great question was whether wealth should be allowed to gravitate into the hands of the few and control over all the instruments of production be concentrated unhampered by restrictive legislation, or whether some effort should be made to regulate economic processes in the interest of the people at large. Society was viewing with increasing apprehension the waste of human life and natural resources in the industrial process. It was groping for a philosophy which would justify public regulation of industry, and for formulae which would establish and maintain standards sufficiently high to relieve society of the presence of so much human wreckage. It was a matter of simple justice to some, conscience to others and dollars and cents to many. The efficacy of the doctrine of *laissez faire* was under indictment. There was general dissatisfaction with the system of taxation which fell heaviest upon the home owner and touched but lightly or not at all the vast resources of intangible wealth. Henry George sought to correct the inequality by advocating in his *Progress and Poverty* a single tax upon the economic rent of land. Others demanded the simpler method of income, estate and corporation taxes. The workers were in revolt against the barbarism of a common law which threw upon helpless widows and orphans the entire burden of industrial accidents by relieving employers of all financial responsibility. Forward-looking intellectuals were viewing with askance the operation of rugged individualism in the employment of women and children for long hours and ofttimes at the merest coolie wages. The more daring among the discontented were proposing a program of complete socialization of industry.

A gradual shifting of emphasis from aiding unfortunate individuals to correcting the social maladjustments which produced them resulted in the evolution of charities and corrections into social service and public welfare. By 1908, the Protestant Episcopal, Congregational, Presbyterian and Methodist churches had established industrial commissions and were advocating protection of workers from dangerous machinery, abolition of child labor and sweatshops, shorter hours, social insurance and a more equitable distribution of the returns from production. The General Federation of Women's Clubs was organized in 1890 and had increased its membership to 500,000 by 1905. It had its committees on Education, Pure Food, Forestry Conservation; and a legislative committee pressing for Juvenile Court Laws and general security legislation for women and children. A group of reform mayors had attracted wide attention with their crusade against public utilities: Samuel M. Jones of Toledo, Thomas L. Johnson of Cleveland and Max Fagan of Jersey City. New York City added a Tenement House Department to its city government in 1902. The movement rapidly spread to other cities suffering either from tall tenement houses with improper lighting and ventilation or from back alley slums. Governor Franklin Murphy of New Jersey, Mayor Patrick Collins of Boston and Jacob Riis initiated and popularized the movement. State legislatures were gradually enacting legislation requiring factories to install fire-escapes, devices for the removal of dust, guards on exposed machinery, and forbidding the use of explosive oils, cleaning of machinery in motion and the fining of employees for defective work. Laxity of enforcement, however, indicates that much of this legislation was passed to still the clamors of reformers without any serious intention of enforcement.

Then came the journalists. Frank Norris published his *Octopus* in 1901 and *The Pit* in 1902. The third of his proposed trilogy of wheat was never finished; but in these volumes dealing with the growing and marketing of the West's staple crop, he revealed the havoc wrought by the railroads and the grain markets in the lives of those who till the soil. Upton Sinclair, more frankly hostile to the capitalistic system, struck viciously at the profit motive and its social effects in his *The Jungle* (1906)—a story of immigrant exploitation in the famous stockyards and packing houses of Chicago. William Allen White added his protest against economic centralization in *A Certain Rich Man* (1909). Ida M. Tarbell, Lincoln Steffens and Ray

Stannard Baker contributed to *McClure's Magazine* in the short space of three years (1903-1905) the *History of the Standard Oil Company*, *Shame of the Cities*, and *Railroads on Trial* respectively. Jane Addams, Ernst Freund, Roscoe Pound, Walter Lippmann and Herbert Croly re-examined, in a series of brilliant monographs, many of our social and economic doctrines and found them inadequate. Not every one accepted these exposés of unpleasant realities with graceful complacency. Men and women motivated by a desire for preferment and notoriety were inevitably drawn into the movement. Convinced of their own righteousness and possessing few qualifications except the use of invective, they resorted to sensational denunciations generally spoken of as yellow journalism. Their activities injured the cause established by the careful and painstaking research of earlier writers. Finally, in the spring of 1906, President Roosevelt called attention to the excesses in these words: "Gross and reckless assaults on character, whether on stump or in newspaper, magazine or both, create a marked and vicious public sentiment, and at the same time act as a professed detriment to noble men of normal sensitiveness and tend to prevent them from entering the public service at any price. . . . It is because I feel that there should be no rest in the endless war against the forces of evil that I ask that the war be conducted with sanity as well as with resolution." His application of the term "muckrakers" to these enthusiastic young realists probably arose as much from his own conservatism as from their over-indulgence in sensationalism. The reform movement could not have moved forward without their contributions; and Roosevelt's action probably injured the cause as much as the reformers' excesses had done.

Political Reform

There followed a full decade of reform legislation. Its first objective was to break down the restraints upon the will of the majority provided by undemocratic governmental machinery. It involved the changing of parts of the system, the adding of new devices and, ultimately, an attack upon the written constitution and the power of judicial review. Oregon introduced more of these innovations than any other state: the initiative and referendum (1902), the direct election of United States Senators (1904), the recall of all elected officials (1908), and the preferential primaries for presidential nominations (1910). Wisconsin enacted the first direct primary law (1903). Arizona succeeded in gaining admission to the Union in 1911 only after promising to remove from her constitution a provision for the recall of judges. Colorado provided for the recall of judicial decisions (1912). Woman's suffrage, the most difficult of all the reforms to secure, had its beginning in the Territory of Wyoming in 1896. Not all of these changes were widely accepted. The Seventeenth Amendment to the Constitution, providing for the popular election of United States Senators, was ratified and became a part of the Constitution in 1913. Its wisdom had been discussed for many years. The power of accumulated wealth in the legislatures, the urge to undemocratic gerrymandering of states, and the unresponsiveness of Senators to popular will under the old system were responsible for the change. The Senate itself, however, under the leadership of conservatives like George F. Hoar of Massachusetts, had delayed the change for many years. The House of Representatives had passed resolutions in 1894, 1898, 1900 and 1902, but the Senate was adamant. The change was advocated by such men as William Jennings Bryan and Senator Cullom of Illinois, opposed by prominent men like Chauncey M. Depew. Finally, Senators William E. Borah of Idaho and Joseph L. Bristow of Kansas forced the amending resolution through the Senate in January, 1911. Woman's suffrage encountered such widespread hostility from prominent men like William H. Taft and Henry Watterson, editor of the Louisville *Courier Journal*, that it required an intensive campaign in legislatures, party conventions and Congress before the Nineteenth Amendment was finally ratified and declared a part of the Constitution in 1920. No one, aside from their over-enthusiastic sponsors, expected these two changes to bring immediate results in the correction of political abuses. Women showed a disposition to work within the party system instead of maintaining an independent position and thus bringing united pressure upon both parties for the enactment of legislation they desired. In the early twenties, however, the Women's Joint Congressional Committee, representing a score of national women's organizations, was formed. It succeeded in getting the Maternity and Infancy Law (1921) enacted and the Cable Act (1922) granting to married women the right of independent citizenship. Their success in securing state legislation for child welfare, women's legal rights, social hygiene and education have been little less than phenomenal. More money was spent, because more was required, on occasion to buy senatorial seats from the voters than had ever been spent in the state legislatures; but it could not be concealed so easily and most attempts have ended disastrously because of an aroused public opinion.

The direct primary, the initiative, the referendum and the recall were all devised to encourage a wider popular participation in public affairs, break up the evils of machine politics and create responsible party government. The direct primary system was adopted by thirty-seven states, the preferential primary system by thirteen and the initiative and referendum by twenty before the first phase of the movement came to an end. The use of the recall was confined largely to city administration. None of these changes accomplished what its sponsors had expected. The preferential primary, devised by Senator Jonathan Bourne of Oregon to give every voter an opportunity to register his choice among candidates, failed to work from the beginning. President Wilson and Charles Evans Hughes failed to enter the direct primaries in 1916. As a result, Alabama, Indiana, Iowa, Michigan, Minnesota, Montana, North Carolina and Vermont repealed their laws. The next presidential campaign introduced the obnoxious practice of entering favorite sons in the primaries. Men who were handling the pre-convention campaigns of certain candidates refused to enter their candidates in doubtful states. Instead, by previous arrangement, a favorite son would be entered against opponents in each such state with the understanding that after a courtesy ballot in the convention the state delegation would shift its ballot to the machine candidate. The initiative and referendum failed almost as completely and fell into disuse. Three decades later another movement was started to make government more responsive to popular opinion. Regular referendums of public opinion were taken by the *Literary Digest* and a New Institute of Public Opinion launched by a bi-partizan group of newspapers. Congress fell into line by specifying that a popular referendum must be taken on the question of prohibition repeal, and a constitutional amendment was adopted eliminating the "lame duck" sessions of Congress and the long period between the election of a President and his inauguration. Senator Norris of Nebraska, whose political career extends from the early reform period to the present, sponsored the latter reform as well as the establishment of a unicameral legislature in his own state (1935). They may point to the ultimate introduction of a parliamentary system in one of the states and its acceptance by all. Laws to prevent the election of state officials by minority votes and to give proportional representation to minorities were adopted in Michigan (1889), Pennsylvania (1895), New Jersey (1901) and at various times in Ohio and Rhode Island. All were invalidated by the courts.

Social Legislation

The second phase of the movement, that to provide social and economic security, was the most important. It included social insurance legislation, the regulation of child labor and safety and health codes. Social insurance legislation began with workmen's compensation laws. The old rule of the common law had enabled employers to evade the cost of industrial accidents unless the injured employee could prove that the employer had been unduly careless in some respect, that a fellow servant had not caused the accident by carelessness, that he himself had not contributed in any way to the cause and that he had been compelled to assume an unusual risk. Needless to say, under such a system of jurisprudence, the cases in which an injured employee could recover damages were few and far between. Long hours, unprotected machinery, and the urge to profit took their annual toll of dead and injured, leaving behind an appalling wreckage of broken homes, destitute widows and orphans.

By the turn of the century, there was a growing conviction that accidents with their resulting loss of time, medical care, burial fees and support of minor dependents were as much a part of the cost of production as raw materials and should be borne by the consumer of the products. Congress passed an Employers' Liability Act in 1906, relieving railway employers from the operation of the contributory negligence and fellow servant rules of the common law. A revision was made two years later limiting it specifically to employees engaged in interstate commerce in conformity with a Supreme Court ruling. Five states adopted workmen's compensation laws in 1911. Twenty-five more followed their example before 1916 and all but Florida, Mississippi, South Carolina and Arkansas by 1929. Steady progress was made in transferring jurisdiction from the courts to special administrative boards, in increasing the amounts payable to the injured employee or his estate and in extending the benefits to a wider range of occupations.

Other types of social security legislation did not fare so well. Labor unions, completely dominated by men, were on the whole opposed to regulation of hours or wages. Women, not being organized, were peculiarly subject to exploitation in the form of long hours, low wages, unsatisfactory and indecent working conditions. The census of 1900 had shown that more than 2,500,000 girls under 25 years of age were employed as wage earners and that most of them were under 21 years of age. The dangers to health and morality, particularly of those employed in factories at night and for low wages, did not need to be argued. Only four states prohibited the employment of women at night in 1900: Indiana, New York, Massachusetts and Nebraska. Not more than twenty states prohibited the night work of children and, in some of those, regulations were little short of criminal. South Carolina, for instance, forbade the employment of "women" at night who were under 12 years of age. Thirty-three states had no legal restrictions upon the number of hours per day or week that women might be gainfully employed; and there were no restrictions upon tenement-house work of the cities where all sorts of clothing, cigars, cigarettes and other artifacts were made during long hours at starvation wages. The humanitarian desire to throw the protecting mantle of the law over the defenseless victim of economic distress, as well as the desire to protect the future of the social state from the physiological damages visited upon its wives and mothers by ruthless exploitation, led to corrective legislation. Acting under the police powers of the state, Massachusetts had inaugurated a maximum ten-hour day for women employees as early as 1875 and the state courts had held the act to be constitutional (*Hamilton Manufacturing Co.* v. *Massachusetts*). A similar law passed by Oregon in 1908 was upheld by the United States Supreme Court (*Muller* v. *Oregon*). The decision in this case stands as a permanent monument to the brilliant labors of Louis D. Brandeis who prepared the arguments for the Oregon case before being appointed to the Supreme Court. From that point there was a succession of such laws until, by 1930, all but four states had regulated hours of work and a considerable number had provided commissions with wide discretionary powers to deal with the conditions of employment of both women and children. A companion movement to establish minimum wage laws was completely thwarted when the Supreme Court in 1923 held such laws to be a violation of the Fifth Amendment of the Constitution (*Children's Hospital* v. *Adkins*). This decision dealt with an act of Congress requiring that the wages of women in the District of Columbia be sufficient to "maintain them in health and to protect their morals." Justice Brandeis did not join in the decision because his daughter was a member of the minimum wage commission of the District. The decision was 5 to 3—Holmes and Taft writing as vigorous dissenting opinions as had ever appeared. Later events gave this case far greater significance than it appeared to have at the time. The Court said:

"We cannot accept the doctrine that women of mature age require or may be subjected to restrictions upon their liberty of contract which could not lawfully be imposed in the case of men under similar circumstances. To do so would be to ignore all the implications to be drawn from the present day trend of legislation, as well as that of common thought and usage, by which woman is accorded emancipation from the old doctrine that she must be given special protection or be subjected to special restraint in her contractual and civil relationships. Enough has been said to show that the authority to fix hours of labor cannot be exercised except in respect to those occupations where work of long continued duration is detrimental to health. This Court has been careful in every case where the question has been raised, to place its decision upon this limited authority of the Legislature to regulate hours of labor and to disclaim any purpose to uphold the legislation as fixing wages, thus recognizing an essential difference between the two." Those words might well have ended the attempts of state legislatures to fix minimum wages; but the Court also said: "A statute requiring an employer to pay in money, to pay at prescribed and regular intervals, to pay the value of the services rendered, even to pay with fair relation to the extent of the benefit obtained from the service, would be understandable." Taking these words at face value, the Legislature of New York passed a statute in 1933 fixing minimum wages for women in laundries. The law was carefully drawn. No attempt was made at broad social reform and the regulation was limited to one industry. The case came before the Court in 1936 and, on June 1, it left no further doubt of its position, holding that state legislatures are "without power by any form of legislation to prohibit, change or nullify contracts between employers and adult woman workers as to the amount of wages to be paid." This was a 5 to 4 decision with Justices Hughes, Brandeis, Stone and Cardozo dissenting. Justices McReynolds, Butler, Sutherland and Van Deventer were opposed to both the act of Congress in 1923 and the act of New York in 1936. Their decisions designated a field into which neither the federal nor state governments might enter with regulatory legislation and limited the scope of the states in their most valuable function: social experimentation.

Child labor, strangely, has been very difficult to control by state legislation. It was one of the earliest recognized evils of our modern industrial system but, after thirty years of agitation for reform, it remained to plague the nation at the time of the last great depression. Statistics show that in 1900 one of every five children between the ages of ten and fifteen were gainfully employed. By 1930, it had decreased to one in twenty. Nevertheless, the census of 1930 showed 2,145,000 employed children between the ages of ten and seventeen, and the census figures were far from complete. They included no children under ten, although thousands below that age are employed in agriculture, in the street trades, etc., and there is some doubt if all types of agricultural employment were included even for those above the age of ten. A nation with two million juvenile employees at a time when millions of men were idle and on the relief rolls has not progressed far in that type of social reform.

The difficulty lay in securing effective uniform legislation in the several states and in the constitutional restraints upon action by Congress. Senator Albert J. Beveridge introduced a bill in Congress in 1906 which was so designed as to exclude from interstate commerce the products of factories and mines employing children less than fourteen years of age. The bill did not pass and nothing more was accomplished for ten years. Then the Keating-Owen bill was sponsored by President Wilson and enacted into law. This Act excluded from interstate commerce the products of any factory employing children under fourteen years of age, or children between the ages of fourteen and sixteen at night or for longer than an eight-hour day. Mines were forbidden to employ children under sixteen years of age. The Act was contested in the courts and declared unconstitutional by a 5 to 4 decision as an improper use of Congress's control over interstate commerce and an invasion of state rights. The decision was bitterly assailed because in previous decisions Congress had been allowed to exclude from interstate commerce such commodities as lottery tickets, impure foods and drugs, obscene literature, women for immoral purposes, etc. Congress then passed an act (1919) taxing out of existence the products of child labor. It was carelessly drawn and, as was freely predicted at the time, the Supreme Court in a decision written by Chief Justice Taft declared it an unwarranted extension of the power to tax.

In 1924, therefore, Congress passed a Constitutional Amendment giving to Congress "the power to limit, regulate, and prohibit the labor of persons under eighteen years of age." Only six states had ratified before the depression, eighteen more under the pressure of that calamity. Meanwhile, the legislatures of more than thirteen states had rejected the amendment, making ratification extremely doubtful. Opposition to the Amendment was cleverly concealed in an organization known as the National Committee for the Protection of Child, Family, School and Church. It was opposed as an impairment of the freedom of contract, as a threat to parental control, and as an invasion of state rights. Communism, the regimentation of children in concentration camps, and bureaucratic interference with schools and non-religious children's organizations were mentioned as probable consequences of its adoption. The American Legion and the American Federation of Labor both endorsed the amendment. Elihu Root effectively answered the states rights argument when he said: "It is useless for the advocates of state rights to inveigh against the supremacy of the constitutional law of the United States, or against the extension of national authority in the fields of necessary control, where the states themselves fail in the performance of their duty." It was pointed out that Congress no less than the state legislatures was under popular control and that children as well as adults were protected by the Bill of Rights, but to no avail. The only real progress came through compulsory school attendance laws. States gradually increased the minimum age at which children could leave school, raised the degree of proficiency required, and lengthened the school year. The more advanced require attendance until eighteen years of age unless high school has been completed and place the employment of all children who have not completed the educational requirements under the supervision of school superintendents. Other laws requiring physical examinations before securing employment, and excluding minors from certain types of employment altogether have done something to correct the situation.

A further extension of social legislation had to do with the care of dependent children. Illinois established a juvenile court system in 1899 and the plan had spread to all but two of the states by 1930. Mothers' pensions, established to preserve the home influence over children whose fathers were dead, in prison or had deserted, were first established in 1911. Eighteen states enacted some form of assistance to mothers during the next two years and, by 1930, all but four had done so. The White House Conference of 1930 reported that during the previous year 220,000 children were thus cared for at a cost of thirty million dollars. Old age pensions and unemployment insurance lagged definitely behind in the movement. They occupy such a prominent part in the revival of reform legislation during the early thirties that it is better to deal with them later.

The most dilatory states in the enactment of social legislation were in the South. That was the stronghold of economic as well as religious fundamentalism. They were the great agricultural states whose cotton crop depended so heavily upon the labor of women and children. They were the states in which industry was still in its growing pains; where parental authority and individual liberty still made a strong appeal; and where the

Negro question still hampered the development of a critical attitude toward social and economic reform. Mississippi, South Carolina, Florida and Arkansas have no workmen's compensation laws. Alabama, Louisiana and Tennessee have compensation laws but no industrial commissions for their administration. South Carolina, Mississippi, Georgia and Alabama have more than twenty-five per cent of their women employed. Eighty-four per cent of the children employed in agriculture in the country are in the cotton states. Georgia and South Carolina are the only two states without mother's pension laws.

Industrial Relations

Legislation for the regulation of industry and trade fell, for the most part, within the province of the federal government. The Constitution expressly granted to Congress control over interstate commerce, and the Supreme Court had given that clause a broad interpretation in many cases, especially in *Gibbons* v. *Ogden* (1824), *Covington Bridge Company* v. *Kentucky* (1899), and *Champion* v. *Ames* (1903). In the last of these cases, the Court had said: "In this connection it must not be forgotten that the power of Congress to regulate commerce among the states is plenary, is complete in itself, and is subject to no limitations, except as may be found in the Constitution."

Three developments of the late nineteenth century had aroused wide discussion of the entire question. The railroads had always been a vital part of our national life. They were absolutely essential to industrial development and to the life of any business enterprise. In their haste to promote the development of transportation, the people had recklessly granted charters and bestowed favors upon railroad promotors. The mighty railway system, embracing a total of 160 thousand miles when federal regulation began and 250 thousand miles in 1930, could not have been built on any such scale without the government's generous donations of land and loans of public money. Land grants by the federal government, the states of the Mississippi

Valley and Texas amounted to more than 200 million acres, and money grants to more than a billion dollars. Eventually, the people came to realize that the roads were public highways and demanded that they no longer be operated as private enterprises. The railroad owners, particularly where large blocks of stock were held by industrial corporations, insisted upon the same freedom as was accorded other businesses under the prevailing doctrine of *laissez faire*. The period of rapid railway building between 1850 and 1890 witnessed the unique situation of governmental units, even down to towns and counties, straining their credit to furnish the nation transportation facilities while promotors of the roads stretched moral and legal restraints to the limit in a mad scramble for private gain. It was this excessive will to profit, rather than to serve communities through which the roads passed, that eventually led to government regulation; and it was the original public investment in the system which finally broke down the resistance of the roads to public control of rates and services. The people of the several states had established in the Granger laws, during the 1870's, the principle that states had the power to regulate corporations rendering a public service and the principle had been confirmed by the Supreme Court in the Granger Cases (1876). About the turn of the century, the states began to set up public utility commissions with control over banks as well as railroads. The North Carolina and Virginia commissions were established in 1902; that of New York in 1905.

The second development was the growth of corporations and corporate practices. These creatures of the law possessed the qualities of permanence, impersonality, limited liability and a division of interest among many owners. The people at large became both the owners of and money lenders to them, the former being the stockholders, the latter the bondholders. Their capitalization was based not upon original investment nor upon replacement valuation, but upon probable earning power. They were so constituted that the officers and directors exercised control without personal responsibility, and they came more and more under the power of banking interests. In the decade of the seventies, they were largely industrial combinations based upon agreements between otherwise independent companies to fix prices, divide sales territory, limit production or share profits. These were followed by trusts, in which the controlling company exchanged its trust certificates for the stock of the several constitutent corporations. These, in turn, were followed by the holding companies: corporations whose property consisted of shares of stock in other corporations. Their evolution resulted in the strangulation of small competitive enterprises, in the establishment of monopolies, in over-capitalization, and in tremendous amounts of watered stock; and the public at large insisted upon intervention by the government to protect stockholders, employees, the consumers, and the government itself from the tremendous pressure of accumulated wealth.

The third development was that of organized labor. The modern history of organized labor in the United States may be divided roughly into three periods. The first began with a series of events between 1886 and 1894. It gradually terminated between 1914 and 1917. The second period came to an end in 1933. Within these dates occurred certain definite trends with respect to the type and degree of organization among wage earners, the attitude of government toward labor and of organized labor toward government, and general aspects of American life vitally effecting the status and condition of wage earners though not directly pertaining to labor.

The Noble Order of the Knights of Labor was organized in 1869. It was a secret order under the control of Uriah S. Stephens until 1879 when it dropped the cloak of secrecy and passed under the direction of Terence V. Powderly. It reached a peak membership of 700,000 in 1886, almost disappeared by 1890 and was absorbed by the Populist movement in 1892-93. Previous to the Knights of Labor, in the Civil War period, labor had been organized on the basis of crafts. These early trade unions were at a serious disadvantage in the contest with capital. Composed of skilled workmen, their membership was peculiarly vulnerable to the black list and their organization to prosecution under the state conspiracy laws. The Knights of Labor, therefore, was organized along radically different lines. It was secret; it admitted every one to membership who gained a living by honest toil; and the membership of each chapter included every one living in the locality who belonged to the organization. Legislatures and courts generally had legalized unionization by the time it ceased to regard secrecy as a virtue. Its chief attribute, however, and its greatest weakness lay in its type of organization. Craft distinctions were ignored and three classes of labor were brought into the organization whose relative importance in the labor market steadily increased through the years, becoming paramount in the modern machine age: women, Negroes and unskilled laborers. The order deprecated strikes though not outlawing them. Failing to develop the technique of conducting strikes, it nevertheless supported the May Day strikes of 1886, called to gain the eight-hour day in industry, and their failure marked the beginning of a new era in labor history.

The second aspect of this short but highly dynamic period of labor history was the organization of the American Federation of Labor on the ruins of the Knights of Labor. The Federation was first organized as the Federation of Organized Trades and Labor Unions of the United States and Canada in 1881 and assumed its present form in 1886. It was under the presidency of Samuel Gompers from the date of its organization until his death in 1924 and then of William Green. It had 550,000 members in 1900, 2,000,000 in 1914, 2,725,000 in 1918, and about 3,500,000 in 1929. It was never able to bring the Railway Brotherhoods into membership, but was not seriously threatened by competitive organizations until after the World War when the Communist Party sought to gain control of it by boring from within. Again, in 1933, capital sought to thwart its growing prestige under the National Industrial Recovery Act by organizing a host of company unions.

With the founding of the Federation, organized labor purged

its ranks of all but skilled craftsmen and started the way of becoming the most conservative labor body in the world. All schemes for the socialization of industry were repudiated. The Federation was composed of Labor's aristocracy. It fought bitterly to maintain its privileged position, against capital with the strike and boycott; against alien radicals by supporting restrictions on immigration; against unskilled labor with apprenticeship rules and the closed shop; against foreign competitions with a protective tariff. Its officers and those of the affiliated unions drew salaries comparable to the salaries of United States Senators. The operating unit of the organization was the local craft union. In a given locality, there were unions of teamsters, bricklayers, stone-cutters, stationary engineers, etc., with no common interest or contact except that each was part of state and national unions, all of which were loosely joined in the Federation. The representation of each of the national craft unions in the Federation was based on its membership.

Organized Labor and Government

The disastrous Haymarket riot of 1886 and the Pullman strike of 1894, both in Chicago, precipitated a sharp divergence in the attitude of the public and of government toward organized labor. The Haymarket riot introduced into labor controversies the most persistent feature of all such tests of strength since that time: the confusion of rational consideration of issues involved with alien radicalism. In this instance, violence followed police interference with an orderly assemblage of labor sympathizers. Some one threw a bomb, and several policemen were killed. Unable to find the guilty parties, they rounded up the leaders of the Black International, an anarchists' organization of some two thousand persons. The court ruling, that it was only necessary to show that their teachings were of such nature as to have provoked the violence, led to the hanging of four, the suicide of a fifth and imprisonment of three others. Seven of the eight were of foreign birth. From that time until the present, radicalism has been dragged into so many cases involving the struggle for social and economic justice that the historian can not ignore its significance if he would. It inflamed the public mind against Illinois's humanitarian governor, John P. Altgeld, and weakened his position in the controversy with President Cleveland on a really vital constitutional question. It silenced popular resistance to equally fundamental violations of the safeguards of personal liberty by the Department of Justice's raids upon aliens in 1920. It deprived the textile workers of Elizabethton, Tennessee, and Gastonia, North Carolina, in 1929, of the public support needed to win their strike against atrocious conditions in the mills of those towns. It deprived the defendants in the famous Scottsboro Case of an impartial consideration of guilt. It was harped upon continuously by the defense in the Tampa flogging cases in 1936. Back of all these and myriad other specific cases was the psychological effect upon general public opinion when labor disturbances ensued and the cry of radicalism was raised.

Even more important than the question of radicalism, however, was the realization that labor unions could be just as destructive of individual freedom and initiative of the laboring man as industrial combinations were of the small business man, and that strikes were as injurious, even more annoying, to the peace, safety and good order of the community.

The first step toward federal regulation of industrial relations was taken by Congress in 1887 when it passed the Interstate Commerce Act. Its primary purpose was to require equitable service to all patrons of the railroads by outlawing rebates and pools; but it was also an indirect blow at the trusts. Three years later Congress passed the Sherman Anti-Trust Law, designed to prohibit contracts in restraint of trade and monopolies. It declared "every contract, combination in the form of trust or otherwise, or conspiracy in restraint of trade or commerce among the several states, or with foreign nations," to be illegal. It imposed upon District Attorneys the duty of instituting proceedings against such combinations; and it permitted those injured by such illegal acts to recover threefold damages.

The Interstate Commerce Commission created by the Act of 1887 was little more than a fact-finding agency for many years. Congress had not intended it to be merely that, but the appointments of Presidents Cleveland and McKinley and the several Supreme Court decisions had stripped it of both the will and the power to regulate rates or exercise judicial functions. The real history of regulation began in 1906 when President Roosevelt and Senator La Follette forced the Hepburn Act through Congress. Later legislation included the Mann-Elkins Act (1910), the Physical Valuation Act (1913), the Transportation Act (1920), and the Emergency Railroad Transportation Act (1933). For the most part, these acts dealt with the regulation of rates and services, capital structures, the sale of securities, consolidations and the extension of the jurisdiction of the Interstate Commerce Commission over other, but not necessarily competing, communication.

The Interstate Commerce Act had stated that all rates "shall be reasonable and just." The Supreme Court held in 1897 that this did not give to the Interstate Commerce Commission the power to require a reduction of rates nor to set maximum rates. The statement of the Court in *Smyth* v. *Ames* (1897) contains the fundamentals of the rate-making problem. Said the Court: "We hold—that the basis of all calculations as to the reasonableness of rates to be charged by a corporation maintaining a highway under legislative sanction just be the fair value of the property being used by it for the convenience of the public. And, in order to ascertain that value, the original cost of construction, the amount expended in permanent improvements, the amount and market value of its bonds and stocks, the present as compared with the original cost of construction, the probable earning capacity of the property, under particular rates prescribed by statute, and the sum required to meet operating expenses, are all matters for consideration, and are to be given such weight as may be just and right in each case."

The items here listed by the Court as a basis for determining reasonable rates contained such a medley of contradictions as to render their use as a formula impossible. The original cost of constructing the roads bore no relation to the amount of stocks and bonds outstanding because of the tremendous amount of water that had been pumped into the latter. The original cost of constructing the Erie Railroad had been $15,000,000, but when Daniel Drew and Jay Gould finished their fight for its control by manipulating the market, bribing legislatures and printing stock its capitalization was $60,000,000. The Union Pacific had cost $50,000,000 to build, but because of the exorbitant profits taken by its promotors through the medium of the Crédit Mobilier, its stocks and bonds amounted to $94,000,000. The New York Central alone had nearly $50,000,000 of watered stock before the Interstate Commerce Act was passed. By 1930, there was an estimated $8,000,000,000 of watered stock in the capital structure of the roads. Likewise, there was no relation between the market value of stocks and bonds and any other item except probable earning power or probable bankruptcy, because the roads were wrecked by irresponsible management so frequently as to ruin thousands of small investors throughout the country.

The Sherman Anti-Trust Law, like all such laws, depended for its effectiveness upon vigorous action and eternal vigilance on the part of the Department of Justice for its enforcement. So far as the trusts were concerned, it was allowed to languish by the Attorney-Generals until Roosevelt became President. Meanwhile, it was invoked against the labor unions and given its first test in the courts. The Pullman strike of 1894 marked a significant step in labor history. When the American Railway Union refused to handle trains carrying Pullman coaches, Attorney-General Olney directed its prosecution under the Sherman Act of 1890. This Act declared illegal "every contract, combination in the form of trust or otherwise, or conspiracy, in restraint of trade or commerce among the several states or with foreign nations." An injunction was issued against its head, Eugene V. Debs, and he was given a six months' prison sentence for contempt of court. The Supreme Court upheld the sentence, May 27, 1895 (*In Re Debs*). Injunctions had been used against the Knights of Labor in the eighties; but they became very prevalent after the Debs decision. Their scope was broadened gradually until they were issued finally against the attempted organization of unions, picketing, strikes, the payment of strike benefits, boycotts, and even the assembling of strikers or members of their families. Almost all the damage done to organized labor was through temporary injunctions which required neither hearing nor trial, but violations of which were punishable as contempt of court. Strikes were broken ordinarily by temporary injunctions before the time arrived for a hearing on the question of making the injunction permanent. The Supreme Court had based its decision upholding injunctions in the Debs Case on broader grounds than the Sherman Act. As a consequence, both the rights of labor under the Sherman Act and the scope of injunction became political question.

The meaning of the Sherman Act with respect to industry and trade was still a disputed question at the turn of the century. Moreover, this was the one phase of the reform movement in which the reformers themselves disagreed both as to objectives and methods. There were men who would have been satisfied to remove the influence of industrial corporations from legislative bodies, believing such activities to be outside their legitimate sphere of action and inimical to the public welfare. There were others who believed that full publicity of financial and trading practices would make the corporations honest in their relations with competitors and the public. Some authorities regarded industrial combinations as indispensable to modern economic life and asked that they be preserved under regulation. They took the realistic view that the nation could never again return to the era of small individual business, but that competition must not give way to monopoly. There were others who insisted that the trusts must be destroyed with despatch and great fanfare. It was a question of the relative merits of combination as opposed to unrestricted competition. There was a question of whether competition could be restored by any sort of legislation. James M. Beck held that the Sherman Act had "not altered the underlying basis of any industry, and it never will, because you cannot compel men to compete if they do not want to compete." Senator Francis G. Newlands of Nevada, a member of the Interstate Commerce Committee, found men from all types of business and professions demanding either a federal incorporation law or an amendment to the Sherman Act clearly defining the words "reasonable or unreasonable" as used by the Supreme Court and specifically stating what should be considered evidence of conspiracy in restraint of trade. Louis D. Brandeis and Senator La Follette favored such an amendment. Beck took much the same position when he said: "If the Supreme Court of the United States, after two years of deliberation and the use of sixteen thousand words, cannot give a plain definition of what a business man may do or may not do, then business men ought not to be charted with violation of law if they mistake their way in this jungle of legal terms." Attorney-General Wickersham, who believed that 50 per cent of evil corporate practices arose from lax incorporation laws of the several states, and President Taft favored federal incorporations. Senator John Sharpe Williams of Mississippi favored a national law barring from interstate commerce all corporations operating under charters from states whose incorporation laws did not meet requirements laid down by Congress. The trouble, as he saw it, was in "charter-enacted legislation," but he opposed federal incorporation as likely to result in "government and industrial centralization . . . more laws and more offices." The final suggestion was embodied in a bill introduced shortly after the decision of the Supreme Court in the Standard Oil Case. It provided for a federal administrative agency similar to the Interstate Commerce Commission, which would gradually build up through administrative procedure a body of law for the conduct of industry and trade. When men like William H. Taft, George W. Wickersham, Robert La Follette, James M.

Beck and John Sharpe Williams could not agree on the remedial legislation required, it is conclusive evidence that there was no well-defined program among the reform element of the country.

Conservation

Conservation of natural resources, particularly coal and timber lands, soil and water power sites was an integral part of the general reform program. Its purpose was to withhold from exploitation for private gain the exhaustible resources such as public coal lands, to place restrictions in the public interest upon the development of inexhaustible resources such as water power, and to restore to normalcy those resources already partially destroyed, such as forests and soils. It was a movement close to the hearts of men like Theodore Roosevelt and Gifford Pinchot (Director of the United States Forestry Service), heartily endorsed by William H. Taft and supported by all lovers of wild life and out-door recreation, opponents of monopolistic tendencies and those interested in the future prosperity and economic democracy of the nation. In its broader aspects, it marked the period of transition from the exploitive philosophy of pioneering days to the conservative philosophy of a mature people concerned over the adequacy of its original inheritance to meet the needs of present and future generations.

The demand for action by the federal government arose from (1) a realization that private enterprise would not engage in a general plan of conservation for the public good at the expense of private gain, (2) the close inter-relation between forest areas, the flow of water in navigable streams, flood control and soil erosion by wind and water in regions far beyond the limits of one or even a group of states, (3) the riparian rights of the federal government along navigable streams and its control over the transmission of power across state lines in the realm of interstate commerce, and (4) the proved ineffectiveness of state control over large corporations. It was opposed by special interests engaged in lumbering, mining and water power development, by individualists who feared the stifling of individual enterprise, and by state rights devotees, particularly in the new western states, who resented radical departure from traditional policies by the federal government while they were in the stage of early development.

The most important part of the Roosevelt program involved the public land policy and reclamation of arid and semi-arid areas, both in the Far West. Roosevelt called a White House Conference, in 1908, of governors, members of Congress, justices of the courts and technical authorities for the purpose of formulating a national conservation program. It made two important recommendations: (1) that timber lands on the head-waters of all navigable streams be preserved, lumbering operations on all other lands, public and private, be placed under strict regulation, and vigorous measures for the control of forest fires be adopted; (2) that the government should retain all lands containing deposits of phosphates, natural gas, oil and coal, and retain title to all mineral deposits in other lands that it might sell. The establishment of state and national conservation commissions dates from this conference. Roosevelt, acting with his characteristic vigor and impulsiveness, had closed 64,000,000 acres of public lands in 1906. Following the establishment of the National Conservation Commission in 1908, he closed to entry over 200,000 acres, including valuable forest areas, waterpower sites and mineral deposits; and requested Congress to enact the necessary legislation to fulfill the second recommendation of the White House Conference, namely, the retention by the government of all mineral and water power sites and their development under lease. Congress refused to do this and Taft took up the burden where Roosevelt left off. He succeeded in getting legalization for the Roosevelt withdrawals, for the right to separate titles to land and mineral deposits and to withhold permanently waterpower sites and some mineral lands. He was embarrassed politically by an open controversy between his Secretary of the Interior, Ballinger, and Pinchot, who had been retained as Director of the Forestry Service, over the restoration to private interests of certain water power in the West and the alienation of coal lands in Alaska. The controversy, which reached the proportions of a national scandal, contributed to the growing unpopularity of Taft. Roosevelt made a great deal of political capital out of it in spite of the fact that Ballinger was one of his own appointees and that Taft probably was correct in questioning the legality of the public land withdrawals. The Ballinger scandal was not the last such episode in the administration of public lands, those of Harding's Administration after the World War being far more serious but having less political repercussion.

Irrigation projects were first begun in 1902 and continued without intermission to the present time. The program succeeded in restoring to cultivation millions of acres of productive soil; and eventually evolved into gigantic enterprises for the production of hydro-electric power and still greater projects for reforestation and flood control. No progress was made toward flood control, however, until after the disastrous flood of 1913, and none in the direction of government power production, except as a World War activity, until after 1932. It is a mistake to think that agitation over the power trust and for the control of public utilities began in the late twenties. The whole question was thoroughly discussed during the first decade of the century, leaving little to be added except the aggravation of then existing evils by the rapid increase in power production and the perfection of an intricate system of holding companies.

The same may be said about the arbitration of industrial disputes and the tariff. At the turn of the century, industrial relations were governed almost entirely by the common law. Intimidation or coercion by strikers, picketing during strikes, and attempts to gain the closed shop were generally held to be illegal. The individual workingman was secure in his right to quit work at will by virtue of the Thirteenth Amendment of the Constitution, but often in danger of losing all semblance of personal liberty through punishment for contempt of court in violation of injunctions. The demand was for some provision in law which would eliminate industrial warfare. It was suggested that the Interstate Commerce Commission and the State Public Service Commissions be given power to investigate controversies and enforce their studied decisions; that emphasis be placed upon forestalling violence by eliminating the cause rather than upon the suppression of rioting; that machinery for conciliation and compromise be substituted for strong-arm police activity. Slason Thompson published in *The Outlook*, December 17, 1904, statistics showing that, during the previous two and one-half years, 180 persons had been killed, 1651 injured and 5533 arrested in industrial warfare in the United States. Concerning the Pennsylvania coal strike of 1902, he said:

"From beginning to end it was attended by every conceivable description and degree of human fiendishness. Malicious and criminal mischief held carnival in many districts. Outbreaks of minor deviltry did not spare the mother bearing her infant in her arms, or innocent children on their way to school. Clergymen were notified not to bury dead non-unionists, and union men refused to worship at the same altar with the industrious 'scab' who preferred to work rather than see his family starve."

It was this strike of the anthracite coal miners which furnished Roosevelt one of his many opportunities to keep before the public. The striking miners numbered no less than 150,000, and they had succeeded in completely suspending operations for more than five months. The operators refused to meet their demands for a nine-hour day and 20 per cent increase of wages and made no effort to compromise. Early in October, Roosevelt called representatives of both sides to Washington, reminded them of approaching winter and the needs of the public, and suggested that it was time for conciliation. The operators scorned the offer of mediation and asked that Roosevelt suppress the strike by using the army and prosecuting the miners' union for violation of the Sherman Anti-Trust Law. Instead, he made arrangements to appoint an investigating commission and to seize the mines and operate them with army labor. J. P. Morgan hastened to bring the operators to terms while there was still time and they suddenly petitioned Roosevelt to undertake mediation. The miners resumed operations and the Commission awarded them the nine-hour day and a 10 per cent increase in wages. Nothing was accomplished, however, in the way of establishing labor courts, compulsory arbitration, or even relief for the workers from the widespread use of the injunction, during Roosevelt's and Taft's Administrations. Wilson's Administration brought important federal legislation and compulsory arbitration laws in some of the states.

The tariff was also under discussion as a part of the reform movement. Tariff rates had been raised to the highest levels in the nation's history during McKinley's Administration. The primary object of our tariff laws had always been to safeguard home industries with incidental revenue to the government. They represented an exercise of the taxing power beyond its normal purpose. The Dingley tariff rates, established in 1897, had gone beyond the point of taxation for public purposes and had come dangerously close to establishing an embargo—thus creating a partnership between the government and certain industries for the exclusion from the country of relief from oppressively high prices. The demand for tariff reform, therefore, did not emanate entirely from the agrarians as it largely had at other times. It arose from a more scientific approach to the problem, with a definite claim that excessive rates were helping to create and perpetuate monopolies, fostering an inequitable distribution of wealth, restricting foreign markets, undermining the normal functions of our political institutions, and imposing excessive prices on all consumers, agrarians and others alike. Roosevelt was a protectionist, and so was Taft. Roosevelt said with regard to protection:

"Conditions change, and the laws must be modified from time to time to fit new exigencies. But the genuine underlying principle of protection, as it has been embodied in all but one of the American tariff laws for the last forty years, has worked out results so beneficial, so evenly and widely spread . . . that the American people, if they show their usual practical business sense, will insist when these laws are modified that they shall be modified with the utmost care and conservatism, and by the friends and not the enemies of the protective system."

Taft has said more bluntly: "The present business system of the country rests on the protective tariff and any attempt to change it to a free trade basis will certainly lead to disaster." There was the difference between the political sagacity of the two men. Roosevelt's Administration closed without anything being attempted in the way of revision. Taft's Administration opened with the greatest tariff debate in three-quarters of a century.

The public was demanding that rates be revised downward to the point where cost of production at home and abroad would be equalized. The Republican platform of 1908 promised as much. The House of Representatives, after an exhaustive study by the Ways and Means Committee, passed a bill which not only honestly met the requirement but provided for free trade with the Philippines and a progressive inheritance tax. The reactionary Finance Committee of the Senate, however, went all the way in catering to the demands of special interests, restored rates to their old levels, and repudiated the inheritance tax. The Progressives, who were by this time numerous enough to make their presence in the Senate felt, denounced the bill as a repudiation of party pledges and a reversion to unadulterated class legislation. The issue was fairly joined in the greatest of our public forums and, while the Progressives failed to defeat the tariff bill, they materially advanced their cause in the country at large. The debate marked the beginning of party schism, with Taft failing to rise to the occasion as the leader of his party. The bill passed both Houses by narrow margins, substantially as the Senate had written it. The inheritance tax was not included, although some concession was made in the form of a low corporation tax and a resolution presenting the income tax amendment to the states for ratification.

CHAPTER IV

POLITICAL PHILOSOPHY—ROOSEVELT TO WILSON

Political parties have long served as the cement of the nation. Men seeking public office must not only go upon the hustings and satisfy their constituents of their soundness on particular questions, but must meet in national convention, compose their differences and agree upon a platform satisfactory to all sections. The system operates neither perfectly nor smoothly at all times, and in seasons of great reform agitation there is a tendency toward evasion and subtle deception in many quarters. Practically, it means that many men in a party are far in advance of its published principles, many lagging behind. That is why the final test on any question cuts across party lines. It gives meaning to party regularity, to party leadership, to political independence. It makes men's records their own platforms. It nullifies sweeping claims of partisan achievement. It enhances the worth of a minority party and gives victory to its principles though it languish and die.

The success of a national administration depends upon the degree to which it fulfills the mandates of public opinion and meets the exigencies of the times while in power. The need for social and economic security makes and breaks political parties. The disposition of the people to hold the government responsible for that security is one of the soundest virtues of democratic institutions. It teaches men in public life the responsibility of their positions. It teaches them to remain responsive to the changing needs of society during their tenure of office. Men who falter in that respect are thrust aside, regardless of past achievements or intellectual brilliance.

Theodore Roosevelt and William H. Taft

The accession of Theodore Roosevelt to the presidency in 1901 ushered in the twilight of Republican party solidarity. No longer were the stalwarts to rule their party with an iron hand or shape the policies of the government with selfish impunity. Not that Roosevelt himself was to pioneer in the realm of non-partisanship. He was a career politician. He rose to the heights of popular acclaim, but he rode the crest of the great reform movement initiated and carried along by countless other men. He bore the same relation to La Follette, Bryan, Norris and others, in that respect, that Lincoln had borne to Weld, Garrison and Phillips, or Jackson to John Taylor of Caroline. How much the philosophy of any one man in public life creates the prevailing attitudes of a people and how much it indicates his recognition of the people's desires and obedience to them, is difficult to determine. In the case of Roosevelt, it is still a matter of conjecture.

William McKinley, whose assassination enabled Roosevelt to escape from the political graveyard of the vice-presidency, and Marcus A. Hanna, whose death fortuitously opened the way to Roosevelt's leadership in the party, both represented Republican stalwartism. McKinley was the foremost champion of a high protective tariff. Hanna was a business man, manufacturer, banker and promoter of public utilities who preached and practiced the faith of rugged individualism, willing to assist men into office, to pay them on occasion for what he wanted, and wanting reform less than anything else. Thomas A. Platt, who had placed Roosevelt in the governorship of New York at a time when he was a resident of Washington, D. C., represented the party boss—that class of men who seldom sought public office but wielded tremendous power as directors of machine politics and *liaison* with big business. Henry Cabot Lodge of Massachusetts, a close personal friend and confidential advisor of Roosevelt, represented the social and economic aristocracy of the East. Roosevelt, himself, was the scion of an old, aristocratic family and was rated a wealthy man. His party was the party of big business, of wealth, of economic fundamentalism; the champion of rugged individualism and *laissez faire*, of government by precedent rather than by impulse, by tradition rather than by experiment, and of Senatorial dignity and superiority. It was thoroughly institutionalized, conforming to the established procedure of holding local, state and national conventions, but controlled by a closed corporation of machine politicians rather than by the rank and file of Republican voters.

Roosevelt knew the system; he had served his apprenticeship in it, had been found wanting, and had been shunted into the vice-presidency as a means of getting him out of New York. He entered the legislature of New York state within two years after graduating from Harvard, served for three terms and then retired to his Dakota ranch. For three years he rode the range, delved into the history of the westward movement, perfectly identified himself with the spirit of the West and formed many lasting friendships. In 1886, he was back again in New York City contesting with Henry George and Abram S. Hewitt for the mayoralty. He lost to Hewitt and travelled abroad. From 1889 to 1895, he served as a member of the federal Civil Service Commission, then for two years as Police Commissioner of New York City, and for a short time as Assistant Secretary of the Navy. He resigned from that position to lead a famous company, known as the Rough Riders, through the Spanish-American War and emerged from the war a national figure. He was chosen by Boss Platt for the governorship, because the party stood in need of his popularity in the election, and made himself so obnoxious to the machine politicians that they pushed him into the vice-presidency to get him out of the way.

Roosevelt knew how to win and hold the confidence of other men. He enjoyed life to the full—a bundle of nervous energy which sought and found expression in the restless spirit of the age. He was impulsive, too much so for the conservative men of his party, but it gave to his official acts and utterances a dramatic touch that caught the fancy of the people. He knew how to speak in vigorous generalities that exactly satisfied the imperious longing for reform without committing himself to a definite program impossible of fulfillment; he capitalized on the achievements of La Follette and Bryan and all those who had borne the burden of reform when to champion the cause of human rights was to drink the poison hemlock of political ostracism. He knew his people, but he knew his party, too, and for four years he scrupulously followed the rules of a first term presidency, feeling his way into the leadership of his party and the hearts of the people.

He did nothing and said very little until after his re-election, which would alienate the industrialists and financiers. It was not until the closing days of his Presidency that anything was attempted in the way of monetary reform and then nothing more than the appointment of a National Monetary Commission to study the question. He urged Congress, in his first message, to extend the powers of the Interstate Commerce Commission and bring corporations under stricter regulation, but did not push the issue beyond the Elkins Act of 1903; and, in 1906, he did not throw his support back of La Follette to write a physical valuations clause into the Hepburn Act. He pushed the prosecution of trusts under the Sherman Act, settled the anthracite coal strike and concluded the preliminary steps for the building of a Panama Canal, all in dramatic fashion. He vigorously supported the conservation program, being peculiarly suited to the rôle as a devotee of outdoor life and being closer to the soil than most men of his inheritance. That subject, too, was free from political heresy, being opposed only by certain elements in the Far West and viewed with askance as a prospective danger by the power interests. He endorsed the pension policy of his party, avoided any controversy over the protective tariff, and remained on intimate terms with the oligarchy of party conservatives. His re-nomination was by acclamation and his re-election a foregone conclusion. No man before him had ever received a 2,000,000 majority of all the popular votes nor as many as 336 electoral votes. Whatever doubts were expressed as to the welfare of the country in the ensuing four years arose from the fear that Roosevelt's impulsiveness would lead to his accidental death and the elevation of Charles W. Fairbanks to the Presidency.

His real service to the cause of reform came during his second administration, not in the form of Congressional legislation, but through his influence over public opinion. No President since Lincoln had spoken so often and intimately to the people. None cherished popular acclaim more, nor received it so generously. We must remember that the great reform movement gathered momentum throughout the eight years of his Presidency, and reached its crest in a flood of liberal state legislation during Taft's Administration and of national legislation during Wilson's Administration. Conservative wealth was firmly entrenched when he came into office. It controlled the economic life of the nation and, consequently, the state itself. It wielded tremendous influence in legislative assemblies, too often dictated judicial decisions, silenced the press and closed the mouths of its critics. What he could or would have accomplished with the more liberal Congress following the 1910 elections must remain a matter of speculation. He had no such forward-looking legislators. His life-long intimacy with reactionary stalwarts, his occasional petulance toward the more outspoken reformers, and his failure to press reform legislation in Congress more energetically might have been due to inheritance and association; but it is not likely. His whole-hearted denunciation of selfish greed, of judicial conservatism and machine politics, and his endorsement of income and inheritance taxes toward the end of his second administration belie that interpretation. The fact is, that his tremendous popularity and the confidence placed in his judgment by the common man counted heavily for reform at a time when they were most needed to convert those unmoved by the appeals of extremists.

He was not a political philosopher, certainly; but then, neither was Taft, who excelled in intellectual attainments and never came under the blighting influence of practical politics; nor Wilson, the political scientist, whose life was not spent in a wilderness of intellectual depravity and who had the benefit of a number of brilliant monographs denied to Roosevelt: Gustavus Myers' *History of the Great American Fortunes* (1909-1910), Walter Lippmann's *A Preface to Politics* (1913), Charles A. Beard's *An Economic Interpretation of the Constitution of the United States* (1913) and Louis D. Brandeis' *Other People's Money* (1913).

It is significant, too, that Roosevelt was regarded as far more radical than the Democratic candidate, Alton B. Parker, in the campaign of 1904. Bryan temporarily lost control of his party in that campaign and supported this conservative New York friend of corporations in a half-hearted fashion. Many Bryan Democrats threw their votes to Roosevelt, which helped to swell his exceedingly large popular majority. The corporate interests did not openly oppose Roosevelt because they felt secure behind a friendly Senate; but, in a larger measure than events of the period indicate, the schism in the party was widening rapidly. Roosevelt's strength in the country at large was identical with reform strength and, to that degree, non-partisan. It made the campaign of 1908 one of men and not of party platforms. Roosevelt and Bryan were their own platforms. The dark shadows of 1896 and 1900, free silver and anti-imperialism, still followed Bryan. Roosevelt named Taft, his Secretary of War and former Governor-General of the Philippines, as his successor, and that was sufficient to elect him. He did not receive the votes of those independent Democrats who had voted, four years earlier, for Roosevelt or had remained away from the polls. He did receive the votes of many conservative Democrats who had voted for Parker but would not endorse Bryan. His popular vote of 7,677,000 was slightly larger than Roosevelt's had been four years before. Bryan's, on the contrary, was 6,407,000, more than 1,323,000 greater than Parker's had been.

The forward surge of progressivism and the final stand of conservatism combined to make Taft's Administration anything but an era of good feeling. The enactment of the Payne-Aldrich tariff bill, representing as it did a repudiation of Republican party pledges and Democratic principles, has already been indicated. It was the final victory of reaction in the Senate. Taft signed the bill and publicly praised it as a great achievement, thus assuming an unnecessary burden of popular resentment in much the same fashion as Hoover was to do many years later. Public opinion made no allowance for his known preference for reduced rates and his support of the measure because of its administrative features: the introduction of maximum and minimum rates and the establishment of a tariff commission. His restoration to entry of a million and one half acres of public lands in Montana and Wyoming, upon the advice of Secretary Ballinger, alienated the conservation enthusiasts. His dismissal of Gifford Pinchot from the office of Chief Forester for insubordination aggravated his offence in the judgment of Roosevelt's followers. His refusal to approve the admission of Arizona until the provision for recall of judges was eliminated from her constitution antagonized the more extreme advocates of governmental reform. The effort of his Postmaster-General, Hitchcock, to increase postage rates was interpreted as an attempt to silence cheap magazines, conspicuous for their attacks upon vested interests. The attention which these politically unfortunate episodes received to the exclusion of a vast amount of constructive measures, serves to indicate how completely the spirit of reform dominated the changing scene. Few first term presidents could boast of such a formidable list of constructive acts: the Interstate Commerce Act, strengthening the Interstate Commerce Commission; the Land Grant Act designed to preserve mineral deposits and water power sites; the Mann Act for the suppression of the white slave traffic; the admission of Arizona and New Mexico; the establishment of the postal banking system; the Campaign Expense Publicity Act providing publicity for congressional campaign funds; the Radio Act requiring the installation of wireless telegraphy on passenger vessels; the transfer of second class and third class postmasters to the civil service lists; and the passage of a Canadian reciprocity agreement.

Taft was an embodiment of the spirit of deliberation in government. He was instinctively opposed to all reform measures designed to introduce quick and impulsive action: the Initiative and Referendum, the Recall, the Direct Primary. He believed implicitly in the party system and in party discipline. He opposed all tendencies toward socialism and toward excessive regulation of individual conduct. He was, in short, unsympathetic to the prevailing spirit of the times, constitutionally ill-adapted to the task of leadership bestowed upon him by Roosevelt. His life of public service, begun soon after graduation from Law School, had been spent in appointive positions. His election to the Presidency, the one time advancement depended upon popular support, was in no sense a test of his ability as a practical politician. He was conservative, congenial, intellectually brilliant, and an unusually skillful public speaker; but his judicial mind, his too great readiness to trust executive responsibilities to other men, his unwillingness to encroach upon congressional independence and his simple faith in the virtue of individualism and self-reliance unfitted him for the Presidency at a time of political and social turmoil. Roosevelt left him to his own resources, going off to Africa on a hunting trip, and by the time he returned Taft's political fortunes were beyond salvaging.

Republican Insurgency

Meanwhile, the Progressive movement had registered important gains in the sphere of politics. A major revolution was in the making. The first skirmish of the forces which were to make the campaign of 1912 memorable in history occurred in the House of Representatives. On March 18, 1910, George W. Norris of Nebraska offered a resolution to make the Committee on Rules elective and deprive the Speaker of membership on the Committee. The Speaker was Joseph Cannon of Illinois, one of the most popular men, personally, who had ever held that position. The insurgency was not against Cannon but against the system—a system which had developed by precedent to the point where the Speaker was the most powerful man in the government next to the President. He appointed committees and the House operated on the basis of a committee system. He was chairman of the Committee on Rules. He held the power to deny recognition to a member in debate; and he could, as a member of the House, thwart any resort to unanimous consent. The group of insurgent Republicans, assisted by the Democrats, carried the resolution; and, in Wilson's first Congress, the Speaker was deprived of all power to appoint committees, that function being assigned to the elected Ways and Means Committee in conjunction with the leader of the minority party. In the Senate, a group of insurgent Republicans, led by La Follette, waged a bitter battle against the Payne-Aldrich tariff bill. They were unsuccessful in preventing its passage or that of the Canadian reciprocity measure, but their continuous obstructionist tactics and brilliant debate played an important part in keeping their cause before the people.

The three outstanding leaders of Republican Insurgency were George W. Norris of Nebraska, Robert La Follette of Wisconsin and William E. Borah of Idaho. Norris was a native of Ohio, an adopted son of Nebraska. He entered the national House of Representatives in 1904 and the Senate in 1913. For more than thirty years he has continued in public life as an outstanding progressive, always fighting machine politics, always opposing special interests, always confident of the ultimate survival of democratic institutions. His victory against Speaker Cannon was followed subsequently by three other equally significant ones. The greatest battle of his career centered about the disposal of Muscle Shoals. For years he studied the question from every angle: the needs of the Tennessee Valley, the effect of cheaper power upon the manufacturing industry, the utility of government ownership and operation. His interest in the labor question, particularly the use of the injunction in labor disputes, was equally great. Finally, he took the lead in carrying on that phase of the reform movement having to do with political machinery. The Tennessee Valley Authority established in 1933, the Norris-La Guardia anti-Injunction Act of 1932, the Twentieth Amendment abolishing the lame-duck session of Congress and the unicameral legislature of Nebraska were to represent the achievements of three decades of public service. His non-partisanship was as distinctive as his record of public service. He followed Roosevelt out of the Republican party in 1912, supported La Follette in 1924, Alfred E. Smith in 1928 and Franklin D. Roosevelt in 1932 and again in 1936. Senator Arthur Capper of Kansas once spoke of him as "a perambulating Declaration of Independence." Nominally a Republican, he remained through the years consistently opposed to the demands for party regularity, and consistently in favor of whatever public policies he believed would promote political and economic democracy.

Robert La Follette, regarded by many as the greatest of the three outstanding political leaders of the reform movement, was not a showman in the way of Roosevelt. He was as democratic as had been John P. Altgeld of Illinois, with great faith in the common man. He was, moreover, a man of action, not impulsive but patient, indomitably courageous, indefatigable in labor. As governor of Wisconsin, he had learned to rely upon the faculty of that state's great university for the facts and theories upon which he based all his political action, for he was not a career politician nor an opportunist. He thoroughly understood the economic basis of politics. All the great battles he waged in his own state and in Congress were against monopolies and the influence of organized wealth in government and, unlike Roosevelt, he never compromised. His first battle in Wisconsin was with the railroads. He succeeded in breaking their hold upon the state and in writing into the statutes a law which gave them rates sufficient only to provide a fair return on their physical valuation. That was his objective in Congress. He bitterly denounced Roosevelt's acceptance of the Hepburn compromise because, without a physical valuations clause, it was little more than a pretense at rate regulation. He continued his campaign until the Interstate Commerce Commission was authorized to make a thorough study of railroad valuations and then went on to advocate public ownership. He was responsible for the first state primary law (1903), a progressive inheritance tax, a state civil service commission and a workmen's compensation law. The Department of Labor, the Federal Trade Commission, the Employers' Liability Act, and the initiation of the naval oil lease investigations were in large measure his handiwork. Damned, in later years, because of his opposition to our entry into the World War and to the Versailles Peace Treaty, he carried on to poll five million votes without a party organization on a platform of hostility to the Supreme Court's power of Judicial Review. Hated, loved and feared; denounced as a fanatic, a demagogue and a dangerous radical; discourteously treated and his cause betrayed by the friends of Roosevelt; denounced by Wilson—all this notwithstanding, he stands out as the foremost leader of those forces which were seeking to make democracy function, and his high place in history is unalterably secure.

The third of the leading western insurgents was William E. Borah of Idaho. Like Roosevelt, La Follette and Norris, he believed that the special interests must be curbed, that corporate wealth was becoming too powerful in the political and economic life of the nation. His hostility to concentration of economic power, however, was matched by an equal hostility to concentration of governmental power. It was this which gave his career a flavor of inconsistency and made him the despair of conservatives and liberals alike. All of these men—from Roosevelt to Wilson and from Brandeis to Borah—believed in the efficacy of competition to keep wealth widely distributed and economic opportunity a living force in American life; but while other Progressives, for the most part, moved in the direction of Socialism, Borah instinctively moved away from governmental control in the direction of individualism. Virtually all of the others, Roosevelt included, advocated curtailment of the Supreme Court at one time or another. Borah became the staunchest defender of the Court, the most able expounder of the Constitution, and probably the leading debater in the Senate.

The elections of 1910 revealed the amazing strength of progressive forces throughout the nation, represented by Democratic victories in some instances and by insurgent Republican victories in others. It was a situation in which the Democratic party and the minority seeking control of the Republican party were fighting for substantially the same principles. In Kansas, Senator Bristow and the Congressmen who had been prominent in the fight against the Aldrich tariff interests, captured control of the Republican party. In Wisconsin, Democrats again rallied to the support of Insurgent La Follette and returned him to the Senate. Hiram Johnson, insurgent candidate for the governorship of California, captured his party and won the election on a platform of hostility to the Southern Pacific Railway and boss-ridden politics in the state. In Nebraska, the Democrats administered a smashing blow to the prestige of Bryanism by defeating his candidates in the primaries and opened the way to new leadership in the presidential campaign. The people of Ohio did likewise, re-electing Judson Harmon, Democratic governor of that state, by a large majority. In New Jersey, the people elected Woodrow Wilson, previously unknown in politics, who had based his campaign upon an appeal to the intelligence of the voters. In New Hampshire, Winston Churchill won his fight to purify the Republican party by electing Robert P. Bass as governor. The Democrats also elected governors in Maine, Massachusetts, Connecticut, North Dakota, Colorado and Oregon, normally Republican states, and captured control of the National House of Representatives, 223 to 168. Eighteen

Republican Senators saw the legislatures which had elected them replaced by Democratic legislatures.

During the summer, Roosevelt made an extended speaking tour through the West—not the West of his earlier campaigns, but a new West in which the tariff was now a great moral issue, in which the fight was not against rates nor based primarily upon agrarian economy, but against the industrialists and financiers who were using the government to enrich themselves at the expense of every one else. It turned out to be one of the most amazing performances ever seen in the country. The economic and political philosopsy revealed in his public utterances was more socialistic than ever before advanced by either Democrat or Republican, Bryan included. At Osawatomie, he said:

"We grudge no man a fortune which represents his own power and sagacity, when exercised with entire regard to the welfare of his fellows. But the fortune must be honorably obtained and well used. It is not even enough that it should have been gained without doing damage to the community. We should permit it to be gained only so long as the gaining represents benefit to the community. This, I know, implies a policy of a far more active governmental interference with social and economic conditions in this country than we have yet had, but I think we have got to face the fact that such an increase in governmental control is now necessary."

The implications of such a philosophy practically applied were tremendous, involving as they necessarily would a radical departure from fundamental principles of government and an explicit faith in the efficacy of law to remedy social and economic maladjustments. Returning to New York, he dominated the Republican State convention without so much as lifting his voice against a strong endorsement of the Payne-Aldrich Tariff Act. His speeches in the West crystallized, for the first time, the ultra-conservative forces in the East against him. His action in New York, designed to allay their fears, only brought chagrin and resentment in the West. Fundamentally, however, the consequences were much more far reaching. His following among the rank and file voters was a personal one. He recovered it sufficiently to impair seriously La Follette's chances of capturing control of the Republican convention. At the same time, he revealed, in the East, his fatal weakness for compromise of principles in order, as a practical politician, once more to place himself at the head of the Administration forces. No one saw more clearly what had happened than La Follette.

The result of the 1910 elections placed the Democratic party in the strongest position it had occupied for years. Bryanism was no longer an issue, the party was united. It was not in power and, therefore, not responsible for the administration of the government during the ensuing two years. Its close agreement with the insurgent Republicans, particularly on the tariff question, gave it an opportunity to make a vigorous assault upon the conservatives in Congress. It did so, passing a new tariff bill with greatly reduced rates and an *ad valorem* system instead of specific duties, which was vetoed by President Taft. The following year, it established an eight-hour day for government employees, an act for the management of the Panama Canal and the Amendment to the Constitution providing for the popular election of United States Senators.

Early in January, 1911, the National Republican Progressive League was formed by the Insurgent Congressmen and a group of western governors. It was the beginning of organized opposition to Taft's renomination and the initial step in La Follete's campaign which was formally announced in the early summer. What happened between that time and the nominating convention one year later is a tangled maze of contradictions. By successive stages, Roosevelt informed the country that he was not a candidate, that he would support no one, that he would not consider himself bound by his previous renunciation of a third term, that he would accept the nomination if the people demanded it, and, finally, that he was a candidate. An attempt was made to read La Follette out of the race by the announcement that he had suffered a nervous breakdown, but he refused to be sidetracked and bitterly denounced Roosevelt for his betrayal. The weight of precedent demanded Taft's renomination. Roosevelt never succeeded in presenting specific indictments of Taft's Administration which did not apply with equal severity to his own. Taft, being a Republican President, controlled the convention delegates from the South and was able to renominate himself; but there was only slight enthusiasm for him even in the convention. His greatest handicap, from first to last, was having permitted Roosevelt to place him in the Presidency four years before. It left him under a great personal obligation, which he fulfilled with such dignity as becomes a gentleman, replying in the most restrained language to Roosevelt's rancorous assaults. There is no longer any question but that Roosevelt did misrepresent him in the campaign, deliberately and repeatedly. He exaggerated Taft's weaknesses and belittled his accomplishments. He even questioned his personal character. There is no question, also, but that Roosevelt's strength in the preferential primaries was not a test of his progressivism but of his availability. He won too easily in states like Illinois and Pennsylvania. Illinois gave him 266,000 in the primary to Taft's 127,000, but in the election Roosevelt received 437,000 and Taft 631,000. In Pennsylvania, Roosevelt received 298,000 and Taft received 193,000 in the primary, while in the November election they received, respectively, 492,000 and 720,000. Moreover, it is extremely improbable that a man, even Roosevelt, could have secured the backing of an estimated $3,000,000 in a primary campaign on the basis of his liberalism. Finally, there were not enough contested seats in the convention to have given Roosevelt the nomination had all of the contests been decided in his favor. He did not wait for the nomination, however, choosing to make the issue upon the election of Elihu Root as temporary chairman. He issued a statement which said in part: "Under the direction, and with the encouragement of Mr. Taft, the majority of the National Committee . . . with scandalous disregard of every principle of elementary honesty and decency, stole eighty or ninety delegates. . . . The Convention as now composed has no claims to represent the voters of the Republican party. . . . It would be deeply discreditable to any man to accept the Convention nomination under these circumstances, and any man thus accepting it would have no claim to the support of any Republican on party grounds, and would have forfeited the right to ask the support of any honest man of any party on moral grounds." The Roosevelt faction took little part, thereafter, in the proceedings of the convention, but organized a convention of its own and made plans for a third party movement with Roosevelt as their candidate. Its call for a convention at Chicago, on August 5, was addressed to all persons who "realize that today the power of the crooked political bosses and of the privileged classes behind them is so strong in the two old party organizations that no helpful movement in the real interest of our country can come out of either."

This Convention was unique in three respects: (1) It was not a true convention, because Roosevelt had already been tendered the nomination and had accepted. (2) That circumstance and the irregularity of choosing delegates made of it, in reality, an emotional mass meeting, a political resuscitation of the several reform elements. (3) It was the first attempt at a lily white movement, Negroes from the South being excluded from the Convention in the hope of breaking the Democratic ranks within the Solid South. Albert J. Beveridge of Indiana presided over the Convention. The platform endorsed such reform measures as the direct primary, short ballot and initiative, referendum and recall. It promised an easier method of amending the Constitution, without specifying details. It endorsed woman suffrage, publicity for campaign contributions and expenditures, registration of lobbyists, jury trial for contempt cases arising out of labor disputes, safety and health codes, prohibition of child labor, the eight-hour day, a Department of Labor, a federal administrative commission for the supervision of corporations, a revised currency system, downward revision of the tariff, a graduated inheritance tax, etc. Roosevelt and

Hiram W. Johnson of California were nominated by acclamation for President and Vice-president.

Woodrow Wilson was recognized, from the very first, as the strongest potential candidate for the nomination the Democratic party possessed. He was attacked by Tom Watson of Georgia as a tool of the Papacy because his secretary, Joseph Tumulty, was a Catholic. So, too, was Taft indicted by Watson for having completed negotiations for the purchase of the church lands in the Philippines. Wilson, having been president of the oldest Presbyterian University in the country, probably did not suffer much loss from Watson's demagoguery. Governor Harmon, of Ohio, was Wilson's most prominent opponent for the nomination during the early months of the campaign, but Bryan opposed him as a reactionary. Champ Clark, Joseph Cannon's successor as Speaker of the House of Representatives, finally forged to the front as Wilson's most formidable opponent, but his great weakness was his alliance with William Randolph Hearst and his suspected opportunism. Bryan was still a power to be reckoned with and, in the end, he threw his support to Wilson, thus breaking a deadlock in the convention. Wilson's nomination, however, was in response to the wishes of the rank and file of his party to a much greater degree than is ordinarily true. His nomination was accomplished without previous pledges or promises of the sort that so frequently prove embarrassing later.

Not all of the Progressive Republicans supported Roosevelt. William E. Borah of Idaho had sought to secure his nomination instead of Taft, but refused to desert the party. Governor Hadley of Missouri, who had led the Roosevelt forces in the Republican Convention, did likewise. Roosevelt lost heavily from the incontrovertible fact that parties are born, not made, and his was gotten together without previous impulse and under the spell of a magnetic personality. Many discerning men saw more promise for the future in a blistering defeat for the Republican party than in the temporary success of an incongruous expedient. More, too, than is commonly supposed, realized how completely the cause of reform had been sold out to the special interests when it embraced the patron saint of the system, George W. Perkins, who financed the movement. On the other hand, Roosevelt received many votes which otherwise would have gone to the Socialist candidate. He devoted the greater part of his campaign to denouncing Taft as a reactionary. Taft took very little part in the controversy and refused to meet Roosevelt on the plane of personal abuse.

Wilson, seeing clearly how the greatest modern resurgence of Jeffersonian liberalism was being compromised, assumed the responsibility of leadership. He conducted his campaign with dignity and good judgment. He was not a practical politician and his mental processes were pitched far above the economic basis upon which politics so largely rest; but circumstances permitted a superior quality of appeal. He did not talk about opponents but about the system the nation had permitted to develop. Fundamentally, there was not a great deal of difference between Roosevelt's New Nationalism and Wilson's New Freedom, except the method of approach. Wilson's campaign addresses constituted a really stimulating discipline in the science of government. Not since Calhoun's day had any man contributed so freely to political thinking. It was the first step by which he ascended to a position never before occupied by an American and equalled, probably if at all, by any statesman anywhere: ambassador of human rights in the Court of World Opinion and trustee by faith of humanity's hopes for justice and liberty throughout the world.

Woodrow Wilson

In the realm of moral and political philosophy, Wilson belonged to that select group, small in number, whose intellectual achievements taken together have created social progress. He fought strenuously for principles, as a basis for individual conduct, for party action and for international relationship. The search for truth and its application to rules of conduct was the consuming passion of his life. He was a thorough student of

American history, had delved deeply into the impelling forces of human progress. He stepped upon the stage of politics at the very moment when the United States had completed its national growth, when the intricacies of modern commerce and our adventures in imperialism had unconsciously destroyed the possibility of continued isolation, and when traditional methods of international relationship had broken down. As the war clouds gathered, he saw beyond the narrowing horizon the greatest opportunity for service in the century and a half of our national existence, and his vision gave him immortality. Service based in character as the motive of all human action was the secret of his ideals. It was not to him a thing of limitations, nor the peculiar province of professional men. Service of the individual to the common interest of the nation and of the nation to the world of humanity was the ideal. He believed that political parties existed to serve the nation and, in the spirit of the reform movement, he would have the material wealth, the boundless energies and the enterprise of individual men placed at the service of the whole people, that waste of natural resources and human life might be eliminated.

Wilson has often been spoken of derisively as a preacher. He was that, in the sense that he believed the essence of national life to be moral power, drawn from the whole of the people. It was not genius but character which made him the great leader he was, and he looked not to genius but to character to sustain the nation. This wholesome faith in the ultimate judgment of the common man is revealed in his efforts to encourage public discussion of domestic issues, open transactions in the field of foreign diplomacy, and the application of the principle of self-determination, that in every important issue the verdict of an enlightened public opinion might be registered.

In keeping with his ideal that governments exist for service to the people, Wilson advocated such changes in our political system as to provide for a more responsible government: resistance to further separation of powers and the fixation of responsibility upon individuals. He suggested the abolition of the committee system with its attendant evils of secrecy and control by special interests and a return to free and unlimited debate in the House of Representatives. He suggested the advisability of giving Cabinet members seats in the Congress with the responsibility of defending their executive action and directing legislation. The principle was that somehow responsibility be fixed. At no time, did he indicate sympathy for the idea that credits government with omnipotent power and seeks in legislation the corrective for all social evils. He was a conservative in the sense of realizing that the character of national life can not rise above its source; that as the individual citizen thinks and lives so will the national character take shape. Certainly, as no other man in public life, he sought to impress that idea upon the people. He believed in the right of a people to establish and alter on occasion their own form of government. Self-determination is an indefinite thing; it presents difficult problems in application; but the principle of a people's responsibility for its own destiny and perfect freedom of choice are present. This principle he advocated for our territorial administration. He regarded it as inevitable that the welfare of subject people would be forgotten if profits were the aim of business enterprise and the government controlled by special interests. He advocated, therefore, administration by the United States of Hawaii and Puerto Rico in the interest of the native people, that sympathy born of understanding and kindred institutions might form the basis of lasting unity. He advocated administration of the Philippines in such manner as to develop a sense of responsibility on their part for their own destiny, looking to ultimate independence.

The New Freedom

The years between 1910 and 1917 witnessed the culmination of the economic reform movement. They were the years in which the generalities of reform oratory were translated into constructive legislative realities and subjected to the test of constitutionality. The broader aspects of this intensely human drama were too obscured from view to attract general attention. The enactment of the several legislative measures in Wilson's Administration, climaxing a decade of such activity, was simplicity itself compared to the tremendous battle being waged between the ideas of economic fundamentalism, firmly entrenched in constitution and judicial precedent on the one hand, and the ideas of social reform arising out of the economic revolution on the other.

We are accustomed to speak of the "New Freedom" of Wilson's Administration. It was new only in the sense that for the first time, a man occupied the Presidency whose social philosophy envisaged the hope of preserving economic as well as political freedom for the individual, and whose political philosophy embraced the responsibility of government for the social security of the people. The task of harnessing the new economic institutions, depriving them of their anti-social tendencies and forcing them to accept responsibilities to society as well as to property interests was not begun, but was carried farther than ever before, under Wilson's guidance.

In his inaugural address, he said: "We have itemized with some degree of particularity the things that ought to be altered and here are some of the chief items: a tariff which cuts us off from our proper part in the commerce of the world, violates the just principles of taxation, and makes the Government a facile instrument in the hands of private interests; a banking and currency system based upon the necessity of the Government to sell its bonds fifty years ago and perfectly adapted to concentrating cash and restricting credits; an industrial system which, take it on all its sides, financial as well as administrative, holds capital in leading strings, restricts the liberties and limits the opportunities cf labor, and exploits without renewing or conserving the natural resources of the country; a body of agricultural activities never yet given the efficiency of great business undertakings . . . or afforded the facilities of credit best suited to its practical needs; water-courses undeveloped, waste places unreclaimed, forests untended, fast disappearing without plan or prospect of renewal, unregarded waste heaps at every mine. We have studied as perhaps no other nation has the most effective means of production, but we have not studied cost or economy as we should either as organizers of industry, as statesmen, or as individuals.

"Nor have we studied and perfected the means by which government may be put at the service of humanity, in safeguarding the health of the Nation, the health of its men and its women and its children, as well as their rights in the struggle for existence."

The program here set forth was carried through by a series of sweeping legislative enactments: the Underwood Tariff, the Federal Reserve Act, the Federal Trade Commission Act, the Clayton Anti-Trust Act, the Federal Farm Loan Act, and the Seamen's Act.

Wilson's election by a strict party vote and a minority vote as well, placed in the Presidency a man who was far more progressive than a large segment of his own party. His leadership, extending far beyond the limits of his own party, produced a flood of legislation in the ensuing five years more sweeping in its objectives than the country had witnessed since the days of Andrew Jackson. The Progressives were seeking to establish some system of control over the new plutocracy in order to restore the economic freedom of an earlier day. They aimed to free the people from economic slavery, to humanize the industrial process through control legislation, not to change the underlying principles of the system itself. They were individualists rather than collectivists, striving to save the democratic system somewhere short of socialism and, at the same time, promote the common welfare. The system they were seeking to displace had been disposed to extend to business a maximum of freedom and a minimum of interference aside from gratuities in the form of tariffs and special subsidies. That system had used the government to serve vested interests. The Progressives sought to use the government to control vested interests and thus rescue freedom of economic opportunity from the threat of oligarchic monopolies. Radically different from these two concepts of government, was that of the socialists.

The socialists, unlike the Progressives, did not approach the problem from the standpoint of restoring and preserving competition in order to save the small business man from extinction. They had no faith in the ability of the government either to control the trusts or to force their disintegration, but looked to the collective ownership and democratic control of all the instruments of production as the only escape from industrial feudalism. Looking to the ultimate realization of this objective, the national convention of the Socialist party, meeting at Indianapolis, May 12-18, 1912, drew up and submitted to popular referendum a platform of principles. It advocated public ownership of "all grain elevators, stock yards, warehouses and other distributing agencies," mines, quarries, oil wells, forests, water power, land, banking and currency. It demanded the relief of unemployment by public works; adjustment of hours of labor to increased productiveness of machinery; abolition of child labor and prison contract labor; minimum wage laws, unemployment insurance, workmen's compensation laws and old-age pensions; income and inheritance taxes, the proceeds to be used for the socialization of industry; reduction of tariff duties; woman's suffrage; the initiative, referendum, recall, and proportional representation; abolition of the Senate and presidential veto; direct election of the President and Vice-president; abolition of the power of judicial review; amendment of the Constitution by a majority vote in a majority of the states; vocational education; a Bureau of Health and an independent Department of Labor; abolition of all Federal District and Circuit Courts; and the calling of a national constitutional convention. Eugene V. Debs of Indiana and Emil Seidel of Wisconsin were chosen the party's candidates for the Presidency and Vice-presidency. The party had made tremendous growth since its organization in 1899 under the leadership of Debs and Victor L. Berger. By 1912, it had an extensive press and polled 897,000 votes in the presidential election. How many more votes Debs would have received had Roosevelt not been in the race is purely a matter of conjecture, but probably a great many.

Socialism reached its peak in 1912 and declined steadily thereafter. It is true that eight years later Debs received over 919,000 votes. But he was then a prisoner in Atlanta penitentiary at the time and much of his vote was in the nature of protest against his persecution. Twenty years after the 1912 campaign, Norman Thomas, the most able candidate the party has ever presented, received considerably less than a million votes and the electorate was almost double what it was in 1912. Widespread fear of foreign radicalism, hostility to a centralized dictatorship of boards and bureaus and the inherent individualism of the people account for its decline as a party. On the other hand, its platform of 1912 remained through the years a veritable fountainhead of ideas and the party's activity provoked an intellectual ferment which men in public life could not ignore. Socialism preceded communism and regimentation as the nightmare of those people who evinced apprehension for the safety of American institutions. It furnished convenient copy for the conservative press and abundant inspiration for timorous politicians, who dragged its ghastly terrors into every political campaign to the confusion of real and important issues. Many of the specific demands of socialism have been adopted into the platforms of the two major parties and have been written into law. One has only to look at the platform of 1912, with its demands of federal loans to states, public work for the relief of unemployment, old age pensions, workmen's compensation laws, income and inheritance taxes, reforestation, and woman's suffrage or to the Socialist platform of 1932 to realize how much the needs of modern industrial society have promoted a modified program of socialism. On the other hand, one has only to look at the progressive platform of 1912, to realize that virtually every demand of the Socialists which has been adopted was also on the agenda of the Progressives at that time; and that it is the fundamental principle of the Progressives, of men like La Follette, Wilson and Brandeis, rather than that of Socialists like Debs that remains the basis of present-day objectives.

CHAPTER V

IN DEFENSE OF ECONOMIC FREEDOM

Railroads

In his first message to Congress, December 3, 1901, Roosevelt demanded increased attention to corporate practices and an increase in the powers of the Interstate Commerce Commission. Shortly thereafter he suggested, in a series of public addresses, that the Sherman Anti-Trust Law would be enforced and that legislation should be passed providing protection to the public through publicity of corporate affairs and a prohibition of over-capitalization. This meant, as a minimum, that the Sherman Anti-Trust Law would be given an interpretation by the Supreme Court with respect to corporations as it had been with respect to Labor Unions in 1894. Congress had, in 1893, passed a law compelling witnesses to testify before the Interstate Commerce Commission, and another providing for the installation of safety appliances on all railroad equipment. In 1901, they ordered the roads to make monthly reports to the Commission. These slight gains in regulation, however, were more than balanced by the Supreme Court decision in the case of *Smyth* v. *Ames* which stripped the Commission of most of its power to adjust rates. The powerful influence of Roosevelt and of the Senate progressives under La Follette's leadership secured some decidedly important legislation in 1903 and again in 1906. In the former year a Bureau of Corporations was set up in the Department of Commerce and Labor. James R. Garfield was appointed Commissioner with the power to investigate corporations engaged in interstate commerce. His duties were those of a fact-finding agent whose reports were to be the basis of presidential recommendations to Congress and a contribution to an enlightened public opinion. The Elkins Act was passed primarily as anti-trust legislation, although it applied specifically to railroads. In addition to giving the Department of Commerce and Labor the power to inquire into corporate practices, it provided punishment for the receiver as well as the giver of railway rebates. The purpose was to eliminate rate discriminations and thus deprive large corporations of their most potent weapon for stifling competition. At the same time, it was provided that in all cases in which the government was the complainant, either under the Interstate Commerce Act or the Sherman Act, a direct appeal could be taken to the Supreme Court.

In 1906, Congress passed the Hepburn Act, regarded at the time as the greatest achievement of the Roosevelt Administration because it gave renewed vigor to the Interstate Commerce Commission. It gave that body the power to compel uniform bookkeeping practices on all railroads, and the power to establish maximum rates after complaints and investigations had been made; but it was not a general grant of rate-making authority. Senator La Follette insisted, when the Hepburn Act was under consideration, that to give the Commission power only to fix rates sufficiently high as to give the roads a reasonable return on their own valuations was little more than a pretense at rate regulation. He demanded that the roads be given no more than a fair return on their investment, the physical valuations to be determined by the Interstate Commerce Commission. Roosevelt would not support him and the rate-making power of the Commission remained paralyzed although the act did outlaw discriminations, abolish passes and separate railway management from that of other productive enterprises such as mining. It also extended the jurisdiction of the Interstate Commerce Commission over express companies, sleeping car companies and pipe lines. In 1910, the Mann-Elkins Act was passed. It was recommended by Taft and forced through Congress by the Progressives against stiff opposition. It brought telephone and telegraph companies, sleeping car companies and pipe lines under the provisions of the act, gave the Interstate Commerce Commission power to initiate investigations as well as to hear complaints and to suspend rates during the period of investigation, placed the burden of proof on the railroads in all cases of appeal, created a special commission to investigate the marketing of railway securities, and established a special commerce court. This court was to be composed of five United States Circuit Judges appointed by the Chief Justice of the Supreme Court for a period of five years. It was to have the same powers as the Circuit Courts, but was to deal only with cases arising out of the activities of the Interstate Commerce Commission. Appeals from its decisions were to be taken to the Supreme Court, and the United States government was to be represented in such cases by the Attorney-General. It did not represent a complete victory for the progressives, because the power of the Commission to fix the physical valuations of the railroads and federal control of stock issues were eliminated from the bill as previously drawn.

La Follette continued his crusade and, at the very end of President Taft's Administration (March 1, 1913) a Physical Valuations Act was approved.

Tariff

The Ways and Means Committee of the House of Representatives under the leadership of Oscar Underwood of Alabama had spent the interval between 1910 and Wilson's first Congress studying the tariff. The Payne-Aldrich Tariff then in existence was a frank subsidy to industry, the Republican platform of 1908 having guaranteed a "reasonable profit" to American manufacturers. The Democratic House and combined Democratic-Insurgent majority in the Senate had passed a new act lowering many rates and setting up a new free list during Taft's last Congress only to be met with the presidential veto. There was no question as to the desire of the country at large in the 1912 canvass and Wilson called Congress into special session in April following his inauguration. On April 8, he delivered his tariff message in person; but it was more than a tariff message. In its broad implications, as may be seen from the following passages, it chartered the path Wilson was to follow in his entire attitude toward economic reform. "Consciously or unconsciously, we have built up a set of privileges and exemptions from competition behind which it was easy by any, even the crudest, forms of combination to organize monopoly; until at last nothing is normal, nothing is obliged to stand the tests of efficiency and economy, in our world of big business, but everything thrives by concerted arrangement. Only new principles of action will save us from a final hard crystallization of monopoly and a complete loss of the influences that quicken enterprise and keep independent energy alive.

"It is plain what those principles must be. We must abolish everything that bears even the semblance of privilege or of any kind of artificial advantage, and put our business men and producers under the stimulation of a constant necessity to be efficient, economical, and enterprising, masters of competitive supremacy, better workers and merchants than any in the world. . . . It is best, indeed it is necessary to begin with the tariff. . . ."

The House of Representatives, shortly thereafter, passed the new tariff measure prepared in advance by the Ways and Means Committee. The Senate debated the measure until early in September before passing it substantially as it had come from the House. Party discipline played an important part in the proceedings, and the new act was strictly a Democratic measure, the division in each House being along party lines to a larger degree than usual on tariff measures. Four Democrats in the House of Representatives voted against it: Broussard, Morgan and Lazaro of Louisiana and Donohoe of Pennsylvania. Republicans Cary and Stafford of Wisconsin and Manahan of Minnesota voted for the act. Fourteen Republican Senators were absent when the vote was taken. The remainder, with the exception of La Follette of Wisconsin and Poindexter of Washington, voted against the bill as did the two Democratic Senators from Louisiana. Wilson had not asked for a strict adherence to the revenue principle, having been careful to caution against sudden and ruinous reductions without allowing time for business to adjust itself to the new principle of action. In all cases where it could be shown that American products were occupying a dominant position in world trade, rates were reduced. There were more than nine hundred reductions as against eighty-six increases and some three hundred unchanged rates. The average reduction was approximately one-fourth of the former rates, and there was an extended list of free articles. The free list included such foodstuffs as sugar (after May 1, 1916), wheat, cattle, swine, eggs, milk and cream, potatoes, rye, and cornmeal. Rates were reduced on butter from 6 cents a pound to 2½ cents, rice from 2 cents to 1 cent, beans from 45 cents a bushel to 25 cents, chocolate from 21½ per cent to 8 per cent, and onions from 40 cents a bushel to 20 cents. Wool, flax, boots, shoes, leather, and lumber were placed on the free list. Woolen and cotton fabric goods were reduced from a high of 99 per cent to a low of 20 per cent. Steel rails, iron ore, agricultural machinery, cash registers, typesetting machinery, sewing machines, typewriters and shoe machinery were placed on the free list as a definite stroke at monopolies. In addition to all types of machinery necessary to agriculture, there was placed on the free list for farmers: cotton and burlap bagging, band iron, harness, horse-shoes, and barbed wire. Phosphorus matches, cigarettes and the plumes and feathers of wild birds were excluded entirely.

Ratification of the Income Tax Amendment in February, 1913, after four years of intensive controversy made possible the inclusion of an income tax in the Underwood Tariff Act to provide for any revenue losses from reduced import duties. The contest over the adoption of the Amendment was extremely bitter. It was not intended to be simply a revenue measure. Tax laws had ceased to be simply fiscal measures and had become measures of social control. This principle, inaugurated in the levying of special taxes upon amusements, liquors, tobaccos, etc., and in the protective tariff was amplified and given new meaning after the advent of the reform movement. The income tax was regarded as the most just of all forms of taxation when graduated on the principle of ability to pay. It was advanced as the easiest way for society to recapture for use in the new governmental services a portion of the wealth which the new industrial processes were converging into a relatively few hands. Organized wealth opposed the principle then, and never ceased thereafter its efforts to substitute excise or sales taxes for it. It was urged that income taxes should be reserved for special use at times of great national emergency; that any effective program of enforcement would lead to bureaucratic spying into private affairs; that, being class legislation, it would lead to demagogic appeals to the voting masses; that it would retard the development of industrial enterprise; and that, unlike import duties, rational rates could not be maintained because the point of diminishing returns was not so readily discernible. These arguments were of little avail until the World War reaction had reduced the once powerful progressive bloc in Congress to a mere remnant. The difficult part of writing an income tax into the Underwood Tariff was to reach agreement upon the basic exemption and method of collection. It was finally agreed to exempt all incomes under $3000 for single men and $4000 for the joint incomes of husband and wife and to impose a progressive tax of from one to six per cent on all incomes above these amounts. There was a further exemption of $500 for each dependent child, not exceeding two. The rate of taxation was extremely low, amounting to one per cent below $50,000, two per cent between $50,000 and $75,000, three per cent between $75,000 and $100,000, four per cent between $100,000 and $250,000, five per cent between $250,000 and $500,000 and six per cent above $500,000. Deductions were allowed for interest on indebtedness, taxes, business losses, worthless debts, depreciation, interest on federal, state, city or county bonds. The salaries of all state and local employees were exempt and that of the President and United

States Judges then in office. The importance of the adoption of the income tax in 1913 cannot be overestimated. The World War, coming soon afterward, placed enormous burdens upon the federal fiscal system. The need for additional revenue was met in large measure by increased income taxes on individuals and corporations. The corporations tax of one per cent imposed upon incomes in excess of $5000 in 1909 amounted to slightly more than $35,000,000 in the year the new income tax was imposed. In 1916, Congress raised the basic income tax to two per cent; in 1917 to four per cent; and, in 1918, to twelve per cent. Surtaxes were increased to a maximum of fifty per cent in 1917, corporation taxes to six per cent and an excess profits tax imposed. In 1918, surtaxes were raised to a maximum of sixty-five per cent on all incomes in excess of $500,000. From 1913 on, the country became increasingly concerned not only with financing the War and paying the War debt, but with the problem of how to care for its paupers and discipline its wealth. Income taxes supplied the controversial formula for unending strife over every proposal for increased governmental expenditures, public debts and redistribution of wealth. They provided a liberal patronage to members of the legal profession and taught the country new finesse in tax evasion and tax collection.

Finally, the Underwood Tariff gave the Secretary of the Treasury authority to levy additional duties upon goods produced under subsidies in foreign nations, gave the President authority to negotiate reciprocity agreements subject to final Congressional approval, established free trade with the Philippines, and placed all rates upon an *ad valorem* basis instead of the previous arrangement of specific rates on some individual items and *ad valorem* rates on others. The first two of these provisions were in line with the effort to reduce the whole tariff system to a realistic basis. Foreign trade had remained fairly stationary at about $3,000,000,000 annually from 1906 to 1910, but had increased to more than $4,000,000,000 in 1912. Manufacturers were reaching out for foreign markets. The day when nations were to revert to intense nationalism and seek self-sufficiency behind high tariff walls was still in the future; but men were beginning to recognize that tariffs erected by legislative action could only be reduced successfully by negotiation; and that dumping of foreign goods in our markets could be prevented also by executive action alone. These provisions, too, were congenial to Wilson's dictation of the tariff program. He had thrown his full force back of the Underwood bill, had, in fact, dictated many of its provisions, to prevent a recurrence of what had happened in Taft's Administration to the Payne-Aldrich Tariff bill and Canadian reciprocity. The President was no longer suggesting a legislative program to Congress; he was dictating it.

The Federal Reserve Act

The second part of the Wilson reform program dealt with the banking and monetary system. The National Bank Act of 1862 had been devised to serve two purposes: the sale of government bonds, and the erection of a uniform banking system under federal control. That act had been followed by another placing a prohibitive tax upon the note issues of state banks in order to establish a uniform currency system. In 1787, the circulating medium of the country, what there was of it, consisted of specie. State banks emerged during the early part of the nineteenth century and eventually put into circulation some six thousand varieties of bank notes. These notes were good, bad or indifferent according to the life of the bank and the distance from it that its notes were circulated. They gave rise to many losses and great inconvenience. Their destruction forced most banks into the national banking system, created a uniform currency based upon the national debt and made that currency inflexible and rigid. The advent of personal checks toward the end of the century reversed the process, gave state banks a new lease on life and restored the old evil of lax state banking laws without remedying the rigidity of the monetary system or supplying long term credits to the agrarian interests. The deflation of 1907 leveled off without precipitating an economic disaster similar to that of the seventies and nineties; but discerning men, finally freed from the emotional insanity of the free silver controversy, began to comprehend the need for revision. Congress passed the Aldrich-Vreeland Act in 1908, near the close of Roosevelt's Administration. This act made a feeble effort to introduce flexibility into the currency by authorizing issues of national bank notes against state and local bonds as well as against those of the federal government, and against limited amounts of commercial paper; but required the formation of national currency associations as places of deposit and placed heavy taxes upon such currency. A more important feature of the act, however, was its provision for a national monetary commission. This commission carried out a four-year research into foreign fiscal systems and drew up a new banking bill based upon its findings. This bill, presented to Congress near the end of Taft's Administration, was not even considered; but the Commission's report, consisting of many volumes, furnished much valuable data for the Committee on Banking and Currency to use in drafting the new Federal Reserve Act. It was helpful, also, in devising a program for agricultural credits and provided ideas for several commercial savings and loan associations throughout the country.

There was a recognized need for some system by which banking reserves could be brought together for rediscount purposes, for a safe and elastic circulating medium, and for strict supervision of rediscount rates. As the banking system then operated, the volume of currency in circulation was limited by the something less than $1,000,000,000 bonded indebtedness of the United States. The amount of currency any national bank could issue was limited by the amount of its government bonds on deposit with the Comptroller of the Currency and bore no relation to the commercial needs of its community which might at times greatly exceed the bank's liquid assets. Moreover, banks throughout the entire country became so integrated that available reserves were sent to the money centers where they were used as "call money" for speculation purposes, and were not readily available to meet urgent demands for local credit.

Wilson proposed, in a special message to Congress, that these be provided by basing the currency upon commercial paper instead of government bonds and by placing the new banking system under government control. The Federal Reserve Act as first introduced in the House of Representatives by Carter Glass of Virginia, modified in the Senate and finally passed in December, 1913, completely remodeled the banking and currency system of the nation. National banks, state banks and trust companies continued to serve the public as before; but the national banks were compelled and others permitted to purchase stock in new federal reserve banks to the amount of six per cent of their capital and surplus. Twelve such banks were provided, one in each of twelve districts. The function of these new banks in no way touched directly the commercial life of the nation. They were to serve their stockholding banks by rediscounting their commercial paper and granting loans on government securities with new federal reserve bank notes. These new bank notes were to replace the former national bank notes, and were limited in amount only by a required 40 per cent gold reserve. Thus every bank belonging to the system was placed under uniform regulation with respect to loans and cash reserves, but was assured sufficient liquid assets at all times to meet the needs of its community. The volume of currency in circulation was expected to rise and fall in each locality and in the nation as a whole in response to seasonal demands and business fluctuations.

Supervision of this new banking structure in the public interest was assured by placing it under a Federal Reserve Board of seven members, including the Secretary of the Treasury and the Comptroller of the Currency. District banks were likewise controlled by a board, consisting of nine members, three of whom were to be appointed by the Federal Reserve Board and six elected by the stockholding banks. The five (six after 1922) members of the Federal Reserve Board were to be appointed by the President with the approval of the Senate. The federal bonds, bearing two per cent interest, which had been the basis for the old bank notes, were to be retired at the rate of $25,000,000 each year. Speculative inflation was guarded against by prohibiting rediscounting of loans for speculative purposes, by requiring 35 per cent reserves in the Federal Reserve banks and 18 per cent reserves in member banks, by requiring the issuing bank to retire all rediscounted paper, and by limiting rediscounts to a period of three months for commercial paper and six months for agricultural paper.

The system thus established was designed to serve the needs of agriculture better than the old national banking system had done. It was expected to provide a uniform, flexible currency, to prevent financial panics, and to lessen the influence of private banking monopolies over the commercial life of the nation and the fiscal policies of the government. In spite of its excellence, however, it proved to be deficient in two respects: participation in the Federal Reserve System was not required of state banks, and commercial banking was not divorced from investment banking.

It was assumed at the time that the merits of the Federal Reserve System would prove too attractive for state banks to resist, but events proved otherwise. Not more than one-third of the country's banks ever joined although those that did join controlled more than eighty per cent of the combined banking resources. Outstanding leaders in the financial and commercial world urged from time to time that all banks be brought under the system. Action was opposed by others on the ground that it would be an unwarranted assumption of federal power and nothing was done, although the power of Congress to regulate the currency would seem to extend to banks operating a check and deposit business. In 1927, the McFadden Amendment to the Federal Reserve Act was passed, permitting branch-banking by national banks, but only within the limits of their city or county and where state banks were allowed the same privilege. The banking crisis of 1933 forced Congress to take further steps to strengthen the banking structure. The branch-banking privilege was extended to state-wide areas but was still contingent upon state laws only nine of which permitted it at the time. In the same act, however, was a provision designed to compel by indirect action state banks to join the federal system. It created a federal deposit insurance corporation to protect small deposits and extended its benefits to those banks only which were members of the Federal Reserve System, with the expectation that the depositors' desire for security would force all banks to join.

Investment banking was in its infancy at the time the Federal Reserve System was being organized. The National City Bank of New York, desiring to engage in the marketing of securities, which it could not do under the national banking laws, organized the National City Company in July, 1911. Attorney-General George Wickersham was requested to investigate its legality by President Taft. Solicitor-General Frederick W. Lehmann made his report in November of that year, saying in part: "The other enterprise in which the company is engaged may stand in need of credit and of funds, and it is too much to expect that the company's banks will deal simply as banks, equitably and impartially as between its own subsidiaries and persons and corporations with whom it is not affiliated. The temptation to the speculative use of the funds of the banks at opportune times will prove to be irresistible. . . . If many enterprises and many banks are brought and bound together in the nexus of a great holding corporation, the failure of one may involve all in a common disaster. And if the plan should prosper it would mean a union of power in the same hands over industry, commerce, and finance, with a resulting power over public affairs, which was the gravamen of objection to the United States Bank." This opinion was not given to the Comptroller of the Currency, nor was it made public until Senator Carter Glass discovered it in the Attorney-General's office and had it printed as a Senate Document in May, 1932. What influenced Wickersham and his successor to keep it hidden has never been disclosed. It is certain that Attorney-General McReynolds and Secretary of the Treasury McAdoo both knew about it at the time the

Federal Reserve Act was being written, but took no action. The investment affiliates continued to grow in numbers and influence until, nearly two decades later, they were, in the opinion of Senator Glass, "the greatest contributors to the riot of credit and inflation" which ultimately led to the closing of the banks by presidential order.

Industrial Relations

The importance of the investment banking phase of the problem can only be understood by remembering how closely the Federal Reserve Act and the anti-trust legislation of Wilson's Administration are related.

Great emphasis was placed upon destroying the huge industrial corporations during Roosevelt's and Taft's administrations. Roosevelt had won popular acclaim by prosecuting the Northern Securities Company and winning a verdict of dissolution from the Supreme Court in 1904. There followed, during the next eight years, more than one hundred suits against such outstanding corporations as the Standard Oil Company, the American Tobacco Company, the United States Steel Corporation, the International Harvester Company, the National Cash Register Company and the General Electric Company. Roosevelt had, in addition, advocated federal charters for all corporations engaged in interstate commerce; and both he and Taft had urged that specific practices such as holding companies, stock watering, etc., be outlawed. In spite of all the public agitation and government activity it was clearly evident by 1913 that competition had not been restored nor monopolistic growth retarded. There was a definite trend, therefore, of sentiment in favor of regulation of trusts instead of attempted dissolution. Congress responded to that sentiment with the Federal Trade Commission Act. There was also a clearer conception of how the huge corporations were formed and popular attention shifted from the corporations themselves to the financiers who controlled them.

Woodrow Wilson, Governor of New Jersey, had said in

1911: "The great monopoly in this country is the money monopoly. So long as that exists, our old variety and freedom and individual energy of development are out of the question." One year later, the House of Representatives had appointed a committee, under the chairmanship of Arsene P. Pujo of Louisiana, to investigate the money trust. Its report, submitted to the House, February 28, 1913, created a sensation. It revealed that J. P. Morgan and Company held sixty-three directorships in thirty-nine corporations; the First National Bank of New York eighty-nine directorships in forty-nine corporations; the Guaranty Trust Company of New York 160 directorships in seventy-six corporations; the Bankers' Trust Company of New York 113 directorships in fifty-five corporations; the National City Bank of New York 86 directorships in forty-seven corporations; the National Bank of Commerce of New York 149 directorships in eighty-two companies; the Chase National Bank of New York 67 directorships in forty-eight corporations; the Astor Trust Company 144 directorships in sixty-three corporations; the New York Trust Company 74 directorships in forty-seven corporations; and similar control of banks, insurance companies, transportation systems, producing and trading corporations and public utilities by numerous other banking houses in New York, Boston and Chicago. It showed an amazing system of interlocking control among the several great banking houses through directorship held by J. P. Morgan, Thomas W. Lamont, Henry P. Davidson and William H. Porter. Concerning this situation, the Pujo Committee reported: "Far more dangerous than all that has happened to us in the past in the way of elimination of competition in industry is the control of credit through the domination of these groups over our banks and industries."

The following November (1913), there appeared the first of two remarkable books on the subject: *Other People's Money* by Louis D. Brandeis. This study carried the story beyond that of the Pujo report and showed how the large profits to be gleaned from promoting corporate mergers had revolutionized banking, combining investment and commercial banking in the same hands and subjecting industries, railroads and public utilities to ever-increasing banking control. For the first time, the public at large learned how J. P. Morgan and Company received the major portion of $62,500,000 for promoting the Steel Trust and equally large commissions for their services in organizing other corporations including the International Harvester Company, the American Telephone and Telegraph Company and the General Electric Company. Brandeis' principle admonition was that "the Sherman Law should be supplemented both by providing more efficient judicial machinery, and by creating a commission with administrative functions to aid in enforcing the law."

In writing the Federal Reserve Act, Congress made an honest effort to reach the roots of the evil by impounding the reserve funds of the nation's banks in the twelve Federal Reserve banks and by forbidding the rediscounting of "notes, drafts, or bills covering merely investments or issued or drawn for the purpose of carrying or trading in stock, bonds, or other investment securities, except bonds and notes of the Government of the United States." At that time there was less than $100,000,000 in government bonds available for rediscount purposes. The reluctance of many banks to enter the Federal Reserve System and the tremendous increase in government bonds during the World War made available to the investment banker and to the gambling public tremendous sums for the sale and purchase of securities which those who drafted the Federal Reserve Act never intended the new system to provide.

Congress followed this act with the Federal Trade Commission Act and the Clayton Act. The Sherman Act had attempted to regulate the relationships of business enterprise and preserve competition by outlawing combination in restraint of trade. The broad language of the act was purposely used in order to prevent corporations from evading the law and to enable the Department of Justice to bring them before the Court for a wide range of offences. In actual practice, however, that purpose was defeated because the Supreme Court found it necessary to determine in each case whether the corporate act complained of could reasonably be regarded as in restraint of trade. The Senate Interstate Commerce Committee recommended in March, 1913, that the Sherman Act should be amended to specifically prescribe certain conditions upon which persons and corporations might engage in commerce and that a commission be created to supervise corporations in the same manner as the Interstate Commerce Commission supervised the railroads. Wilson, in his trust message to Congress, January 20, 1914, more definitely requested a commission with wider powers than those enjoyed by the Bureau of Corporations. The Clayton Act, passed October 15, 1914, outlawed price discriminations which tended to lessen competition or create monopolies; tying contracts; inter-corporate stock holdings; interlocking directorates of banks having "deposits, capital, surplus, and undivided profits aggregating more than $5,000,000"; interlocking directorates of competing corporations capitalized at more than one billion dollars, and of corporations and common carriers. The former provision for three-fold damages to persons injured by discrimination was continued, officers of corporations were made personally responsible for violations of the law and complaints could be taken directly to the Federal Trade Commission for relief through cease and desist orders.

The Federal Trade Commission Act set up an administrative agency to search out and eliminate abuses in business life. It was designed for a dual purpose: to compel business enterprises to be fair to each other and to serve the public interest. It was to be composed of five members, appointed by the President with the consent of the Senate for a period of seven years. The act declared "unfair methods of competition in commerce" to be unlawful. It gave to the Commission the power to investigate all corporations engaged in commerce, to require reports from such corporations, and to issue cease and desist orders against specific practices. It charged the Commission specifically with the duty of following up all court decrees obtained under the anti-trust laws and reporting its findings to the Attorney-General. Thus the Commission was charged with performing the duties of the former Bureau of Corporations, was made the special agent of the Department of Justice and was given the independent and primary responsibility of purging business of its dishonest practices. The expectation that the Commission would succeed in restoring the competition which the Sherman Act had failed to preserve was never realized, partly because economic security rather than economic opportunity became the aspiration of most people in society and partly because purging business of its dishonest practices was a herculean task as revealed by the experience of the NRA in later years. The Commission did, however, through its fact-finding activities, become one of the most valuable departments of the government in the service of the people. In fact, for some time, it seemed to be the only government commission interested in protecting the consumer. During Wilson's Administration it received more than two thousand complaints and issued 379 cease and desist orders against specific unfair practices, including false advertising, false statements about competitors, bribery, adulteration of goods, misbranding of fabrics, etc. Cooperating with the Department of Justice, it secured the dissolution of the International Harvester Company (1918), and the Corn Products Refining Company (1919), and an agreement from the five great meat-packing companies (Swift, Armour, Morris, Wilson and Cudahy) not to operate stockyards, terminal railways, market newspapers, retail meat or grocery markets or to sell milk and cream.

Little was accomplished in the way of consent decrees during the next twelve years. It was a period in which business was given a free hand by the government. Economic pathology was distinctly foreign to the prevailing philosophy. In 1933, however, the Commission scored its greatest victory since the meat packers' consent decree of 1920. The General Electric and Westinghouse companies surrendered their stock holdings in the Radio Corporation and the radio industry was purged of its interlocking control. The monopoly of radio patents which had so seriously restricted competition and maintained discriminatory prices was eliminated. Meanwhile, however, an investigation of the power and light industry had such far-reaching consequences as alone to have justified the Commission's existence. Senator Thomas Walsh of Montana introduced a resolution in the Senate in 1928 designed to set up a Senate Committee to investigate that industry. Power interests, fearful of Walsh who had been instrumental in pushing the oil lease fraud cases to a conclusion, succeeded in having the task assigned to the Federal Trade Commission. The Commission, after a long and searching scrutiny of financial and propaganda practices of the power interests, presented a monumental report to the Senate. That report was so widely quoted and furnished the data for such an amazing number of books, magazine articles and newspaper editorials, that it actually reversed the entire nation's attitude toward the question of government regulation of public utilities. It served, more than any other factor, to purge the educational system of subtle propaganda which was beginning to creep in. It altered the course of the prevailing economic thought in the nation at large. It forced the utilities, themselves, to make some gesture in the direction of better business practices.

Labor

The section of the Clayton Act which provoked more comment at the time than the anti-trust provisions was Section 20, relating to labor.

The open hostility toward labor shown by President Cleveland when he sent federal troops to Chicago during the Pullman strike and authorized the railway operators to deputize 5000 private guards as United States marshals, was not repeated in the twentieth century. The first evidence of a changed attitude by the two major parties was in the Democratic platform of 1900 which denounced the black list and government by injunction and advocated both arbitration in industrial disputes and the establishment of a Department of Labor. The party did not deviate from this attitude during its minority position and some action was certain following Wilson's election. Labor had suffered a severe handicap from the widespread use of injunctions and from the common law doctrine of "malicious combination" which placed it at the mercy of the social and economic ideas of the judges and left it at a loss as to what action was or was not lawful.

Roosevelt denied the coal operators the use of federal troops to break the strike of 1902. Instead, he indicated a willingness to seize and operate the mines to the extent of supplying public needs unless operation were resumed while the issues involved were being studied by a commission of his choice. In his message to Congress, December 5, 1905, he said: "There has been a demand for depriving the courts of the power to issue injunctions in labor disputes. Such special limitations of the equity powers of our courts would be most unwise. It is true that some judges have misused this power; but this does not justify a denial of the power any more than an improper exercise of the power to call a strike by a labor leader would justify the denial of the right to strike." One year later, he said: "It is at least doubtful whether a law abolishing altogether the use of injunctions in such cases would stand the test of courts." He did advocate, however, a required hearing after due notice before the issuance of an injunction, and (April 27, 1908) trials for contempt before another judge. His position with respect to the question was admirably stated in his message of December 3, 1907, when he said: "Instances of abuse in the granting of injunctions in labor disputes continue to occur. . . . The question is becoming more and more one of prime importance and unless the courts themselves deal with it in effective manner, it is certain ultimately to demand some form of legislative action. It would be most unfortunate for our social welfare if we should permit many honest and law-abiding citizens to feel that they had just cause for regarding our courts with hostility."

In the election of 1908, violent attacks upon the judiciary were made by labor leaders. They demanded that all injunctions should be prohibited except for the protection of property rights and that jury trials should be required in all contempt cases. Roosevelt disapproved most heartily of these suggested remedies and President Taft (March 4, 1909) said: "Take away from the Courts, if it could be taken away, the power to issue injunctions in labor disputes, and it would create a privileged class among the laborers and save the lawless among their number from a most needful remedy available for all men for the protection of their business against lawless invasion. The proposition that business is not a property or pecuniary right which can be protected by equitable injunction is utterly without foundation in precedent or reason."

Congress failed to act concerning the Sherman Act or injunctions during Roosevelt's Administration. Meanwhile, in *Gompers* v. *Bucks Stove and Range Co.* (1911), the Supreme Court gave a sweeping interpretation to the Sherman Act with respect to labor unions in these words, "It covered any illegal means by which interstate commerce is restrained, whether by unlawful combinations of capital, or . . . of labor; and we think also whether the restraint be occasioned by unlawful contracts, trusts, pooling arrangements, black lists, boycotts, coercion, threats, intimidation, and whether these be made effective, in whole or in part, by acts, words or printed matter." In Taft's Administration, however, Congress added a provision to the appropriation bill prohibiting the use of any funds for the prosecution of labor unions under the Sherman Act. President Taft vetoed the measure, but a similar one was signed by President Wilson under protest. Each succeeding appropriation bill contained the same restraint without protest from any executive after Wilson. Organized labor would have benefited greatly had Congress refrained from further action, because only the government could prosecute unions under the Sherman Act; but the Clayton Act was passed and approved on October 14, 1914. Section 6 of this act said:

"That the labor of a human being is not a commodity or article of commerce. Nothing contained in the anti-trust laws shall be construed to forbid the existence and operation of labor, agricultural, or horticultural organizations . . . or to forbid or restrain individual members of such organizations from lawfully carrying out the legitimate objects thereof; nor shall such organizations or the members thereof, be held or construed to be illegal combinations or conspiracies in restraint of trade, under the anti-trust laws."

It forbade any judge or court to issue injunctions in labor disputes "unless necessary to prevent irreparable injury to property, or to a property right." It legalized strikes and strike benefits. It forbade injunctions prohibiting strikers from "recommending, advising, or persuading others by peaceful means" to cease work; "or from attending at any place where any such person or persons may lawfully be, for the purpose of peacefully obtaining or communicating information . . . or from ceasing to patronize or to employ any party to such dispute . . . or from peaceable assembling in a lawful manner, and for lawful purposes; or from doing any act or thing which might lawfully be done in the absence of such dispute by any party thereto." This statute marked the culmination of two decades of agitation to place workingmen and their employers on the same plane in industrial warfare. It appeared to be and the public was led to believe that it was an assertion of the principle that the legislative and not the judicial branch of the government should define public policy toward industrial warfare. It appeared to the layman that certain acts had been made legal at all times and under all circumstances. Every act specified in the law had previously been held unlawful by the courts to some degree. It was the aim of the progressives in Congress to apply to relations between capital and labor the same principle of competition that was regarded so essential in industrial and business life. They recognized the value of competitive economic strength between capital and labor and sought to justify whatever damages might result from testing that strength according to certain rules. In that respect, it stands out in sharp contrast to the principle of compulsory arbitration of industrial disputes then being widely discussed throughout the country. It was the last attempt of Congress to deal with the fundamental aspects of the labor problem until Section 7a of the National Recovery Act, based upon an entirely different principle, was written in 1933.

The Clayton Act was hailed, prematurely, as the Magna Charta of labor. It was in line with the philosophy of Samuel Gompers, President of the American Federation of Labor from 1886 to 1924. Gompers always insisted that labor should remain unhampered by government interference to pit its economic strength against that of capital. He said, over and over again, that compulsory arbitration would lead to the establishment of labor courts and bitter strife between capital and labor for control of the government in order to control those courts. He stood, therefore, for absolute freedom of labor to organize its strength and thus increase its bargaining power in its relations with capital. There had been no agreement in Congress, however, as to whether the act as finally passed merely legalized unions or went further and relieved them from injunctions against their activities. It was another case of Congress, unable to agree upon the terms of an act, writing it in ambiguous language and dumping the dispute into the lap of the Supreme Court for settlement by interpretation of the law. The Court decided that the words lawfully and legitimate gave meaning to the act and merely legalized the past practices of the Courts with respect to injunctions (*Duplex Printing Press Co.* v. *Deering*, 1921). Even more important, however, was the fact that the Clayton Act opened the federal courts to direct suits for injunctions by corporations as well as by the government. But the failure of the Clayton Act to relieve labor organizations fully from the handicaps of the common law and the failure of labor to utilize its potential strength advantageously are two separate and distinct things. Labor's failure, as we shall see later, was largely due to its own incompetence and is not chargeable to the Courts or to the failure of the Clayton Act.

In addition to the labor provisions of the Clayton Act, Congress passed the Adamson Act (1916) in consequence of a threatened tie-up of the nation's transportation facilities, establishing the eight-hour day as the standard for computing wages of employees of common carriers engaged in interstate commerce. The Act was promptly challenged in the courts but its constitutionality was upheld by the Supreme Court in the case of *Wilson* v. *New*.

The next important step in government attitude toward labor was validation by the Supreme Court of yellow dog contracts. The simplest form of yellow dog contracts consisted of an agreement dictated by the employer and signed by the worker that he would not join a union so long as he remained in the employ of the company. There were many variations from this simple form but, for the most part, they were anti-union contracts, open shop contracts, or company union contracts. They made their appearance in the West Virginia coal fields in 1907, spread into the Pennsylvania coal fields in the early twenties, to the Lynn, Massachusetts, shoe industry in 1923, and then to the Union Pacific and the Chicago, Rock Island and Pacific railroads. They possessed few of the fundamental elements of a contract at law because coercion of the worst sort entered into the signing of the agreement. Few laborers ever signed them except through fear of losing their jobs, back of which, of course, was the cruel certainty of starvation or worse for their families. They were given sanctity by the courts, however, and added significance by the granting of injunctions for their enforcement. They became the favorite non-union weapon of capital after the *Hitchman Coal Company* v. *Mitchell* decision (1917) legalized them, and forbade union organizers from proselytizing among workers who were bound by them. The broader economic significance of the combination of yellow dog contracts and injunctions was clearly revealed in the Hitchman case. The coal fields of Ohio, Pennsylvania, Indiana and Illinois were already unionized and hours and wages fairly stabilized before the coal fields of West Virginia were opened with non-union labor working under yellow dog contracts. The United Mine Workers of America set out to unionize the West Virginia field as the only possible way to save their existing security from the devastating effects of cheap coal mined by non-union labor. They were enjoined from doing so by the Circuit Court in 1907 and the injunction was sustained by the Supreme Court in the Hitchman case. The result was chaos in the coal industry and the most deplorable exploitation of labor in southern coal mines of any industrial section of the United States. State legislatures, meanwhile, in large industrial states like Massachusetts, Connecticut, New York, Pennsylvania, Ohio and Illinios, had passed laws outlawing yellow dogs contracts; but the Supreme Court in *Coppage* v. *Kansas* (1915) had invalidated such laws as a denial of the freedom of contract.

The Clayton Act and Hitchman decision were followed closely by the World War. Little progress was made during the period of post-war reaction toward finding a more satisfactory formula for solving the problems of capital and labor than the traditional trial of economic strength within the limits set by the courts. The next action by Congress was the Norris-La Guardia Act of March 20, 1932.

Agriculture

The farming population of the country received its share of attention from the Wilson Administration. The farmers' simple agrarian economy of earlier days had disappeared. As a producer of staple crops for sale abroad and in the eastern industrial centers, his fortunes were closely linked to the management of the great railway systems and the protective tariff. The Interstate Commerce Act, the Sherman Anti-Trust Act, the Elkins Act, and the Hepburn Act had sought to free him from the tyranny of the railroads by eliminating rate discriminations, rebates, etc. The Underwood Tariff Act removed import duties from a greatly expanded list of commodities he purchased as a consumer. The rapid introduction of farm machinery had placed the farmer at the mercy of the manufacturing monopolies. The new tariff act aimed to correct that, indirectly, by reducing the tariff rates behind which monopolies were sustained; and the Clayton and Federal Trade Commission Acts, directly, by challenging the fundamental structure and trade practices of such industrial combinations. The Clayton Act went still farther and exempted agricultural cooperatives from the operation of the anti-trust laws. In 1918, Congress passed the Webb-Pomerene Act permitting the organization of export trade associations, a distinct concession to agriculture as well as to those manufacturers selling in the world markets. The farmer had found difficulty in financing his operations even to the extent of obtaining short-term loans for seed, fertilizer and new farm machinery. The Federal Reserve Act removed the restrictions of the National Bank Act against loans by national banks on farm mortgages and permitted such loans for five-year periods to the amount of 50 per cent of the valuation. It allowed the new Federal Reserve banks to rediscount agricultural paper for periods up to six months; and it impounded reserves in the regional banks in order to keep them available for local needs of agriculture and business.

The most distressing aspect of the farm problem, however, was the increase in farm mortgages. A long period of small profits or operating deficits coupled with the increase of land values through extraneous forces (immigration and the westward movement), larger initial costs and ultimate replacement expenses had placed mortgages on 31 per cent of the farms in the United States before 1900. These were fixed charges against the returns of a better day which never came. The worst situation in this respect was in the agricultural region of the North Central States. Congress debated the situation for nearly two years and then, in May, 1916, passed the Federal Farm Loan Act. The purpose of the act was to create banking machinery suited to the farmers' needs for long time credits at reduced interest rates and to place farm finances upon a sound and stable basis sufficient to make them an attractive field of investment for conservative private capital.

The Federal Farm Loan Act created twelve Federal Land

banks. Their initial capital had to be secured in a different way from that of the Federal Reserve banks because there were no existing land banks similar to the commercial banks which could be brought into the system. The federal government, therefore, undertook to subscribe for all stock not taken by private capital. Each of the banks was capitalized at $750,000 and of the $9,000,000 required, the government supplied all but $200,000. There was a steady reduction thereafter until, by 1930, it had withdrawn almost entirely from the system. The banks were under the supervision of a board of five members, including the Secretary of the Treasury. There were no subsidiary banks, but farm loan associations instead. The membership of these farm loan associations was made up of farmers who wished to borrow from the land banks and who bought stock in the associations to the amount of five per cent of their loans. Loans, as in the Federal Reserve System, were restricted to 50 per cent of valuation, but an additional 20 per cent of the value of buildings and other improvements could be secured. The farm loan associations were to recommend the loans, the land banks furnish the money. The banks were authorized to sell bonds secured by the mortgages and such bonds bore the tax exempt privileges of government bonds. Loans were to be amortized over a period of thirty-three years, interest rates not to exceed six per cent and profits distributed to the members of the loan associations. There were 4659 farm loan associations by 1930 and about $1,000,000,000 of farm mortgages owned by the twelve land banks. That sum represented little more than the total annual interest payment on the total indebtedness of the American farmer. The combined holdings of the Federal Land banks and the Joint Stock Land banks in that year were not more than one-fifth of the total value of farm mortgages. Insurance companies held 23 per cent of the total, commercial banks 10 per cent, farmers and other individuals in rural communities 30 per cent. The land bank system did much to set uniform, reasonable standards in agricultural financing; but it did not fulfill the complete expectations of its sponsors.

CHAPTER VI

LAW ADMINISTRATION AND THE COURTS

We have seen how the period under discussion was preeminently a period of social and economic change; how the individual no less than society as a whole was compelled by forces entirely beyond his control to alter his mode of living, his habits of thought, his attitudes toward old and strange, new institutions. It was a bewildering age; an age of intellectual as well as social ferment; an age in which men and women were groping, often ignorantly and blindly, for new values in life. The legislative program discussed in the preceding chapters represents their effort to solve their problems and crystallize their experiences by experimental legislation; but from the enactment of legislation to the fulfillment of its objectives is a long and difficult process. It involves the support of public opinion, the vigilance and capacity of enforcement agencies, the development of administrative procedure, and the process of judicial review. It is essential for the student of history to remember that the individual citizen lives under the protection of a formidable list of safeguards provided in the common law and the constitutions of both state and nation; that, in recognition of the diverse social and economic interests of widely separated sections, specific powers only are delegated to the federal government; that, because legislators represent the people and are directly responsible to their ever-changing moods, the protection of legislative prerogatives is of vital importance; and that society functions under the rules of the common law in every case where it has not been modified or superseded by statute law. The subsequent history of reform legislation is of more historical importance than its enactment.

Every reform movement spawns its demagogues. Change and progress are not synonymous terms; but it is not always possible to know where statesmanship ends and politics begin. Moreover, the purging of political parties is ofttimes an indispensable preliminary step to legitimate reform; but when party discipline weakens, pressure politics flourish. The result is sumptuary laws which remain unenforced because they invade the accepted limits of personal judgment or are invalidated by the courts because they violate the constitutional guarantees of individual liberty. In the first instance, their over-zealous sponsors denounce the non-conformists, seek to destroy them and succeed only in weakening the majesty of the law in general. In the second instance, they denounce the courts as reactionary and demand that they be shorn of the power of judicial review. Laws against the dissemination of birth control information, the teaching of evolution, the sale of cigarettes, amusements on Sunday, etc., proved unenforceable and were gradually abandoned or modified. They reached their climax in the momentous contest over prohibition. Another type of reform legislation was that which was clearly experimental in character or arose out of social conditions peculiar to a limited geographical section. Either because they proved to be unsatisfactory where tried or had a limited appeal, such laws were confined to a relatively few states. Direct primary, preferential primary, initiative, referendum and recall legislation belonged to this class. It included the Jim Crow laws of the southern states, the peculiar divorce laws of Nevada and South Carolina, the farmers' cooperative laws of Nebraska and Wisconsin. Laws which failed to accomplish fully the purpose for which they were enacted because of lax or inefficient efforts at enforcement include the school attendance laws, the anti-trust laws, safety and health codes, anti-lynching laws, etc. The purposes of the Federal Reserve Act were thwarted, in part, by the inefficiency of the Federal Reserve Board. The same may be said of the subsequent history of the Interstate Commerce Act and the several state utility laws. Finally, the test of constitutionality upset the plans of those who sought by state legislation to abolish private schools and restrict the freedom of the press; of states which attempted to regulate interstate commerce; of Congress when it attempted to reach behind interstate commerce and control child labor in the factories or when it delegated legislative prerogatives to the executive or to administrative agencies. Obviously, space does not permit nor relative historical importance justify a detailed treatment of much of this administrative and judicial history. There are, however, certain laws in the enactment and subsequent history of which are revealed all the surging impulsiveness of reform, the effective use of pressure politics by minority groups, the conflict of opposing philosophies, the problems of law enforcement and the human frailties of judicial bodies.

Public Opinion and Reform

Back in the winter of 1873, Congress was prevailed upon by Anthony Comstock to pass the first of a series of laws known as the "Comstock Laws." Comstock was a fanatic on the subject of moral reform. He believed that the salvation of the human race depended upon driving out of existence every reference to sex life with which young people might come into contact; and he took advantage of the prevailing sentiment against obscenity to write into the national statutes the most drastic prohibitions ever attempted before the Volstead Act. It excluded from the mails, on penalty of five thousand dollars fine and five years imprisonment "every obscene, lewd, or lascivious, and every filthy book, pamphlet, picture, paper, letter, writing, print, or other publication of an indecent character, and every article or thing designed, adapted, or intended for preventing conception . . . and every written or printed card, letter, circular, book, pamphlet, advertisement, or notice of any kind giving information directly or indirectly . . . by what means conception may be prevented. . . ." There followed a series of laws in all but two states, some directly forbidding the dissemination of birth control information and others directed against obscenity which required definition by the courts and, because the two terms were definitely linked in the federal statute, proved to be as effective as the direct prohibition itself.

Comstock was then made a special agent by Postmaster-General Jewell, with authorization from Congress to enforce the postal laws. He held the position without salary until Taft's Postmaster-General Cortelyou forced him to become a regularly appointed postal inspector in 1910. His salary of $100 per month was paid meanwhile by the Y.M.C.A. At the same time he was Secretary of the Society for the Suppression of Vice. The society was incorporated in New York, authorized by the state to enforce its law, make arrests and receive one-half of all fines imposed by the courts. No more typical example exists in the history of the country of the evils of conferring law enforcement powers upon private individuals and associations. Comstock's career was a dreary succession of 3873 arrests and 2911 convictions, the hounding of physicians and social hygienists and the persecution of liberals everywhere.

Few people have been arrested and convicted under the federal statute in spite of its widespread violation; but it, and the several state laws, remained upon the statute books as insidious implements for the persecution of individuals who could not otherwise be reached. They deterred honorable physicians, hospitals, and clinics from applying scientific methods in individual cases, stimulated surreptitious circulation of harmful or worthless contraceptives and denied information to the class of people who needed it most. Soon after the federal law was enacted a petition for its repeal signed by several thousand people was presented to Congress. The petition said in part: "That mental, moral and physical health and safety are better secured and preserved by virtue resting upon liberty and knowledge, than upon ignorance enforced by governmental supervision. That even error may be safely let free, where truth is free to combat it. That the greatest danger to a republic is the insidious repression of the liberties of the people." Nothing was accomplished and little more attempted toward repeal until

Margaret Sanger was arrested in 1914. Her indictment led to the organization of the National Birth Control League. Thereafter, there was ever-increasing agitation of the subject with the opposition to repeal both of national and state statutes coming principally from the National Council of Catholic Women. It is interesting to note that the Methodist Church came out strongly for birth control; and that, on another phase of the reform movement, prohibition of the liquor traffic, the two groups should have taken exactly opposite positions. The religious aspects of the alignment, however, can easily be over-emphasized. Far more significant in the reluctance of Congress and state legislatures to repeal these laws was the deeply ingrained inhibition against discussion of matters pertaining to sex and fear of the consequences of repeal upon the moral life of young people. They preferred to allow the laws to remain upon the statute books and gradually fall into disuse and be forgotten.

The history of the prohibition of the liquor traffic is quite different. The Eighteenth Amendment became a part of the Constitution of the United States on January 29, 1919. It was the crowning achievement of the temperance and prohibition forces. It was the beginning, also, of a disastrous experiment: that of writing a prohibitory statute into the fundamental law. The prohibition appeal was not dependent upon the agitation of a small reform group. It flourished because of the persistent lawlessness of the liquor interests, the reeking vileness of the saloon, and the inability of state and local governments to control effectually the liquor traffic. The saloon was a colorful institution. It served a useful social function as the chummery of the proletariat. It fostered intemperance; but that was its least objectionable feature. It sheltered vice and crime, maintained a consortium with politics and resisted all efforts at control in the interest of decency and respectability. It was an open defiance of good government, clean living and social security. Its relation to the prohibition movement is clearly shown by the platforms of the political parties in 1932 which pledged the Democrats to "effectively prevent the return of the saloon" and the Republicans to "safeguard our citizens everywhere from the return of the saloon."

The second factor was the inability of state governments to control the liquor traffic. New Hampshire and Massachusetts established state liquor license systems in the 1840's. The laws were reviewed by the Supreme Court in 1847. The decision of the Court, written by Chief Justice Taney, held that liquor shipments into a state were under the control of Congress by virtue of the interstate commerce clause of the Constitution; but, since Congress had not assumed control, a state might do so under its police powers. In 1886, Iowa placed restrictions on importations of liquor into the state and the subject again came before the Supreme Court in the case of *Bowman* v. *Railway Company* (1888). This time the Court pronounced the Iowa statute unconstitutional in a new doctrine: that when Congress failed to legislate on a particular phase of interstate commerce, the presumption was that Congress desired it to remain unregulated. This decision rendered state governments impotent to prevent liquor shipments into dry territory and Congress failed to supply the deficiency.

Congress then passed the Wilson Law delegating the power over the liquor traffic in interstate commerce to the states; but the Supreme Court (*Rhodes* v. *Iowa*) held that a commodity remained in interstate commerce until delivered to the consignee. The Wilson Act was then amended by the Webb-Kenyon Act. This act regulated interstate commerce by removing all immunities of liquors in interstate commerce. The Supreme Court upheld its constitutionality by a five to four decision; but President Taft, afterward Chief Justice of the Supreme Court, had vetoed it as being unconstitutional, Attorney-General Wickersham held it to be unconstitutional, so did Sutherland, later a Supreme Court Justice, and Elihu Root, a distinguished authority on constitutional law. This fear of a future reversal by the Court in a new case which might arise accounts for the provision in the Twenty-first Amendment giving Congress authority to protect dry states.

It was the southern states with their heavy Negro population and the agricultural states of the Middle West that fostered the national prohibition movement. The industrial states of the East were opposed to it. The Constitution could be amended, however, against the wishes of the twelve states having more than a majority of the total population of the country; and such an amendment could only be removed by another which twelve of the smaller states, with a combined population of less than 6,000,000 in a total of more than 100,000,000, could prevent. The full possibilities of this minority rule system were not applied to the prohibition question, but approximately that is what happened. The Methodist Church fostered the Women's Christian Temperance Union, the Board of Temperance, Prohibition and Public Morals, and the Anti-Saloon League. The stronghold of the movement was in the Middle West and South. Skilfully organized independently of political parties, the prohibition forces represented a minority in most governmental units, but were able to control both parties by pressure politics. State prohibition laws were forced through legislatures contrary to the wishes of a majority of the people. The fight was carried into Congress on the eve of the World War, conducted under the direction of Wayne B. Wheeler, General Counsel of the Anti-Saloon League, and through the agency of the most powerful lobby ever established at Washington.

The resolution submitting the Eighteenth Amendment to the states was passed in December, 1917, when the country was in a mood to make any sacrifices congenial to a successful prosecution of the war. Patriotism was added to the already strong appeal. A seven-year limit on ratification was engineered by Senator Penrose with the confident expectation that the amendment would go by default. To the surprise of many, however, the amendment was quickly ratified by all the states except Connecticut and Rhode Island. It was a unique amendment in the sense that it did not transfer power from the states to Congress but wrote an inflexible police regulation into the Constitution. Congress then passed the National Prohibition Act

(Volstead Act) over Wilson's veto on October 28, 1919. The Amendment prohibited the manufacture, transportation, import and sale of intoxicating liquors and the Prohibition Act defined intoxicating liquors as those containing more than one-half of one per cent alcohol.

The subsequent history of the movement belongs to a later chapter, but certain aspects of it are important at this point. The prohibition was in the fundamental law and not subject to change either by state legislatures or by Congress. It was a regulation of the customs and habits of the people in the interest of uniform standards of conduct. It took no account of the widely diverse social environments of the rural and urban communities or of the industrial East and rural South. It did not have sufficient public opinion back of it to make it effective in spite of the fanatical zeal of its sponsors. The ensuing years present a tragic record of death, of decreasing respect for law, and of a corrupting alliance between government officials and the criminal underworld. Bootlegging, smuggling and moonshining flourished through the patronage of all classes of society. Enforcement agencies broke down. The fiction that the federal government could always enforce its laws irrespective of state and local impotence was disproved. The entire system of safeguards for individual liberty was seriously impaired. A half million were convicted for violating the law. Thirty thousand intoxicants were arrested in Cleveland alone in one year and their average age was only 25 years. The federal government spent nearly five hundred million dollars annually for enforcement over a twelve-year period. The net result was the most dismal failure in the history of the republic.

A third aspect of the intricate interrelationship between law, law enforcement and the complexities of human impulses is furnished in the record of lynchings. A lynching is not a secret, premeditated murder; it is a bold and open defiance of the law by any number of people, ranging into the thousands, in which the victim is subjected to variable punishments between the extremes of instant death and all the tortures and indignities unrestrained sadism can devise. There were 1958 people lynched in the United States between 1889 and 1900; 885 during the first decade of the century; 606 during the second decade; and 275 between 1920 and 1930. Seven hundred and sixty-eight of the victims were whites, the remainder Negroes. This appalling record of barbarism in twentieth-century America is of no small historical importance. It stands in sharp contrast to the humanitarian solicitude for the victims of industrial exploitation, organized vice and demon rum. Lynchings occurred most frequently in the rural South, in localities of economic and cultural decadence, where the religious emotionalism of the Baptist and Methodist churches still prevailed. They arose out of widespread inferiority complexes on the part of the ignorant, depraved whites who lived on the margin of civilization and found satisfaction in sudden assertions of racial superiority. Lynchings were not all in the southern states nor were the victims always Negroes; but 90 per cent of them were in the South, in the very sections which most actively supported the prohibition, fundamentalist and Ku Klux Klan movements. The surviving heritage of earlier days—lawlessness of the frontier, low value placed on human life during slavery, and the need for self-preservation during reconstruction—contributed to the basic pattern. Economic rivalry between competing racial groups; the craving for emotional excitement, stimulated by the lurid publicity of mob scenes; distrust of legal processes; and the indifference of the general public to the situation, all were in part responsible for the continued lawlessness. The essential facts are (1) that lynchings were always in open defiance of the law; (2) that they variously occurred before arrests were made, after arrests but before trial, while trials were in progress, after conviction but before sentence was executed, and after commutation of sentence by executive clemency; (3) that only rarely was there more than a feeble effort to punish these violations of the law; and (4) that public sentiment, through inaction or perversion, condoned lynchings, elevated men to public office who capitalized on racial prejudices and resisted all efforts to secure federal or effective state anti-lynching laws.

The same people who championed federal legislation to solve the local problem of keeping liquor away from the Negro, became ardent defenders of state rights when the Dyer bill, and later the Wagner-Costigan bill, were before Congress. This proposed legislation would have given the federal courts jurisdiction where state courts failed to act against persons suspected of participating in lynchings. There were serious doubts as to the constitutionality of both; there were doubts as to whether juries would be any more disposed to convict in federal courts than in state courts; but, of all the states, Virginia was the only one really to make an effort to devise an effective state statute. Its success with a law defining participation in a lynching as murder and authorizing the governor to use state prosecutors and state funds to convict stands as clear proof that the continued record of barbarism is directly chargeable to the attitude of the public. Thus was the theory of law modified in practice by the elusive factors in human behavior.

Administration of the Law

Equally enigmatic was the administration of the law. Every extension of government in the direction of social control or of social service added to the total responsibilities of administrative personnel. The expansion of administrative units in local, state and national governments, together with the evolution of administrative procedure, grew so rapidly as to constitute a revolutionary change in government at a time when training for government service was almost wholly lacking and the spoils system was rampant. The more capable men were, the less likely they were to enter public service, not only because the vulgarity of practical politics was distasteful to them but because service to private interests was more remunerative than service to the public interest. Nor did the public welcome the intrusion of specially trained men into public life. The explosive thrusts at the "Brain Trust" of Franklin D. Roosevelt were only repetitions of the widespread derision of the professor in the White House of Wilson's day—contemptuous expressions that were so frequent as to be nauseating in the whispering campaigns of presidential elections. This willingness of the people to permit politicians to run the country for them was a fundamental cause of the prevailing disrespect for law and order. It was cumulative and deep rooted in the lives of the people. One only needs a cursory glance at the panorama of national life to see its ultimate results. Millions of traffic tickets torn up with a shrug of the shoulders because the offender knew some one who could "fix" the matter with the enforcement officers, until the whole business became a national disgrace and the annual toll of traffic deaths alone reached more than thirty-six thousand. Hundreds of helpless men and women hunted like beasts, torn from the custody of officers and courts, tortured and burned by howling mobs of men, women and children without semblance of trial or effort to determine guilt, not only because of the lack of laws, but because of a complete break-down in their proper administration. The federal prohibition enforcement machinery included the Bureau of Internal Revenue in the Treasury Department and the Department of Justice which conducted prosecutions. They had at their service all the combined resources of internal revenue officers, customs inspectors, postal inspectors and the coast guard. The federal enforcement was reinforced by prohibitory laws in all but two states and the combined activities of state and local police, deputies and law courts. Never in history did such a horde of public officials infest the land for the enforcement of a single law. Never were they assisted so assiduously by self-appointed spies among the people. Never was conformity to the requirements of the law enforced with such utter disregard of human life and the sanctity of the rights and liberties of the individual. Yet enforcement broke down completely, partly because the combined sentiment of the majority of the people in the most densely populated sections of the country was hostile to the spirit of the law; but, in larger measure, because the tyranny of enforcement was directed at only a portion of the people. Too many enforcement officers turned out to be bootleggers who replenished their stock in trade from seizures made in the course of arrests. Too many justices of the peace and judges sentenced men to prison in the afternoon and enjoyed their cocktails at home in the evening. Thousands of barrels of alcohol were illegally withdrawn from government warehouses with the connivance of Department of Justice agents. Government officials, in short, not only considered themselves and their friends above the law but did not hesitate, in the enforcement of a single law, to violate others equally sacred.

The same situation prevailed with little variation in other fields of enforcement. School attendance laws became a vital adjunct to the control of child labor, but they might as well never have been placed upon the statute books so far as Negro children were concerned in some sections of the rural South, because little effort was made to enforce them. Theodore Roosevelt's Attorney-Generals, Knox and Bonaparte, instituted forty-four proceedings under the law in seven and one-half years; and Attorney-General Wickersham began ninety suits during the four years of Taft's Administration. Zealous enforcement from the beginning might not have accomplished the objectives for which the law was designed; but that is of little importance. The historical fact is, that so long as it remained on the statute books with no attention from the executive departments of the government, the representatives of the people in Congress were unaware of the necessity of approaching the problem in a different and more realistic way. The Federal Reserve Act was intended and confidently expected to establish a sound banking system. The President and Senate were given the responsibility of appointing the governing board which was to include the Secretary of the Treasury and the Comptroller of the Currency, but Senator Carter Glass could say in the Senate, May 10, 1932: "While we intended to preclude all idea of central banking, we designed that the Government, through its agencies, should keep a strict supervisory control of the system, and we appointed a Government agent, one of three of the Government directors at the Federal Reserve bank, who should be the presiding officer, and whom we intended to be the head officer of the bank. He has been literally brushed aside. He is a mere custodian of evidence of credit. They have set up in each of these banks a government of their own.

"For a while this 'board of governors' came well-nigh usurping important functions of the Federal Reserve Board here in Washington. They would have their meetings at their pleasure and convenience, resolve this, that, or the other thing, and graciously let the supervising authority here know what they had done."

The Fordney-McCumber Tariff Act of 1922, although it established the highest rates in American history, set up a tariff commission to make a study of the differences in costs of production in foreign countries and in the United States. This commission was to make reports to the President who was given power to raise or lower rates by as much as 50 per cent. In March, 1928, Edward P. Costigan resigned from the commission and, in a letter to Senator Joseph T. Robinson charged President Coolidge with having packed the commission, overruled its recommendations and thwarted its every effort to accomplish what Congress intended it to do. Whatever the truth of his charges may be, and the evidence seems convincing, the President did, over a six-year period, lower rates on millfeed, bobwhite quail, paint-brush handles, phenol and cresylic acid, raise them the maximum amount on eighteen items including iron ore, and refuse to lower them in accordance with the commission's recommendation on many items, including sugar.

On the other hand, there were important developments in the direction of improved administration of public affairs. President Taft appointed a Commission on Economy and Efficiency in 1911. The most important result of its report was the Budget and Accounting Act of 1921 and the Classification Act of 1923. These two acts created the Bureau of the Budget and the Personnel Classification Board. In 1930, the two agencies were brought into coordination by making the Director of the Budget the Chairman of the Personnel Board. Budget systems were also established in all of the states except Arkansas between 1912 and 1913. The concerted effort to improve public service by bringing into it highly trained and specialized employees and by placing them under the civil service made steady progress for many years. As administrative boards and bureaus multiplied, the task of appointing competent men to the many new posts placed a heavy responsibility upon the President. There was always pressure from partisans, lame-duck Congressmen and special interests to have these agencies manned by other than specially qualified persons. This was particularly true when the government passed from the control of one party to the other. The number of federal employees under civil service reached a high point of approximately 80 per cent by the close of Hoover's Administration; but the percentage dropped rapidly as new boards and bureaus were created in Roosevelt's Administration, and low administrative efficiency due to the spoil system was accentuated by conflicting views of desirable policies within the administration.

Congressional Decadence

In writing its reform legislation, Congress did nothing more or less than attempt to express the policy of society on a given question. Public opinion was frequently so divided as to what that policy should be that Congress was unable to agree upon any legislation. It was frequently only a general demand for action which the intelligence of Congress was incapable of meeting. Congress ofttimes refused to be specific, framing legislation in broad terms in order (1) to exercise the full limits of legislative power under the Constitution, and (2) to relieve itself of the onerous task of specifically saying what the rules of competition should be in industrial relations. This practice forced the Court to give meaning to the law by its decisions and directed criticism away from Congress and upon the Court when one side to a controversy failed to get from the Court the full returns to which it felt entitled under the laws. Later Congress went even farther in its failure to define legislative policies in intelligible language and delegated more and more power to the President and to administrative agencies. This was particularly true in the history of legislation touching industrial relations. Economic conditions changed so rapidly that they were years ahead of public policy at all times which complicated the problem. If we would understand this relationship between public opinion and the three coordinate branches of the federal government, we must go, not to the tirades of disgruntled reformers, but to the great minds of those upon whom the responsibility of applying the nation's policies devolved: to men like Taft, Wickersham, Hughes, Holmes and Brandeis, of whose intellectual integrity there can be no question.

Public opinion in the United States throughout this period was concerned with a minimum of four things: (1) the conservation of natural resources; (2) the freedom of the individual, whether laborer, producer, or trader, to rise in the economic scale; (3) a well-balanced economic life which should function evenly and smoothly through the years; and (4) protection for the consumer, the laborer and the producer of raw materials from exploitation. With respect to the policies which should be pursued to accomplish these things there was disagreement. Complete inaction by the government (*laissez faire*) and complete public ownership and control (socialism) were both rejected except by an insignificant minority. Enforced competition by action of the Congress and the Courts was the first experiment. This was the period of the Sherman Act before 1913, of the inaction by Cleveland and McKinley and "trust-busting" by Roosevelt and Taft. The second period was that of regulation by law and supervision by administrative agencies. This was the period of the Clayton Act and the Federal Trade Commission Act of Wilson's Administration. The third period was that in which concentration was regarded as inevitable and desirable. In Coolidge's and Hoover's administrations, it was undisturbed except by advice. In Roosevelt's Administration, it was legalized to the full extent of price and wage regulation with restraints upon excesses attempted through administrative machinery.

Congress made three notable failures during the period in dealing with the problem. Public opinion was aroused first by revelations concerning rebates received by the Standard Oil Company from the railroads. It was thought that corporations were growing to enormous size by destroying their competitors through unfair practices. Congress was forced to act and passed the Sherman Act. This declaration of public policy outlawed all "combinations in restraint of trade." It made such combinations a criminal offense. It gave the Department of Justice a mandate to destroy them, and private individuals were encouraged to assist by allowing suits for threefold damages. Here was a case, however, where Congress was unable to agree and wrote the law in indefinite terms. Senator Sherman said in debate: "It is difficult to define in legal language the precise line between lawful and unlawful combinations. This must be left for the Courts to determine in each particular case. All that we, as lawmakers, can do is to declare general principles. . . ." The burden thus thrust upon the Supreme Court by Congress may be judged from the words of Justice Brandeis (*American Column Co.* v. *United States*, 1921):

"Restraint of trade may be exerted upon rivals; upon buyers or upon sellers; upon employers or upon employed. Restraint may be exerted through force or fraud or agreement. It may be exerted through moral or through legal obligations; through fear or through hope. It may exist, although it is not manifested in any overt act, and even though there is no intent to restrain. Words of advice, seemingly innocent and perhaps benevolent, may restrain, when uttered under circumstances that make advice equivalent to command. For the essence of restraint is power; and power may arise merely out of position. Wherever a dominant position has been attained, restraint necessarily arises. And when dominance is attained, or is sought, through combination—however good the motives or the manners of those participating—the Sherman law is violated; provided, of course, that the restraint be what is called unreasonable."

It was generally believed, at first, that the language of the Act was so sweeping as to ruin business; but the Supreme Court adopted the attitude that Congress must bear the responsibility (*United States* v. *Trans-Missouri Freight Association*, 1897). In 1895, however, the Court had refused to allow the contention of the government that the American Sugar Refining Company was illegally restraining commerce among the states by bring under its control 98 per cent of the sugar-refining industry (*United States* v. *E. C. Knight Company*). President McKinley and Attorney-General Harmon used this decision as an excuse to say that the act was unenforceable. President Taft later contended that the case had been presented very inadequately by the government. In 1898, the government won its case, by a unanimous decision of the Court, against a division of sales territory (*United States* v. *Addystone Pipe and Steel Company*). These two cases were clear indication to producers that they could not enter into agreements for the elimination of competition, but that they could accomplish the same purpose by bringing their productive enterprises into one large corporation. New Jersey offered them attractive corporation laws, and the legal profession generally advised them that the federal government had no authority under the commerce clause over ownership, investments and form of corporate organization. There had been no decision concerning this because of the inactivity of the Department of Justice. There followed several years of very active combinations of corporations into trusts, and a revival of popular agitation.

President Roosevelt took cognizance of the popular unrest and began his anti-trust prosecutions with proceedings against the Northern Securities Company. The case arose out of a contest between James J. Hill, backed by J. P. Morgan, and Henry I. Harriman for control of the Burlington Railroad.

Hill controlled the Great Northern and the Northern Pacific. Harriman controlled the Union Pacific. Each wanted the Burlington as a Chicago connection. Harriman lost in the stock market contest and the Northern Securities Company was organized. The government sought to restore competition between the two trans-continental railroads, and the Supreme Court handed down its decision in 1904 (*Northern Securities Co.* v. *United States*). It was a five to four decision against the Northern Securities Company, but Justice Holmes dissented on the ground that if control of two railroads in the same hands were a penal offense "then a partnership between two stage drivers who have been competitors in driving across a state line, or two merchants once engaged in rival commerce among the States, whether made after or before the Act, if now continued, is a crime." He continued: "I am happy to know that only a minority of my brethren adopt an interpretation of the law which in my opinion would . . . disintegrate society so far as it could into individual atoms. If that were its intent, I should regard calling such a law a regulation of commerce as a mere pretense. It would be an attempt to reconstruct society. I am not concerned with the wisdom of such an attempt, but I believe that Congress was not entrusted by the Constitution with the power to make it and I am deeply persuaded that it has not tried."

This minority opinion of Holmes, that the words of the Sherman Act must be interpreted by their meaning in the Common Law and that there must be an *attempt* to restrain trade for a combination in restraint of trade to exist (actual monopoly instead of power to monopolize), became the opinion of the majority in 1911 (*Standard Oil Co.* v. *United States* and *American Tobacco Co.* v. *United States*) and was clearly sustained in 1920 (*United States* v. *United States Steel Corporation*).

Meanwhile, investigations by the newly created Bureau of Corporations into the oil, tobacco, steel and farm implements industries, and of a special congressional committee into the steel industry, revealed that the Sherman Anti-Trust Law had not checked the process of industrial integration. Juries had shown an indisposition to convict and the government had emphasized disintegration of the trust rather than punishment for violations of the law. The decision of the Court, in 1911, that the law prohibited only unreasonable restraints of trade, precipitated the third period of violent public agitation and resulted in the legislation of Wilson's Administration. There was, however, still no unanimity of opinion as to what public policy should be. Taft's attitude toward the trusts was realistic and in line with actual achievements under the Sherman Act. He said: "We are not engaged in trying to strike down the business of this country. Where combinations of this sort show themselves willing to come within the law, the Attorney-General is only too willing to enter a decree by consent, if need be, enforcing the law and dividing up the great combinations into lesser combinations." Attorney-General Wickersham, however, pointed out that there were those who "were disappointed because, as with the wave of a wand, conditions that had existed twenty years ago were not restored . . . who regretted greatly that the national administration should have succeeded in working out a problem of this character without the embarrassment which would have attended upon a ruin of vast interests and the destruction of great businesses."

In 1913, Congress again placed the question under discussion. They put into legislative form the "rule of reason" enunciated by the Supreme Court, defined "combinations in restraint of trade" and enumerated the unfair methods of competition which public opinion condemned. It was a far more definite statement of policy than the Sherman Act had been and it remedied, by the creation of the Federal Trade Commission, the error of shifting responsibility to the Courts. The importance of creating these industrial commissions was well stated by Charles Evans Hughes, Governor of New York, in 1907, in defense of his proposal for a state public utilities commission: "We are under a Constitution, but the Constitution is what the Judges say it is, and the judiciary is the safeguard of our liberty and of our property under the Constitution. I do not want to see any direct assault upon the Courts, nor do I want to see any indirect assault upon the Courts. And I tell you, ladies and gentlemen, no more insidious assault could be made upon the independence and esteem of the judiciary than to burden it with these questions of administration—questions which lie close to the public impatience, and in regard to which the people are going to insist on having administration by officers directly accountable to them."

In establishing such administrative agencies as the Federal Trade Commission, however, there were certain fundamental principles so self-evident that it never should have been necessary for the Supreme Court to restate them. Congress, as the legislative branch of the government, could not divest itself of the legislative function. It must lay down policies and establish standards, although it might leave to "selected instrumentalities the making of subordinate rules within prescribed limits and the determination of facts to which the policy as declared" was to apply. Gradually, in practice, the Commission worked out an administrative procedure. It received complaints of unfair trade practices and elicited answers from the accused. It examined and cross-examined witnesses. It submitted its proposed findings to the contestants with opportunity to file exceptions. It concluded its case in each instance with a hearing before the full Commission, a finding of facts, and the issuance of an order. The Commission might appeal to the Circuit Courts to have its orders enforced. The defendant might appeal to have the order rescinded. In either case, it remained the duty of the Supreme Court to determine if the evidence in the case justified the findings of facts and if the facts were sufficient under the law to justify the cease and desist order. In no case could the Commission usurp the legislative function of declaring policies or deprive the individual of his constitutional right of appealing to the Courts. Furthermore, the Federal Trade Commission was independent of the executive department. Congress limited the reasons for removal to "inefficiency, neglect of duty or malfeasance in office" and, when President F. D. Roosevelt sought to remove Commissioner William E. Humphrey because "the aims and purposes of the Administration with respect to the work of the Commission can be carried out most effectually with personnel of my own selection," he was restrained from doing so.

The second important phase of industrial control in which Congress found itself unable or unwilling to define a policy, thus shifting the burden to the Courts, was in the matter of utility valuations. Through the entire history of rate regulations, Congress has refused to say what basis for fixing valuations shall be followed. Public opinion, at times of property depreciation and in order to protect society against watered stocks, urged the rule of reproduction cost new. A considerable minority, however, including the State of Massachusetts, a majority of the Interstate Commerce Commission and a minority of the Supreme Court including Justices Holmes, Stone and Brandeis endorsed the principle of honest and prudent investment. The majority of the Court in the St. Louis and O'Fallon Railway Case endorsed the principle of reproduction cost new, but only because it believed Congress had stated that to be its policy in the Transportation Act of 1920. That Congress openly shrank from the duty of enunciating a definite policy is clearly revealed by its order to the commission to capture one-half of all earnings above six per cent and to give "due consideration to all the elements of value recognized by the law of the land for rate making purposes."

In addition to writing its laws in language which required definition by the Courts, and to shifting responsibility to the new administrative agencies, Congress showed an increasing unconcern about the constitutionality of its acts. The practice is not of recent origin. President Taft was constrained to say: "It is said that it should be left to the Supreme Court to say whether this proposed act violates the Constitution. I dissent utterly from this proposition. The oath that the chief executive takes, and which each member of Congress takes, does not bind him any less sacredly to observe the Constitution than the oaths which Justices of the Supreme Court take."

The Constitution and the Law

Public agitation about social and economic questions receded into the background when the United States entered the World War. It remained in abeyance during the greater part of the twenties but reappeared with a vengeance during the depression. Meanwhile, the flood of state and federal legislation designed to meet the problems of the new economic order continued to come before the Supreme Court. Most of the congressional legislation had been passed under the constitutional power of Congress to control interstate commerce and to tax and spend. Most of the state legislation was passed under the police powers. Since it was impossible to draw the line between interstate and intrastate commerce or to define the guaranteed rights of freedom of contract, due process, and equal protection except as individual cases arose, legislative action and judicial interpretation combined through the years to give them meaning. Even so, they did not admit of non-contradictory interpretation, and the members of the Supreme Court, of Congress and of society generally often disagreed over the constitutionality of legislative acts. Except for a few cases, however, the Supreme Court displayed a remarkable unanimity in its interpretations of the fundamental law.

In fixing the limits of the powers of Congress over interstate commerce, the Court defined regulation very liberally to mean foster, protect and promote (*Austin* v. *Tennessee,* 1911), but it limited the extent of interstate commerce to the movement of goods from the point of origin to its destination (*United States* v. *E. C. Knight Co.,* 1895). Within those limits, Congress could keep the channels of commerce free from shipments of goods considered harmful to the health and morals of recipients. The first of these cases was *Champion* v. *Ames* (1903), in which the Court upheld a law of 1895 prohibiting the shipment of lottery tickets. This decision came just as the reform movement was getting well started and Congress made full use of the newly discovered power. The Court sustained the Pure Food Act of 1906 (*Hipolite Egg Co.* v. *United States*, 1911), the Narcotics Acts of 1909 and 1914 (*United States* v. *Jim Fuey Moy*, 1916), the Mann Act of 1910 for the suppression of the white slave traffic (*Hoke* v. *United States*, 1913) and the exclusion of prizefight films (*Weber* v. *Freed*, 1915). The decision in the E. C. Knight case contained this interesting observation: "If it be held that the term [commerce] includes the regulation of all such manufactures as are intended to be the subject of commercial transactions in the future, it is impossible to deny that it would also include all productive industries that contemplate the same thing. The result would be that Congress would be invested, to the exclusion of the states, with the power to regulate, not only manufactures, but also agriculture, horticulture, stock raising, domestic fisheries, mining . . . interests which in their nature are and must be local in all the details of their successful management." Changing economic conditions through three decades destroyed the validity of the statement. Production ceased to be local in all its details, and the state governments found difficulty in meeting the requirements of regulation. Public opinion condemned child labor no less than it had condemned the white slave traffic, and Congress, acting under the same constitutional power of regulating commerce, decreed that the channels of trade should remain free of the products of child labor. But the decision in the E. C. Knight case and in *Adair* v. *United States* (1908) that Congress could not reach back of interstate commerce to regulate production rendered their efforts futile (*Hammer* v. *Dagenhart*, 1918). It was a five to four decision, Justices Holmes, McKenna, Brandeis and Clarke dissenting. Justice Holmes said in his dissent: "The act does not meddle with anything belonging to the States. They may regulate their internal affairs and their domestic commerce as they like. But when they seek to send their products across the state line they are no longer within their rights. If there were no Constitution and no Congress their power to cross the line would depend upon their neighbors. Under the Constitution such commerce belongs not to the States but to Congress to regulate. It may carry out its views of public policy whatever indirect effect they may have upon the activities of the States. Instead of being encountered by a prohibitive tariff at her boundaries the State encounters the public policy of the United States which it is for Congress to express." In addition to defining the limits of the power of Congress to control interstate and foreign commerce, the Court was called upon to restrain the states from invading that field. It said that, if Congress did not legislate in a particular case, the presumption was, it wished no regulation and the states might not intrude (*Di Santo* v. *Pennsylvania*, 1927). The states might not interfere with things sent in interstate commerce so long as they remained in the original package (*Schollenberger* v. *Pennsylvania*, 1898; *Austin* v. *Tennessee*, 1900; *Cook* v. *Marshall Co.*, 1905).

The Supreme Court also reduced to a minimum the constitutional limitations on the taxing power of Congress; but, again, the cases in which it was impelled to restrain dealt with questions about which there were violent prejudices rather than unanimity of public opinion. Having failed in its efforts to reach back of the point where goods entered interstate commerce and eliminate conditions in production which were contrary to public policy, Congress turned to the taxing power and, February 24, 1919, imposed a 10 per cent excise tax on all products of mines and factories employing children under fourteen years of age. The case came before the Supreme Court in *Bailey* v. *Drexel Furniture Co.* (1922) and was declared unconstitutional with but one dissent, that of Justice Clarke. Regulation of the conduct of manufacturing and production was again held to belong to the states and, therefore, beyond control by a tax imposed by the federal government. Two years previously, the Court had held that stock dividends were not subject to the income tax (*Eisner* v. *Macomber*, 1920). This, also, was a five to four decision, with Justices Holmes, Day, Brandeis and Clarke dissenting.

In the matter of state legislation, the Supreme Court was

called upon to decide many cases under the Fourteenth Amendment which were cases of degree and could not be decided on point of law, because the terms "due process" and "equal protection" did not permit exact definition. The eternal problem was to protect the rights of the individual without seriously restricting the right of the states to legislate for the general welfare. The states were allowed wide latitude in the imposition of taxes, the one general limitation being that they must not reach the point of confiscation of property. They were allowed to use their power of taxation to curb the operations of chain stores (*Indiana* v. *Jackson*, 1931) and to tax out of existence business thought to be undesirable (*McCray* v. *United States*, 1904; *State of Washington* v. *Magnano Co.*, 1934). They were allowed to regulate hours of labor for both men and women (*Muller* v. *Oregon*, 1908; *Bunting* v. *Oregon*, 1916). They were allowed to license and supervise small loan companies. But neither the state nor the federal government was allowed to regulate the wages of women in industry.

This brief survey is sufficient to show how Congress and the several state legislatures sought to cope with changing social and economic conditions; and how the Supreme Court attempted to keep them within their respective fields, protect the individual's rights of person and property, and still keep the Constitution a living instrument for progress. There were people, however, who felt that the necessity of keeping legislation within the limits of the Constitution made it difficult, if not impossible, to translate public policy into legislation. They urged that the Court be deprived of the power of judicial review. There were those who made much of the occasional five to four decisions, and advocated the requirement of a six to three or seven to two majority of the Court for invalidation of an act of Congress. There were those who felt that changing economic conditions rendered futile the attempts of the states to regulate production. They urged that the limits of the powers of Congress be expanded either by Constitutional amendment or by appointment of more liberals to the Supreme Court.

The Supreme Court

The relationship between the personnel of the Court, the Constitution and the laws was never absent from public discussion after the turn of the century. When Theodore Roosevelt was faced with the task of appointing a successor to Justice Gray in 1902, he wrote that "the majority of the present Court who have, although without satisfactory unanimity, upheld the policies of President McKinley and the Republican party in Congress, have rendered a great service to mankind and to this nation"; and he added: "I should hold myself guilty of an irreparable wrong to the nation if I should put in his place any man who was not absolutely sane and sound on the great national policies for which we stand in public life." After satisfying himself that Oliver Wendell Holmes could be trusted in that respect, Roosevelt gave him the appointment. He was then sixty-one years of age, a veteran of the Civil War, a graduate of Harvard, Chief Justice of the Supreme Court of Massachusetts. He was destined to serve upon the Supreme Bench for nearly thirty years, to retire in 1932, and to live until he reached the age of ninety-four. During those thirty years, he exercised a greater influence upon legal thought in the country than any other living man. Chief Justice Hughes spoke of him as having been "the apostle of the latest generation. . . . More modern than the modernist, for he knows what is not modern; truer to the old than many a conservative, for he is more likely to know how the old became such and what in it is worth conserving." One year before his appointment by Roosevelt, the Northern Securities holding company had been incorporated in New Jersey to bring control of the Northern Pacific Railroad and the Great Northern Railroad into the same hands. The government moved against the Northern Securities trust as a combination in restraint of trade and won a five to four decision from the Supreme Court; but Holmes wrote the dissenting opinion.

President Wilson elevated his Attorney-General, McReynolds, to the Supreme Court and also appointed Louis D. Brandeis. Roosevelt had been favorably inclined to Holmes because in his labor decisions he had "been able to preserve his aloofness of mind so as to keep his broad humanity of feeling and his sympathy for the class from which he has not drawn his clients." Brandeis's whole career had been devoted to the interests of the masses, so much so that only a Wilson in the White House and the overwhelming predominance of liberal sentiment by 1916 could have secured his appointment. He was the outstanding social pathologist of his day, the champion of individuals caught in the bewildering growth of institutions, the foe of monopolistic exploitation whether by public utilities, industrial combinations or labor unions. Ratification of his appointment was opposed by the legal profession and by business men in general. His social and economic views, of which his entire legal career was an expression, did not coincide with the long prevailing and accepted principles under which economic life had been allowed to develop. It was feared that the reform movement was about to invade the sacred chambers of the Supreme Court. Specifically, his ability was not questioned; but his fitness for judicial service was thought to have been impaired by his uncompromising advocacy of reform measures which were still to be brought within the purview of the Court. The Senate ratified his appointment after an extensive investigation, and there came to sit upon the bench one who looked beyond the rigidity of the fundamental law to the changing needs of the social order.

In 1930, President Hoover nominated Charles Evans Hughes to succeed Chief Justice Taft. This time the opposition came from the liberal and progressive elements throughout the country. Hughes had resigned from the Court to be the Republican candidate for the presidency in 1916 to the utter chagrin of those who believed the Justices superior to the allurements of politics. He had been a member of Harding's cabinet during the years of disgraceful malfeasance on the part of so many public servants. He had served as attorney for many of the vested interests. His previous record upon the Supreme Bench was regarded by many as evidence of an inherent narrow vision and obstinacy. He was, in short, regarded as wholly unfit by temperament and previous record for judicial service; but his nomination was confirmed and his record for guidance of the Court during the trying period of the depression may well give him a place in history among the greatest of Chief Justices. Shortly thereafter, President Hoover was called upon to fill another vacancy and nominated John J. Parker of North Carolina. The Senate refused to confirm the nomination. Opposition to Parker was based on two facts: (1) that, as a member of the Circuit Court for the Fourth District, he had supported an injunction restraining the United Mine Workers from soliciting members who were working under yellow dog contracts; and (2) that he was sympathetic to the Lily White movement —an effort to purge the Republican party in the South of its Negro membership. The attitude of the nominee on two great social questions, race and labor, therefore, stamped him as a reactionary and deprived him of a place on the Supreme Bench. Later on, another vacancy occurred and President Hoover nominated Benjamin N. Cardozo of New York. There was severe criticism in many quarters because the membership of the Court was tending to be drawn too much from one section of the country; a criticism which was directed at the industrial East and indicative of the increasing cleavage between the agricultural and industrial sections.

Subsequently, Franklin D. Roosevelt, Democratic candidate for the Presidency, remarked that the opposition party had been in complete control of the Supreme Court. This statement was denounced by Silas Strawn, sometime President of the American Bar Association, as destructive of fundamental principles of the government and contrary to the established historical fact that there had never been "any politics in our Supreme Court and that no political party could control the actions of the Court." Two years later, three laws of singular importance came before the Court for review. One was the Agricultural Adjustment

Act, representing the latest effort of Congress to solve the perplexing agricultural problem. It was strongly supported in the West and opposed in the industrial East. The second was the Tennessee Valley Authority Act involving the controversial question of public utilities and a government project of incalculable benefit to Tennessee Valley states. The third was the National Industrial Recovery Act designed to legalize trade and industrial associations, eliminate vicious trade practices, child labor and starvation wages. It was supported alike by the United States Chamber of Commerce and the labor unions, but opposed by the consuming public. Justices Butler, Van Devanter and Sutherland were of the majority against the constitutionality of the AAA, and Justices Stone, Brandeis and Cardozo of the minority supporting it. Justice McReynolds of Tennessee disagreed with every other Justice of the Court and rendered a minority opinion against the constitutionality of the TVA. Every Justice of the Court united in one of the most strongly-worded opinions of the century to invalidate the NIRA.

The above record is very revealing because, and only because, it does not vary in any important respect from the history of Supreme Court appointments and Supreme Court decisions since the founding of the Republic. Justices of the Court do not render decisions on the basis of previous party affiliations or sectional origins; but not because the judicial process of reasoning is susceptible to mathematical precision nor because elevation to the Bench obliterates the human addiction to the social and economic philosophy of earlier days. The point is that Presidents and Presidents-to-be, Senators and political parties generally believe that the future welfare of the country depends upon their principles being written into the law of the land and are rightfully concerned about securing a Supreme Court which will not hold their acts to be contrary to the fundamental law. History proves the futility of their efforts. They are never certain what the fundamental convictions of their appointees are with respect to government and its relation to social and economic questions, nor are they certain what the principles of their own party will be in relation to all situations which may arise. The dynamic social changes of the twentieth century greatly compounded the difficulty. It would have required a greater omniscience than any President from Roosevelt to Roosevelt possessed to have predicted how his appointees to the Supreme Bench would react to the perplexing problems of the thirties.

In spite of all these facts, criticism of the Court because of its adverse decisions on economic and social legislation continued unabated. Politicians and students of political science, reformers and organized labor, special interests and disinterested intellectuals joined in the chorus. The Court was frequently referred to as a House of Lords, a usurper of legislative powers, a reactionary barrier to majority will. Theodore Roosevelt was particularly incensed at the state courts as a result of the invalidation by the New York Court of Appeals of laws prohibiting the processing of tobacco in tenement houses, limiting hours of labor of women in factories and working men's Compensation Acts. He publicly endorsed a statement by a British newspaper that the Court's determination of the legality of income taxes and factory legislation constituted "one of the most galling of all possible tyrannies." Senator Robert La Follette denounced the Court as a bulwark of special privilege and conducted his presidential campaign of 1924 on a demand for abolition of judicial review. Said he: "By a process of gradual encroachments now confident and aggressive, sovereignty has been wrested from the people and usurped by the Court." Morrison Q. Swift spoke of "the destiny of a nation of ninety millions . . . chiseled by the mental temper of five practically irresponsible men." Among the many changes suggested from time to time were (1) limiting the term of office of the justices; (2) giving Congress the power to remove them; (3) allowing the Court only a suspensory veto, Congress being empowered to enact finally a measure after an intervening election; (4) transferring the Court's functions to the United States Senate; (5) requiring more than a mere majority vote of the Court to render an act of Congress invalid; (6) depriving inferior courts of the power to pass upon the constitutionality of acts of Congress. Resolutions embodying one or more of these provisions were introduced in Congress from time to time by such prominent men as Senators William E. Borah of Idaho, Simeon D. Fess of Ohio and George W. Norris of Nebraska. Criticism of the Court died down during the twenties only to burst forth with renewed vigor, as we shall see, when the legislation passed by the first Congress of Roosevelt's Administration came up for review.

CHAPTER VII

NATIONAL EXPANSION

Territorial Policy and Precedents

The historic policy of the United States with respect to the acquisition and government of territory outside the limits of the several states was first established in the Ordinance of 1787 and was developed gradually in the several treaties of cession, the acts of the President as Commander-in-Chief of the Army and Navy, the legislation of Congress, and the decisions of the Supreme Court. The matured policy of the nation, consisting of these many precedents, served as a basis for the control and administration of the several dependencies in the twentieth century—territories acquired, with the exception of Alaska, after an interlude of fifty years of inactivity. Without exception, all previous accessions of territory had consisted of regions contiguous to the several states of the United States. They were regions sparsely inhabited by Indian tribes and a few thousand people of European extraction, and already known to be attractive for settlement. Indeed, in most cases, it was the previous infiltration of hunters, traders and even settlers, which constituted the pressure for their acquisition. Congress, in re-enacting the Ordinance of 1787, and the treaty making power in arranging the terms of transfer for Louisiana, Florida, Oregon and the Mexican Cession, clearly indicated the policy which should be followed with respect to their future status. They should be opened to settlement as rapidly as land surveys and Indian relations would permit. None of the fundamental principles of Americanism: freedom of speech, the press, assembly, religion, etc., should be denied the people. The full measure of self-government should be extended to them as rapidly as circumstances allowed. The government would facilitate, in every possible way, the early incorporation of these new possessions into the Union of States on a basis of perfect equality with the rest. So long as they remained under the jurisdiction of Congress, the best interest of the dependent people, regardless of expense or inconvenience to the people of the states, would be the determining factor in all legislation. To that end, the people would be expected to manage their domestic affairs and administer their local governments to the limit of their capacity for self-government as determined by Congress. In only one respect may this traditional policy be said to have been modified in the recent period of expansion: ultimate incorporation into the Union of States.

Chief Justice William H. Taft said in 1922 (*Balzac* v. *People of Porto Rico*), "Few questions have been the subject of such discussion and dispute in our country as the status of our territory acquired from Spain in 1899. The division between the political parties in respect to it, the diversity of the views of the members of this Court in regard to its constitutional aspects, and the constant recurrence of the subject in the Houses of Congress, fixed the attention of all on the future relation of this acquired territory to the United States." The territorial possessions of the United States as the twentieth century opened were not contiguous to the states. Some of them were already densely populated with foreign peoples. None of them proved attractive to settlers. American penetration was commercial in character. Even Alaska, the only possession approaching the traditional character of our territorial domain, was some distance away and thought to be undesirable as a haven for surplus population. There were, therefore, no such disturbing problems as land surveys and sales, the status of slavery or the admission of states, which had consumed so much of the energy of government and aroused such tempestuous strife during the decades before 1860. The fact that precedents in territorial government were not wholly applicable, however, created many questions of national policy for Congress to determine, questions of constitutional law to tax the ingenuity of the Supreme Court, problems of administration for Executives to ponder and arguments for political campaigns.

The subject of much of the contemporary discussion was whether, as the Supreme Court said, some of these lands had been incorporated as a part of the United States by treaty and congressional legislation and others were merely owned by and under the jurisdiction of the United States. The question was of immediate importance as determining the status of children born in the Philippines and Puerto Rico. The inhabitants of these islands had not been accorded United States citizenship either by treaty or act of Congress. Their children, however, would be citizens under the provisions of the Fourteenth Amendment if the opinion of Justice Harlan prevailed that the Constitution became the Supreme Law for any and all peoples immediately upon their coming under the jurisdiction of the United States and that Congress, a creature of the Constitution, could not suspend the Constitution in any particular, in any place, or for any length of time.

The distinction between what the Supreme Court chose to call incorporated and unincorporated territories seems, in reality, to have been made by the treaty making power and to have been confirmed as a national policy by Congress. Its endorsement by the Supreme Court was by a five to four decision. The interpretation of the Constitution with respect to territorial government as made by the combined action of Congress and the Court included the following pertinent points.

1. Incorporation into the United States of acquired territory had been left to the discretion of Congress, though the treaty-making power, at times, may have committed the government to such ultimate action.

2. The Constitution did not extend to acquired territories except by Congressional Action. "The liberality of Congress in legislating the Constitution into all our contiguous territories has undoubtedly fostered the impression that it went there by its own force, but there is nothing in the Constitution itself,

and little in the interpretation put upon it, to confirm that impression" (*Downes* v. *Bidwell*, 1901).

3. The legislative power of Congress over the territories was complete. It might establish, change or abolish territorial governments; legislate directly for the people of a territory; supplement or set aside acts of the territorial government provided for in its organic act.

4. The executive and legislative departments of the government, in administering territorial affairs, were restrained by certain constitutional limitations. "The guaranties of certain fundamental personal rights declared in the Constitution, as for instance that no person could be deprived of life, liberty or property without due process of law, had from the beginning full application in the Philippines and Porto Rico . . ." (*Balzac* v. *People of Porto Rico*, 1922).

5. It was locality and not the status of people living in it which determined the application of constitutional provisions. Thus, a citizen of the United States and of a state, enjoying the right of trial by jury, did not carry this right with him in removing to Puerto Rico. A citizen of the United States and of Puerto Rico, denied the right of trial by jury at home, possessed it while residing in one of the several states. It was within the province of Congress to extend to the people of the territorial possessions, at its own pleasure, United States citizenship; to levy tariff duties upon their products shipped into the states; to establish civil government for them or to retain them under arbitrary rule; to elevate them through successive stages to statehood or to grant them their independence.

Congress was thus given a free hand to work out a colonial policy, if it so desired, distinct from the traditional territorial policy of the nation. Every state carved out of what had been unorganized territory had passed through successive stages of government before reaching statehood. Territory acquired in the midst of war was governed by the President as Commander-in-Chief of the Army and Navy. He was responsible in every respect until Congress assumed its legislative prerogatives. His authority was absolute and was frequently used to make drastic modifications necessary to insure the success of whatever new system of civil government Congress might choose to devise. It frequently continued the governing agencies established in this way but, thenceforth, the President ceased to govern in his capacity as head of the defense forces and acted as a civil official on authority from Congress. This stage of government was utilized by Congress to acquaint itself, usually through the investigations of special commissions, with conditions in the new possessions as a basis for intelligent action. The third, fourth and fifth stages were those first outlined in the Ordinance of 1787. The President, with the consent of the Senate, appointed executive officers, usually consisting of a governor, a secretary and a judge. These officials were to govern the district under laws selected from the statutes of any of the several states, such laws always to be subject to the approval of Congress. The next stage was reached when there were five thousand free males in the district, and was generally known as that of an organized territory. It was the adolescent period of statehood. The boundaries of the anticipated state were fixed, and the inhabitants were given a measure of self-government. The territorial legislature consisted of two houses. The House of Representatives was elected and the upper house was chosen by Congress from a list presented by the territorial house or by the President. A territorial delegate to Congress was always provided. The only important change in this procedure came in 1836 when, in organizing the Territory of Wisconsin, both houses of the legislature were made elective and property qualifications for voting were abandoned. The final stage, when there were sixty thousand inhabitants in the Territory, consisted of a congressional enabling act, a constitutional convention and admission as a state. California did not pass through the territorial stage, and the population requirement was very flexible. Otherwise, there were no important deviations from this procedure. All territory acquired before the Civil War had been incorporated, organized into territories and, with the exception of Oklahoma, New Mexico and Arizona, admitted to the Union as states before 1900.

Alaska and Hawaii

The two possessions which Congress chose to incorporate and organize into Territories in the traditional manner, as if contemplating eventual statehood for them, were Alaska and Hawaii. Alaska was purchased from Russia in 1867. It was the first accession of territory in the history of the United States without some indication in the treaty that eventual statehood was contemplated for the region, with the exception that inhabitants of Alaska were accorded United States citizenship. It was sparsely settled by about an equal number of whites and Indians and, as late as 1900, there were no more than 63,000 people in a region one-fifth as large as the United States. Congress provided no form of government for several years. It was controlled intermittently by army and navy officers until 1884. Congress then (May 17, 1884) established the traditional first stage of territorial government with a governor, district judge and four commissioners appointed by the President. Instead of permitting these officials to make a selection of appropriate laws from the statutes of the several states, the laws of the state of Oregon were extended to Alaska except where inapplicable. During this period education was under the supervision of the Department of Interior at Washington, justice under the Attorney-General and customs duties under the Treasury Department. Between 1898 and 1903, Congress legislated directly for Alaska, enacting civil and criminal codes, transportation and homestead laws. The most important of these acts was the Civil Code of June 6, 1900, which provided for a new taxation system, a Surveyor-General and municipal incorporation. This was the period in which exploiters of natural resources were reaching beyond the limits of the United States for the buried riches of Alaska. It was, also, the period of an awakening national consciousness of the need for conservation. The result was a bitter contest in Congress, with the financial interests represented in the Alaskan Syndicate able to prevent the organization of the Territory of Alaska until 1912. Meanwhile, President Roosevelt withdrew the coal lands from entry in 1906 and, when the interests which had been exploiting transportation, fishing and copper attempted to patent the coal lands a major scandal broke over the actions of Secretary of Interior Ballinger. It was an embarrassing situation for President Taft with the Roosevelt-Pinchot forces gaining much the better of the argument so far as public opinion was concerned. The final result was the advancement of Alaska to the status of an organized territory on August 24, 1912. This act provided for a two house legislature: a Senate of eight members and a House of Representatives of sixteen members, both elective as in the case of Wisconsin, 1836. The franchise was given to all male citizens of the United States who were twenty-one years of age and who had resided in Alaska for one year. The legislature was authorized to extend the suffrage to women at its discretion and to elect a delegate to Congress. Provision was made for the building of a government railroad and coal lands were placed under the leasing system. Oil lands and water power sites were brought under the same system during Wilson's Administration. The several departments of the President's Cabinet were given the responsibility of administering timber lands, homesteads, water power (agriculture), coaling and wireless stations (Navy), roads (War), customs and taxes (Treasury), and mails (Post Office).

The Hawaiian Islands, lying in mid-Pacific, have an area of 6,449 square miles and, at the time of annexation, had 154,000 inhabitants, about 30,000 of whom were native Hawaiians, a slightly less number Americans and the remainder Asiatics. They were brought into the possession of the United States by the same slow manner of penetration as western territory had been. Missionaries went to the islands as early as 1820 to Christianize, educate and give industrial training to the natives. It was there that Samuel C. Armstrong received the inspiration which later went into the establishment of Hampton Normal and Industrial Institute. Merchantmen used the islands as a vantage point for their Far Eastern trade and the whaling industry before the Civil War. Financial interests were attracted by the sugar industry in the early fifties. Following the war, they led the movement for domination of the islands by and their annexation to the United States. They were virtually a protectorate of the United States after 1851. Hawaiian sugar was placed on the free list of imports by Congress in 1875. Pearl Harbor was ceded to the United States as a naval base in 1884. The feudal land system of the islands was broken down and large private land holdings established by the commercial sugar companies, who introduced Asiatic laborers. The natives bitterly resisted their system of labor exploitation and the native government was overthrown. A revolution was engineered, an American protectorate was proclaimed by the United States minister with the assistance of naval officers and annexation was arranged. It would have been approved by Congress (1893) except that delay in the Senate permitted the newly inaugurated President, Grover Cleveland, to withdraw the treaty before final action was taken. An independent republic was created in the islands in 1894. President McKinley re-opened the question of annexation, and it was carried to a conclusion by joint resolution of Congress, July 7, 1898. The treaty of annexation placed every department of government in the hands of the President until Congress should take further action.

Congress passed the organic act creating the Territory of Hawaii April 30, 1900. This act conferred United States citizenship upon citizens of the United States resident there on that date. It provided for an elected legislature of two houses and for a governor and secretary to be appointed by the President and Senate of the United States. Other administrative officials were to be appointed by the governor with the approval of the Hawaiian Senate. The franchise was granted to all male citizens at least 21 years of age who could speak, read and write Hawaiian or English. The territorial legislature was given a delegate to Congress and the responsibility of organizing a system of local government. It could not pass legislation with less than a majority vote of all members, and appropriation laws were to continue in effect if a legislature failed to act. All public lands were placed under the control of the territorial government.

Puerto Rico and the Philippines

The two most important Spanish possessions obtained by the Treaty of Paris, 1898, were Puerto Rico and the Philippine Islands. Public opinion was sharply divided over the advisability of acquiring them and it remained so over the problems of their administration and ultimate status. Alaska and Hawaii had been acquired with very little opposition and largely without public agitation. There was some discussion about the methods employed in Hawaii and doubts on the part of President Cleveland as to whether the proposed annexation really was the expressed will of the people in the islands. The case of the Philippines, however, was quite different. The islands were gained by purchase and conquest. Spain was paid $20,000,000 to relinquish her claim to them and 400,000 acres of church lands were purchased from the Papacy in 1903 for $7,239,000. Meanwhile, a three year military campaign was required to subjugate the natives who were fighting for independence under Aguinaldo. Few people in the United States knew anything about the Philippines when the Spanish-American War began. The peace commission was entirely at a loss as to what to demand with respect to them. Two of the Commissioners, former Secretary of State, W. R. Day, and Senator George Gray of Delaware, were both opposed to their acquisition. Mid-Western Democrats and New England Republicans joined forces to oppose the terms of the treaty, and only the insistence of William Jennings Bryan that it be ratified and imperialism be made the ensuing campaign issue secured its ratification. The opposition insisted that the entire procedure was contrary to the fundamental principles of Americanism and would lead to nothing but disastrous foreign complications. Those who favored the purchase—Alfred T. Mahan, John Hay, Theodore Roosevelt,

Henry Cabot Lodge, President McKinley and others—variously based their position upon the needs of national defense, Asiatic trading centers and the responsibility of extending the blessings of American civilization to a benighted and oppressed people. Their position was strengthened by the support of American missionaries, the difficulty of withdrawal under pressure from a native insurrection and the desire of Great Britain to encourage our expansion as a restriction upon German imperialism. The determining factor was our unwillingness to shirk a responsibility created by the destruction of Spanish authority and prestige. Having joined forces with the native Filipinos in driving the Spanish out of the islands, we could not, with honor, do less than protect them against the imperialistic ambitions of other nations, and we were not disposed to assume a position of responsibility without authority.

Both Puerto Rico and the Philippines were governed by the President as Commander-in-Chief of the Army for some time. The Foraker Act, establishing civil government in Puerto Rico, was passed by Congress on April 12, 1900. Actually, army rule extended from July 25, 1898, to May 1, 1900. The army took over the administration of the Philippines on August 13, 1898. The revolt of the Filipinos, under the leadership of Aguinaldo, began on February 4, 1899, and continued until early in 1902. It was not until then that Congress passed an organic act for the islands (July 1, 1902). Meanwhile, in December, 1898, President McKinley ordered the Secretary of War, Elihu Root, to establish civil government in the islands under army administration. The First Philippine Commission, under the chairmanship of President Jacob F. Schurman of Cornell University, was sent out on January 20, 1899. This Commission, the other members of which were Rear Admiral George Dewey, Major General Elwell S. Otis, Charles Denby and Dean C. Worcester, made its final report on December 31, 1900. It was a lengthy description of the islands, of the attitude of the people and of the Commissioners' opinions with respect to their government. The Second Philippine Commission, under the chairmanship of

Judge William H. Taft, was sent to the islands on March 16, 1900. It was given authority to enact legislation, to create a court system and to appoint administrative officials. Its authority was derived from the war powers of the President until March 2, 1901, when Congress passed the Spooner Amendment to the Army appropriation bill, authorizing President McKinley to continue to govern the islands as a civil official until Congress should pass additional legislation. Acting under this authorization, the President gave Taft the position of Civil Governor of the Philippines and, September 1, 1901, ordered three Filipinos added to the Commission and four executive departments created: interior, commerce and police, finance and justice, and education.

The new colonial policy gradually took shape from the investigations of the commissions, the experiences of administration under the War Department and the discussions during the Presidential campaign of 1900. Colonial policy was a major issue in that campaign. Few people in the country, Republicans or Democrats, would have endorsed as a deliberate policy the expansion incident to the war. An anti-imperialist League was formed in New England in 1898, under the leadership of Ex-Secretary of the Treasury, George S. Boutwell. The purchase or conquest of distant territory, inhabited by a foreign race, was denounced as hostile to the spirit of Americanism as expressed in the Declaration of Independence and as likely to foster militarism, entail enormous expense and involve the country in foreign complications. The Administration's defense of its action as a solemn duty arising from the destruction of Spanish authority in the Islands was ridiculed as a pretense. The Democrats, under the leadership of Bryan, promised to grant independence to the Philippines and condemned the war of subjugation in strong terms. There were anti-imperialists in the Republican party, particularly Senator George F. Hoar and Speaker Thomas B. Reed, but they did not desert their party to support Bryan. Likewise, there were Democrats who supported the Administration's Philippine policy. The Populists, who ultimately supported Bryan, spoke of the Philippine policy as "in conflict with all the precedents of our national life; at war with the Declaration of Independence, the Constitution, and the plain precepts of humanity." They endorsed the addition of Puerto Rico to the United States, but insisted that the Constitution followed the flag. The Democratic platform held that "no nation can long endure half republic and half empire." It said further: "The Filipinos cannot be citizens without endangering our civilization; they cannot be subjects without imperilling our form of government; and as we are not willing to surrender our civilization, or to convert the Republic into an empire, we favor an immediate declaration of the Nation's purpose to give the Filipinos, first, a stable form of government; second, independence; and third, protection from outside interference such as has been given for nearly a century to the republics of Central and South America." The Republican platform endorsed the war record of the Administration as having given "to ten millions of the human race . . . a new birth of freedom, and to the American people a new and noble responsibility." It merely promised to extend to the Filipinos "the largest measure of self-government consistent with their welfare and our duties. . . ." The question of colonial policy can not be said to have exercised a determining influence in the re-election of President McKinley, but it did leave the Republican party free to continue the organization of governments in Puerto Rico and the Philippines along lines established by the Foraker Act and the Taft Commission.

Puerto Rico had a population of 953,000 of whom 589,000 were whites. They were a civilized people with Spanish institutions. The Philippine Islands had a population of eleven million of whom about nine million belonged to the principal cultural group of Christian Filipinos. The government of both Puerto Rico and the Philippines, under Spanish rule, was highly centralized. In each, the important administrative officials held office at the pleasure of the governor general, and the judiciary, public works, transportation, education and police were under the control of this representative of royal prerogative. Their legal systems were based on the Roman law. The Catholic Church was the established church. The basic problem, therefore, was to bring the institutions of these people into harmony with those of the United States; to extend to them the American system of decentralization and self-government with freedom of speech and press, the jury system, habeas corpus, etc. The greatest administrative problem was to maintain efficient government while training the native people to govern themselves. The question of incorporation or independence was postponed to some future date, when the people should have demonstrated the extent of their ability to adapt themselves to American institutions.

Preliminary steps in the establishment of a new regime were taken by the Army officers both in the Philippines and in Puerto Rico. The most important work in Puerto Rico was done by the medical, engineer, and paymaster departments of the Army of Occupation in introducing new methods of sanitation, road building and public finance. Administrative costs were reduced drastically and a new provisional court system was installed. The same procedure was followed in the Philippines. Army rule there extended over a longer period and, in addition to the reforms mentioned above, preliminary steps were taken toward establishing an educational system, civil marriages, public trials and popular elections with a limited suffrage. When President McKinley first sent the Taft Commission to the Philippines, it was with instructions to be guided in all matters by the best interests of the native people; to grant them as much autonomy as was consistent with good government; and to place the responsibility for local government upon them. Congress then passed the Foraker Act (April 12, 1900) for the government of Puerto Rico. It was to the new colonial policy what the Ordinance of 1787 had been to the territorial policy, containing the basic principles of government for the new dependencies.

The Foraker Act provided that the President, with the approval of the Senate, should appoint for Puerto Rico a Governor and Commission of six administrative officers: Secretary, Attorney-General, Treasurer, Auditor, Commissioner of Interior and Commissioner of Education. These Commissioners might be either Americans or Puerto Ricans. To this group of administrative officers, the Puerto Rican government added (1904) a Commissioner of Public Health and a Commissioner of Charities and Corrections. Each Commissioner had full discretionary power to administer the affairs of his own department and was responsible to the several Cabinet members in Washington rather than to the Governor. The House of Delegates, consisting of thirty-five members, was to be elected bi-annually. The Delegates were to be not less than twenty-five years of age, be able to read and write Spanish, and own taxable property, but they need not live in the districts from which they were elected and franchise qualifications were left to the determination of the legislature. The six Commissioners and five others to be named by the President were to serve as an Executive Council. Not less than five of the eleven members must be Puerto Ricans. The Executive Council was to serve as the upper house of the legislature and was to sit permanently as a supervisory body for the granting of franchises, determining the salaries of all officials not appointed by the President, and approving municipal ordinances. Thus, the House of Delegates was, from the first, controlled by native Puerto Ricans and they were given a majority in the Executive Council during President Wilson's Administration. The Spanish Court system was abolished and the American legal system, both criminal and civil, was introduced by the territorial legislature. Justices of the seven District Courts received their appointments from the Governor and Executive Council and the five Justices of the Supreme Court at San Juan from the President and Senate. The Justices of the municipal courts were made elective. The Island was given a Resident Commissioner at Washington rather than a Delegate to Congress. The Foraker Act also gave Puerto Rico control of its own customs duties. It levied a duty equal to 15 per cent of normal tariffs on all commerce to and from the United States. These duties were to be assessed only until the Puerto Ricans had established a sound revenue system, when free trade was to prevail. In no case was the collection of tariff duties to extend beyond March 1, 1902. Actually, none were collected after July 25, 1901. The money which had been collected at the ports of the United States was placed in a trust fund and used for the construction of highways and schools in the Island. The monetary system of the United States was extended to Puerto Rico. The territorial legislature was given control of its own revenue system, but borrowings were limited to 7 per cent of assessed property valuations. Inhabitants of the Island were declared citizens of Puerto Rico. They were not given United States citizenship until 1917.

The Philippine Act of July 1, 1902, was passed before the conquest of the Islands had been completed. This Act approved and continued in force the work already accomplished under the governorship of Taft, which included the establishment of a Philippine Constabulary, Bureaus of Agriculture and Forestry, a rigid civil service, a highway department, and a public school system. The Act made provision for a Census after the conclusion of peace, to be followed by an election of representatives to the Philippine Assembly. Meanwhile, until 1907, the government of the Islands was the Philippine Commission, consisting of the Civil Governor (Governor-General after 1905) and seven other members, four Americans and three Filipinos. This Commission was to serve as the upper house of the legislature. The Justices of the Supreme Court were to be appointed by the President and Senate. Local government was to be created by the territorial legislature. There were to be two resident commissioners in Washington. The Act, also, specifically extended to the Philippine people such fundamental rights as due process of law and freedom of speech and assembly. Municipal indebtedness was limited to five per cent of assessed property valuations. A Philippine currency system was created, but it was tied to the currency of the United States by giving the peso one-half the value of the gold dollar. Tariff duties of 75 per cent of those on commerce with foreign nations were levied on trade with the United States. During the interval before the election of an Assembly, the Commission created a complete administrative system of Bureaus including agriculture, public lands, biologicals, statistics, forestry, mines, archives, public buildings, ethnology, printing, coast guard, prisons and education. The most important part of this work was accomplished before Taft returned to the United States in 1903 and during his Presidency when W. Cameron Forbes was Governor-General of the Islands.

The Canal Zone

The United States had long been interested in an inter-oceanic canal across either the Isthmus of Panama or Nicaragua or both. A rational consideration of the question of expansion in the Caribbean had been impossible before the Civil War because of the slavery controversy. Filibustering expeditions went out from time to time to Nicaragua and to Cuba, but official action by the government was limited to restraining British encroachments in the region. The Clayton-Bulwer Treaty (1850) with that nation bound both governments to guarantee the international character, joint-control and non-fortification of any canal which might be constructed. Treaties with Colombia (New Granada) in 1846 and with Nicaragua in 1867 further committed the United States to respect the sovereignty of those nations and the interests of all nations in any project which might be undertaken. The Clayton-Bulwer Treaty was regarded at the time as a diplomatic victory by the United States. The increasing prestige of the country in international affairs following the Civil War changed the complexion of the treaty and caused it to be regarded as a hindrance to freedom of action. While Great Britain hesitated to revise it, French and American commercial interests began work on both canals. The French company, under De Lesseps, spent $260,000,000 on the Panama project before going bankrupt in 1889, and the American interests lost heavily on the Nicaraguan project during the panic of 1893. Uneasiness over the activities of these private companies was plainly evident in official circles and it became acute after the acquisition of territorial possessions in the Caribbean and Pacific. Great Britain agreed in 1901 to revise the Clayton-Bulwer Treaty. The Hay-Pauncefote Treaty was ratified on February 21, 1902, giving the United States freedom to construct and fortify a canal with the single requirement that it was to be open for use by all nations on terms of equality.

Fortunately, the proposed canal was no longer a political question in the United States. Both major parties favored the project, the Republicans as a part of their colonial policy and the agrarian Democrats because of their long-standing grievances over trans-continental freight rates. There was, however, much debate over the respective merits of the two routes. The French Company's desire to salvage as much as possible from its ill-starred venture introduced intrigue into negotiations with the Republic of Colombia. Congress authorized President Roosevelt in June, 1902, to proceed with the undertaking in Nicaragua unless satisfactory agreements could be reached with the French company and Colombia within a reasonable time. This authorization, together with the impending expiration of the Company's rights under its agreement with Colombia caused it to reduce its price for its property to the reasonable figure of $40,000,000, but the Colombian Senate, hopeful of more favorable returns at the expense of the company, refused to take final action on the Hay-Herran Convention of January, 1903. By that agreement, Colombia was to receive $10,000,000 in cash and $250,000 in gold annually for a Canal Zone six miles wide. The failure of Colombia to act was directly contrary to the interests of the French Company, of the United States and of the people of Panama. The combined resentment of the three interested parties, finding expression in the acts of President Roosevelt, Attorney W. K. Cromwell of the French Company, and Manuel Amador of Panama, provoked a revolution in Panama. If the United States government did not instigate the revolution, it certainly prevented its suppression, and President Roosevelt departed radically from the traditional policies of the nation in recognizing the new Republic of Panama within a few hours after it came into existence. A treaty with the Republic of Panama, November 18, 1903, formally ratified recognition and gave a United States guarantee of independence. Panama received $10,000,000 in cash and $250,000 annually in return for the Canal Zone ten miles wide. The work of constructing the canal began in 1906 and was completed in 1914 at a total cost of $350,000,000.

Congress placed the government of the Canal Zone in the hands of the President on April 28, 1904, having previously provided for the appointment of an Isthmian Canal Commission. The Commission, appointed March 6, 1904, consisted of the Governor of the Canal Zone and six other members. It was given complete legislative and administrative powers. It established several departments of administration, including Public Health, Justice and Education. The Zone was divided into four administrative districts, each with a district court. A Supreme Court of three Justices was provided and both Civil and Criminal Codes enacted. The Commission continued to govern until the Panama Canal Act was passed by Congress August 24, 1912. By this act, Congress resumed direct legislative authority over the Zone, provided for the eventual removal of all persons except government employees, and gave the President administrative authority only over it. Governors thereafter were appointed from the Engineers Corps of the Army. The Act also created the Zone into a judicial district with appeals to the Fifth Circuit Court of the United States.

The Virgin Islands

Negotiations for the purchase of the Virgin Islands were begun in 1901 as a part of the Isthmian policy. They were of no value except as outer defenses for the proposed Panama and Nicaraguan Canals, having an area of only 132 square miles and a population of only 25,000, most of whom were illiterate and poverty-stricken Negroes and half-breeds. They were not finally secured from Denmark until 1917. Framing a government, March 3, 1917, Congress retained the Danish Code of Laws, allowed Danish citizens either to retain their citizenship or to become citizens of the United States and gave all others the status of nationals. The President was authorized to appoint a governor with the approval of the Senate. Jurisdiction was given to the Secretary of the Navy, as was the case with Samoa and Guam. The latter Island had been seized by the United States during the Spanish-American War. American Samoa, important for the harbor of Pago Pago on the island of Tutuila, was acquired in a tripartite agreement with Great Britain and Germany in 1900. Congress did not make provision for their government and they continued under the absolute authority of the President as Commander-in-Chief of the Navy.

The New Colonial Policy

The platforms of the Democratic party, adopted at Denver, July 10, 1908, and at Baltimore, June 27, 1912, condemned in identical language "the experiment in imperialism as an inexcusable blunder which has involved us in enormous expense, brought us weakness instead of strength, and laid our nation open to the charge of abandoning a fundamental doctrine of self-government." Both platforms favored independence for the Philippines "as soon as a stable government" could be established and the "full enjoyment of the rights and privileges of a territorial form of government" for Alaska and Puerto Rico. The Progressive party, meeting at Chicago, August 5, 1912, promised "the people of the Territory of Alaska the same measure of local self-government that was given to other American Territories." Shortly afterward (August 24) the Democrats and Republican Insurgents forced through Congress the act organizing a territorial government in Alaska, and Wilson's election assured a definite change of policy in Puerto Rico and the Philippines. Congress passed the Jones Act, reorganizing the government of the Philippines on August 29, 1916; an Organic Act for Puerto Rico on March 2, 1917; and, the following day, an Act for the Government of the Virgin Islands which had been purchased from Denmark on January 25, 1917.

From 1901 to 1907, the governing body in the Philippines was the Philippine Commission, consisting of seven members only three of whom were Filipinos. It was both a legislative and administrative body. The first Philippine Assembly was elected in 1907 and, thereafter, the Commission served as the upper house of the legislature. The Filipinos were given a fourth member of the Commission by Act of Congress in 1908. President Wilson's first action was to appoint a fifth Filipino to the Commission, thus giving the native people control of both houses of the legislature. He appointed Francis B. Harrison Governor-General with instructions to allow the legislature wide latitude in the exercise of their new power of self-government. The most significant feature of the new regime was an experiment in state socialism including government enterprises in the fields of transportation, banking, mining and manufacturing. The Jones Act definitely committed the United States to Philippine independence as soon as they had demonstrated their ability to maintain a stable government under the new policy of self-government. It abolished the Philippine Commission and the Assembly, replacing them with a Senate and House of Representatives, both elective. Senators and Representatives were required to be able to read and write English or Spanish and reside in the district from which they were elected. The legislature was given control of the franchise, power to over-ride the veto of the Governor-General by a two-thirds vote of each house, and complete authority to organize all executive departments except the Department of the Interior and that of Instruction. The latter was placed under the control of a newly created executive official: the vice-governor. The Governor-General and the vice-governor were the only officials appointed by the President and Senate of the United States. Governor-General Harrison, by executive order, created a Council of State (1918) consisting of the Governor-General, the President of the Senate, the Speaker of the House of Representatives and the Secretaries of the six executive departments. Its purpose was to promote cooperation between the executive and legislative branches of the government, but it actually determined the policies of the government until abolished by executive order of Governor-General Leonard Wood, Harrison's successor.

The Organic Act for the government of Puerto Rico gave that dependency the same measure of self-government accorded to territories in their final stage without, however, incorporating it as a territory preparatory to statehood. United States citizenship and virtually all of the fundamental rights guaranteed to the individual in the Constitution were extended to the citizens of Puerto Rico. The legislature was to consist of a Senate and House of Representatives, both elective. It was given power to over-ride the Governor's veto by a two-thirds vote of each house. Only the Governor, the Commissioner of Education, the Attorney-General and the Justices of the Supreme Court were to be appointed by the President of the United States. The Secretaries of the other executive departments were to be appointed by the Governor with the approval of the Puerto Rican Senate. A Delegate to Congress replaced the resident Commissioner at Washington.

The independence promised to the Philippines by the Jones Act was indefinitely postponed with the return of the Republican party to power in 1921. President Harding sent Major-General Leonard Wood and W. Cameron Forbes to investigate conditions in the Islands. Wood was a Republican, seeking to restore his political fortunes, and violently opposed to Philippine independence. His report, so far as recommendations were concerned, might well have been written before his departure from the United States. It was so clearly biased that the legislature promptly sent a committee to the United States to refute its charges that the people had misused their powers of self-government. The spirit of independence was so general that even Wood could find no opposition to it except among the 400,000 Mohammedan Moros and the American Colony. In spite of popular resentment in the Islands over Wood's report,

Presidents Harding and Coolidge kept him in the Islands as Governor-General until 1927. It was a period of strife and misunderstanding, during which most of the progress made under Harrison's Administration was undone. Government enterprises were turned over to private capital, and the Council of State was abolished. At one time, the entire Cabinet resigned. Hostility to the Wood regime became so open in the Islands and criticism so severe in the United States that President Coolidge sent Carmi A. Thompson out to investigate in 1926. Governor Wood died while in the United States fighting to retain his position.

Thompson's report was a masterful politician's compromise between the demands for immediate independence by the Filipinos, for more autocratic power by Wood and for relief from a trying situation by President Coolidge. He advised that "independence be postponed for some time to come" (1) because of the Islands' lack of financial resources, common language and controlling public opinion; (2) because they were necessary to the United States as a commercial base and free trade with the United States was essential to their economic security; and (3) because granting their independence "might complicate international relations in the Orient." He just as definitely, however, condemned the proposed repeal of the Jones Act and the land laws which stood in the way of large scale exploitation by the rubber interests of the United States. He recommended immediate restoration of cooperation between the Governor-General and Philippine Legislature, presumably by the appointment of a new Governor-General from other than Army ranks, extension of the Federal Reserve System to the Islands, and sale of Philippine national properties to private capital. Finally, he recommended a new department of Colonial Administration of Alaska, Hawaii, Puerto Rico, and the Philippines. President Coolidge was himself opposed to independence for the Islands, offering as his reasons the additional economic burden which would be thrown upon them in providing for their own defense and in becoming subject to the tariff duties on foreign commerce with the United States. Governor-General Wood was succeeded by Henry L. Stimson, who restored the Council of State, subjected department heads to legislative control and, in other ways, adopted a policy of conciliation.

The refusal of Congress to tamper with the Jones Act, coupled with the return to the Harrison policies by Governor-General Stimson, ended whatever hopes had existed on the part of industrial interests that the Philippines would be turned over to economic exploitation. There were no large investments of American capital in the Islands to influence their retention. They had proved valueless as a base for developing commerce in the Orient. Naval experts regarded them a liability rather than an asset in event of war. Importations of sugar, cocoanut oil and tobacco on a free trade basis after 1913 added to the advocates of Philippine independence all those domestic producers who suffered from this competition. Finally, there was a growing consciousness that the task undertaken at the conclusion of the war with Spain was completed. It had cost several hundred million dollars; but it stood as a magnificent monument to the benevolence of the American people. The Philippine people longed for independence. Neither they nor the United States had anything further to gain by longer delay. Congress passed the Hawes-Cutting Act on December 29, 1932. This act provided for the adoption of a Philippine constitution acceptable both to the Filipinos and to the Congress of the United States which would serve as an instrument of government during a ten year period. During this period the Islands were to be a protectorate of the United States with a High Commissioner in the Philippines and a Philippine Commissioner in the United States. The United States was to retain naval coaling stations and military posts in the Islands. Philippine foreign relations were to be under the supervision of the United States and appeals permitted from the insular courts to the Supreme Court of the United States. Philippine immigration to the United States was limited to 50 annually and imports of sugar and cocoanut oil were placed on a quota basis. American exports to the Islands were to be duty free. President Hoover vetoed the bill on the grounds that it would project the Philippines into economic and social chaos with subsequent collapse of government and degeneration of free institutions; that it would lead to peaceful infiltration or forcible entry of neighboring peoples; and that it would weaken the authority of the United States to a dangerous point during the probationary period. Congress promptly passed the act over the President's veto but the Philippine legislature objected strenuously to its economic and immigration features and permitted it to lapse by default, failing to call a constitutional convention within the prescribed twelve months period.

President Roosevelt requested, March 2, 1934, that the Hawes-Cutting bill be revived and amended. It was revived and passed as the Tydings-McDuffie Act and signed by President Roosevelt on March 24, 1934. The only change from the original act was the surrender by the United States of its right to maintain military establishments in the Islands. The Filipinos accepted the act and all American officials were withdrawn except a High Commissioner who was to have only powers of investigation and advice. Ten years were allotted to the two governments to solve the problems of economic independence for the Islands, involving the necessity of finding new markets at a time of world-wide economic nationalism. Equally important was the necessity of providing international guarantees of the Islands' independence. Failure to do these two things would make independence a mockery and vindicate the dire prophecies of Presidents Coolidge and Hoover.

Protected Independent States

When Congress (April 19, 1898) authorized President McKinley to use the armed forces to free the people of Cuba from Spanish sovereignty, it pledged the United States to respect Cuban independence. The treaty-making power, by the Treaty of Paris, pledged the United States to restore order in the Island and provide protection to persons and property. The

Army, under command of General Leonard Wood, remained in the Island until May 20, 1902. During this period of occupation, the arbitrary power of the President as Commander-in-Chief of the Army was used to disestablish the Catholic Church, inaugurate a program of sanitation, establish schools, and reconstruct the financial system. Congress then passed the Platt Amendment, drafted by Secretary Elihu Root, which Cuba was forced to append to her Constitution of 1901 and sign as a part of a permanent treaty in 1903. This amendment bound Cuba to make no treaties impairing her independence, contract no debts beyond her ability to meet from ordinary revenues, continue the sanitation program and lease naval stations to the United States. Its main purpose, however, was to protect the young Republic in its infancy and, for this reason, it gave the United States "the right to intervene for the preservation of Cuban independence, the maintenance of a government adequate for the protection of life, property and individual liberty. . . ." Secretary Root interpreted this provision as an application of the Monroe Doctrine and gave assurances that there would be no intervention except in cases of anarchy or foreign invasion. In three decades, however, American troops were landed four times. The first occupation, resulting from the 1906 elections, lasted from 1906 to 1909. The second, in 1912, was on the pretense of suppressing race riots. The third, in 1917, resulted from a minor revolution growing out of an election. The fourth, in 1920, was clearly at the behest of financial interests to protect their investments. There can be no question that the readiness of the United States government to interfere in the internal affairs of the Republic retarded political development there. The very existence of the Platt Amendment stood as an expression of skepticism as to the Cubans' capacity for self-government and fostered irresponsibility on the part of her public officials. A minority in the Republic, opposed to independence from the first, remained ever ready to create situations which would lead to intervention. The reserved right of intervention, therefore, defeated its purpose of establishing responsible government, tempted the exercise of dollar diplomacy, and engendered uneasiness among other Latin American republics. Its abrogation by the Senate during Roosevelt's first administration was but one of the indications that the experiment in imperialism was being abandoned.

The second excuse for the dominance of other peoples came in 1904 as a result of political disorders extending over several years in Santo Domingo. Revolutions and unsound fiscal policies had placed the Republic in debt to European nations, and raised the question of how far those creditors might go in forcing payment without violating the Monroe Doctrine. In his message to Congress, December 2, 1904, President Roosevelt placed an interpretation upon the Monroe Doctrine which remained the official interpretation until 1928. He said: "Chronic wrong-doing, or an impotence which results in a general loosening of the ties of civilized society may in America, as elsewhere, ultimately require intervention by some civilized nation, and in the Western Hemisphere the adherence of the United States to the Monroe Doctrine may force the United States, however reluctantly, in flagrant cases of such wrong doing or impotence, to the exercise of an international police power." Congress refused to approve an agreement negotiated by Roosevelt under which an official representative of the United States would be placed in control of the Republic's finances. Nevertheless, Roosevelt kept naval vessels in Dominican waters, marines in the Island and secured the appointment of an acceptable financial dictator who succeeded in reducing the claims of the European nations by nearly 50 per cent and placing the Republic on a sound financial basis.

In 1912, a third excuse was found for intervention, this time in Nicaragua. Secretary of State, Philander C. Knox, negotiated conventions with Nicaragua and Honduras in 1911, by which American bankers were to loan the two countries substantial sums, such loans to be protected by the appointment of an American customs collector. Again the Senate proved recalcitrant, and again the President sent marines on his own responsibility to Nicaragua and Bluefields. Three million dollars were paid to Nicaragua for the right to build a canal. Private financial interests in the United States took over the Nicaragua national bank and undertook to develop the country. Eventually their investments amounted to $15,648,700. Meanwhile, marines were kept in the country to protect these investments, but officially to protect our canal rights, at a cost of $6,076,000 before 1932. This was what came to be known as "dollar diplomacy." The Wilson Administration followed the path marked by the Taft Administration and negotiated in 1916 the lease of a naval base at the Gulf of Fonseca and of the Great Corn and Little Corn Islands. This policy, as in Cuba, led to instability in Nicaragua with the United States attempting to supervise elections and the patriots under Sandino engaging the marines in constant guerilla warfare. This adventure in Nicaragua and a similar one in Hayti were the two most deplorable incidents in our attempt to follow investments with armed forces. The evacuation of the country, begun in 1932, closed what was regarded by many people as a disgraceful episode, and placed relations between the two countries once more on a civilized basis.

President Wilson not only continued the Roosevelt policies in Santo Domingo and the Taft policies in Nicaragua, but extended them to Hayti. Marines were landed in the latter Republic in 1915 where they remained for nearly twenty years. A dictated treaty of May 3, 1916, gave the United States virtual control of the government. Popular government ceased to exist. Elections were controlled by the armed forces of the United States. Roads were built by forced labor. Natives who rebelled were subdued in what was little else than official slaughter. Under pressure of growing criticism in the United States, President Hoover sent the Forbes Commission to investigate in 1930. The result was the adoption of a policy of gradual withdrawal.

Mexico

Abandonment of American intervention in the internal affairs of other Republics to the south of the United States grew out of the Mexican policy of President Wilson. The dictatorship of Porfirio Diaz, extending from 1877 to 1911, had reduced the population of that country to the status of agricultural peonage, given foreign capital control of transportation, mining, oil lands, and rubber production, and destroyed all semblance of popular government. Revolution broke out in 1911 under the leadership of Francisco Madero, who was unable to retain power after gaining it largely because of the hostility of the Taft Administration. He was overthrown by the counterrevolution of Victoriano Huerta in February, 1913. Soon after President Wilson's inauguration he announced his Mexican policy. It was: (1) that the United States would not recognize governments founded by force; (2) that it would assist, in every way possible, the establishment of democratic government; (3) that the armed forces of the United States would not be used to protect capital investments; (4) that the United States would tolerate no interference with its leadership in Latin American affairs. Applying this policy, Wilson blockaded the Mexican harbors and in April, 1914, seized the port of Vera Cruz. He sent a punitive expedition into Mexico after the rebel Francisco Villa in 1916, but firmly resisted all efforts of American oil and mining interests to precipitate further intervention. The demand for intervention arose out of the Constitution adopted by Mexico in May, 1917, which included provisions for protection of labor against capitalistic exploitation, nationalized church property, secularized the schools, and prohibited further acquisition of land and water rights by foreign capital. It further declared all land, water, and mineral deposits to be the property of the state. Oil interests in the United States brought pressure in Congress and upon the Department of State, at the close of the War and during Wilson's illness, to intervene. Only the timely action of President Wilson prevented war.

Wilson's refusal to violate the rights of the Mexican people to control their own domestic affairs, and his championship of democratic government, laid the basis for a solution of the Mexican problem in President Coolidge's Administration. It constituted, also, the beginning of the end of imperialism and the formulation of a new national policy in Latin American affairs. Secretary of State Hughes and his successor, Frank B. Kellogg, sought to follow the old dictatorial policy between 1921 and 1927 without success. Mexico went ahead with her Petroleum and Alien Land Laws of 1925, substituting fifty-year concessions for existing titles and public sentiment in the United States restrained any application of the policy threatened by Secretary Kellogg when he said: "We have been patient and realize, of course, that it takes time to bring about a stable government, but we cannot countenance violation of her obligations and failure to protect American citizens." Dwight W. Morrow, of J. P. Morgan and Company, was sent to Mexico as Ambassador in 1927. His skill as a diplomatist and, more particularly, his appreciation of the domestic problems of the Mexican government, secured a modification of the Petroleum Law, an adjustment of the controversy between the government and the Church and a spirit of mutual sympathy and cooperation between the two neighboring peoples which had never existed before.

Secretary of State, Henry L. Stimson, in 1930, completely repudiated the Roosevelt interpretation of the Monroe Doctrine, and justified whatever action had been taken in the Caribbean region on the needs of national defense as related to the Isthumian Canal. Meanwhile, military occupation of Santo Domingo was terminated in 1924. President Hoover announced in 1930 that marines would be withdrawn from Hayti after the expiration of the ten year treaty in 1936. In 1931, he announced that military occupation of Nicaragua would be terminated after the election in that country in 1932. President Roosevelt and Secretary of State Cordell Hull speeded the movement already begun. Troops were withdrawn from Hayti without waiting for the termination of the treaty. The Platt Amendment was speedily abrogated by the Senate. The Philippine Independence bill was passed. Three decades of expensive dominance of neighboring people was at an end.

New Ventures in Foreign Diplomacy

Traditional American foreign policy had included the principles of (1) no foreign alliances; (2) non-interference in European affairs; (3) non-aggression by European nations in the Western Hemisphere; (4) equal commercial privileges for all nations in the Far East. The rise of Japan to the rank of a first class power beginning with the Chinese War of 1895, and the extension of United States sovereignty over Alaska, Hawaii and the Philippines, brought new problems in foreign diplomacy. While the United States was engaged in war with Spain, Germany, France, Russia and Great Britain were wresting from China important spheres of influence diverging from the ports of Kiaochow, Kwangchow, Port Arthur, and Wei-hai-wei. This action seriously threatened the principle of equal trading privileges. National monopolies, recognized by international treaties, of the right to exploit natural resources, transportation and opportunities for investment were recognized as inimical to American commercial and financial interests. Secretary of State, John Hay, therefore, approached the European powers with a request that they agree to respect the right of all nations to equality of treatment in the use of harbors and transportation facilities, and in the application of tariffs, and that they guarantee the integrity of existing vested interests. All nations agreed to this Open Door policy which, however, took no account of the embryonic giant of international rivalry: capital investments. Shortly thereafter, the United States again assumed leadership in the expedition to quell the Boxer uprising, restraining the powers from using the incident to further dismember the ancient empire, and keeping the indemnity within somewhat reasonable limits.

Five years later, Russia and Japan were nearing exhaustion in the war which had broken out in 1904. Japan, whose economic system was bordering on collapse, requested President Roosevelt to mediate. American peace advocates had done likewise. His motive for acting, however, was fear that the newly acquired position of the United States in the Pacific might be endangered by a Japanese victory. His policy was that of curbing Japan in order to maintain a balance of power in the Far East. He arranged a peace conference at Portsmouth, New Hampshire, and guided its deliberations in such a way as to accomplish his desired object by avoiding a humiliating peace for either nation. Japan's agreement to forgo a 600 million dollar cash indemnity remained a source of irritation against the United States for many years. While the peace negotiations were under way, Roosevelt entered into a secret, personal agreement with the Prime Minister of Japan by which the sovereignty of the respective nations over the Philippines and Korea was recognized and the United States agreed to support the principles of the Anglo-Japanese Alliance of August 12, 1905. This agreement was not submitted to the Senate, nor was it publicly known for many years.

Meanwhile, the eyes of all America were turned to the Pacific by the trend of world events. It was generally believed that the coming decades would unfold a mighty drama in that region with Japan and the United States playing the leading rôles. Fear of Japanese power was responsible for Roosevelt's action. The inevitability of war between the two races became a common topic of conversation. We made no effort, as with China, to cultivate friendship between the two nations. Instead, fortifications were pushed on the West Coast. Naval bases were planned for Alaska, Hawaii and the Philippines. Exclusion of Japanese immigrants was insisted upon. California took the lead among the states in enacting discriminatory laws against Japanese residents whose children, at least, were citizens. The stage was set for some move on the part of persons in authority in either nation to precipitate a conflict. The public mind was made agreeable to new naval construction although our navy already was the third largest in the world.

There may have been excuse for Roosevelt's action in the Caribbean and the Far East, but there was no precedent for his interference in the Moroccan Crisis of 1905. In this case, he exerted considerable pressure upon France to agree to the Algeciras Conference to which he sent as representatives Henry White, United States Ambassador to Italy, and S. R. Gummere, Consul-General to Morocco. The Conference adopted a settlement similar to Hay's Open Door policy in China, but the Senate, in ratifying that settlement, was constrained to say that there was no intention to depart from the traditional policy of non-interference in strictly European affairs.

The United States and Great Britain

The clash of interests between Japan and the United States producing mutual fear and distrust was matched by an exactly opposite development in relations between Great Britain and the United States. How much weight can be given to the cohesive influences of similar culture and institutional life is a matter of opinion. The Treaty of Ghent in 1815 ushered in lasting peace between the two nations, in spite of the fact that the causes of the war were scarcely mentioned in the Treaty. Many irritating circumstances arose thereafter, all of which could have served, and have served many times in history, as excuses for armed conflict; but the inherent good sense and friendliness of leading private citizens in both nations simply would not permit it. The same can not be said for their governments, nor for certain jingoistic elements of their populations.

The same insatiable desire for expansion which had contributed to the cause of war in 1812, had again rendered difficult an amicable settlement of the controversies arising out of the Civil War period. Charles Sumner, who was Chairman of the Senate Foreign Relations Committee, insisted that Great Britain had erred not only in permitting cruisers to be built for the Confederate States of America but also in according her the status of a belligerent. She could only expiate the crime by severing Canada and its people from the British Empire and passing them over to the United States. It required all the ingenuity of Ambassador Reverdy Johnson, Secretaries of State

William H. Seward and Hamilton Fish and President Grant, not to mention the labors of such peace advocates as A. J. Mundella, Newman Hall and James B. Miles, to counteract the martial spirit in the United States and bring the controversy before an international court of arbitration in 1871-1872. The Senate was equally bellicose in the controversy arising over the rights of American fishermen to operate within the three mile limits of the coast of British North America. New England fishing interests insisted upon continuing the practice without making reciprocal concessions of free trade to Canadian fishing interests. Congress went so far as to provide in 1887 for the exclusion of Canadian vessels from the ports of the United States and for a complete embargo upon Canadian products. By independent action, the Department of State nursed the situation along without further complications until a settlement could be effected in 1910.

Further trouble of a serious nature was experienced in the administrations of Grover Cleveland and Theodore Roosevelt. The first incident arose out of a boundary dispute between British Guiana and Venezuela which caused a severance of diplomatic relations between the two countries in 1887. The dispute dragged on without resort to arms until, in 1895, Secretary of State Richard Olney began a spirited correspondence with the British Foreign Minister Lord Salisbury. Olney went so far as to express doubts as to the permanency of British sovereignty over any portion of America and proclaimed the amazing thesis that the United States is "practically sovereign on this continent, and its fiat is law upon the subjects to which it confines its interposition . . . because, in addition to all other grounds, its infinite resources combined with its isolated position render it master of the situation and practically invulnerable as against any or all other powers." Lord Salisbury's rejection of Olney's claims led President Cleveland to request authority from Congress to run the boundary line and enforce the decision against any counter-claims of Great Britain. His belligerent attitude was lauded by such men as Theodore Roosevelt, Chauncey M.

Depew, and Andrew D. White. Once more, however, the peace advocates won, partly because increasing tension in South Africa and the Caribbean turned the attention of both governments to other matters. Great Britain lent every assistance to the investigating commission of the United States and, in 1899, the entire controversy was settled by the findings of an international board of arbitration.

It was only natural that President Roosevelt, who believed strongly in preparedness and the benefits of an occasional war, should precipitate the next crisis. The discovery of gold in Alaska had brought the two governments into a dispute as to whether the boundary between Alaska and Canada should follow the sinuosities of the coast or run from mountain peak to mountain peak. Secretary of State Hay finally succeeded, in 1903, in getting the controversy submitted to a commission consisting of three representatives from the United States, two from Canada and one from England. Failure of the Commission to act promptly caused Roosevelt to say that, unless a satisfactory decision were arrived at, the United States would assert its claims without further consideration of those of Canada and Great Britain. The British government averted further complications by instructing its Commissioner to support the American claim.

CHAPTER VIII

WAR TO END WARS

THE SPIRIT OF AMERICA

THE last years of the nineteenth century had witnessed a distinct departure from the isolationist attitude of the United States. It emerged from the war with Spain as a world power. The same forces within the nation that had striven mightily to counteract the drift toward imperialism now sought to direct national policy toward internationalism and world peace. It was a short twenty years from the day that the United States embarked upon its crusade to liberate the Cubans from tyranny to the day it threw its strength into a world cataclysm with the avowed purpose of bringing liberty, freedom and justice to all peoples, everywhere. A cursory glance at the powerful forces which struggled for supremacy during those years shows the futility of any effort to explain our entry into the war on economic factors alone. There were Americans—Jane Addams and Eugene V. Debs certainly were two—who believed in, preached and practiced the principles of human brotherhood irrespective of nationality, race or creed. The idea cannot be said, however, to have penetrated very far into the consciousness of the Amercian Colony in the Philippines, the champions of white supremacy in the southern states, the immigrants from the Emerald Isle, or the readers of the anti-Catholic *Menace*. There were men like Speaker T. B. Reed who believed that the dispute with Spain should have been submitted to arbitration, but not William Randolph Hearst, Joseph Pulitzer, Henry Cabot Lodge, or Theodore Roosevelt. There were men like Gamaliel Bradford, William Jennings Bryan and William James who believed that Americanism and "imperialism" were incompatible: that government should rest always upon the consent of the governed; but not Senator Albert G. Beveridge, Major-General Leonard Wood, or William Howard Taft. There were business men like Edward A. Filene of Boston who insisted that no profit was to be gained by our ventures into imperialism, but not the Wall Street bankers. There were those like Washington Gladden who insisted that armaments create fear and distrust and provoke wars rather than prevent them, but not the Navy League founded in 1902 and sponsored by Captain Richmond P. Hobson and Theodore Roosevelt. Those who refused to look upon other nations as the presumptive enemies of our own, to agree that armaments were an insurance against war, to regard tariff barriers as the key to general prosperity, to become deliriously intoxicated by the victory over Spain, a third rate power, or by the spectacle of the Navy passing in review—all such were but lonely souls in an atmosphere of glorified patriotism. The paramount idea in the minds of the people was that the American way of life was the best way. They supported unquestioningly the activities of their missionaries in the Fast East. They brushed aside as irrelevant the methods by which the Philippine people were pacified. They never questioned the righteousness of uprooting the Latin culture of dependent peoples to make way for their own. They dug down in their pockets for billions of dollars to vindicate the pagan theory that the way to preserve peace was to prepare for war. They displayed an amazing simplicity of thought in lauding the agreements to humanize war, as if war could ever be humanized. Underlying all else was a very real spirit of humanitarianism and love of peace; but there was an unfortunate lack of realism in both. Most people were deeply concerned over the plight of oppressed peoples in foreign lands and perfectly oblivious to conditions at home. They did not want war, but failed to understand the part that economic rivalry, national bigotry and irresponsible governments play in creating wars. Finally people were too absorbed in making a living and in carrying through the program of domestic reform to be aware of the destiny toward which subtle forces were leading them. The Spanish-American War and Theodore Roosevelt made the United States a world power. The war in Europe which broke out in August, 1914, set the stage for the assumption of world leadership. Failure to anticipate the problems of neutrality drew the nation inevitably into the conflict. The preparedness program made our entry possible. The peace movement, sympathy for oppressed peoples, and cultural affinity with Great Britain made rationalization of our decision less difficult. The intellectual brilliance and emotional fervor of Woodrow Wilson inspired a crusading zeal not equalled since the French Revolution and almost, but not quite, made justice for all men the guiding principle in international relationships.

Peace and Humanitarianism

The peace movement in the United States cannot be used as a criterion by which to measure repugnance for war. Isolation and opposition to large military establishments were deep-rooted and ingrained characteristics of the American temperament. They cannot be interpreted in any other way than a desire to remain out of European embroilments and to refrain from setting up any instruments even remotely threatening to democratic institutions. The desire of the American people was freedom to carry on the ordinary peaceful pursuits of life. It must not be forgotten that, at the turn of the century, the world was in an extraordinarily belligerent mood, while governments were protesting peace and peoples everywhere were bankrupting themselves to pay for armaments, not for the purpose of making war but to keep the peace. That one man believed in the efficacy of arbitration treaties and another in the efficacy of larger navies and armies does not make one less desirous of peace, though perhaps more naïve, than the other. There is no evidence that the vast majority of Americans desired anything else than international peace and good will as a permanent condition. At the same time, they did not rush to the support of the program advanced by the devotees of peace, nor lend financial aid to their organizations. Nor did pacifists succeed in securing the aid of those powerful agencies of propaganda—the press, the churches, and the schools—to the same degree as the advocates of abolition and temperance had done. The fourth agency—the political forums—was all but closed to them because politicians too often were compelled to cater to minority groups such as the Irish-Americans. There was, also, a pronounced strain of emotionalism and humanitarianism in the American temperament. It militated against the continuity of the peace movement, neutralized its appeal. Men were willing to forget their ideals of peace and wage war to abolish slavery. They supported the war against Spanish in order to free the Spanish colonies from the iron hand of tyranny. Few outstanding pacifists were able to remain true to their convictions in either case. Each war revived the martial spirit, temporarily stimulated business, created new vested interests and veterans' organizations, none of them helpful to the cause of peace. The World War was without precedent in that it was waged in the name of permanent peace; it was a war to end wars.

The peace movement in the United States was financed by a few philanthropists of whom Edwin Ginn and Andrew Carnegie were most prominent. Ginn gave one million dollars to finance the World Peace Foundation in 1910. Carnegie was influential in securing the first Pan-American Conference in 1889. He was a tower of strength at the first Hague Conference ten years later. He tried to induce the Emperor of Germany to head an international peace movement. He was President of the New York Peace Society, organized in 1906. He gave enormous sums to the Carnegie Endowment for International Peace and the Church Peace Union. Those pacifists, mostly Quakers and socialists, who pledged themselves never to participate in any war are of little consequence so far as our entry into the World War is concerned. The same may be said of those who were opposed merely to wars of aggression. The real significance of the peace movement in the twentieth century lies in the effort to set up political machinery to prevent wars. Nothing was attempted in the way of disarmament.

The idea of a World Court for the adjudication of international disputes was first advanced by William Ladd in 1840. No practical steps were taken to establish such a court until 1899 when twenty-six nations, at the invitation of the Czar of Russia, sent representatives to a conference at the Hague. There was some suggestion that the conference might undertake to deal with the question of disarmament, but its only practical accomplishment was the creation of a Permanent Court at the Hague for the voluntary arbitration of international disputes. President Roosevelt, after much persuasion by D'Estournelles de Constant, Andrew Carnegie and Richard Bartholdt, called a second conference at the Hague in 1907. Its most important action was an agreement of the leading naval powers to meet at London in 1908. This conference drew up what came to be known as the Declaration of London in 1909. It included, among other things, the agreement that a blockade should not discriminate between nations, nor bar ships from non-blockaded or neutral ports, and that it must be effective to be legal. It classified articles of commerce as contraband and non-contraband, including in the latter things essential to the life of non-combatants. Ratifications of this treaty were never exchanged between the signatories because the British House of Lords refused to agree to many of its commitments. Meanwhile, an effort was made to secure permanent treaties of arbitration between the United States and other nations. This was the particular objective of the Universal Peace Union, founded in 1866. Many men in public life, including President Grant, had spoken in favor of compulsory arbitration of international disputes, without the usual reservation of those involving national honor. An arbitration treaty with Great Britain, however, was rejected by the Senate in 1897 due to the combined opposition of the Irish-Americans, armament manufacturers, western silver advocates, and the jealous champions of the Monroe Doctrine and Senate prestige. In 1904, the Senate again refused to approve the principle of arbitration. Secretary of State Hay had negotiated agreements with several nations, including Great Britain, Germany and France, by which the several nations agreed to submit to the Hague Court all disputes between themselves and the United States except when vital interests, independence or national honor were involved. The Senate so amended the treaties as to cause President Roosevelt to regard them as lowering standards of international relations already established by the State Department and he refused to exchange ratifications. They were revived and approved by the several nations at the instance of Secretary of State Elihu Root in President Taft's Administration.

In 1910, Taft announced that he was in favor of submitting to arbitration even those questions which were regarded as involving national honor. This was the vital point in the whole program of arbitration. To advocate less was to evade the principle, and Taft's pronouncement was a shining example of intellectual honesty and forthrightness so sadly lacking in public discussions of foreign relations. Following Taft's pronouncement, Secretary of State Knox negotiated treaties with Great Britain and France providing for arbitration of all questions, except that those about which there was delicacy, at the request of either nation, should first be surveyed by a commission. By unanimous consent of its membership, the commission could invoke arbitration. In case of disagreement, it could recommend a settlement. Taft favored a treaty of this kind with Japan. The treaties were supported by leading European statesmen and by men and women from all walks of life in the United States. Taft's political fortunes were at low ebb at the time and all his efforts to secure ratification by the Senate were in vain against the combined hostility of Theodore Roosevelt, the German- and Irish-Americans, and the Midwestern isolationists.

The inauguration of Woodrow Wilson in 1913 gave new life to the peace movement. In the first place, he led the forces of domestic reform to new achievements in social and economic change. The emotional fervor of the reform movement, which placed new values on human life, reached its peak between 1913 and 1917, and we entered the war at a time when it was at a point of hyper-tension. In the second place, Wilson himself was a member of the American Peace Society and he appointed a devotee of peace, William Jennings Bryan, to the position of Secretary of State. Bryan was the leading champion of the idea that international disputes could be settled without war if a crisis could be delayed until a thorough investigation by an impartial commission had been made and the force of public opinion allowed to operate. He proceeded, with the full knowledge and approval of the Senate Foreign Relations Committee, to negotiate treaties with thirty nations, not including Germany, Austria, Mexico and Japan, which provided for the submission of all questions in dispute, without exceptions, to investigating commissions. There was to be no resort to war nor increase in armaments during the deliberations of the commissions. The treaties were ratified by the Senate without opposition. Congress went still further in the direction of international good-will when it repealed (1914) the Panama Canal Tolls Act of 1912. This act had exempted American vessels engaged in coastwise trade from the payment of tolls. Great Britain protested the exemption as a violation of the Hay-Pauncefote Treaty, and the action of Congress did much to promote friendly relations between the two nations. On the other hand, Congress refused to ratify a treaty negotiated by Bryan with Colombia because it included an expression of "regret that anything should have occurred to interrupt or mar" friendly relations between the two nations. This language was thought to be a reflection upon the procedure of President Roosevelt, and it was not until 1921 that a somewhat differently worded treaty was ratified.

The Great Decision

The search by historians for the causes of the World War and our entry into it probably will continue for many decades. The important point is not what historians believe now or will come to believe were its causes, but what the people of the

United States believed at the time. No people could have made so momentous a decision without deep convictions. Four stand out most prominently: (1) that the War represented a failure of political institutions, particularly of secret diplomacy; (2) that the piling up of armaments had created mutual distrust, powerful interests with a stake in war, arrogance and sharp practices in foreign relations; (3) that the success of the central powers—Germany, Austria and Turkey—would constitute a threat to democratic institutions everywhere; and (4) that the liberation of millions of oppressed peoples in Central and Eastern Europe depended upon an Allied victory. There was wide discussion of the struggle for colonies, markets and world trade. The latent devotion of millions of people to the land of their birth was aroused by the conflict. But there never was a remote possibility that the United States would go into the war on the side of the Central Powers. The question was not between assistance to one side or the other, but (1) between the two strong traditions of isolation and humanitarianism and (2) between the theory that the United States could best aid in achieving a lasting peace for all nations by isolation and that it could best do so by international cooperation.

Isolation soon became an impossibility, because little thought had been given to the problems of neutrality created by modern warfare. The Government was forced to rely upon the established principles of international law because Great Britain refused to abide by the Declaration of London and, in several important instances, the old rules were inapplicable to new conditions. The severity of the conflict led to the establishment of what amounted to totalitarian states by all of the belligerents. Distinctions between combatants and non-combatants were narrowly restricted. Conscription of man power and material resources shattered the old conceptions of contraband of war. Blockades of enemy ports were rendered ineffective by the rapid transportation of supplies through neutral countries. The old rules of search and seizure were rendered obsolete by the advent of submarines. Great Britain established her supremacy on the high seas and then, March 11, 1915, announced a blockade of German ports. Unwilling to risk patrolling the North Sea ports and unable to control the Baltic Sea, she closed the North Sea to normal traffic by establishing a patrol between Scotland and Norway and in the English Channel. She then rationed the neutral countries of Northern Europe on the basis of peace-time imports, and licensed neutral traders with these nations to prevent supplies from reaching Germany. Successive Orders in Council extended the list of contraband until virtually all commodities were included. Unable to stop vessels and search them on the high seas because of submarines, she forced them to call at British ports for inspection. She interfered with the mails. She forbade export from Germany to the United States of items essential to industry and even to health. In short, freedom of the seas as that term was understood in the United States and used in international law succumbed to the stern necessities of a war for national survival.

The United States Government protested vigorously against these annoyances to trade and violations of neutral rights, but without avail. The natural sympathies of the American people were with the Allied cause. From the very beginning of the conflict, the Carnegie Endowment had taken the attitude that there could be no permanent peace in the world until Germany was defeated. Secretary of State Bryan was unwilling to risk war with either side by too vigorous defense of neutral rights. His successor, Robert Lansing, was convinced that the Allied cause was the cause of democracy. Walter Hines Page, Ambassador to Great Britain, and Colonel Edward M. House, Wilson's roving Ambassador to Europe, were both engaged in softening the force of the State Department's protests. Ambassador Robert Herrick had endeared himself to the French people at the outbreak of the war. However much the Allied governments might have interfered with trade and modified the rules of international law to fit the new conditions, they never needlessly endangered the lives of American citizens. Nor did Great Britain engage in acrimonious debate with the State Department, being content with a categorical statement of her position or preferring to delay answering our protests until new situations relieved the tension. Moreover, the natural sympathies of the American people were re-enforced by their economic interests. Foreign trade grew rapidly as the warring nations, marshaling all resources for war, relinquished their foreign markets and the Allies turned to the United States for still greater supplies of war materials and foodstuffs. Losses incurred by American traders because of the blockade and new rules of search were small indeed compared to the profits from Allied trade, a situation which did much to ease the demands for redress. American securities held abroad and then gold were used for purchases in this country. Private loans, foreign bond flotations and, after we entered the war, government loans made possible a demand which taxed the productive capacity of the United States and gave it the greatest peace time prosperity in history. Foreign trade reached such proportions that Congress set up a United States Shipping Board in September, 1916, and embarked upon a program of acquiring a government-owned merchant marine. J. P. Morgan and Company acted as the agent for Great Britain, France and Russia, purchasing their supplies, selling their bonds and short term notes and furnishing needed private credits. Bonds worth more than $1,500,000,000 were sold by the Allied governments in this country before we entered the war. The Federal Reserve Board finally became concerned about the supply of available credit for domestic use and, November 27, 1916, cautioned member banks against further purchases. Their supply of credit for further purchases was dangerously low when the United States entered the war.

Germany, reluctant to risk a decisive naval battle, permitted her merchant marine to be swept from the seas and then sought to destroy British morale by unrestricted submarine warfare. The waters about the British Isles were declared a war zone and all merchant vessels entering them were marked for destruction. Submarines, as Germany insisted upon using them, were in a class with the tomahawk and stiletto, a fit companion weapon to poison gas which the Germans also introduced into the war. International law did not recognize the mode of warfare required by the very nature of the submarine. It would not have made much difference in any case. They had to strike without warning. They could not remove crews or passengers from the vessels they destroyed. They could make no distinction between combatants and non-combatants. The people of the United States simply refused to condone such barbarism. At a time when the reform movement was placing increasing emphasis upon human rights as opposed to property rights, they made a sharp distinction between British and German violations of the rules of international law. The submarine warfare was not conducive, either, to a critical examination of reported German atrocities. British propaganda, including lies manufactured out of whole cloth, continued unchecked and unchallenged.

Germany's submarine campaign began on February 18, 1915, with the announcement that the waters about the British Isles were a war zone in which all enemy merchant vessels would be subject to destruction at sight. Citizens and vessels of neutral nations were to enter this zone at their own risk. President Wilson warned Germany, February 24, that she would be held to "strict accountability" for any losses of American vessels or lives. Some American lives were lost when the British vessel *Falaba* was sunk on March 28 and the American vessel *Gulflight* was torpedoed on May 1 but, before action could be taken, the large British passenger and merchant vessel *Lusitania* was sent to the bottom with the loss of more than 1100 lives, including 124 Americans, on May 7. There would have been very little opposition to a declaration of war at that moment, in spite of the fact that the *Lusitania* was armed and carrying contraband. Within a week, President Wilson sent his first *Lusitania* note to the German government. He called their attention to the stupidly irregular procedure of warning the American people through the newspapers that the vessel would be sunk, and announced as unacceptable the idea that warning of an "unlawful and inhumane act" about to be committed was an excuse or "abatement of the responsibility" for it. Speaking of the use of submarines, he said: "Objection to their present method of attack against the trade of their enemies lies in the practical impossibility of employing submarines in the destruction of commerce without disregarding those rules of fairness, reason, justice, and humanity which all modern opinion regards as imperative. . . . Manifestly submarines can not be used against merchantmen, as the last few weeks have shown, without an inevitable violation of many sacred principles of justice and humanity."

A series of notes followed the first without any admission by Germany that the sinking had been an illegal act; but she promised to sink no more vessels without warning and providing for the safety of non-combatants. Secretary of State Bryan resigned rather than sign the second note and was replaced by Robert Lansing. Bryan then threw his support to those Congressmen who were attempting to preserve the neutrality of the United States in a different way, chief among them being Horace Towner of Iowa, Charles A. Lindbergh of Minnesota, and Senators Robert La Follette of Wisconsin, Hitchcock of Nebraska and Bartholdt of Missouri. They insisted (1) that continued trade with and loans to the Allies would inevitably drag us into the war; and (2) that citizens of the United States should be refused permission to travel on armed merchant or passenger vessels. The latter thesis was presented to Congress in the form of the Gore-McLemore resolution. The administration forces were thrown against its adoption. President Wilson's position, as announced in a letter to Senator Stone, February 24, 1916, was that neither Germany nor any other nation was justified in setting aside the restraints agreed upon by civilized nations in mitigation of the horrors of war; that the United States could not maintain her dignity among the nations of the world much less her position as a sovereign power if she failed to protect the rights of her citizens; and that, if she receded from her position in this instance, all the principles of international law would be weakened, perhaps destroyed.

Conversations with Germany were renewed again when the French liner *Sussex* was sunk on March 24, 1916. President Wilson's note of April 19 stated very plainly that the United States had accepted previous explanations in good faith in the hope that it would "be possible for the German Government so to order and control the acts of its naval Commanders as to square its policy with the principles of humanity as embodied in the law of nations." Since the German government had failed to accomplish this, the United States must revert to its former conclusions "that the use of submarines for the destruction of an enemy's commerce is, of necessity, because of the very methods of attack which their employment of course involves, incompatible with the principles of humanity, the long-established and incontrovertible rights of neutrals, and the sacred immunities of non-combatants." He further threatened immediate severance of diplomatic relations unless Germany abandoned unrestricted submarine warfare. She promised to do so, May 4, but reserved to herself "complete liberty of decision" unless Great Britain were compelled to observe the rules of international law.

Meanwhile, an intensive preparedness campaign and a new peace program had been launched in the United States in the midst of the presidential campaign. The agitation for a stronger army and navy was strongly supported by men like Theodore Roosevelt, Major-General Leonard Wood and Samuel Gompers, and there were ample subsidies for the National Security League from the munitions interests and financiers. Fear of a victorious Germany, increasing concern over radical labor activities, and a desire to discipline the youth of the country were advanced as arguments by the sponsors. Samuel Gompers endorsed the program early in the war period, President Wilson in December, 1915. William Jennings Bryan, Henry Ford and Jane Addams, the Debs Socialists and the Industrial Workers of the World were among the opposition. In June, 1916,

Congress increased the size of the navy and national army, brought the state militia under national control, provided for the training of civilians and students, and authorized a Council of National Defense for the mobilization of war time industry.

The new peace program was the work of the League to Enforce Peace and embraced the plan of Anna B. Eckstein of Boston for a League of Nations to enforce peace with economic boycotts and a court of arbitration. The idea was supported from the beginning by Andrew Carnegie, Theodore Roosevelt, Hamilton Holt and William Howard Taft. President Wilson appropriated the idea in May, 1916, and by broad resolution of Congress in August of that year the President was authorized to call an international conference at the conclusion of the war for its consideration. There was a general discussion of what should constitute a just peace at this time and, eventually, the plan won the support of Bryan. Bryan and Wilson had parted company over the question of keeping Americans out of the war zone. Bryan was, at that time, in favor of resorting to a popular referendum before entering the war. The great question in the late summer of 1916 and the following winter was whether permanent peace could better be secured by our going into the war or remaining out of it. Germany, herself, left the country little choice in the end. The presidential election did not hinge on the war issue. The Republican candidate, Charles E. Hughes, was defeated because neither he nor his party would endorse or offer a substitute for the social and economic reform program. The independent voters, therefore, supported Wilson. The Republicans' disparagements of Wilson's speeches as "shifty expedients" may have won some votes and lost others. If Wilson received votes in the Middle West because "he kept us out of war," he lost the German-American vote because of the manner in which he had accomplished it. But the German government incorrectly interpreted the reelection of Wilson as a mandate to remain neutral.

Having canvassed the several warring nations as to their war aims, President Wilson appeared before the Senate, January 22,

1917, with his Peace without Victory address. Beginning with the thesis that the United States was directly concerned with the problems of ultimate and permanent peace, he stated the conditions on which the United States would participate in the postwar deliberations and "add their authority and their power to the authority and force of other nations to guarantee peace and justice throughout the world . . . the conditions upon which it [the Government] would feel justified in asking our people to approve its formal and solemn adherence to a League for Peace." He mentioned specifically equality of rights between nations irrespective of size; independence for subject peoples such as Poland; an outlet to the seas, the highways of world commerce, for all large nations; absolute freedom of the seas; and limitation of armaments. In general terms, he implied that responsible governments must be established and non-aggression policies must be adopted. That part of the address which caused the most comment was his statement that the peace must be without victory: "Victory would mean peace forced upon the loser, a victor's terms imposed upon the vanquished. It would be accepted in humiliation, under duress, at an intolerable sacrifice, and would leave a sting, a resentment, a bitter memory upon which terms of peace would rest, not permanently, but only as upon quicksand. Only a peace between equals can last." These were, substantially, the objectives of the American people when they finally entered the war. That they were to be lost sight of, bartered away, and rise again as a bitter memory, of course no one could then perceive.

Three days previously, the German Foreign Minister had written to the German Minister in Mexico that the German government would resume unrestricted submarine warfare on February 1. Germany proposed, if the United States entered the war, an alliance with Mexico by which that nation was to receive as compensation her lost provinces of New Mexico, Texas and Arizona. The German Minister was also instructed to promote an alliance with Japan. The contents of the dispatch were delivered to the American government by the British

Intelligence Service on February 26 and promptly published. Meanwhile, the German government had notified the United States of its intention to resume submarine activities and Ambassador Bernstorff had been given his passports on February 3. Three American ships were sunk shortly afterward. Congress was called into extraordinary session and President Wilson delivered his war message in person on April 2, 1917. The message belongs among the greatest of our state papers. Careful to make a distinction between the German people and the German government, he spoke of the latter as "an irresponsible government which had thrown aside all considerations of humanity and of right and is running amuck." Speaking of America's war aims, he said: "The world must be made safe for democracy. Its peace must be planted upon the tested foundations of political liberty. We have no selfish ends to serve. We desire no conquests, no dominion. We seek no indemnities for ourselves, no material compensation for the sacrifices we shall freely make. We are but one of the champions of the rights of mankind. We shall be satisfied when those rights have been made as secure as the faith and the freedom of nations can make them." Touching but briefly the possibilities of a just peace, he said, "We shall fight for the things which we have always carried nearest our hearts, for democracy, for the right of those who submit to authority to have a voice in their own Governments, for the rights and liberties of small nations, for a universal dominion of right—by such a concert of free people as shall bring peace and safety to all nations and make the world itself at last free." It is no exaggeration to say that these words lifted Wilson to a position of moral leadership among the war-weary peoples of the earth.

No nation had ever before undertaken such an enterprise as the United States entered upon when, four days later, Congress declared war upon Germany: a war to end wars. The time is past when we can longer afford to ignore the fact that in winning the war we lost the peace, and the peace—a lasting, enduring peace of justice for all peoples—was the reason for our appeal to arms. It has been customary to blame the failure to achieve a lasting peace settlement upon the secret treaties, grasping selfishness and vindictiveness of the European powers. They were contributing factors, of course, but that explanation is too self-satisfying, too much of a rationalization of our own action. The war had brought more people in the world into a receptive mood for the sort of program we had conceived than probably will be true again for generations. We had the power to dictate a peace in 1917, but not two years later and the fault was our own. We proved incapable of going to war and retaining the dispassionate attitude which the Wilson peace program demanded. Moreover, we ignored too many fundamental principles of Americanism in our haste to throw the full force of the nation's strength into the contest. The declaration of war was followed immediately by an unprecedented regimentation of man-power, industry, transportation and public opinion. The resulting distrust, hatred and fear destroyed the fine idealism in which the crusade was conceived.

National Regimentation

The Administration insisted upon conscription of man power and Congress passed a Selective Service Act on May 18, 1917. It was the first radical departure from precedent in that it empowered the President to select for military service one million men between the ages of 21 and 30, with exemptions for clergymen, objectors on religious grounds and defectives, and with deferred status for persons engaged in public service and in industries essential to war, including agriculture. The act also increased the strength of the National Guard and the Regular Army to 750,000. 9,586,000 young men were enrolled on June 5, 1917, approximately 1,000,000 more on June 5, 1918, and 13,000,000 between the ages of 18 and 45 in September, 1918. Five hundred thousand of the first registrants were called into service on July 20, 1917, and nearly 3,000,000 before the close of the war. The three units of the military forces were kept separate, consisting of (1) seventeen divisions of National Guard

(26-42); (2) eighteen divisions of conscripts, known as the National Army (76-93); and (3) twenty divisions of the Regular Army (1-20). All of the National Guard divisions, all but one division of the National Army, and eight divisions of the Regular Army were sent to France. They were trained in thirty-two hastily constructed camps, each equipped to accommodate between 40,000 and 50,000 men. Many veteran French and British officers were sent to assist in the training. Five hundred thousand troops were in France at the end of the first year and about four times that number before the Armistice was signed in November, 1918. No one who went up the Seine with the first handful of untrained men on May 25, 1917, could fail to understand what the mere sight of American troops meant to the drooping spirits of the French people. Several hospital units were hastily organized within a few days after war was declared, rushed to England and then on to various parts of the British lines in France for no other reason than the psychological effect upon the British and French people. American destroyers were already in British waters to convoy them through the submarine zone. The Commander-in-Chief of the American Expeditionary Force, General John J. Pershing, followed shortly afterward, arriving in London June 9 and in Paris June 13. From that time on, detachments of troops from every department of the Army moved in ever increasing numbers into the war zone. They were brigaded with the French and British troops all through the winter of 1917-1918. The United States was not prepared to equip them properly for modern warfare and relied heavily upon the British and French for artillery, machine guns and, particularly, airplanes. Nor were we prepared to transport troops to France, Great Britain carrying no less than one-half of our army across the Atlantic.

Having made a feeble gesture at regimenting man power in such way as to place every individual in the position, civil and military, for which he was best equipped, the government next undertook to regiment the economic life of the nation under six regulatory agencies: the War Industries Board, the War Trade Board, the Food Administration, the Fuel Administration, the Railroad Administration and the National War Labor Board. These agencies were created to increase production and reduce domestic consumption, to insure maximum efficiency in transportation, and to prevent disputes between capital and labor from interfering with the smooth functioning of the industrial process. The aggregate powers of these several boards and administrators constituted an economic dictatorship. Prices of many commodities, including steel, aluminum, copper, cement, lumber, wheat and sugar, were fixed. Products were standardized. Sub-marginal mines were opened and sub-marginal land cultivated. No new industrial enterprise could be initiated without government consent. Processors were dependent upon the good-will of bureaucrats for raw materials, for priorities in shipment and for export permits. The housewife was no less irritated by the rationing of grocers and butchers and the assumed importance of the local dispensers of sugars. Meatless and wheatless days and fuelless Sundays were borne without protest or even with zealous show of patriotism, but in the hearts of millions was harbored a dull resentment against the attempt to put everyone in leading strings.

The War Industries Board originated as a Committee of the Council of National Defense and was created a separate agency by executive order on July 8, 1917. Its chief members were Bernard M. Baruch, Judge Robert S. Brookings and Robert S. Lovett. It maintained strict control of all manufacturing and mining and approved all purchases by the United States and foreign governments. The War Trade Board, under the chairmanship of Vance C. McCormick, was empowered to regulate all exports and deny licenses to trade to any firm even remotely connected with German and Austrian commerce, to refuse permission for the export of certain commodities, and to allot shipping space to exporters. The Food Administration Board, supervised by Herbert Hoover, exercised the same powers over the production and consumption of foodstuffs as the War Industries Board over manufacturing. The task was infinitely more difficult because of the tremendous number of units of production and total lack of cooperative enterprises. Nevertheless, through the control of exports, purchases and shipping, it did bring the production and distribution of agricultural products under control. Six months after wheat was selling for $3.45 a bushel in May, 1917, it set a price of $2.20 for the 1917 crop, increased wheat acreage from 45,000,000 in 1917 to nearly 76,000,000 in 1919, and set in motion an amazing voluntary conservation program in the use of foodstuffs, particularly of bread and meat. The Fuel Administration, headed by Harry A. Garfield, closed factories at will to conserve fuel, introduced daylight saving time and encouraged the expansion of the coal industry into what were previously regarded as sub-marginal deposits. The Railroad Administration was created in December, 1917, and placed under the supervision of Secretary of the Treasury William G. McAdoo. Inland water transportation and express companies were also brought under the same control. They were operated as a single unit with little thought for improvements, profits or even replacements except as required by the single objective of quick and adequate transportation of the sinews of war.

The character of the war was such that most industries shared in the orders for war supplies. Others profited from the widespread prosperity created by the prodigious spending of our own and foreign governments between 1914 and 1919. Men became wealthy over night. Property values soared, especially those of agricultural lands. The cost of living rose steadily. Labor was in a strategic position during those years. Immigration from Europe virtually ceased at the outbreak of the war. Production speeded up to supply the demands of the warring nations. The labor supply was further reduced by our entry into the war and the operations of the draft. A friendly administration was in power at Washington. Organized labor took advantage of conditions to increase its membership from 2,000,000 in 1913 to nearly 3,000,000 at the end of the war. Huge profits from the manufacture of war supplies made possible an increase in wages even more rapid than the increase in living costs. But the gains of labor were not made easily. The friendliness of the Wilson Administration for organized labor provoked stubborn opposition from capital. Fresh labor supplies were tapped in the agricultural South and violence was resorted to in the West against the Industrial Workers of the World. Industrial warfare was general during 1916 and 1917. The Wilson Administration was faced with the necessity of keeping production at a maximum and, to its everlasting credit, it refused to use its war powers to labor's disadvantage. An advisory council was given to the Secretary of Labor and a War Labor Conference Board was established in the winter of 1917-1918. Finally a National War Labor Board was created by executive order on April 8, 1918. The formulation of labor policies was largely the work of Felix Frankfurter and the direction of the War Labor Board was assigned to Ex-President William H. Taft and Frank P. Walsh. The purpose of this machinery was to settle by mediation and conciliation every controversy which might arise between employers and employees in essential war industries and related fields. This was to be done through mediation committees in local communities which were given power to summon all parties for a hearing and refer questions it failed to settle to the National Board. This Board, in such instances, was to choose an arbiter by unanimous vote or by lot from ten disinterested persons nominated by the President of the United States. The machinery of the Department of Labor was placed at the disposal of the Board, and the Secretary of that Department or either party to a controversy might bring a case to the attention of the Board. All committees appointed by the Board were to have equal representation from capital and labor. The principles laid down by law were as follows: (1) strikes and lockouts were banned for the duration of the war; (2) the right of collective bargaining was affirmed and could not be denied; (3) employees could not be discharged for union activities; (4) unions were forbidden to coerce non-union workers or employers; (5) standards of work and wages established by unions must be maintained where already existing; (6) equal pay for men and women in the same work was required; (7) existing eight-hour day agreements were to be continued and all other cases determined on the basis of governmental requirements and the best interests of the employees; (8) a national card index of available skilled labor was to be prepared by the Department of Labor; and (9) wages were to be maintained on a level insuring "health and reasonable comfort" to the worker's family.

The cost of the war amounted to $32,000,000,000. Nearly $1,000,000,000 was loaned to the allied nations within six months after our declaration of war and a total of $10,338,-000,000 went for war and rehabilitation purposes to the Allies and to the newly created states of eastern Europe after the war. Great Britain borrowed $4,277,000,000; France, $3,404,-000,000; Italy, $1,648,000,000; Belgium, $379,000,000; and Russia, $192,000,000. Of the other nations, Poland received $159,000,000; Czechoslovakia, $92,000,000; Jugoslavia, $52,-000,000; Austria, $24,000,000; Esthonia, $14,000,000; Armenia, $12,000,000; Latvia and Lithuania each $5,000,000; and Hungary, $1,685,000. Practically all of this money was advanced in the form of credit for the purchase of foodstuffs and supplies in the United States. The government secured approximately the amount loaned to these nations, or one-third the total expenditures of the war period, from taxes, largely income taxes on individuals and corporations, excess profits taxes, and excise taxes on telegraph and telephone messages, railroad and theater tickets, etc. The larger part, of course, came from income taxes which amounted to three billion dollars in the fiscal year 1917-1918. Twenty and one-half billion dollars, about the cost of our own war establishment, was secured by the sale of Liberty Loan Bonds, Victory Loan Bonds and War Savings Certificates. The amounts, dates and interest rates of these bond issues were as follows:

First Liberty Loan—June, 1917—3½%—$2,000,000,000
Second Liberty Loan—November, 1917—4%—$3,800,000,000
Third Liberty Loan—May, 1918—4¼%—$4,200,000,000
Fourth Liberty Loan—October, 1918—4¼%—$6,000,000,000
Victory Loan—April, 1919—4¾%—$4,500,000,000

The public had no more choice about buying bonds than the soldiers had about buying government insurance. The government did not directly coerce the purchase of its securities, but it worked the people into such a frenzy of patriotic hysteria that few people dared risk the disfavor of their neighbors by not purchasing irrespective of their ability to do so. Not only did the people respond to the government's appeal for funds, they supported most magnanimously such agencies of relief as the American Red Cross, the Young Men's Christian Association and the Salvation Army as well as the several religious organizations for soldiers' aid.

The United States Shipping Board, created in September before war was declared, set up an Emergency Fleet Corporation with General George W. Goethals as its chairman. It started out with a fund of fifty million dollars to acquire ships by purchase, charter and construction. Goethals and William Densman, Chairman of the Shipping Board, soon disagreed and were replaced by Charles M. Schwab and Edward M. Hurley. Shipyards were built and a huge construction program was initiated. Ships were purchased from other nations and the interned German ships were reconditioned. From all sources, the Shipping Board assembled ten million tons of shipping before the Armistice. Its efforts enabled the government to carry about half of its own troops and all supplies to France and to return them all to the United States in record time after the war.

More important than all of these activities, over the long view, was the government's zealous effort to regiment public opinion. On April 14, 1917, George Creel was placed in charge of a Committee on Public Information. The work of this agency was little short of sensational. Millions of pamphlets were distributed. Seventy-five thousand speakers were engaged to promote the sale of bonds and stimulate patriotism. The foreign language press was censored and other newspapers persuaded to establish their own censorship. Every conceivable channel for the dissemination of propaganda in the country was utilized from motion pictures to stereopticon slides and foreign missions were sent out to convert the world to America's war for peace program. When Creel's work was finished every one confidently expected that a new world order was in the making and the repercussions which followed their disillusionment continued to reverberate throughout the world for many years. In the United States, the result was equally tragic. Carried away by the war hysteria, Congress passed the Espionage Act of June 15, 1917, and amended it with the Sedition Act of May 6, 1918, sweeping away at one stroke the most cherished principles of the American people: freedom of speech and of the press under all circumstances.

When Woodrow Wilson delivered his war message to Congress, he said: "We act without animus, not in enmity toward a people . . . but only in armed opposition to an irresponsible government which has thrown aside all considerations of humanity and of right and is running amuck." Wilson continued to differentiate between that government and the German people; but the people of this country made no such distinction. They came to hate the German people as well as their government; they permitted suspicion to supplant facts in judging disloyalty, hurling bitter terms of denunciation at citizens of foreign birth and aliens; they discharged such persons from positions of honorable employment which they had long filled; they sought to ban the study of the German language and German literature from the schools by legislation, all but destroying it through force of public opinion; they inaugurated a widespread witch-hunt in the public schools, colleges and universities in an effort to crush every one who was pacifically inclined or internationally minded; they found it impossible to go to war and remain true to their traditions of justice and tolerance.

It is important to remember that war legislation set up a vast centralized control of nearly every phase of activity and, especially, that the Selective Service Acts made every man between the ages of eighteen and forty-five a potential member of the armed forces. An individual, therefore, could scarcely speak, write or print anything, however selected his audiences, without influencing the armed forces. Whether the memory of Civil War dissent, the difficulties already experienced by the Allied governments, or Wilson's personal fear of criticism was responsible for federal legislation is a matter of conjecture. There are strong reasons for believing that it was the latter. A war time President usually gets the type of legislation he desires from Congress. The original Espionage Act was an administration measure and was modified only after a bitter attack upon it by the press and a small group of Senators led by Borah. Moreover, Wilson said: "If there should be disloyalty, it will be dealt with with a firm hand of stern repression." The Espionage Act was introduced shortly after the declaration of war and, certainly, was not a response to popular demand. It was followed, in point of time, by the activities of the Committee on Public Information. Then came the many repressive state statutes from one of which, that of Montana, the language was taken for the amendment to the Espionage Act, popularly known as the Sedition Act of May 16, 1918. It was under the original Espionage Act, however, that most of the government prosecutions were conducted. Wilson rose to such heights of leadership, not of power alone, that he could have done much to modify the popular attitude had he chosen to do so.

The Committee on Public Information was designed to perform the two-fold function of promoting publicity and invoking censorship. It established precedents in disseminating propaganda which were followed up with equal fervor and small regard for the truth by a host of self-anointed patriots and patriotic societies. Some stories, such as the mutilation of Belgian babies and soap-making from the cadavers of their soldiers fallen in battle by the Germans, emanated from foreign propaganda machines. A thousand others, manufactured out of whole cloth by suspicious individuals alarmed at unusual but harmless incidents, set the people everlastingly to suspecting every one of subversive activities. The number of actual spies thus apprehended was relatively so small that failure to discover them probably would not have resulted in any serious consequences. The historical importance of the whole phenomenon does not lie in the number of guilty individuals caught, nor in the inconvenience, injustices and injuries inflicted upon unfortunate innocents, deplorable as such incidents were. It lies in the self-imposed restraints of free discussion and rational criticism through fear by every one. It lies, too, in the fact that intolerance, which is a vicious disease, carried over into the post-war period to follow the psychopathic trail into many phases of social and economic life. If there is one fact clearly revealed by the history of the abolition movement, the Civil War and the reform movement, it is that the right of free discussion was an unquestioned principle of American life. We emerged from the war with the right of the individual to advocate publicly and freely whatever ideas he might have little more than a hollow pretense.

The Espionage Act of June 15, 1917, imposed a maximum penalty of $10,000 fine and twenty years imprisonment upon any one who interfered with the operations of the draft, made false statements with intent to retard the success of the armed forces, or attempted to incite disloyalty. It was amended drastically, May 16, 1918, to include any one who discouraged the sale of government bonds; obstructed the making of loans by or to the United States; incited insubordination, disloyalty, or mutiny; uttered, printed, wrote or published any "disloyal, profane, scurrilous or abusive language about the form of government of the United States," constitution, armed forces, or uniform; issued language intended to bring them into "contempt, scorn, contumely or disrepute"; discouraged production of war necessities; or taught, defended, or suggested the doing of any of these things.

These acts gave the Postmaster-General power to exclude from the mails not only anything which in his sole judgment violated the prohibitions but to deny the offender all use of the postal service for any purpose whatsoever. Postmaster Burleson did exercise the power thus conferred upon him to the extreme limit, excluding from the mails *The Masses* edited by Max Eastman, the *Milwaukee Leader* edited by Victor L. Berger, an issue of the *Nation* and many books and pamphlets, including Thorstein Veblen's *Imperial Germany and the Industrial Revolution.* The Department of Justice, under the control of A. Mitchell Palmer, ably assisted by courts and juries, sent nearly two thousand men and women to prison for terms ranging up to twenty years, including Eugene V. Debs, Victor L. Berger and William D. Haywood. Several aspects of the trials and convictions under these war-time statutes are significant. The courts gave a broad construction to the law, holding all utterances to be in violation which had a tendency to do the things prohibited. Jury trial failed to safeguard the traditional principle of freedom of speech because of the widespread determination to suppress dissent. The Department of Justice and the Post Office, rather than Congress and President Wilson, were responsible for converting the law into an instrument for the persecution of pacifists and economic dissenters. It was the first establishment of political crimes in a century of national development. The defense that government severity was necessary to forestall mob actions and the expressed fear of radical influence upon the Negro were pregnant with meaning for the future.

The extreme penalties provided in the law and the militant activities of the enforcement agencies thwarted all rational consideration of public questions. There could be no free discussion of fiscal policies with respect to taxation, bond issues, or war loans to the allies; of the relative merits of conscription and volunteer enlistments; of mistaken administration policies touching upon neutrality; of the economic and imperialistic basis of Allied war aims; of profiteering and official corruption; or of the many other issues about which there are always honest differences of opinion and which can be approached intelligently only after free interchange of opinions. Many of these issues which carried over to test the wisdom of the post-war generation were far more perplexing than they necessarily would have been had the government been satisfied with an almost unanimous support of the people and not attempted to create an artificial unanimity of opinion. The period presents the unique spectacle of a nation, whose President was the recognized champion of human rights everywhere, sending men to prison for twenty years whose humanitarianism was no less sincere, but whose formula for reaching the millennium differed from the prevailing one.

War at the Front

The American Army was assigned the southern sector of the war zone with General Pershing's headquarters at Chaumont, supply headquarters at Tours and the principal seaports at Brest, Saint-Nazaire and Bordeaux. Railway lines, motor transport roads, telegraph and telephone lines were constructed from the ports of debarkation to the front lines and connecting the dozens of training camps, storage depots and hospitals within the triangle from Le Havre to Chaumont to Bordeaux. The construction of docks, barracks, warehouses, recreation centers, etc., went on unceasingly until the Armistice. Millions of tons of equipment, food, munitions and other supplies including railway rolling stock and motor trucks had to be transported through the submarine zone. So efficiently did the navy perform its services that the loss was almost negligible. The navy was not called upon to participate in any major engagements but effectively protected American convoys, engaged in planting mines and destroying submarines. Its presence may have been the deciding factor in the decision of the German government not to risk a decisive naval engagement. It was almost a year before American troops in any numbers participated in actual fighting and not until August, 1918, that a separate American Army was created. Until that time, detachments were brigaded with British and French troops. Beginning in October, 1917, however, one division after another entered the lines on the more quiet southern sector. The final German offensive began on March 21, 1918, and finally ended on July 18. These four months were critical. Germany had transferred her finest troops to the western front, marshaled all her resources and was making a desperate bid for victory before the American Army could be assembled. The stimulating effect of our entry into the war was wearing off and the morale of the British troops particularly was reaching a new low point as the weary months of the winter dragged on without hope of immediate victory. The German attack was launched viciously and at the proper psychological moment to break the British lines. It almost succeeded in doing so, giving the Allied command some anxious hours until fresh support could be rushed into the breach. In desperation, American troops were rushed to critical points all along the line to the north, and plans for the immediate formation of an American Army appeared to be doomed. More important still was the decision of the Allied governments to surrender all differences among themselves and place their armies under the absolute authority of a supreme command. The French General Foch was chosen for the post and Foch consented to the American demands for united forces in their own section of the line. While this was being accomplished and during the German offensive, American troops engaged in strenuous fighting in the battles of the Aisne, Noyon-Montdidier, and Champagne-Marne.

The Allied counter-offensive began on July 18. It was the last drive of the war, ending with the signing of the Armistice on November 11, 1918. This was the ninety day period in which the combined activities of the American Army, numbering at the last more than a million men, and the diplomatic representations of President Wilson destroyed the German morale and brought the war to a close. Between July 18 and

August 6, an American force of about 250,000 men, cooperating with the French Army, regained the ground previously lost between Rheims and Soissons and straightened out the salient which, at its farthest point, included Château-Thierry. Two days later, the British began an attack which did not cease until November 11 on the Somme east of Amiens. Ten days later (August 18), the French and American armies resumed their attack on the Oise-Aisne line between Rheims and Soissons and, the following day, the British and Belgians drove south and east from Ypres on a line toward Brussels. These concerted and continuous attacks made the shifting of troops by the German command precarious business and set the stage for the final drive of the full American Army through the almost impenetrable Argonne Forest to Sedan. The St. Mihiel salient was straightened out between September 12 and 16 and, on September 20, the drive began north of Verdun. The Germans sent their finest troop to stay the American advance but without success. It was the beginning of the end for Germany because that sector of the line protected the iron mines of Lorraine and the central transportation center at Sedan. The British Army broke through into Belgium and the American Army pushed forward to cut the German line of communications at Sedan.

German Capitulation

The disintegration of the German Empire began with the failure of the last German offensive. Had the government not taken advantage of the Wilson peace program and sued for peace, the Allied armies would have driven straight to Berlin. Knowing that utter defeat was near and unwilling to risk the havoc of an invasion, the Germans hastened to capitulate before the armies reached the frontier. A parliamentary form of government was set up under the Chancellorship of Prince Max of Baden. President Wilson was notified on October 5 of their willingness to make peace on the basis of the Fourteen Points.

President Wilson had elaborated from time to time upon the theme of his war message to Congress. The more important of these pronouncements were an address at Washington, June 14, 1917, and his messages to Congress, December 4, 1917, and January 8, 1918. They contained the American program for a just and lasting peace. Secret treaties, tariffs and armaments were to be renounced. Freedom of the seas and self-determination for all subject peoples, particularly in the Turkish and Austro-Hungarian empires, were to be guaranteed. Alsace-Lorraine was to be restored to France. Belgium was to be evacuated and restored as a "healing act" without which "the whole structure and validity of international law is forever impaired." Russia was to be evacuated and all questions touching that nation settled in such manner as would obtain for her "an unhampered and unembarrassed opportunity for the independent determination of her own political development . . . under institutions of her own choosing." An independent Poland was to be created under international guarantee and with an outlet to the sea. Boundaries of the Balkan States were to be re-defined. There were to be no annexations and all territorial settlements were to be made on the basis of the best interests of the people involved rather than for the benefit of rival nations. All such settlements were to be consistent with permanent peace and without discrimination arising from war hatreds. Finally, there was to be a League or General Association of Nations, which was to replace all alliances between nations or groups of nations and have sole control of economic discriminations for the purpose of enforcing its mandates.

An exchange of notes between the United States and Germany and between the United States and the Allies occurred during the month of October. It was agreed that Germany was to surrender on terms to be dictated by the High Command of the Allied armies; that submarine activities were to cease; and that the principles contained in Wilson's addresses would be adhered to in the peace treaty with two exceptions. The Allies refused to be bound by any committments on "freedom of the seas" before entering the peace conference, and they interpreted "evacuation and restoration of territory" to mean that Germany would make compensation "for all damage done to the civilian populations of the Allies and their property by the aggression of Germany by land, by sea and from the air." This reservation left the way open for the imposition of heavy reparations. The terms of an Armistice were agreed to on November 11 and the war came to a close.

CHAPTER IX

WHAT PRICE VICTORY?

Making the Peace

Looking back after nearly two decades one may well ask the question, What price victory? Millions of men must have pondered the thought, Woodrow Wilson among them. This was no exception to the rule that wars create more problems than they solve. Making the peace was incomparably more difficult than winning the war. Making the peace and demobilizing the vast war machine were very much in men's minds in the summer of 1918, the latter more than the former. The question for determination was whether government should continue its control of industry, whether the nation should move farther away from or back to individualism in economic life. Specifically there were the questions of foreign and domestic debts, of the railroads, of submarginal land and mines, of finding new markets, of the merchant marine, of veterans and disarmament and tolerance for minority groups. Reaction had already set in before firing ceased on the western front. Its first fruit was a sordid sacrifice of lofty idealism to political expediency which weakened Wilson's position at the Peace Conference and then prevented our entry into the League of Nations. Wilson began it when, in October, 1918, he placed the question of supporting his policies on a partisan basis, implying, in an appeal to the electorate, that to be a righteous patriot one must first be a Democrat. Warren G. Harding followed with an open bid for the Presidency by repudiating the idea that nations can be anything but potential enemies or that mankind can recognize higher motives for human conduct than mere selfishness. The spirit of the irreconcilable isolationists was permitted to prevail as the mass of people, deprived of inspired leadership, turned indifferently to other things. The United States remained out of the League and the World Court, insisting upon acting always according to its own judgment in any situation which might arise. Germany and Japan ultimately did likewise. Economic warfare followed. Irresponsible governments rose to power. National hatreds accumulated. National bigotry passed for patriotism. The eternal peace for which men fought turned out to be a sadly elusive goal as human life turned back many decades to isolation, violence and despotism. The price of victory was the damaged morale of a generation of young people who grew up to know only idleness, starvation, turmoil and oppression. The theory of safety in armaments, shattered and discredited by the events of the World War, was repeated and believed. Armaments piled upon armaments, adding their billions of dollars to the burden of taxpayers and kindling distrust in the hearts of men.

On October 24 before the congressional elections of 1918, Woodrow Wilson made the following appeal to the people of the United States: "If you have approved of my leadership and wish me to continue to be your unembarrassed spokesman in affairs at home and abroad, I earnestly beg that you will express yourself unmistakably to that effect by returning a Democratic majority to both Senate and House of Representatives." A few days later the people went to the polls and gave the Republicans a majority of two in the Senate and forty-five in the House of Representatives. Wilson's appeal was in no way responsible for the results of the election. Its significance lies much deeper than that. For eighteen months the government had been attempting to destroy all diversity of thought by compulsion and regimentation. Congress was the tool of the President. He had demanded explicit faith and unquestioning support of his policies. What he asked of the electorate was the right to continue to dictate to Congress, to determine the national policies, and to draft men for their support. Only a few Republicans were courageous enough to resist his dictatorship from the first.

Norris and La Follette were two and he had denounced them and their associates as the "wilful twelve." But now that the war was virtually over and the necessity of formulating a reconstruction program approached, this question of executive power vs. Congressional prerogatives assumed new importance. Wilson's base appeal to partisan politics swept away the shroud of idealism which had given him the support of most Republicans and loosed the torrent of pent-up discussion and hostile criticism. It was then that Wilson's intolerance of others' desires, his dictatorial attitude with respect to policy, and his lack of followers genuinely devoted to him personally, counted so heavily against him.

There was another aspect to the situation which is too often ignored. For months, a mob spirit had been abroad in the land masquerading under the cloak of patriotism. Tarring and feathering, deporting, beating and downright murders, had finally impelled Wilson to say in July, 1918: "How shall we commend democracy to the acceptance of other peoples if we disgrace our own by proving that it is, after all, no protection to the weak?" But he did nothing about it and government agencies went on making America unsafe for liberalism with their bureaucratic autocracy while the President insisted the world must be made safe for democracy. The Department of Justice and the Post Office Department were particularly active during September, 1918, and the protest, however strong it may have been, was silently registered on election day.

Finally, there were four points on which Wilson lacked the united support of either party, all vital to the peace program he had enunciated. They were (1) moderation in dealing with the vanquished nations; (2) reduction of economic barriers; (3) an association of nations; and (4) reduction of armaments. For the first time, Wilson needed the support of all the liberal forces in the country and they were completely disorganized, some of them in prisons. He did not lose the peace at Versailles. He lost it when he permitted the proscription of freedom of speech and freedom of conscience in the United States, when he permitted government agencies and a narrow patriotism to prevent a full and complete discussion of war and peace aims. There had been so little discussion of the peace program developed by Wilson that no strong public opinion was created to strengthen his position at the Peace Conference. It was impossible, with the government insisting upon conformity even to the point of denying individuals the right to discuss and publish their opinions, to criticize the government or to disagree with the majority. The strategic control of world diplomacy which passed into Wilson's hands with our entry into the war, and which even the publication of the secret treaties in the summer of 1918 did not damage, was lost by the election. He went to Europe the repudiated leader of the American people. He came back the discredited leader of liberalism throughout the world. All of which should not obscure the fact that men like Lodge, Roosevelt and Taft had endorsed a militaristic approach to the problem of peace and were demanding the prosecution of the war to the point of unconditional surrender, a dictated peace in Berlin; that the opposition was already demanding a return to high protective tariffs and government aid in the anticipated mad scramble for world markets; that fear of Bolshevism was rapidly replacing fear of Prussianism and not only reviving the spirit of isolation, but threatening the proposal that Russia be left free to adopt institutions of her own choosing; and that the farmers of the Middle West were hostile to Wilson because they regarded their war profits so very small compared to those of the industrialists.

President Wilson sailed for Europe late in the year, arriving in France on December 13. He had ignored the Senate, the practical politicians, and the Republicans completely, taking with him a large assembly of "experts," Colonel Edward M. House, Secretary Robert Lansing, General Tasher H. Bliss, and ex-Ambassador Henry White. He had brushed aside as unimportant the secret treaties by which the principal Allies had agreed to dismember the Central Powers and divest them of all their outlying possessions, never having confronted their governments with these treaties during the negotiations leading up to the Armistice. He knew the announced intention of the British and the French to destroy Germany as a great power by depriving her of her economic resources and imposing punitive reparations. This question of dealing with Germany is so important that it is best to consider again Wilson's previous pronouncements:

January 22, 1917—"Victory would mean peace forced upon the loser, a victor's terms imposed upon the vanquished. It would be accepted in humiliation, under duress, at an intolerable sacrifice, and would leave a sting, a resentment, a bitter memory upon which terms of peace would rest, not permanently, but only as upon quicksand."

April 2, 1917—"We have no quarrel with the German people. . . . We are, let me say again, the sincere friends of the German people, and shall desire nothing so much as the early reestablishment of intimate relations of mutual advantage between us—however hard it may be for them, for the time being, to believe that this is spoken from our hearts."

August 27, 1917—"Punitive damages, the dismemberment of empires, the establishment of selfish and exclusive economic leagues, we deem inexpedient and in the end worse than futile, no proper basis for a peace of any kind, least of all for an enduring peace."

December 4, 1917—"You catch, with me, the voices of humanity that are in the air. They grow daily more audible, more articulate, more persuasive, and they come from the hearts of men everywhere. They insist that the war shall not end in vindictive action of any kind; that no nation or people shall be robbed or punished because the irresponsible rulers of a single country have themselves done deep and abominable wrongs."

January 26, 1918—"The people won this war, not the governments, and the people must reap the benefits of the war. At every turn we must see to it that it is not an adjustment between Governments merely, but an arrangement for the peace and security of men and women everywhere."

February 24, 1919—"The men who are in Conference in Paris realize as keenly as any American can realize . . . that no man dare go home from that Conference and report anything less noble than was expected of it."

The Treaty was drawn up at Versailles between January 18 and May 7, 1919, not by the delegates to the Peace Conference but by Wilson, Lloyd George and Clemenceau. It was a disgraceful repudiation of all the generous promises with respect to Germany. The socialists of France denounced it as a settlement which violated justice "in nearly every phrase." The *London Herald* could say: "There is no honor left for any of us." The Women's International Conference for Permanent Peace saw in it "discords and animosities which can only lead to future wars." Germany was forced to sign a confession of guilt for the outbreak of the war and all damages to the Allied governments and their people. She was stripped of all her overseas possessions, together with commercial rights in Morocco, Egypt and China. She lost Alsace-Lorraine, Schleswig, German Poland, Danzig and the Polish Corridor. The Saar Basin was placed under the control of the League of Nations and its coal mines given to France. Her army was reduced to 100,000 and compulsory military service abolished. She was forbidden to manufacture or import arms, munitions or war materials; to construct fortifications within thirty miles of the Rhine; to own any submarines or more than six battleships; to manufacture or import any airplanes or engines for airplanes. She was required to pay $5,000,000,000 in gold before May 1, 1921, for rehabilitation purposes and ultimately a sum, to be fixed by a Commission, sufficiently large to completely restore the Belgian and French war zones. Meanwhile, she was to deliver to the Commission live stock, coal, and manufactured products, all merchant ships above 1600 tons, one-half of those between 1000 and 1600 tons, and build for the Allies 200,000 tons of shipping annually for five years. By these terms, Germany lost control of her transportation system, taxation, exports and imports, navy, air service and merchant marine. She was reduced to economic impotence.

The important omissions of the treaty provisions were as significant as the punitive sections. An economic basis for this supposedly permanent peace was completely lacking. There were no provisions for the disarmament of nations other than the vanquished. Germany and Russia were excluded from the League of Nations. Finally, the manner in which the representatives of the three great powers drew up the terms of the treaty, sitting in secret and dictating to all the world, without counsel and advice from the leading neutral powers or opportunity of protest from the Germans, without representation from the important social and economic groups in the leading nations—all of this was looked upon as autocratic rule by the three powers, a repudiation of self-determination, and a return to the oft-condemned practices of secret diplomacy. These were the things which caused liberals in the United States, Great Britain and France to reject the treaty and, many of them, to consider Wilson's previous confessions of faith as mere camouflage.

The other provision of the treaty which aroused strenuous opposition in the United States was the provision for a League of Nations. The governing agencies of the League were to consist (1) of an Assembly in which all member nations were to have equal representation and voting power; (2) a Council of nine members, consisting of one each from the United States, Great Britain, France, Japan and Italy; and four to be chosen by the Assembly; (3) a Secretariat at Geneva; and (4) a World Court. The function of the League was to preserve peace by eliminating and curbing the development of all conditions leading to war. It was to guarantee the "territorial integrity and existing political independence" of its members; arbitrate international disputes; impose economic sanctions and, perhaps, military pressure, against violators of the Covenant's provisions; supervise the mandates over the territories of the former Central Powers; control slavery and traffic in women, drugs and implements of war.

This provision for a League of Nations was the one point on which Wilson refused to yield either to the other nations or to the Senate of the United States. Other mistakes in the settlement could be rectified peacefully and by agreement only if the whole process of international relations was changed. Cooperative action to preserve peace and work toward a better world order required a permanent agency for the purpose. That agency, however much it might require future modification, was the League of Nations. He returned to the United States in February, 1919, for the purpose of consulting with the Foreign Relations Committees of Congress and succeeded in having some alterations made in the final draft of the Treaty to insure its ratification by the Senate; but thirty-nine Senators of the new Congress agreed to reject any Treaty of Peace which included the Covenant of the League of Nations. The principal objections to the first draft of the Treaty which were rectified on Wilson's return to Paris were (1) that it did not recognize the Monroe Doctrine; (2) that it failed specifically to exclude the authority of the League over domestic questions such as immigration and tariffs; (3) that the right of a nation to withdraw was not recognized; and (4) that no cognizance was taken of the powers of Congress to make war and peace.

The text of the Treaty was withheld from the Senate until July 10, but copies were secured unofficially and a bitter attack was launched against it. It was opposed by the liberals, both because of its harsh treatment of Germany and its guarantees of the territorial integrity of nations which had appropriated to themselves the former possessions of the Central Powers. It was opposed by the western Progressives who represented the deep-seated tradition of isolation and abstention from foreign entanglements. It was opposed by the group of American Imperialists who shuddered for the safety of the Monroe Doctrine and protective tariffs. These several forces brought together in opposition to its ratification such powerful men as Elihu

Root, Charles Evans Hughes, William Howard Taft, and Senators Brandegee, Borah, Johnson, Knox, La Follette, Lodge, McCormick, Moses, and Poindexter. The Senate Foreign Relations Committee under the Chairmanship of Lodge insisted upon amendments to the Treaty and President Wilson refused to accept them. He left Washington on September 4, 1919, for a direct appeal to the people but suffered a paralytic stroke at Pueblo, Colorado, three weeks later. The Senate Committee added forty-five amendments to the Treaty, all but fifteen of which were rejected by the Senate. That body then refused to ratify the Treaty with reservations (41-51) and without reservations (38-53). The discussion was renewed in the next Congress and the Treaty was again rejected on March 19, 1920, by a vote of 49 to 35. Wilson vetoed a joint resolution declaring the war with Germany at an end and it was not until July, 1921, that President Harding signed another resolution bringing the war officially to a close.

Interallied Debts

If one may regard the American people as reasonably entitled to expect repayment of loans made to European nations, then the cost of the war to American taxpayers had scarcely begun when the Armistice was signed. Numerous problems created by that great adventure remained to plague the nation, none more perplexing and costly than war debts, veterans benefits, armaments and the merchant marine. The total loans of the United States Government to foreign nations amounted to $10,-350,490,000. The loans of $4,277,000,000 to Great Britain, $3,404,818,000 to France, $1,648,034,000 to Italy, $379,-087,000 to Belgium, and $192,601,000 to Russia were in the nature of financial assistance to allied nations engaged in a common undertaking and for rehabilitation work; but, of the three billion post-Armistice loans, much went to the new nations created by the Versailles settlement, some to the recent enemy nations. Austria received $24,055,000; Czechoslovakia, $91,-879,000; Jugoslavia, $51,759,000; Poland, $159,668,000; Latvia, $5,132,000; Lithuania, $4,981,000; Esthonia, $13,999,000; and other nations smaller amounts.

The Versailles Conference of 1918-1919 did not attempt to decide upon the total amount of indemnity to be imposed upon Germany but amounts as high as one hundred twenty-five billion dollars were mentioned. By June, 1920, the allied nations had considered the matter more calmly and talked about $64,000,000,000. In April of the following year, the Reparations Commission set up by the Versailles Treaty notified Germany that her bill for the war was $31,680,000,000. This action was based upon the theory that Germany was solely responsible for the war. The major portions of this amount, approximately nine-tenths, was to go to the four largest debtors to the United States, and in about the same relative proportions as their debts.

On February 9, 1922, Congress created a World War Foreign Debt Commission to arrange terms of settlement between the United States and its debtors without reference to the question of German reparations. This act of Congress laid down certain rules which must be followed in the negotiations. All debts were to be paid before June 15, 1947, interest was not to be less than 4¼ per cent per year, and there was to be no reduction in the principal amounts due. France refused to discuss such terms, and the commission was forced to make important modifications in the arrangements with Great Britain which were ratified by Congress. Payment was extended over a period of sixty-two years and the interest rate was modified sufficiently to reduce the total amount, principal and interest combined, to slightly less than $10,000,000,000. The negotiations with other nations continued over a period of years; and, by 1930, all of the principal debtor nations except Russia had agreed to terms. Their payments were all extended, as in the case of Great Britain, over a period of sixty-two years. Belgium was granted an interest rate of 1.8 per cent; France, 1.6 per cent; and Italy, .4 per cent. The other nations were charged an average of 3.3 per cent. These interests reductions lowered the total indebtedness of Great Britain 20 per cent, France 50 per cent and

Italy 75 per cent; but still left the total to be paid more than twice the amount originally borrowed and about equal to the amount of the United States government bonds outstanding as a result of war financing.

Each year that passed saw a more complicated situation developing. The fighting had scarcely ceased in Europe when a reversion to intense nationalism set in. An economic warfare was inaugurated and carried to the point where tariff barriers destroyed fifty per cent of international trade. The rising generation, pushed to the limit of human toleration by starvation, turmoil and oppression, revolted against paying for the devastation of the war. Germany defaulted from the first on her reparations payments. The Allies indicated that their payments to the United States must depend upon German payments to them. The United States Government refused to admit officially that there was any relation between reparations and debts. The combined intelligence of the world was never able to state how the transfer of the huge sums involved could be made from one nation to another in the absence of foreign trade.

An international debt commission, under the chairmanship of Charles G. Dawes, drew up a new reparations arrangement which went into effect in 1924. This plan advanced a loan of 800,000,000 marks to Germany, allowed her a moratorium for one year, and cut her initial annuities to 20 per cent of the original payments. The total amount of reparations was not reduced, but the mystifying problem of finding a method of transfer was shifted to the Allies. Faced with the problem of finding a means of transfer from Germany to themselves and of transferring their own payments to the United States, it was inevitable that they should link the two together officially, if possible. The inability of Germany to meet her obligations under the Dawes plan resulted in a new reparations commission headed by Owen D. Young. In the Young plan, announced in June, 1929, Germany's reparations were cut, for the first time, to $26,000,000,000, a sum still substantially larger than the total amounts due the United States. The most important item in the new arrangement, however, was that which finally fixed the amount due from Germany at $8,800,000,000 plus 5½ per cent interest, making a total of $26,800,000,000 to be paid over a period of fifty-nine years. These payments were separated into two divisions. $165,000,000 annually for thirty-seven years was specifically required. The remainder, amounting to more than $350,000,000 annually over a period of fifty-nine, was to be reduced in proportion to whatever reductions the Allies were able to secure in their debts to the United States.

By 1931, the economic structure of the whole world was in such a state of collapse that President Hoover announced a moratorium for one year on all international debt payments. This was the first official recognition by the United States Government of any connection between debts and reparations. It altered the entire nature of the problem. Premier Laval of France visited Washington in October of that year and issued in conjunction with President Hoover a statement to the effect that further arrangements concerning intergovernmental debts must be made before the expiration of the one year moratorium, the first steps to be taken by European nations relative to German reparations.

The Allied nations—Great Britain, France, Italy, Belgium and Japan—met with Germany at Lausanne and entered into an agreement, July 8, 1932, reducing reparations to two per cent of the original amount, approximately $714,000,000. This amount was to be paid in the form of five per cent German bonds to be delivered to the Bank for International Settlements created by the Young plan. These bonds were to bear no interest until placed upon the market at the end of three years and might be redeemed by Germany at any time. By this action, France completely reversed her post-war attitude, agreeing to virtual cancellation of all further reparations although continuing the fiction of collection. This altered the entire nature of the problem of debts to the United States. The question no longer was how to make the transfer of payments from one nation to another nor how large the payments should be.

It was now a choice of fulfilling the spirit of the Hoover-Laval pronouncement by drastic reduction or cancellation or refusing to act and thus forcing our debtors into repudiation. Shortly before the Lausanne settlement was announced, the Democratic Convention adopted as a plank in its platform a pledge against war debt cancellation. That party was victorious in November, and Congress refused to act. France, therefore, repudiated her debt in December. President Roosevelt announced that nations making partial payments of their annuities would not be considered in default and Great Britain continued to make token payments until December, 1933. At that time France, Poland, Hungary, Belgium and Esthonia paid nothing. The other nations, following the lead of Great Britain, made only small token payments amounting to about nine million dollars in all, slightly more than five per cent of the total amount due.

Congress passed the Johnson Act in 1934, prohibiting any defaulting nation to float loans in the American market. Thereafter, only Finland continued to meet her payments. The question of willingness to pay was never a fundamental part of the war debt question. It was, from the first, a question of how the payments could be made. The United States refused to buy Europe's goods, raising its tariffs three times after the war, in 1922, 1930 and 1932. The collapse of the American market in 1929 reduced the flotation of foreign bonds to zero before Congress passed the Johnson Act. We virtually stopped immigration in 1924, and we subsidized our merchant marine. There was no other way by which the debtor nations could recover for purposes of continuing payments the gold they originally sent to this country. It is true there was some sentiment in European countries against payment in any case. Taxes were far heavier there than in the United States; war losses had been greater; distress was more general; but, from the first, payments had been possible only through sale of securities in this country. It amounted to a lowering of their debt to the United States Government by increasing their debt to the private investors of the United States. When the market for their securities in this country collapsed, payment became impossible. The Johnson Act merely closed the door to a resumption of payments and unjustly attached the stigma of defaulters to nations like Great Britain which were willing to raise the money by taxation but could find no way to transfer it to this country. When President Hoover agreed to payment in pounds sterling to be earmarked and deposited in London, he merely resorted to fictitious payment for the sake of political expediency. Until some way of transferring the sums could be found, there was no payment in fact.

The problem was loaded with political dynamite in this country. Politicians evaded it when possible, or encouraged continued unsound thinking by asserting that the debts must be paid when most of them were too good economists to believe that it was possible. The people of the United States were in personal difficulties financially and confronted with increasing tax burdens. They were even less disposed to think in terms of cancellation than they would have been had Europe used some discretion in expenditures for armaments. They failed to realize that government expenditures within a nation's own domestic economy and payments to another nation were two different things. Congress merely reflected the attitude of the people. The problem which faced the Hoover Administration and the Roosevelt Administration and will continue to face men in public office, was to find some means of cancelling the debts which would be acceptable to the people; in short to cancel without admitting it. Several possibilities existed: (1) to collect the principal of the loans without interest; (2) to regard all moneys lent before the Armistice as a part of this country's contribution to the war, and collect only the post-Armistice loans; (3) to reduce amounts due in proportion to the reduction which had taken place in world price levels, international trade, or on some other fair ratio; (4) to accept the Allied nations' point of view and balance debts to us against German reparations. The unwillingness of the United States to agree upon one or another of these formulae before the debtor nations were forced into repudiation reduced their chances of ever receiving anything either in the way of financial return or concessions toward the stabilization of world trade. The debts gave to the United States strong bargaining power in the field of diplomacy. They could have been sacrificed in the interest of foreign trade through lowering of tariff barriers. They could as an absolute minimum, have been used to purchase international friendship and good-will. All of these possibilities were sacrified on the altar of political expediency.

Veterans' Benefits

The history of veterans' legislation does not begin with the World War, nor does it concern only veterans of that war. No other governmental policy is as consistent and firmly established as that of placing ex-service men in a special class with respect to government gratuities. The principle that the government is responsible for relieving all distress growing out of war service by pensions to disabled veterans and to the widows and children of those killed had never been seriously disputed at any time. The fact that any period of service makes it difficult for the individual to readjust himself to normal civilian life and, also, that wars are invariably followed by disturbed economic conditions, have ever made the government cognizant of the need for some special arrangements for easing the strain of the transition period after a war. Until recently, the great resources of public lands were used for this purpose, veterans being granted special consideration in their disposal since the Revolutionary War. Beyond that, however, the considerable body of veterans in any constituency offered a temptation to men seeking public office to court their favor by supporting the principle of pensions to all veterans, to their widows and minor children. Thus a considerable number of widows remained upon the pension rolls long after the last veteran of a war had answered the final roll-call. The last veteran of the War of 1812 died in 1905, but five widows still received pensions at an annual cost to the government of about four thousand dollars. The last veteran of the Mexican War died in 1929, with 351 widows still on the pension rolls at an annual cost of nearly $300,000. At the close of Hoover's Administration, there were still about 23,000 Civil War veterans and 125,000 widows of Civil War veterans on the rolls at an annual cost to the government of nearly $100,000,000. More than 200,000 Spanish War pensions were costing $110,000,000 annually. By the end of the fiscal year 1933, the country had paid out pension benefits to the following amounts: Revolutionary War, $70,000,000; War of 1812, $46,000,000; Mexican War, $60,000,000; Civil War, $7,500,000,000; Spanish-American War, $800,000,000; Indian Wars, $58,000,000. The principle involved is best shown by the fact that only 392,000 men were brought into the service in the Spanish-American War and there were not more than 10,000 casualties; but payments to veterans—business men, professional men, laborers, rich and poor alike—still amounted to more than $100,000,000 annually after thirty years.

The adoption of the selective draft system, bringing, as it did, several million men into the armed forces at the beginning of the World War, forced the government to consider a substitute for the pension system. A program designed by a commission under the chairmanship of Julian W. Mack drew up a program which was endorsed by President Wilson, Secretary of the Treasury McAdoo, and others and adopted by Congress as the War Risk Insurance Act on October 6, 1917. This act provided (1) for the support of service men's families by a fifteen dollar per month allotment from their pay plus an additional allowance from the government up to fifty dollars; (2) compensation to the amount of $30.00 per month for disabilities arising out of war service; (3) free hospitalization and rehabilitation through vocational training; (4) government war risk insurance. All payments under these provisions were protected against assessments for taxes and debts. Every man in the service was required, not by law but in effect, to buy this insurance up to $10,000. The premiums, based on the usual mortality tables, averaged $6.60 per month on that amount and were deducted from the service man's pay. The face value of the policy was to be paid upon death in monthly installments of $57.50. The cost of administration plus war losses in excess of normal expectancy was borne by the government.

The war brought about four million men into the armed forces in addition to their normal pre-war strength. The Army of 4,057,000 men was composed of 1,274,000 volunteers and the remainder conscripts. The Navy forces numbering 596,000 and the Marine Corps of 104,000 were all volunteers. About half of the Army reached France during the war, but less than 1,000,000 men participated in major engagements. Following the Armistice, these 2,000,000 men were returned to the United States as rapidly as possible and given their discharge with two months' pay or $60. The real history of veterans' legislation begins at this point and, to be honestly understood, must be divided into adjusted compensation for war service and rehabilitation and disability benefits.

Veterans who gave up their jobs and volunteered or who were selected for military service from the more than 12,000,000 men of military age, were assured on every hand that when they returned they would receive fair treatment economically. The general understanding was that the service man would not have to suffer economically by reason of his service. This financial obligation of the country to the men in the service was constantly stressed by public speakers during the war. At the close of the war, they came back to find the country tremendously prosperous, seventeen hundred new millionaires created by war profits with thousands less fortunate but exceedingly well-to-do, and their former jobs occupied by some one else. Dull resentment was the inevitable consequence, and bills were constantly pressed in Congress for adjusted compensation. Meanwhile, seventeen states provided bonuses of from $10 to $30 for each month of service rendered. The first proposal, calling for a fifty dollar bond for each month of service, was bitterly opposed by President Harding who appeared before Congress in person to urge its rejection. Senator Tom Watson of Georgia countered with a proposal to make the payments with greenbacks and a new factor was injected into the controversy. President Harding's objections, as expressed in his veto message of September 19, 1922, were based upon paying a bonus to men who themselves did not expect it at the time of service, or to men who were physically fit and not in distress. He insisted that such a bill must carry additional taxes to provide for the payments, suggesting a sales tax; and he added: "Pledge to the able-bodied ex-service men now will not diminish the later obligation which will have to be met when the younger veterans of today shall contribute to the rolls of the aged, indigent, and dependent. It is as inevitable as that the years will pass that pension provision for World War veterans will be made, as it has been made for those who served in previous wars. It will cost more billions than I venture to suggest." The fight continued in Congress, however, with the issue clearly drawn on the manner of payment and the possibility of future pensions. This question of whether payment should be made by virtue of a sales tax, income and inheritance taxes, or by inflation continued to be troublesome until the matter was finally disposed of in 1936. The other question, that of pensions, was probably not settled even then.

The World War Adjusted Compensation Act was finally passed over President Coolidge's veto on May 5, 1924. Each veteran was given a twenty year endowment insurance policy. These policies matured at death or at the end of twenty years, were non-negotiable, and had a fixed scale of loan values. Their face value was determined by allowing $1.25 per day for foreign service, $1.00 per day for home service with $625 maximum for overseas service and $500 maximum for service at home. To this amount was added 4 per cent compound interest and the whole regarded as a single premium for the purchase of a paid-up insurance policy. The largest single policies were somewhat less than $1600 and the average about $1000. About 3,500,000,000 veterans received the adjusted compensation certificates for a total amount of $3,500,000,000. President Coolidge's veto repeated the fear that pensions would follow and emphasized the effect of the law upon an already overtaxed treasury. The House passed it over his veto by a vote of 331 to 87 and the Senate by a vote of 61 to 27. Thus Congress evaded the necessity of enacting an unpopular sales tax while leaving the way clear to reduce income taxes, which it did five times between 1921 and 1929. It also minimized the probability of an immediate demand for pensions by giving the veterans a payment collectible twenty-six years after the war ended. The matter did not become an important political issue again for six years.

Meanwhile, the costs of payments for disabilities sustained in the service, for disabilities presumed to be of service origin, for vocational rehabilitation, for hospitalization and other benefits had risen to nearly $1,000,000,000 annually by 1933. Congress had established the Veterans Bureau by act of August 9, 1921, bringing together the work formerly handled by the Bureau of War Risk Insurance, the Federal Board for Vocational Education and the Public Health Service. The Bureau was also given charge, by act of July 3, 1930, of the National Soldiers Home and the Bureau of Pensions and renamed the Veterans Administration. It included the central office at Washington under the Administrator of Veterans Affairs, thirty-eight regional offices, forty-four hospitals, and twelve soldiers' homes. The original War Risk Insurance Act of 1917 was amended on June 25, 1918, to provide that all men enrolled in the service were presumed to have been in sound condition at the time. The change was deliberately made to bring under the provisions of the act men who might become mentally deranged as a consequence of having been inducted into the service even though their active term of enlistment did not result in visible injury. An effort had been made, with little success, to weed out mentally infirm before enrolling them into the service, by setting up a special neuropsychiatric bureau, and by use of the army intelligence tests. How complete the failure was is shown by the fact that eventually almost half the ex-service men receiving hospitalization were neuropsychiatric cases. Congress also provided for vocational training at any school or college, with monthly allowances of eighty dollars for single men and one hundred dollars for married men, for all veterans unable to pursue their original vocation.

The second fundamental change in the law came in 1924. This amendment declared that neuropsychiatric disorders, amoebic dysentery and tuberculosis appearing before January 1, 1925, were to be classed as of service origin and the patient entitled to full compensation. Henceforth, these were known as presumptive cases. It also extended hospitalization and compensation to any veteran "blinded or paralyzed" by venereal disease. Compensation was increased to $80 per month with $10 for each child. The act also set up complicated tables by which degrees of disability were to be determined. Meanwhile, special pension acts, granting compensation to individual service men, were continually passed by Congress, nearly 8000 such laws being enacted during the Coolidge Administration, and nearly 15,000 before 1933. Meanwhile, too, the Spanish-American War pension list increased from 23,000 in 1919 to 193,921 on June 30, 1933. The first step toward civil disability allowances was taken in 1930. In that year, Congress provided that certain physical and mental disabilities appearing before January 1, 1930, were to be held as being of service origin and the veteran entitled to from twelve dollars per month for 25 per cent permanent disability to forty dollars for 75 per cent disability.

These liberal provisions had placed upon the pension rolls by the end of 1932, 853,827 World War veterans and dependents at an annual cost of more than $315,000,000. By that time the total cost to the country of veterans' benefits had reached more than $14,000,000,000, including $2,205,000,000 for disabilities presumed to have been of service origin, and $644,943,000 for vocational training.

In the winter of 1930, agitation began for immediate payment of the face value of adjusted compensation certificates. Veterans, like millions of others, were in dire need as a result of the depression and the drouth. The claim was made that the addition of such a sum of money to the nation's purchasing power would break the back of the depression. Congress refused to pay the face value of the certificates but did pass over President Hoover's veto, February 27, 1931, an act enabling the holder of a certificate to borrow from the Treasury one-half of its face value at 4½ per cent interest. Hoover said in his veto message: "We cannot further the restoration of prosperity by borrowing from some of our people, pledging the credit of all of the people, to loan to some of our people who are not in need of the money. . . . If this argument of proponents is correct, we should make government loans to the whole people." How nearly the government came to doing that very thing will be seen later. This act made full payment at an early date an absolute certainty because the interest, if unpaid—and none expected it would be—would cancel the remaining 50 per cent of the value of the policy before 1945.

In September, 1931, President Hoover appeared in person before the American Legion Convention in Detroit with a plea that further agitation for the payment of the adjusted service certificates be abandoned. The following June 20,000 veterans, many of them with their families, made their way to Washington, D. C., encamped on the "flats" and sought by their presence to bring pressure upon the government to meet their demands.

From that point payment of the certificates and demands for inflation were closely connected. Representative Wright Patman of Texas was the leading advocate of payment by a $2,300,000,000 inflation of the currency. A bill bearing his name and backed by both the inflation lobby and the veterans' lobby passed the House of Representatives on June 15, 1932, by a vote of 211 to 176 and again on March 12, 1934, by a vote of 295 to 125. It was defeated each time in the Senate by votes of 62 to 18 and 51 to 31. There then occurred a break between the veterans and the inflationists, the former supporting a bill bearing the name of Representative Vinson of Georgia and providing no method of payment. Frank Belgrano, Commander of the American Legion, strongly supported the payment of the certificates by a bond issue. In May, 1935, the Patman Bill was passed by Congress but vetoed by President Roosevelt in a strongly worded message. He denounced it as a "complete abandonment" of the 1924 settlement and an opening wedge for the payment of service pensions to "all veterans, regardless of need or age." He added: "I hold that the able bodied citizen, because he wore a uniform and for no other reason should be accorded no treatment different from that accorded to other citizens who did not wear a uniform." It was perfectly clear that the bill failed to pass over the President's veto because of its inflationary provisions and that, if a way could be found to eliminate those features, it would pass at the opening session of Congress in January, 1936. In fact, there was strong support from all quarters for the elimination of the question as an issue in the next presidential election and a feeling that in no other way could inflation of the currency be prevented. The inflation bloc in Congress was dangerous largely because it was constantly bidding for the support of the veterans' bloc. Bonus legislation, therefore, was made the special order of business when Congress convened and a bill for immediate payment was drawn up by the Ways and Means Committee of the House with the endorsement of the administration spokesman, Senator Pat Harrison of Mississippi. This bill was promptly passed by Congress with only sixteen Senators and fifty-nine Representatives voting against it. It was vetoed by President Roosevelt but immediately passed over his veto (January 27, 1936) with the support of Congressmen from both parties, even those who had been most insistent upon a balanced budget. The act provided for the exchange of the Adjusted Compensation Certificates for Government Baby Bonds in denominations of fifty dollars each, such bonds to be non-negotiable but to bear three per cent interest and to be redeemable at any post office after June 15, 1936. The problem of finding the necessary funds to redeem whatever portion of the bonds should be presented was left to the Treasury Department. Thus was the final chapter written to a fourteen year controversy. Every President during those years had opposed payment of adjusted compensation, vetoing bills of one kind or another. Not one of the measures passed by Congress, even the final act of 1936, had contained any provision for collecting the necessary funds by taxation, a fact which emphasizes the cumulative effect of pressure politics.

On March 15, 1933, Congress passed An Act to Maintain the Credit of the United States Government, popularly known as the National Economy Act sponsored by President Roosevelt. It superseded all existing pension legislation having to do with the Philippine Insurrection, the Boxer Rebellion, the Spanish-American War and the World War. Opposition to it was based upon the provision delegating to the President the power to make retrenchments in government expenditures. The debate brought from many members of Congress what Senator Simeon D. Fess of Ohio designated a "humiliating confession" that that body was powerless to make economies because of the pressure of organized minorities. Senator William E. Borah led the fight against the act, not because he opposed economies but because, as he said, "I am unwilling myself, in the midst of this awful calamity . . . to single out the Congress of the United States and say that that body, of all who were concerned in the matter, has been the signal failure and therefore we are called upon to abandon our function of seriously considering and passing such measures as we in our judgment feel are necessary for the situation." Under the provisions of the act, President Roosevelt removed 426,000 men from the pension rolls for an annual saving of $460,000,000. He then journeyed to the American Legion Convention at Chicago to explain that the principle involved in his action was simply one of drawing the line between pensions for disabilities incurred in war service and those not incurred in service. The Economy Act was designed to give the President wide discretionary powers in fixing disability rules on the assumption that the executive department is not under as great pressure from the veterans' lobby as is Congress. Within a few weeks after President Roosevelt's action, Senator Connally introduced a bill designed to restore $170,000,000 of the veterans' cuts. The Administration forces compromised on $100,000,000, restoring to the pension rolls 29,500 totally disabled veterans whose disabilities were not incurred in the service and submitting the presumptive cases to special review boards. The review boards, one hundred twenty-eight in number, were composed of five members, including a physician, a veteran and three citizens. These boards rejected forty-three per cent of all cases reviewed, some of whom were discharged a few days after being called in the draft but had drawn stipends of $100 per month.

In March, 1934, Congress passed over President Roosevelt's veto the Independent Office bill, restoring to the pension rolls the 29,000 veterans whose cases were rejected by the review boards, and several thousand Spanish War veterans whose disabilities were not of service origin. It also limited to ten per cent all Spanish War pension reductions. In his veto message, Roosevelt said: "The Spanish-American War veterans' amendment to this act provides for service pensions. . . . I am wholly and irrevocably opposed to the principle of the general service pensions, but I do seek to provide with liberality for all those who suffered because of their service in that war." In August, 1935, Congress passed the Spanish War Veterans Act restoring to veterans of that war, the Boxer Rebellion and the Philippine Insurrection the full allowances taken away by the Economy Act of 1933—a total of about 50,000 at an annual cost of $45,581,000. Only one Senator, Hastings of Delaware, voted against it. President Roosevelt signed the bill with a statement, directly contrary to his former position, that Spanish War veterans and World War veterans were in a different class.

Merchant Marine and Aviation Subsidies

Merchant marine and aviation subsidies have been an integral part of the program of national defense since the World War. National subsidies for merchant vessels date from the beginning of American history. The first subsidy act was passed on July 4, 1789, and was in the nature of an average ten per cent reduction of custom duties on all goods imported in American built and operated vessels. Hyson tea, for example, was taxed 20 cents per pound if imported from the Far East in American vessels, 26 cents per pound if imported from Europe in American vessels and 45 cents per pound if otherwise imported. In 1845, Congress inaugurated indirect subsidies through the postal service. Two years later it permitted ship owners to borrow money from the government to construct vessels for mail service. Some $21,000,000 were expended in indirect subsidies before 1877. There followed an interlude of no subsidies until 1891. In the latter year an act was passed allowing liberal sums beyond the rates for actual poundage carried to ship owners holding mail contracts. This law, which was not repealed by the Jones Act of 1920 but remained in force until 1928, cost the government an estimated thirty million dollars. The early subsidies probably aided materially in the development of our fleet of clipper ships to the point where only Great Britain was superior in total tonnage owned and operated. The outmoding of wooden vessels coupled with the destruction of vessels flying the American flag by Confederate cruisers virtually destroyed the American merchant marine. By 1900, American owned vessels were carrying only 9.3 per cent of the goods entering into our foreign trade.

The entry of the United States into the World War found us without the necessary troop and supply ships. In fact, when President Theodore Roosevelt sent the fleet around the world in 1907, it was necessary to rely upon foreign merchant vessels to provision them. At the outbreak of the war in 1917, Congress created the Emergency Fleet Corporation with a capitalization of fifty million dollars and authority to "purchase, construct, equip, lease, charter, maintain, and operate merchant ships in the commerce of the United States." It was under the direction of George W. Goethals and, later, of Charles M. Schwab. Four large shipyards were constructed, some vessels were built, others were purchased, and the interned

German ships were repaired and placed in service. A total of $3,000,000,000 was spent in one form or another to acquire a merchant fleet during the war. The money thus spent was borrowed as a part of the Liberty Loans and cost in interest alone a minimum of one hundred million dollars annually after the war. Much of it was wasted in poorly constructed and unserviceable vessels. Nevertheless, the United States Shipping Board had under its jurisdiction ten million tons of shipping at the close of the war and these vessels were carrying 42.7 per cent of the country's foreign trade when Congress took up the question of their disposal in 1920.

The Jones Act, sometimes called the Merchant Marine Act of 1920, was passed after long and bitter debate. The one fundamental principle on which every one agreed was the desirability of maintaining permanently an American merchant fleet, either privately or publicly owned, as an auxiliary to the Navy in time of war. National pride was a most important motive in the Congressional decision. The Shipping Board was authorized to sell the vessels under its control to private owners. It was the purpose of Congress, and was clearly understood at the time, that the Board was to sell only when convinced that by so doing the development and maintenance of a permanent merchant marine would be promoted. Purchase of ships was restricted to corporations in which the majority of the stock was held by citizens of the United States, 75 per cent if the vessels were to be operated in coastwise trade. Ships not sold were to be operated by the Shipping Board, which had the authority to map out new trade routes and loan money to companies operating over them. The principle of the act of 1789 was re-established and preferential tariff rates were authorized for goods imported in American owned vessels. Presidents Harding and Coolidge both refused to act under this provision because it violated existing treaties with other nations and succeeding Congresses did not press the point. The act also permitted indirect subsidies in the form of mail contracts. This provision was also ignored for several years, a total of only five million dollars being spent in that manner before 1928. The act contained three fatal defects. It made no provision for building new ships. It did not provide specifically for reconditioning old vessels. It left wide discretionary powers in the administration board. The board did establish thirty-five new trade routes between 1920 and 1928. It sold 1,141 ships and nine shipping lines and guaranteed the losses of companies willing to operate over the new lines. Many of the vessels, however, which had cost an estimated $200 per ton to build, were sold for as low as five dollars per ton and scrapped by the purchasers. The fleet was operating three hundred ninety-two vessels with a tonnage of 3,378,342 in 1923 and two hundred eighty-six vessels with a tonnage of 2,548,648 in 1928. During that period its operating deficits were regularly supplied by Congressional appropriations as follows: 1922—$48,500,000; 1923—$12,000,000; 1924—$50,000,000; 1925—$30,000,000; 1926—$824,000,000; 1927—$13,900,000; 1928—$17,000,000. Many of the vessels, built hastily and for war purposes, were slow-moving and ill-adapted to competitive commerce. Meanwhile, about half of the world's tonnage had been Dieselized while the Shipping Board had no funds for that purpose. By 1928, the percentage of foreign commerce carried in American vessels had shrunk from 42.7 as of 1920 to 32.2. It was a sorry return for the interest on money spent to accumulate the fleet and the operating deficits combined, amounting to more than one hundred fifty million dollars annually.

When Congress again took up the question in 1928, the Shipping Board had a total of four hundred eighty-five vessels permanently inactive. One hundred twenty-nine of them were fit only to be scrapped. The remainder were in need of extensive repairs before being put into service. Congress approached the problem vigorously with strong support for a publicly owned merchant marine. In the end, however, it was decided to fall back upon the same principle followed in railroad construction: liberal subsidies to private builders and operators. Two hundred and fifty million dollars was appropriated in the Jones-White Act for construction loans. Long-term, liberal mail-carrying contracts were authorized. Vessels remaining in the hands of the Shipping Board were to be disposed of at whatever price operators were willing to pay. Between 1928 and 1931, seventeen shipping lines were awarded mail contracts costing $5,588,000 annually. The difference between that sum and an estimated actual cost of carrying the mail of $92,000 annually constituted an indirect subsidy.

The construction of sixty-eight new vessels to operate over thirty-nine new routes at a cost of $281,000,000 was also provided for in mail contracts. Mail subsidies under these contracts brought the total to twenty-three million dollars annually in 1933. Meanwhile, the Shipping Board sold, for $23,000,000, 104 vessels which had cost the government $258,000,000. That the government had failed to accomplish the purpose back of its entire merchant marine policy after the war was clearly evident by 1933. The La Follette Seaman's Act together with the higher standard of living maintained in the United States placed shipping interests at a tremendous disadvantage in competition with foreign operators. Even more important was the devastating effect of tariff barriers, particularly the Hawley-Smoot tariff, which contributed to the decline of foreign trade, drove American manufacturers to establish branch factories in foreign lands, and thoroughly counteracted all efforts to develop shipping by liberal subsidies. The policy of merchant marine subsidies, in the words of the Black Committee of the Senate, had turned out to be "a sad, miserable and corrupting failure."

Equally important as a part of the national defense program was the policy of encouraging the development of aviation by mail subsidies to a total of $20,000,000 annually. Congress undertook to encourage aviation because of its increasing importance in war and the dismal failure of the government to construct an aviation force during the World War. There had been much loose talk at the beginning of the war about throwing a fleet of 100,000 planes into the contest and Congress made ample appropriations for building the planes. Few planes were built, however, in time to be of any service to the fighting forces. The Army in France was compelled to rely heavily upon the Allies for planes. An investigation disclosed that there had been some administrative inefficiency and mismanagement, but that the chief difficulty was almost a complete lack of construction facilities and personnel. Congress decided to subsidize commercial aviation as an integral part of the national defense program.

A Senatorial investigating committee, under the chairmanship of Hugo Black of Alabama, revealed in January, 1934, that these subsidies had been diverted from their original purpose of fostering aviation and prostituted to party politics, private graft and stock promotion schemes. Air mail routes had been divided by the large company operators themselves in May, 1930, without competitive bidding. Postmaster-General Brown had brought pressure upon small companies to merge with larger companies. The testimony revealed that one official had started with forty dollars and manipulated his stock to a market value of five million dollars. Stock-watering, salary bonuses, etc., had ended with more than eighteen million shares of outstanding stock on which only a few thousand dollars of dividends had been paid.

The subsidies themselves had amounted in 1933 to the difference between fifty-four cents per mile paid and the fifteen cents per mile estimated cost of operation. Total subsidies between 1926 and 1933 were estimated at more than sixty million dollars. Following the disclosures, all air mail contracts were cancelled and the duty of carrying the mails thrust upon the Army Air Corps. There followed a series of disasters in which twelve pilots were killed. Extraordinary flying conditions, poor equipment, unskilled pilots and the fact that many pilots had been called back hurriedly from CCC camps all contributed to the debacle. Not the least important result of the disasters was the fact that it drew the attention of the country from the disgraceful situation revealed by the Senatorial investigating committee. The service was again returned to private companies and a special committee was appointed to investigate conditions in the Army Air Corps. Newton D. Baker, former Secretary of War, was chairman of the Committee composed in part of expert aviators. The Committee went beyond the question of Air Corps efficiency and discussed the relative strength of aviation in different countries. It recommended: (1) an increase in the Army Air Corps to 2320 planes; (2) purchase through negotiated contracts; (3) continuation of air defense as a supporting branch of both the Army and Navy Departments; (4) increased attention by Congress to army aviation; (5) the retirement of aviators at forty-five years of age; and (6) aviation training for all West Point cadets.

CHAPTER X

POST-WAR REACTION

Socialists and Aliens

Political crimes having been introduced into the American scheme of things, it was inevitable that proscription of social and economical ideas should follow. The transition was easy because socialists the world over had deprecated the outbreak of the World War, but had been unable to prevent it. Being pacifists and also internationalists, they opposed our entry into the war. It is probable that the government's activities against them increased rather than decreased their strength. The conviction of Eugene V. Debs aroused a great deal of protest. He was nominated for the Presidency in 1920 and received nearly a million votes while a prisoner in Atlanta penitentiary. From his prison cell he wrote in acceptance of the nomination: "I am thinking this morning of the men in the mills and the factories. I am thinking of the women who, for a paltry wage, are compelled to work out their lives; of the little children who, in this system, are robbed of their childhood and in their early, tender years are seized in the remorseless grasp of Mammon and forced into industrial dungeons to feed the machines, while they themselves are being starved in body and soul. I can see them dwarfed, diseased, stunted, their little lives broken and their hopes blasted, because in this high noon of our twentieth-century civilization, money is still so much more important than human life." The following year President Harding released him from prison without the restoration of citizenship. Meanwhile, Victor L. Berger, conservative Socialist editor of the *Milwaukee Leader* and former Congressman, had his paper barred from the mails by Postmaster-General Burleson and was indicted under the Espionage Act. Specifically, he was charged with having said that we entered the war to save our financial interests in Allied success and to maintain munition profits; that war would enable the capitalists to suppress labor disturbances as treason; that insanity was a common consequence of active service; that conscription had a taint of dishonor; and that the Bible was a pacifist document. He was elected to Congress while under indictment, but was refused his seat. In November, 1917, he was sentenced by Judge Kenesaw Mountain Landis to twenty years' imprisonment. An appeal was filed and Berger was meanwhile returned to Congress by an increased vote of 8,000 over that he formerly received; but Congress again rejected him. The peak of Socialist proscription came in January, 1920, when five members of the New York Legislature were expelled for no other reason than that of belonging to the Socialist party. The conservative and liberal press alike protested most vigorously, as did the New York Bar Association under the leadership of Charles Evans Hughes. The protests did not alter the action of the Legislature but the episode marked the beginning of a sharp decline in war-time hysteria and a restoration in part at least of the principle of free political discussion.

The immediate post-war period, however, was one of economic stress—a period in which society felt in grave danger of losing its ideals and customs and struck out in blind intolerance against all who dissented from the established order. In Europe, it was said, the capitalistic system was rapidly passing and with it the Protestant faith; that the middle class economic system of exploitation and production for profit, reenforced by the Protestant virtues of thrift, industry and self-reliance, were on the decline. A new social order was being constructed, painfully and often violently, in many spots on the Continent, particularly in Russia. Lloyd George and President Wilson both offered the menacing unrest in Europe as an excuse for the haste with which the Versailles Treaty was thrown together. There is no space here to enumerate all the interesting aspects of the revolution in human institutions. Suffice it to say that men and women everywhere were facing the facts of their environment in a new and more realistic manner and were undertaking to remodel that environment along new lines. That phase of the change which had to do with human relationships proved most confusing and, therefore, most disconcerting. That is why men said our social institutions had not kept pace with our scientific advance. It was the secret of the amazing appeal of Wilson's promise of a new world order to bewildered humanity everywhere. It was why men turned from him in despair after the Treaty of Versailles and took into their own hands the reconstruction of a new world. It was a vindication of the socialist claim that hope for world peace based on justice was utterly out of the question until the social and economic order at home was reconstructed on the same principle. It was why the socialists who believed in political action came to be tolerated and those who advocated direct action suppressed.

It should be remembered (1) that the Socialist program called for a fundamental reorganization of production under social ownership and control; (2) that the South, still in the growing pains of industrial development, had millions of Negroes in its midst whose status in society was such as to make them peculiarly susceptible to violent reform ideas; (3) that the American Federation of Labor was a conservative organization, representing the aristocracy of labor and in no sense representative of the great groups of unskilled workers: the domestic servants, the agricultural laborers, the western transients, and the Negro; (4) that economic rivalry as the fundamental cause of the World War, President Wilson's grand theme of Democracy versus Aristocracy, and other equally thought-provoking theses had evoked an intellectual ferment non-academic in character and all-inclusive in its evaluation of human institutions; (5) that the rule of the proletariat became an accomplished fact by violent revolution in Russia in 1918; and (6) that there were millions of recent immigrants in the United States, not yet thoroughly assimilated, many of whom had fled to this country to escape the militarism and oppressions of Old World autocracies.

Not the least important aspect of the shifting American scene was political. The Democratic and Republican parties remained definitely middle class in their economic philosophy with some modifications due to the increasing number of extremely wealthy men; but opposed to them were the socialists and the Industrial Workers of the World and Non-Partisan League. Each of these parties had a definite program that touched the fundamental principles of economic life. The Industrial Workers of the World was organized about 1905. Its strength was in the western states among the transient laborers of the mines, lumber camps and farms, a submerged group second, if at all, in that respect only to the agricultural laborers of the South. It was partial to industrial unionism and the general strike rather than to craft organization and the conservatisms of the A. F. of L. Its objective, like that of the socialists, was to overthrow capitalism, but by direct action. Its members were far more outspoken than the socialists in denouncing the war as a capitalistic enterprise and in resistance to its continuance by sabotage, etc. The arrest and conviction of ninety-three members of the party in Chicago, in 1918, including the head of the organization, W. D. Haywood, virtually destroyed it. The mopping up process was continued after the Armistice under state syndicalist laws and the federal Alien Act; but its place at the extreme Left was taken immediately by the Communist party or American Branch of the Third International. The Communist party was organized in Chicago in 1919 and frankly admitted its support of the Russian revolutionary program. Neither the Industrial Workers of the World nor its successor, the Communist party, ever attained a membership of 100,000. Their active supporters at any one time was probably less than half that number. Nevertheless, the mere fact of their existence has vitally affected the course of American history.

The men and women who were convicted under the Espionage Acts, approximately fifteen hundred in number, continued to languish in prison long after the war was officially ended. Many petitions were sent to the Department of Justice, to Congress and to the President in an effort to secure a general amnesty for them. Congress refused to act, President Coolidge insisted upon individual petitions for pardon and President Hoover refused to discuss the matter. Action was finally taken in their behalf by President Roosevelt who issued a blanket amnesty restoring citizenship and civil rights to all of them at Christmas time, 1933.

On October 16, 1918, Congress passed an act authorizing the Secretary of Labor to take into custody and expel from the United States any alien who advocated or who belonged to any organization which advocated the overthrow of government by force, assassination of public officials, no human government, or the unlawful destruction of property. The act was amended, May 10, 1920, to give the Secretary of Labor authority to take into custody and to deport if, after a hearing, he found them "undesirable residents of the United States," all aliens convicted of violation or conspiracy to violate any of the war-time statutes, such as the Espionage Act, the Trading with the Enemy Act, etc. There were two distinctive features of these Alien Acts: (1) they gave into the hands of an administrative officer, the Secretary of Labor, plenary power, without appeal even to the President of the United States or the safeguards of court procedure, to impose upon aliens, irrespective of their length of residence in this country, the most drastic punishment conceivable, namely, that of being summarily torn from family, friends, and property and transported beyond the sea; and (2) they subjected to the possibility of such punishment individuals who had committeed no overt act, who might even not endorse such principles as those designated, but who from some circumstance or other had become affiliated with men who did. The first action under these acts was taken on December 21, 1919, when two hundred forty-nine Russians were deported on the transport *Buford.* The next month over four thousand persons were taken into custody in a carefully planned raid throughout the country, but many were later released for insufficient evidence.

These activities against aliens were vigorously pressed by Attorney-General Palmer. The enforcement of the law was under the jurisdiction of Secretary of Labor, William B. Wilson; but the government agencies were disorganized in the winter of 1919-1920. President Wilson was dangerously ill, the country was drifting, and reactionary elements were in control. The orders for the January raids, for instance, were signed by J. W. Abercrombie, acting solicitor for the Department of Labor but a member of the Department of Justice, and A. Carminette, Commissioner-General of Immigration. Secretary Wilson was ill at the time and, in his absence, important changes were made in the rules of procedure, one such denying the person in custody the benefit of counsel. Everywhere throughout the country, the industrial unrest became much more of a class warfare than it would have been had not the Justice Department taken the lead in pursuing labor agitators suspected of communist leanings.

It is perfectly clear that the Alien Acts and the deportations were popular throughout the country. In the South, much was said and believed about the danger of communist agitation among the Negroes. The American Federation of Labor was not sympathetic to radical labor groups which sought to penetrate their organization and discredit their policies. Industrialists were satisfied to see their adversaries clapped into jail for long terms under the state syndicalist laws or deported to foreign lands. Returned soldiers were unfriendly to a radical labor group which had been so actively identified with opposition to the war. The exhilaration of silencing economic dissenters by suppression was as pleasurable as silencing pacifists and German sympathizers had been, especially when the victims were foreigners against whom there was a prevailing though perhaps subconscious dislike. Many people agreed with Attorney-General Gregory and his successors that free expression of opinion was dangerous to American institutions, and a great many more preferred not to have to think about the social and economic injustices which agitators were constantly bringing to their attention. Many thought, and continue to think, that safety lay in splendid isolation with the minds of mature men and women safeguarded against strange new ideas. These conditions combined to give to the post-war decade an atmosphere of dull resentment and surprising indifference to internal disorders. It was a decade of racial and class hatreds, of open and defiant lawlessness, of religious bigotry, of intolerance and intellectual dishonesty.

Ku Klux Klan

During the early days of the war, a moving picture made its appearance, called *The Birth of a Nation.* The picture, supposedly historical but a grossly inaccurate and distorted portrayal of the reconstruction period, made a sensational appeal to race prejudice. It was shown to packed houses throughout the nation at a time when other disturbing factors in race relations were threatening open warfare. The feeling of hostility between the Negroes and whites had been slowly dying out in the South after the turn of the century. Confidence, born of understanding and cooperation, was taking its place. Booker T. Washington, the great Negro leader and educator, had pioneered in the field. His work at Tuskegee had stimulated racial pride among the Negroes, contributed to improvement in every field of human endeavor, and established the principle that the only solid foundation for sectional advancement was equal justice to all. His thesis that the two races had talked "too much about each other and not enough to each other" was acted upon by several agencies. The National Urban League set up inter-racial boards to assist migrating Negroes to adjust themselves to urban conditions. The Southern Publicity Committee, financed by the Phelps-Stokes Fund made press releases of notable Negro achievements. Dr. Willis

D. Weatherford, President of Southern College, working through the College Y.M.C.A., promoted special studies along scientific lines of the race problem. The organization created inter-racial boards and established a summer school at Blue Ridge, North Carolina, for a study of the question. In 1912, the Southern Sociological Congress, composed of representative southern men from all walks of life, held its first meeting at Nashville. A special committee on race relations, under the chairmanship of James H. Dillard, was created. Its meetings and reports were a real stimulus to continued activity. Dillard, Director of the Anna T. Jeanes Foundation, organized the University Commission on the Southern Race Problem. The Commission, representing all southern state universities, studied the conditions of Negro life, and issued many open letters on lynching, education, migration, etc.

Then came the World War, the most trying period in race relationship since Reconstruction, and a return of all the old passions and misunderstanding. *The Birth of a Nation* with its scenes of Negro terrorism revived the Ku Klux Klan. There probably would have been a proscriptive organization of some sort in any case, but the mere use of the name was an incentive to all the old oppressions fifty years after the event and under strangely different circumstances. The name struck terror into the hearts of the Negroes with their inherited traditions of unlawful persecutions; it revived dormant prejudices in the hearts of competing groups of whites; it gave some degree of legitimacy to the use of robes and masks. The selective service act took nearly 400,000 Negroes into the armed forces, about half of them to Europe. That there was intentional discrimination against them would be difficult to prove; but it is apparent that they had grievances, real or imaginary. It was said and believed that proportionately more Negroes were drafted into the service than whites; that Negro officers were discriminated against in travel; that Negro soldiers were discriminated against by the Y.M.C.A.; etc. More important, however, were the lynchings of thirty-four Negroes in 1917 and sixty in

1918, including five Negro women; and race riots in East St. Louis, Chester, Pa., Philadelphia, Houston, Omaha, Chicago, Washington, D. C., and Elaine, Arkansas. The feelings of Negro soldiers carried off to France to battle against German atrocities, about the situation at home, was not conducive to racial harmony. In addition, there was the fear among the whites that Negro freedom in army life in France would disrupt the normal relationship between the races at the South. This fear led to repressive measures to stop the migratory movement which, in turn, succeeded only in providing further excuse for the migration. More than 600,000 migrated to the North between our entry into the war and 1924. Hundreds of Negroes, waiting at railway stations, were arrested and thrown into jails. Northern labor agents were heavily fined. All these conditions contributed to a sense of impending peril.

Early in 1919, there met in Atlanta five men who had been active in promoting inter-racial cooperation: John J. Eagan, a steel manufacturer of Atlanta; M. Ashby Jones, an Atlanta clergyman; R. H. King, Executive Secretary of the National War Work Council for the Southeast; W. W. Alexander, prominent clergyman and army Y.M.C.A. executive; and J. H. Dillard. These men planned and inaugurated the Atlanta Conference of representative Negroes and whites from all parts of the South. Out of that conference, where there was more honest and frank interchange of opinion than ever before, came a proclamation and the permanent organization of a Commission on Inter-racial Cooperation. The proclamation clearly reveals the gravity of the crisis: "We a group of Christians, deeply interested in the welfare of our entire community, irrespective of race or color distinction, and frankly facing the many evidences of racial unrest, which in some places have already culminated in terrible tragedies, would call the people of our own beloved community to a calm consideration of our situation before extremists are allowed to create a condition where reason is impossible."

The Commission on Inter-racial Cooperation, financed by

the Y.M.C.A., established headquarters at Atlanta. Under its guidance, executive boards were established in each southern state, inter-racial committees in more than eight hundred counties and a network of committees in local communities. The organization was flexible but permanent, devoting its efforts toward insuring justice in the courts, the repression of mob violence, adequate school and recreational facilities for Negroes, etc. It worked in close cooperation with local institutions such as boards of education, chambers of commerce and churches. The presidents of leading Negro schools, Robert R. Moton of Tuskegee Institute, James E. Gregg of Hampton Institute, Isaac Fisher of Fiske University, and John Hope of Morehouse College were active in the organization from its inception. The two fundamental objectives were (1) to correct injustices and inequalities of conditions affecting the Negro; and (2) to improve those inter-racial attitudes out of which intolerable conditions arise. The attainment of the first objectives was specifically the task of local committees; that of the second the function of a press service reaching 2000 publications with a combined circulation of twenty million. The Commission was responsible for the establishment of college courses for the study of race relations in more than sixty institutions, and for the appointment of a committee on race relationship by the Federal Council of Churches of Christ in 1921, and is generally given credit for the sharp reduction in the number of lynchings after that year, in addition to effecting marked improvement in conditions touching household servants, the founding of day nurseries, kindergartens and child clinics.

Meanwhile, the Ku Klux Klan, with its organized defiance of the law and its attempt to direct the affairs of men through an invisible empire, was working in the opposite direction. The Klan was conceived by William J. Simmons of Atlanta, organized under a Georgia charter in 1916, and promoted along lines of high pressure salesmanship by Edward Young Clarke. By 1925, its membership had reached a total of more than five millions with half the total members in New York, Ohio,

Indiana, Texas, and California. Its fundamental creed was religious and racial intoleranace combined in hostility to Negro, Jew and Catholic. Its practices were utterly foreign to the fundamental tenets of Americanism of which it claimed to possess a 100 per cent monopoly: the boycott and proscription of Catholics, foreigners and Jews; secret trial and punishment of Negroes in particular but of all without distinction who incurred its displeasure; the utter disregard of law and Constitutional guarantees of individual liberty. The reasons for its phenomenal growth, estimated at 100,000 per week for a time, are perfectly clear. The deep concern about the large number of foreigners unrestricted immigration was bringing into the country was crystallized by Wilson's denunciation of hyphenated Americanism, the association of aliens and Jews with radical economic theories, and the fear that post-war Europe was about to deluge the country with a new flood of immigrants. The moral reform movement, which reached its dramatic climax in emphasis upon the prohibition of alcoholic beverages, was beginning to encounter serious resistance. The effects of the war were draining the South of its agricultural laborers and creating unrest among the Negro population. More than half of the nation's population was living within fifty miles of its boundary lines. Here were concentrated the wealth, the foreign born, the freedom from religious restraints, the opposition to prohibition, the intellectual heresies, the Catholics. The interior region, predominantly agricultural, native born American and Protestant, was precisely the region which nourished the prohibition movement and fundamentalism, raised its voice against the encroachments of industrialism, viewed with alarm the changing status of Negroes, and harbored a genuine fear of Popery.

The Klan capitalized on all of these things. It was more than a mere organization; it was an attitude of mind—a body of thought—which was the direct antithesis of justice, liberty, and equality. Professional organizers and propagandists were drawn into the movement by the high percentage of initiation fees they were allowed to retain. The result was that the lunatic fringe of society furnished more than its quota of members. The Protestant ministers took up the banner and added a degree of respectability to it. Professional and business men were forced to join as a means of self-preservation. The press was silenced in many places, and politicians feared to lift their voices in protest. Anonymous telephone calls and fiery crosses came to direct the conduct of men. The organization became so strong that neither the Democratic nor the Republican party had the courage to do more than evade the issue. Even after it had ceased to be a force to be reckoned with in politics, its lingering spirit cast a blight over the land. It is doubtful if such organizations ever die out completely. Fiery crosses may still be seen on occasion in the Black Belt. The campaign against the Democratic presidential candidate, Alfred E. Smith, in 1928, was based upon the Ku Klux Klan vendetta. Religious and social hatreds are peculiarly sensitive to sly propaganda, and propaganda has developed into an esoteric art.

Fundamentalism

A second aspect of the post-war reaction was the fundamentalist movement. Economic and religious fundamentalism are inseparable in history. Each represents eighteenth-century dogma in its respective field and are brought into concert by the increasing emphasis upon social welfare in the Protestant churches. Rural Southerner and millionaire Northerner found common ground in opposition to this sociological trend which threatened to interfere with the exploitation of Negro and factory white. The religious fundamentalist remained faithful to the literal interpretation of the Bible; the economic fundamentalist clung to the sacred formulae of parental authority, individual liberty and property rights. The former opposed every effort to reconcile the teachings of Christian religion with modern scientific thought; the latter denied the need for new relationships between the individual and the changing social order. The prestige of the pioneering modernists in the Church —Harry Emerson Fosdick, A. C. McGiffert, Preserved Smith and others—finally reached such heights that the fundamentalists sought to throw up legislative barriers against their heresies. Their efforts were followed by an equally determined minority who hoped to accomplish the same thing with respect to social and economic theories. The public schools have become the clearing house for the accumulated mental pabulum of the human race. Some groups doubted the ability of young people to choose correctly between conflicting theories. Others questioned the impartiality of instructors in their presentation. Others, more certain that their own philosophy constituted the correct way of life, insisted that it be emphasized to the exclusion of everything else. Still others sought to prostitute the educational system to their own selfish ends. The aim of the school personnel, then, to teach children to think and to take what they read and what they hear, not as facts, but as data for their consideration, became increasingly difficult. The campaign of the Ku Klux Klan to require the reading of the Bible in the public schools and to eradicate parochial schools, was followed by the fundamentalist drive against the teaching of evolution; and that, in turn, by the teachers' oath to uphold the Constitution. Interwoven with the whole movement was the effort to use the schools as an agency for propaganda by the prohibition forces, certain elements of the privately owned utilities, etc.

The anti-evolution agitation coursed through the entire nation for a decade after the war. Its great protagonist was William Jennings Bryan who had contributed more than any other individual to the cause of prohibition. His plea for a return to the old-time religion was as eloquent as that of Billy Sunday, but he made it directly to legislative bodies for statutes to stamp out modern heresies. Interest was largely localized with little notice by the press until the Scopes trial at Dayton, Tennessee, in the summer of 1925. The man who introduced the bill in the Tennessee legislature was John W. Butler, a primitive Baptist farmer of Fayetteville. The bill as passed forbade the teaching in state-supported schools of "any theory that denies the story of the Divine Creation of man as taught in the Bible." There were immediate demands for its enforcement. John T. Scopes, a high school teacher of Dayton, acting on the suggestion of a group of friends, made a test case of the law. There followed one of the famous trials in the history of the country. William Jennings Bryan assisted in the prosecution and the Civil Liberties Union employed Clarence Darrow, Dudley Field Malone and Arthur Garfield Hayes for the defense. Scopes was convicted and the state Supreme Court, on an appeal, upheld the constitutionality of the law. Little was said in the trial about the relationship between state and church, or about academic freedom in the broad sense of the term. Bryan summed up the theory of the fundamentalists when he said: "Power in this country comes from the people; and if the majority of the people believe that evolution breaks down a religious faith and threatens Christianity, they have a right to demand that it be suppressed or at least confined to the little group of research men who may study it as a theory not yet proven." The defense made no great effort to prove the law unconstitutional. Instead, it sought to show that the theory of evolution was not contradictory to the Bible. The nature of the controversy accompanying the trial gave further convincing proof of the rural South's conservatism and of its sensitiveness to outside criticism, of the ignorance of many of its religious leaders, and of its lag in general cultural progress. The trial contributed to a general nation-wide introspection which turned the tide against religious fundamentalism, against the Klan, and against lynchings. The reaction was generally favorable to educational processes and more courageous leadership.

The success of the anti-evolutionists in Tennessee encouraged them to greater efforts elsewhere; but their great leader was gone. Bryan had died during the Scopes trial, a crusading reformer to the last. Two organizations were founded about this time to aid in the movement: The Supreme Kingdom and the Bible Crusaders of America. The former was founded by

Edward Young Clarke, former Imperial Wizard of the Ku Klux Klan. The latter was said to have been financed by the millionaire George F. Washburne, who published a list of fifty-four institutions of higher learning where young people could receive an education without their faith in the book of Genesis being disturbed. He was also chairman of a committee for founding a memorial university to Bryan at Dayton. T. T. Martin of the Bible Crusaders of America and author of *Hell and the High Schools,* carried the fight into Mississippi, most rural of all the states, where an anti-evolution act was placed upon the statute books in 1926. A similar measure was defeated in Lousiana only by parliamentary manoeuver and in Kentucky by a vote of 42 to 41. Martin then transferred his lobbying headquarters to Charlotte, North Carolina. Heroic work by President Harry W. Chase of the state's great university defeated his efforts, the fight ending finally in 1927. The same year an act was passed by popular referendum in Arkansas by a majority of 45,000. The anti-evolutionists then turned their attention to text books and teachers, fomenting strife at many schools including the University of Tennessee, the University of Texas, and Southern Methodist University at Dallas. The Southern Baptist convention, in 1926, adopted a resolution stating: "This convention accepts Genesis as teaching man was a special creation of God and rejects every theory, evolutionary or otherwise, which teaches that man originated or came by way of lower animal ancestry." The Southern Presbyterian General Assembly, in 1931, broke away from the Federal Council of Churches of Christ in America because it endorsed the practice of birth control. The burden of the fight against these phases of reaction was carried by a group of independent southern newspapers: the Norfolk *Virginia Pilot,* edited by Louis I. Jaffe; the Raleigh *News and Observer,* owned and edited by Josephus Daniels; the Chattanooga *Times,* edited by L. G. Walker; the Columbus (Ga.) *Enquirer Sun,* edited by Julian Harris; and the Montgomery *Advertiser,* edited by Grover C. Hall. Pulitzer prizes were awarded to the *Vir-*

ginia Pilot for its campaign against lynching and might with equal justice have been given for its bold denunciation of A. Mitchell Palmer's Red hunts; to the *Enquirer Sun* for its relentless crusade against the anti-evolutionists; and to the *Advertiser* for its fight against the Klan. Just as the Klan, anti-evolution, lynchings and anti-communism were inseparable, so too was the fight against them. The combined efforts of this group of newspapers, and others to a lesser degree, constitute a brilliant epoch in American journalism, the more so because they were located in the heart of the reactionary region and were a hundred times more effective than northern newspapers would have been.

The same cannot be said for men in public life. Most politicians fought shy of the Klan issue, insisting that it was of minor importance and would soon disappear. They refused to admit that the Klan was seeking to put its doctrines into practice by seizing control of the government. In fact, politicians turned the situation to their own account, basing their appeals for support upon the prevailing spirit of intolerance. Robert La Follette, in the campaign of 1924, was denounced as a dangerous radical, whose election would sound the death knell of American institutions. Charles G. Dawes and Calvin Coolidge spoke passionately of the menace of Bolshevism and with deep affection for the Constitution. The campaign slogan of the Republican party was *Coolidge or Chaos*. Thus was the attention of the country skillfully turned from the corruption of the previous administration by an appeal to irrational thought. A straw man was set up and every one invited to the kill. The idea worked so well that it was repeated with each presidential campaign. When succeeding generations are able to view the period with a better perspective than the present permits, it may well appear to have been the most damaging blow ever dealt to the country. The worst depression in the nation's history brought financial ruin to millions and forced one man in five into the breadlines. The Roosevelt Administration in 1933 commanded the largest working majorities in history and faced tremendous problems. It was a situation which called for the most vigorous and intelligent minority leadership that could be mustered; but the minority had talked about communism for so long it could not think in any other terms. After a while it began to denounce the administration program as all wrong, un-American, radical, destructive of individual liberty, inspired by Moscow. There was no difference between the appeal of the southern politicians to race prejudice and of northern politicians to the fears of Bolshevism. Both made grand themes for the hustings: dramatic, emotional and non-controversial. Both created an atmosphere in which self-appointed guardians of social security insisted upon banding themselves together into organizations for the purpose of non-legal control. They are variously opposed to Catholics, Negroes, Jews, aliens, communists, labor leaders, liberals of all kinds and, particularly, pacifists. The Silver Shirts, known to have organizations in forty-six states, charge the Jews with responsibility for all the ills from which humanity has ever suffered. The Crusaders for Economic Liberty in Tennessee and the White Legion of Alabama were particularly hostile to agitation among the Negro and white share-croppers. There were, also, the Pioneer American Protective Association of New England; the Union of Fascists of New Jersey; the Order of '76 of New York; the Black Legion of Michigan; and the Vigilantes of San Francisco and Tampa, but who are said to exist in every large city in the country.

The attack of the economic fundamentalists upon the educational system met with greater success than that of the anti-evolutionists because of the subtle fashion in which the meaning of patriotism was broadened to include not only devotion to our democratic political system, but to the existing social order and willingness to defend the latter even to the point of denying the right to discuss freely social and economic questions. Academic freedom was seriously imperilled all over the country by Red hunts and legislative investigations. A group of students was expelled from one university for inviting Harry

Elmer Barnes to speak on the Mooney-Billings case; from another university for vigorous opposition to compulsory military training; from another for various offenses ranging from peace parades to inviting John Strachey to speak on the campus. Some leading educators of the country endorsed the idea of teachers attending summer school at the University of Moscow, there to learn first hand the principles of the social and political system of the Soviet Union. We maintain great universities to teach young people about social practices from the Court of St. James to the cannibalism and eroticism of the heathens; about political theories from Aristotle to Calhoun; and about every conceivable kind of economic institution; but, because some intelligent people proposed to find out what the Russian people were thinking and doing, a great chain of newspapers was ready to drive them into exile. That the movement did not go farther was due to a vigorous counteroffensive. The Board of Regents of the University of Wisconsin went on record as believing that "students should have and do have the right to study social problems and should not be suppressed from expressing or advocating doctrines in which they sincerely believe, provided always the bounds of law or of decency are not exceeded." Secretary of the Interior, Harold Ickes, said before the Teachers Welfare Organization of Chicago: "To justify its existence, a school system in America, from kindergarten to university graduate school, must be staffed by intellectually honest men and women who are undaunted in their search for truth, fearless in its dissemination and unshackled by ancient superstitions or bugaboos, free to think and think aloud." President Robert M. Hutchins of the University of Chicago, Thomas W. Lamont of J. P. Morgan and Company, the *St. Louis Post Dispatch*, the *Baltimore Sun*, the *Christian Science Monitor*, and others added their protests so vigorously that the movement was checked before great damage was done. That was not true, however, of the public schools.

Twenty-two states had adopted teachers oath laws before January 1, 1936. The first of these laws since the period of the

Civil War was enacted in Rhode Island in 1917. This oath, which every teacher in the public schools was required to take, was the only one of its kind until 1935 and, in some respects, still remains in a class by itself. It reads:

RHODE ISLAND—1917

I, as a teacher and citizen pledge allegiance to the United States of America, to the state of Rhode Island and to the American public school system.

I solemnly promise to support the constitution and laws of Nation and State, to acquaint myself with the laws of the State relating to public education, and also the regulation and instruction of my official superiors, and faithfully carry them out.

I further promise to protect the school rights of my pupils, to conserve the democracy of school citizenship, to honor public education as a principle of free government, to respect the profession of education as a public service, and to observe its ethical principles and rules of professional conduct.

I pledge myself to neglect no opportunity to teach the children committed to my care loyalty to Nation and State, honor to the Flag, obedience to law and government, respect for public servants entrusted for the time being with the functions of government, faith in government by the people, fealty to the civic principles of freedom, equal rights and human brotherhood, and the duty of every citizen to render service for the common welfare.

I shall endeavor to exemplify in my own life and conduct in and out of school the social virtues of fairness, kindliness and service as ideals of good citizenship.

I affirm in recognition of my official obligation, that, though as a citizen I have the right of personal opinion, as a teacher of the public's children I have no right, either in school hours or in the presence of my pupils out of school hours, to express opinions that conflict with honor to country, loyalty to American ideals, and obedience to and respect for the laws of the Nation and State.

In all this I pledge my sacred honor and subscribe to a solemn oath that I will faithfully perform to the best of my ability all the duties of the office of teacher in the public schools.

Ohio adopted a teachers oath law in 1919, and Colorado, Oklahoma, Oregon and South Dakota in 1921. Florida required the signing of a pledge after 1925. West Virginia enacted an oath law in 1928 and Indiana in 1929, the latter serving as a model for those adopted in 1931 in California, Montana, North Dakota, and Washington. An oath law was enacted in New York in 1934 and the following year in Arizona, Georgia, Massachusetts, Michigan, New Jersey, Texas and Vermont. Moreover, such bills were introduced in the legislatures of sixteen states in 1935 but were defeated in seven and vetoed by the Governors of Delaware and Maryland. Propaganda behind such laws was thoroughly organized in that year as a part of a broad program including stringent sedition bills and bills barring radical parties from the ballot. All of these laws were similar either to that of Oklahoma or Oregon or Indiana, except those of Georgia, Florida and Vermont which belong in a class with that of Rhode Island. The substance of these laws reveals in a better way than can otherwise be shown, the progression of the movement.

OKLAHOMA—1921

I . . . do solemnly swear (or affirm) that I will support, obey, and defend the constitution of the United States and the constitution of the State of Oklahoma.

OREGON—1921

I solemnly swear, or affirm, that I will support the constitution of the state of Oregon . . . and the laws enacted thereunder, and that I will teach, by precept and example, respect for the flags of the United States and of the state of Oregon; . . . reverence for law and order and undivided allegiance to the government of our country, the United States of America.

INDIANA—1929

I solemnly swear (or affirm) that I will support the constitution of the United States of America, the constitution of the State of Indiana and the laws of the United States and the State of Indiana, and will, by precept and example, promote respect for the flag and the institutions of the United States and of the State of Indiana, reverence for law and order and undivided allegiance to the government of the United States of America.

GEORGIA—1935

Uphold, support and defend the Constitution and laws of this State and of the United States, and will refrain from directly or indirectly subscribing to or teaching any theory of government of economics or of social relations which is inconsistent with the fundamental principles of patriotism and high ideals of Americanism.

VERMONT—1935

I, . . ., do solemnly swear (or affirm) that I will support and defend the Constitution of the United States against all enemies, foreign and domestic; that I will bear true faith and allegiance to the same; that I take this obligation freely, without any mental reservation or purpose of evasion; and that I will well and faithfully discharge the duties of the office on which I am about to enter. SO HELP ME GOD.

FLORIDA—1925

I believe in the United States of America as a government of the people, by the people, for the people, whose just powers are derived from the consent of the governed; a democracy in a republic; a sovereign nation of many sovereign States; a perfect Union, one and inseparable, established upon those principles of freedom, equality, justice, and humanity for which American patriots sacrificed their lives and fortunes.

I therefore believe it is my duty to my country to love it; to support its Constitution; to obey its laws; to respect its flag; and to defend it against all enemies.

This amazing legislative concern with the patriotism of teachers has but one explanation. It is that during the World War and the two periods of economic unrest since the war any one was an object of suspicion by certain vested interests who suggested changes in the economic and social order or who even desired to discuss the merits of suggested changes. Middle class philosophy and intense nationalism were masquerading as patriotism. The prevailing philosophy was the direct antithesis of that expressed by Justices Holmes in the Rosika Schwimmer case when he said: "If there is any principle of the Constitution that more imperatively calls for attachment than any other it is the principle of free thought—not free thought for those who agree with us but freedom for the thought that we hate." The purpose back of every teachers oath was to induce those who took it so to present the facts in class room discussion as to make the *status quo* appear to be the wisest and best of all human endeavor. How could any teacher have sworn in 1850 to promote, by precept and example, the institutions of the United States without being a slaveholder? If ever there was a distinctly American institution, it was slavery in 1850. How could any teacher have taken such an oath in 1920 without being a stanch prohibitionist? The prohibition was a part of the Constitution. How could any teacher have taught pupils respect for some of the public servants at Washington during the Harding Administration? The amazing thing about the whole procedure was that, in setting up the Constitution as a symbol to which teachers must swear allegiance no thought was given to the fact that the Constitution itself provides a form of amendment by which every feature of the government may be altered or abolished if the people so desire.

Every teacher who ever took such an oath in the United States knew that the purpose of those who sponsored its requirement was that, so frankly stated in the Georgia oath, of preventing a full and frank discussion of social, economic and political questions. The damage done to the school system can not be measured in terms of those rare cases where teachers refused to take the required oaths or were dismissed from the service. It can not even be measured by the number of teachers who were dismissed and continue to be dismissed because of "incompetency" or are "frozen out" by being refused salary increases or promotions, or who refuse to accept positions after listening to an hour's tirade by the hiring superintendent on the dangers of Communism. The damage, and no one can adequately measure it, resulted from the fact that teachers, already suffering the effect of drastic salary cuts, concealed whatever spark of liberalism and disposition they might have to acquaint their children with broad knowledge of human thought, rather than antagonize conservative interests in the community. One could find school districts in every state where teachers voluntarily refrained from a discussion of one or another of the questions of banking, dishonest advertising, industrial labor policies, child labor, old age pensions, unemployment insurance, the tariff, crop renters, lynching, or pacifism.

Back of the movement for teachers oath laws was a continuous agitation by the Hearst and Macfadden publications and such organizations as the Daughters of the American Revolution, the American Legion, the American Liberty League, the Sentinels of the Republic, the American Defense Society and the United States Flag Association about the menace of Bolshevism, communism and regimentation. There can be no question but that the widespread denunciation of the Roosevelt Administration on these counts had some connection with the drive for teachers oath laws in 1935. That the movement was definitely checked by the following year was due to the courageous efforts of many men and women in the leading eastern universities including George Counts, Carl Becker, Alice Snyder, Mary Woolley, Christian Gauss, Kirtley Mather, Howard K.

Beale, Charles Beard, Merle Curti, John Dewey and Harold Faulkner.

Meanwhile, the Customs Bureau of the Treasury Department and organizations such as the Boston Watch and Ward Society and the New York and Philadelphia Societies for Suppression of Vice were busy protecting individuals against their own indiscretions by the censorship of books, theater productions, moving pictures and art exhibits. The Tariff Act of 1894 prohibited any person from importing into the United States from any foreign country, "any obscene book, pamphlet, paper, writing, advertisement, circular, print, picture, drawing, or other representations, figures, images, etc." Beginning in 1909, when the Bureau sought to prevent the Field Museum from importing Chinese pictures and manuscripts claimed to be obscene, a black list of hundreds of book titles has been compiled. Among those books which have been excluded at one time or another since then are Rousseau's *Confessions*, Voltaire's *Candide*, Boccaccio's *Decameron*, Joyce's *Ulysses*, and Lawrence's *Lady Chatterley's Lover*. Police censorship in large municipalities of books, plays and movies barred from the bookstores and from the stage such eminent productions as Eugene O'Neill's *Desire Under the Elms* and *Strange Interlude*, Sinclair Lewis' *Elmer Gantry*, Upton Sinclair's *Oil* and *Boston*, Theodore Dreiser's *American Tragedy*, Lee Shubert's *Bunk of 1926*, Maxwell Anderson's *Gods of the Lightning* and *Winterset*, Ernest Hemingway's *Farewell to Arms*, Lion Feuchtwanger's *Power*, Carl Van Vechten's *Nigger Heaven*, Sherwood Anderson's *Dark Laughter*, Samuel Raphaelson's *Young Love*, Clifford Odets' *Waiting for Lefty*, and Jack Kirkland's *Tobacco Road*. Margaret Sanger was refused permission to speak in Boston on the subject of birth control. Mary W. Dennett was arrested and brought to trial for circulating a treatise originally written for her adolescent sons explaining the physiological basis of sex life. Rosika Schwimmer, one of the really fine characters of the age and an internationally known pacifist fifty years of age, was denied citizenship because she refused to agree to bear arms in defense of the country. Charlotte Whitney was convicted for membership in the Communist Labor party which was a criminal offense under the laws of California. Editors of student publications in several colleges and universities were forbidden to discuss compulsory military training. Large radio stations "cut out" of network programs when communist, socialist and pacifist speakers went on the air.

Criminal Syndicalist laws were enacted in thirty-two states; laws punishing the display of the red flag as a political emblem in twenty-eight states; laws requiring the reading of the Protestant Bible in the schools in seventeen states; laws prohibiting atheists from testifying in court or holding public office in six states; laws segregating negroes in public conveyance, schools and recreation centers in seventeen states; and laws establishing censorship of the movies in six states. Laws dating from reconstruction days were revived in some southern states and used against labor organizers. In the cities, ordinances were written against disorderly conduct, disturbing the peace, parades or street meetings without permits, distribution of literature in public places—all of which gave discretionary power into the hands of police officials which was used to deny freedom of speech, press and assemblage to dissentient groups. Bills were introduced into Congress and received substantial support to deport all alien radicals, register all aliens, suppress sedition and syndicalism.

CHAPTER XI

THE AGE OF THE GOLDEN CALF

THERE was a time, when the nation was predominantly agricultural, that the desire for a home, a few acres of land from which to draw sustenance, and a fair start in life for their children was the principal objective of enterprising people. The same was true of those engaged in manufacturing enterprise during the first stages of industrial development. These people were drawn rapidly into the cities, where they lived in a money economy. They went to work in the factories, in business establishments and in the several types of services for a money wage. The factory—the unit of production—was not theirs. They had no voice in determining when it should operate. They were paid only when it did operate—not an annual wage, but a monthly, weekly or hourly wage. If they saved money, it was invested sometimes in a home, but more often in real estate mortgages or industrial stocks and bonds, either directly or through the medium of savings banks, trust companies or insurance companies. The value of these investments, like their wages, depended upon the operation of the factories in which they worked. There was a particular exception in the case of government bonds, foreign, United States or municipal. The manufacturing process could function only so long as there was a market for the artifacts produced. The market was foreign and domestic. The domestic market was urban and agricultural. The agricultural market in turn depended upon the ability of farmers to sell their products at home or abroad. The system was highly dependent upon the proper functioning of each of its parts. It also was vulnerable at many points. Anything which effected the farmers' ability to purchase, destroyed a most important part of the industrial market. Tariffs were one. A currency with a fluctuating purchasing power was another. The urban market was a third. Anything which effected the value of investments likewise destroyed purchasing power. It was one thing to buy securities with the idea of receiving a fairly constant return on the investment, but quite another to purchase them with the idea of selling the next day to some one else for a profit. It was one thing to use that profit to purchase consumers goods and another to re-invest it until one's income passed beyond one's ability to consume. The sale of securities on the stock market, then, was a second important factor. Its relative importance depended upon the disposition of the people to speculate rather than to invest and upon their ability to determine the true investment value of securities. The third important factor was the relative proportion of industrial profits which went to invested capital in the form of dividends, to management in salaries and bonuses, to labor in wages, and to reserves for replacements, expansion, etc. The portion which went to labor for the most part, and to investors in some degree, was used to purchase consumers goods and keep the factories in operation. These fundamental facts, simple as they may seem, are essential to an understanding of the history of the Golden Twenties.

Population

The population of the United States increased 62 per cent between 1900 and 1930, from 75,000,000 to 122,000,000. The rate of increase during this period steadily declined. Estimates for the future vary. Some authorities suggest a possible increase to 145,000,000 by the year 2000. Others predict an actual decrease from the present figure. The movement of rural folk to the urban centers continued until the depression of 1929, the rural population declining during that period from 60 per cent to 44 per cent of the whole. On the other hand, the foreign immigration, which had gone largely to the cities, was drastically reduced.

In 1907, Congress had created an Immigration Commission to study the whole problem. Its report, published in 1911, represented four years of labor and an expenditure of several hundred thousand dollars. It placed emphasis upon three features of a proposed program: (1) selection on the basis of easy assimilation, preferably by the literacy test; (2) government action to encourage naturalization and proper geographic distribution; and (3) consideration of economic aspects to prevent exploitation by industry and injury to American standards of living. These recommendations, embodying the literacy test, were written into the Smith-Burnett bill in 1913, which was vetoed by President Taft. President Wilson vetoed two such bills, in 1915 and 1917.

The second of these acts was passed over the veto, largely by a combination of those elements from the South and West which were soon to enter upon the crusade for 100 per cent Americanism. This law was an extension of the individual desirability principle, with three important additions to the undesirable class: chronic alcoholics, possible public charges, and psychopathics. Immigrants must be able to read some language. They must be deported if convicted of felonies. In May, 1921, Congress established an entirely new principle for admission. Immigrants were to be admitted, not to exceed three per cent of the number of their nationality in this country in 1910. The law did not apply to nations in this hemisphere nor to other aliens resident in those countries for one year. One year later this period of residence was raised to five years. In 1924, the number of immigrants was reduced to two per cent of the nationality resident in the United States in 1890. This was to apply until 1927, when the total number of immigrants in any one year was fixed at 150,000. Each nation was allowed the same proportions of that number as it had nationals in the population of the United States in 1920. Members of the immediate families of American citizens and skilled agriculturists were to be given preference up to 50 per cent of a nation's quota. The change was not made in 1927 because the Secretaries of State, Commerce and Labor were unable to determine the quotas. Congress refused to grant President Hoover's request for a repeal of the provision and it went into effect in 1929. In 1931, the executive department of the government decided any one was likely to become a public charge who possessed less than $1,000 and permitted only 48,500 to enter under the law. Mexican labor was also cut down under this provision of the law. Nearly 500,000 came in during the twenties, but only 3,000 in 1931.

The steady migration of people from Europe and from the rural sections of the United States to the cities before the mid-twenties had furnished expanding industry with a ready supply of mature labor. One may fix the cost of rearing a child at any figure within reasonable limits and it represents a substantial sum if paid out in wages. Industry had never paid for rearing its labor supply. It had come as a gift from Europe and rural America. Industry had never cared for all of its unemployables. The children and aged were left behind when mature young men and women migrated to the industrial centers. Industry was faced with the necessity of doing both if the restrictions on immigration were maintained; of curtailing its previous rate of expansion if the population ceased to grow, the birth rate in the cities being consistently lower than in rural sections; of absorbing within its own economy the loss of sales due to a declining agricultural market.

Insecurity of Labor

Of the 17,000,000 increase of population between 1920 and 1930, less than 2,500,000 was in rural areas. Agricultural production, however, increased nearly 50 per cent between 1900 and 1930: cotton from 10,000,000 bales to 14,000,000 bales; wheat from 602,000,000 bushels to 850,000,000 bushels. Approximately 150,000,000 acres were added to the total farm acreage of the country, although the average size of farms continued to fluctuate slightly around 150 acres. This increased production with less man power was due to the development of labor-saving machinery. To some degree, the shifting population was re-absorbed into other fields of production, particularly manufacturing, transportation and mining, although much of it went into new types of services created by an expanding urban population. The latter group remained an unknown quantity and greatly complicated the formulation of a recovery program after the collapse of 1929-1930. Mining, manufacturing, and transportation industries each increased more than 300 per cent during these thirty years; but the number of workers employed in these industries did not increase in any such proportion. Science and technology entered into the picture to slow up the re-adjustment and in some cases actually displaced men already employed. Labor-saving machinery and power outdistanced the increased consumption of minerals and manufactured goods. The increased cost of mining, for instance, after the more accessible deposits were exhausted, was met by replacing hand labor with machines. By 1930, the average coal miner was producing twice as much coal as he had thirty years earlier. There were only 125 loading machines in the coal fields in 1923. That number had increased to 3089 by 1934. In that year machines were loading 12 per cent of the bituminous coal and 20 per cent of the anthracite. The efficiency of steel workers increased 50 per cent after the World War; that of the automobile worker 300 per cent. There was perfected a steam shovel which would do the work of 200 men; a bread-wrapping machine which would do the work of 20 men; a clothes-making machine which would do the work of 25 men.

This increased output per man hour in industry was greater than the increased demand for their products. The power generated in the oat and hay fields was replaced by that which came from the oil fields as the tractor, truck and passenger automobile came into general use. The coal mining industry suffered from increased production of water power, oil and natural gas. The rate of increased production in iron mining slowed down as more and more scrap from accumulated stocks went back into the manufacturing process. New, rich fields of exploitation were discovered and older fields were abandoned. In some cases it amounted to a migration within the nation's own domestic economy, in others to importation of minerals from Central and South America. The first process always left behind a destroyed local economy as in the copper districts of Upper Michigan, the gold fields of the Cripple Creek area, the oil fields of Pennsylvania and Ohio. In the second process there was competition from richer deposits outside the domestic economy: of anthracite coal from Russia, of copper and oil from Latin America. By 1930, agricultural imports were larger than agricultural exports by more than $300,000,000. Imports of copper were almost negligible in 1900; but, thirty years later, they were only two per cent less than exports. Imports of crude oil were only 30 per cent less than exports. In every case, three factors operated to create unstable conditions in the extractive industries: (1) over-production resulting from unrestricted competition and production for profit; (2) the development of substitute products; and (3) the development of new fields of operation at home or abroad. These unstable conditions in our national economy affected both man and material. 250,000 coal miners and 535,000 railroad men lost their jobs between the close of the World War and 1930. 150,000,000 tons of coal were forever lost each year by destructive processes of extraction. The situation in the oil and gas industries was even worse, with enough gas being wasted in the Texas field to supply large industrial cities of the North and East.

It was customary in the days when the American system was regarded as one hundred per cent perfect to dismiss the subject of technological unemployment with the traditional fiction that other enterprises made possible by invention took up the displaced workmen. A more ridiculous idea was never foisted upon an intelligent people. How many blacksmiths became garage mechanics when automobiles replaced horses? How many piano tuners went into the radio business? How many operatives in the New England textile mills moved south into the Piedmont Crescent when the manufacturers shifted their field of operations? How many employees of the shoe factories of New England moved to St. Louis? How many mountaineer farmers in the South went into the textile mills with their wives and children? The answer in any case is: precious few. How many cotton fields went untended when 135,000 Negroes moved out of Georgia? What became of the millions invested in houses, schools, streets, etc., when a town shrank from several thousand to a few hundred population? Who provided for the aged and infirm when young men and young women left the farms for distant manufacturing centers? The answers to these questions and more provide the dark shadows in an economy of reputed superabundance. One does not have to dig very deep into the life of any community in the twenties to find men whose experience and skill in a particular trade became useless to them when they were past the age of adaptation; men who lost their jobs in periods of seasonal or cyclical unemployment and walked the streets for months before they found some one who would risk employing persons above the age of forty-five; men whose factory or mine or oil field was moved away from them over night and were unable to follow because of age, or homes, or other local attachments. No one can say how many there were at any time because those who suffered these reverses usually found temporary or less desirable employment after using up their savings and passing through a period of despondency, perhaps under-nourishment and despair. Statistics of unemployed are useless in measuring these things; but even so there was not a single year after the World War when ordinary measurements showed less than 2,000,000 unemployed. It was more than 4,000,000 in 1921 and probably close to that figure in the peak year of prosperity, 1928. By 1932, it had increased to an estimated minimum of 15,000,000. Unemployment among laboring men resulting from technological advance, shifting fields of operation and cyclical depressions, was matched by equal casualties among those business and manufacturing enterprises unable to keep up with the rate of increased output per man hour. The increased wealth represented by new factories, homes and civic improvements in the textile districts of the South little more than offset the depreciation represented by idle factories and falling real estate values in New England. So with every phase of the economic system. One man's gain was another man's loss. People began to buy automobiles, radios, electrical appliances, and all the other numerous modern conveniences; but unless their incomes increased proportionately, they purchased less of food, clothing and other commodities. When they turned to fabricated homes, they bought less lumber. The automobile drove down the value of horses. Silk and rayon replaced cotton. The effects of changing standards of living were especially severe upon agriculture. The increased consumption of many of these new artifacts led to the general assumption that standards of living were rising. It was more apparent than real. When the total volume of consumption made possible by mortgages on agricultural lands and on the future earnings of urban residents through installment buying is deducted, the result is startling.

Distribution

The total wealth of the United States rose from an estimated $192,000,000,000 at the outbreak of the war to $362,000,000,000 in 1929; the total national income from $34,000,000,000 to $83,000,000,000. This evident increase in material prosperity was credited to scientific production and management which enabled men to produce vastly more per hour of labor than ever before. There were, however, more things involved in the general process than merely total production and wealth. The ever-increasing supplies of marketable goods had to be distributed at home and abroad. The degree of equitable distribution both of the finished product and of the returns from the industrial process is the only criterion by which to judge the general welfare of the people. In view of the fact that the output of factories operating on the modern system of mass production can not be sold to a small per cent of the population, unless there are extensive foreign markets, it is the only criterion by which to judge the general stability of the industrial system. The shift in population from rural to urban centers made the purchasing power of the urban masses a vital element in the industrial market. At the turn of the century, labor was receiving in wages 17½ per cent of the total value of the goods it produced. In 1929, it was receiving 16½ per cent. Industry increased its output about 50 per cent during the twenties, but the wages received by the workers, translated into real income, amounted to less than a 30 per cent increase. The volume of consumers goods increased about 30 per cent during the same period, while that of capital goods, including machinery, construction other than residential, etc., increased much more rapidly. The volume of unemployment was not due to lack of plant equipment, which has never operated to full capacity, but to lack of consumption. It is estimated that the average man purchased one suit of clothes per year during this period; that nearly one-half the dwellings in many cities were without electric lights and furnace heat; that nine-tenths of the urban homes had no electric refrigeration. This was true, in spite of the fact that an ever larger proportion of family incomes was going into these so-called durable goods. Consumption of food and clothing increased less than 20 per cent, while that of durable goods increased more than 70 per cent.

These things were true because not only the real income, but the money income of the wage earner was pitiably small. There were more than 7,000,000 families living in cities whose income was less than $1500 per year; and 15,000,000 whose income was less than $2500. Not a single study by government or private research investigators has ever been published which would indicate that these families enjoyed more than the barest subsistence. Evidence is conclusive that the capacity of American farms and factories to produce would have been taxed, had every American family enjoyed a liberal allowance of life's simple necessities. Further evidence of a hopelessly inadequate system of distribution was furnished when, in the depression, millions were on the verge of starvation in the midst of an abundance of food. Norman Thomas described it as "breadlines knee-deep in wheat." Secretary Wallace called it "the tragic nonsense of misery and want in the midst of tremendous world stocks of essential goods."

By 1929, three-fifths of the nation's wealth was owned by two per cent of the people. More than half of the corporate wealth was in the possession of 200 corporations, which were under the control of a few hundred men. There had developed, for the most part since 1900, a modern industrial feudalism in which the instruments of production were owned by a relatively few stockholders and controlled by a much smaller number of directors. Almost one-fourth of the total income of the nation flowed from the industrial process. The simple necessities of food, clothing and shelter for millions of people depended upon its uninterrupted operation. It is agreed that nine-tenths of the income of families receiving less than $2500 per year went for goods and services; and that those receiving $100,000 per year spent about one-half for goods and services; and that families receiving $500,000 or more probably spent little more than one-tenth for goods and services. The income tax returns showed that 513 people had incomes above $1,000,000 in 1929. There were only 20 such in 1932, but the increase began again thereafter and rose to 46 in 1933. There were 14,816 families with incomes above $100,000 in 1929; and it was estimated that there was about an equal amount received by 11,000,000 low income families and 36,000 high income families. There was, moreover, a steady growth in the unequal distribution of income.

Investment and Speculation

The decade following the World War was an era of rackets. Man shrank from denouncing another man's racket for fear of having his own exposed. Children were brought up to feel that anything one did was all right providing one could get away with it. They did not need to be told. It was in the very air they breathed. Scarcely a ripple of excitement followed the exposure of corruption in high governmental circles. Few realized then the extent to which this philosophy of life was undermining the economic structure of the nation, for it was a matter of economics as much as a matter of morality and ethics. The idea that a nation of people could become wealthy by gambling was an economic fallacy of the first order; yet every one was trying to get something for nothing.

Farm mortgages rose from $3,500,000,000 in 1910 to $9,500,000,000 in 1925. The number of renters increased proportionately. There were several reasons for it, which will be discussed later; but not the least was the constant appreciation of land values which went on before and during the World War. This appreciation was fictitious. It was not the result of increased productivity of the soil, because the soil was being depleted by erosion and lack of fertilization. It was not due to increasing profits for most farms were being operated at a loss. Nevertheless, land owners, seeing the value of their land increase, thought they were rich and moved to the hundreds of small towns throughout the Mississippi Valley. The same land that had previously provided sustenance for one family as the result of that family's labor now was expected to provide sustenance for two families from the labor of one, the other joining the leisure class. What farm mortgages made possible in agriculture, was equally true in city real estate. Every city had its horde of real estate speculators who reaped their harvest from the unearned increment produced by concentrating populations. Millions of people bought homes, paying for them in part with accumulated savings and from their monthly earnings, only to find themselves unable to continue payments as a result of unemployment or to find their equities wiped out when serious depressions arrived. The social inventions of the people did not include a plan for equal sharing of depreciation and remaining values. The railroads had been burdened down year after year by additions of watered stock to their capital structures until the volume of earnings required to meet interest and dividend payments on bonds and stocks outstanding made reductions of rates to compete with automotive carriers an impossibility.

The last and most important addition to the process, however, was that of corporate stocks. No-par-value stocks lent themselves as readily to the gambling fraternity who played the Big Board as blue chips to those who sat by the poker table. The objective was identical in each case: to get something for nothing. When many industrial enterprises were brought together into one corporation, the amount of the capitalization of the new corporation was always greatly in excess of the actual value of the constituent properties. Whatever else was done in the process of financial organization, a considerable block of common stock always went to the men who engineered the transaction. This stock had no equivalent value in property belonging to the company. The actual assets of the company were represented by bonds and preferred stock outstanding. The common stock was valuable to the promotors only because they could find some one willing to buy it. It was valuable to the purchaser only if the profits of the company were large enough to permit dividend payments. The same thing was done in the organization of virtually every large corporation, and invariably the promotors unloaded this stock upon the investing public through the medium of the Stock Exchange. The whole business would have been impossible had the people who purchased stocks done so for investment purposes rather than for speculation. It is agreed that no less than one million people from all walks of life went to gambling in stocks on margin. They were told that any man could become wealthy by saving a few dollars a week and investing in common stocks.

The result was the wildest orgy of speculation in the history of the nation. Hundreds of thousands of investors were drawn into the net by the promotors of colossal swindles. Foreign bonds were floated without the truth being told about the economic conditions of the debtor nations. Holding companies were pyramided one above another until, when the crash came, neither the promotors nor the courts could untangle the complicated structures. Pools were organized to drive up the price of selected stocks so that those on the inside might profit handsomely from the transaction. The partners of Dillon, Read and Company's investment trust, the United States and International Securities Co., thus disposed of stock which cost them twenty cents a share for $52 per share. Investment trusts and commercial banks were drawn into the operations. Prominent men in all walks of life, including public officials, were placed on preferred lists and sold stock, about to be fed to the public, at tremendous discounts from the market price. Insull Investments was thus sold for $7.48 to insiders before being placed on the Chicago Exchange at $30. Worthless securities were unloaded into trust funds established for the protection of widows and orphans. Thus some people not only speculated with their own money, but unscrupulous financiers, occupying positions of public trust, gambled with the savings of the remainder. Hundreds of millions of dollars were drawn into the market from foreign countries, complicating an already precarious economic situation in foreign nations. It is estimated that 90 per cent of the stock market transactions during the twenties were speculative rather than for investment purposes. The extent of the economic misery throughout the nation following the collapse of the market in 1929 is a measure of how far money was drawn from normal channels of trade for speculative purposes.

The effect of this abnormal condition upon consumption of goods is immediately evident. Money which would otherwise have been used to purchase life's necessities went into the market and was transferred eventually to the bank accounts of men whose incomes were far beyond their capacity to consume. The people probably lost close to $25,000,000,000 through speculation in one short decade. Men who purchased 100 shares of stock for ten dollars a share and saw it rise to twenty dollars a few days later, figured they had one thousand dollars to spend. Retaining the stock for future profits, they bought the new automobile, washing machine or furniture on time payments. How many more who had no money to gamble on the market, thus mortgaged their future earnings through credit accounts is difficult to say. The important points are (1) that a large part of the consumers goods which was sold in the twenties was sold because men were mortgaging their farms or their future wages—living from past savings and prospective earnings; (2) that much of the wealth of millions of people was in stocks which had no real value and was certain to be erased by a sudden slackening in business; (3) that, because of the necessity to pay dividends on large volumes of watered stocks, the directors of industries were forced either to sell their products at a higher price than would have been necessary otherwise or pay labor less, or both.

The actual ownership of agricultural lands, mines, transportation companies and corporations was widely distributed. Farm lands were worth about $78,000,000,000 at the close of the war, $57,000,000,000 in 1930. In addition to the large portion of the returns from agriculture which went to non-producing owners, there was the portion which went to the holders of farm mortgages. The mortgage debt of farm owners was a little less than $10,000,000,000 in 1930, of all farmers about $4,000,000,000 more. The interest payments on this indebtedness was nearly $1,000,000,000 per year. Insurance companies own 23 per cent of the total, Federal Land Banks and Joint Stock Land Banks 20 per cent, private lenders in agricultural communities 25 per cent, and commercial banks 10 per cent. The increased take of absentee landlords and money lenders through the years placed a steadily increasing burden upon the soil and reduced the volume of goods farm operators were able to purchase. The railroads were capitalized at $25,000,000,000, representing an actual investment of about half that amount. The stockholders numbered 850,000. The holders of $11,000,000,000 bonds, having first claim upon the assets of the companies, were largely savings banks, insurance companies and numerous kinds of trusts, representing no less than 60,000,000 policy holders and depositors. At least $2,000,000,000 of that amount was owned by educational, religious and charitable institutions. There were about 4,000,000 holders of corporate stocks in 1900, 20,000,000 in 1930. Making allowance for those who held stock in more than one company, there still was an amazing distribution of ownership. The stimulating effects of inflation and the devastating effects of deflation upon consumer purchasing power are readily discernible.

The effect of the World War upon the economic life of the United States was far reaching. Production was expanded to meet the war needs of the nation and its allies. It began with the outbreak of the war in Europe and continued until nearly two years after the Armistice because of the need for private and public rehabilitation work. Fifty million acres of land were taken out of production in the warring nations of Europe. Thirty-five million Europeans lost their lives in combat or as a result of disease over and above the normal death rate. The efficiency of more millions was lessened by injuries. Every nation emerged from the war with a tremendous internal debt, impoverished beyond belief, and owing the United States Government a combined total of more than $10,000,000,000. They eliminated their internal debts in whole or in part by confiscating the savings of their people with depreciated currencies. They delayed debt-funding negotiations with the United States, made some slight payments and then defaulted. They entered upon intensive industrialization programs, purchasing machinery from the United States with short term and then long term credits; purchased foodstuffs when necessary from those nations possessing an abundance of cheap land—Australia, Canada and South America; and initiated extensive trade wars with tariffs and fluctuating currencies as their weapons. The United States could not escape the effects of this abnormal situation. The farmers, unable to take high-priced land out of production without government subsidies and forced to depend upon the domestic market, accumulated crop surpluses and mortgage debts. Industry cut across tariff barriers by building factories in foreign lands. Private investments and loans in foreign countries were increased to a total of $12,000,000,000.

Government Spending

An historical treatment of public finance during the period under consideration involves more than statistics of expenditures and tax collections. The bitter controversy that raged over every incidental aspect of fiscal policies bear witness to the complexity of the problem. Taxation long ago ceased to be a matter of meeting ordinary governmental expenditures in the most painless manner possible. Tax laws became weapons for controlling the social and economic life of the nation. At times, they came dangerously close to political regimentation as well. Taxation ceased to be a measure of public expenditures, credit and tax exempt securities easing the way for extraordinary services required by the exigencies of the times. The burden was simply passed along to future generations. Almost one-third of public expenditures during the period 1916-1936, not including the World War and the depression, were from borrowed money. Taxation came to serve as a corrective for inequitable distribution of wealth made possible by technological progress. It drove deep cleavages between various classes in society as the real estate owner sought to shift the burden to the consumer by sales taxes and the poor man, in turn, to incomes, inheritances and estates. Fiscal policies also involved the nature of the currency, with a revival of two ancient problems: bimetallism and inflation. They aroused a critical analysis of obsolete units of government, and a violent discussion of the question of judicial review as the Supreme Court indicated probable limits to the legislative prerogatives of taxation and spending. In short, aside from the direct questions of revenues and expenditures, fiscal policies touched almost every phase of American life.

During the period, 1916-1936, the federal and state governments were forced to assume no less than a half dozen extraordinary financial burdens, every one a permanent annual charge against society. They included: (1) greatly increased army and navy budgets; (2) retirement of the World War debt; (3) veterans' benefits; (4) education; (5) highway construction; (6) unemployment relief. In spite of the fact that the revenues of federal and state governments had reached a combined total of $11,500,000,000 annually at the end of the twenty years, every unit of government except the state of Nebraska had greatly increased its bonded indebtedness. The extent to which the items mentioned above figured in the total fiscal pattern is shown by the fact that, in the federal budget of 1934-1935, emergency relief took 41.6 per cent of the total, not including 16 per cent for the Agricultural Adjustment Administration and Civilian Conservation Corps. Included in the remaining 58.4 per cent were 18.9 per cent for interest and retirement on the public debt, 7.2 per cent for defense, 8.2 per cent for veterans' benefits and only 7.5 per cent for regular government services. The public debt of the federal government had been $1,023,479,000 or $13.47 per person in 1900. In 1914, it was $967,953,000 or $9.88 per person. At the close of the World War expenditures, August, 1920, it stood at $24,061,000,000 or $228 per person. On June 30, 1930, it was $16,185,000,000 or $134 per person. Then came the second period in which expenditures exceeded receipts and borrowing was again resorted to, this time for emergency unemployment relief. The debt increased about $14,000,000,000 between July 1, 1930, and July 1, 1935, reaching a total of $30,500,000,000. About one-half of this amount rightly may be assigned to the World War and the other half to the depression. Since debt services claimed 18.9 per cent of the budget in 1935, 9.5 per cent is chargeable to the World War. That, together with 8.2 per cent for veterans and 7.2 per cent for defense, makes a total of almost 25 per cent of all federal expenditures for past and future wars. Assuming that the expenditures for emergency relief were extraordinary and temporary, the costs of wars and defense mounts to a total of nearly 60 per cent of the government's ordinary expenses. Both the annual interest charge of

$750,000,000 and the $744,000,000 defense budget for 1935 exceeded the total federal budget of $734,000,000 for 1916. Meanwhile, the expenses of state, municipal and other local units of government increased largely as a result of expanding educational systems and highway construction. Education, which was costing all units of government less than $1,000,000,000 in 1916, required about $3,000,000,000 in 1936, only an insignificant amount being contributed by the federal government. Highways cost less than $500,000 in 1916, but about $2,000,000,000 in 1930. After 1930, highway construction became an integral part of emergency relief activities in some states and was abandoned in others, so that comparative statistics do not indicate normal trends. If we add together the national defense budget and cost of veterans' benefits, the state and local school and highway budgets, and the $2,500,000,000 interest and amortization costs of all public indebtedness in 1930, it amounts to about 75 per cent of the total public expenditures for that year.

When government revenues dropped off sharply after 1929, nothing was done to reduce the defense budgets. Instead they continued to increase year after year. The cost of veterans' benefits was drastically reduced by the National Economy Act of 1933 and promptly restored within a year, plus an additional increase in the public debt for payment of the Adjusted Service Certificates. The United States Chamber of Commerce and its constituent units began an intensive campaign for a reduction in the costs of the educational establishment which succeeded only in working injury upon isolated units because of the manner in which curtailed budgets were applied. Highway construction was curtailed, but ever larger amounts were poured into the elimination of grade crossings and other public works. The tremendous agitation for curtailing the cost of government by elimination of personnel must be accounted pure political buncombe in view of the small percentage of public funds which went for such purposes. The only action of any note was the refunding of the national debt at a lower rate of interest, which no more than balanced the additional annual cost of interest on borrowings for emergency relief. Moreover, there was added to the permanent annual cost—at least they are generally admitted to be permanent—$500,000,000 for soil conservation and a somewhat slightly smaller sum for the Civilian Conservation Corps.

At the beginning of the Roosevelt Administration the federal government had outstanding $6,268,099,450 of 4½ per cent Fourth Liberty Loan bonds and of the First Liberty Loan bonds $1,392,227,850 at 3½ per cent, $5,002,450 at 4 per cent and $535,983,300 at 4½ per cent. These obligations required an annual interest payment of $337,101,579. Great Britain had converted about $10,000,000,000 worth of war bonds in 1932 for an annual saving of about $150,000,000. France in the same year had converted bonds worth nearly $3,500,000,000 for an annual saving of more than $50,000,000. The example of these two countries, together with the severe financial stringency in the spring of 1933, brought increased demands for conversion in this country, the Senate voting almost unanimously for the Treasury to act. Secretary of the Treasury Woodin announced in October, 1933, that $1,875,000,000 Fourth Liberty Loan bonds would be called in April, 1934. $1,600,000,000 were exchanged for 3¼ per cent bonds and the remainder were paid for in cash. On October 15, 1934, $400,000,000 of bonds were exchanged for 3¼ per cent bonds, $596,000,000 for 2¼ per cent four year notes and $200,000,000 for cash. By April, 1935, an additional $1,870,000,000 of Fourth Liberty Loan bonds were converted into 2¾ per cent bonds and 1½ per cent notes. The government was saved more than $150,000,000 annually by these conversions, the average interest rate of all outstanding federal obligations being reduced to about 2¾ per cent.

Taxation

The extraordinary items included in the complicated tax structure of today should not confuse us with respect to certain general principles involved in the history of taxation during this period. Many taxes were levied on the principle of making government undertakings self-liquidating. Automobile owners demanded paved highways and so special weight taxes and sales taxes on gasoline were levied in most states to provide road funds. The purpose of the Agricultural Adjustment Act was to restore a normal balance between agriculture and manufacturing within a self-contained national economy by diverting some of the benefits of the tariff to the farmers; and so the funds for benefit payments were sought from processing taxes. The fact that they were passed on to the consumer does not alter the principle on which they were first applied. When the unemployment insurance scheme was drawn up, funds were provided for by a tax on pay-rolls.

In addition to taxes for particular purposes, there were taxes for social reform. Excise taxes on cigarettes, liquors and playing cards are favored because they are taxes on non-seasonal and non-depression commodities: but they are also taxes which, when first levied, were on commodities the use of which a considerable portion of the population thought should be discouraged. During the depression many governors and mayors advocated the legalizing of institutions previously outlawed, such as dog and horse racing and lotteries. Not the least argument for the repeal of the Eighteenth Amendment was the expectation of much needed revenue from taxes on liquors and beer. Inheritance and estate taxes have a strong appeal aside from derivative revenues because they serve the popular fancy of promoting equality of economic opportunity for the youngsters of each succeeding generation.

Finally, agricultural prostration, real estate speculations and increasing governmental budgets combined to force the exploration of new fields of taxation for the relief of real property. Not only did sales taxes lift some of the burden from farm lands, but they fell very lightly upon those who derived their living from the soil. Farmers who could, in an emergency, produce most of what they consumed and who figured income from the point of putting cash in the bank, did not hesitate to throw their support to sales and income taxes. Retail grocers demanded special chain store levies to force up the price of consumers goods to a level permitting continued competition. The urban consumer, who, of all groups, had no organization, paid real estate taxes in rents, processing taxes and chain store taxes in food prices, insurance taxes from nearly every type of recreation and amusement, and regarded the income tax with a substantial exemption for the law income groups as most virtuous of all.

At least eight major trends in fiscal history are discernible during the period 1916-1930: (1) the adoption of the Eighteenth Amendment and the Volstead Act reduced annual receipts from liquor excises by approximately $300,000,000. The stagnation in foreign trade resulting from world wide resort to national self-containment, international debts and tariff walls reduced the percentage of customs receipts in the total federal revenues by more than one-half, although actual receipts increased. The collapse of war debt payments from European nations in 1931, with the probability that they never would be renewed, necessitated further heavy additions to the tax burden. (2) Income, estate and inheritance taxes furnished a fair proportion of the extraordinary expenditures of the war period, provided an annual surplus for debt retirement in the post-war period, but failed completely in the crisis of the depression. (3) Congress abandoned most of the nuisance taxes after the war, but hastened to resume them and liquor taxes when the income tax receipts dropped off sharply in 1932. (4) The general property tax remained the principal source of revenue for the state and local governments, furnishing more than half of all public revenues even at the end of the period, but reached the point of diminishing returns in 1930 as real estate values fell and tax delinquencies mounted. Meanwhile North Carolina, Oklahoma, Virginia and Wisconsin, which had income tax laws before the federal law of 1913, were joined by sixteen other states during the twenties, and by seven more during the depression with total returns from such state levies rising to about $250,000,000. All states adopted some form of inheritance and estate taxes. Sales taxes were introduced by West Virginia and tobacco taxes by Iowa in 1921. They were followed by numerous chain store taxes after 1925. (5) The desperate rush for revenues by state legislatures and Congress at the beginning of the depression resulted in general resort to sales and nuisance taxes. (6) Unable to finance the extraordinary burden of relief, all units of government fell back upon the inexhaustible resources of federal credit, which was extended to tottering business enterprises, subordinate units of government, and private individuals. (7) The burden was finally assumed wholly by the federal government through expenditures for direct relief and public works. (8) An entirely new innovation appeared in the process: the delegation to administrative units of discretionary power to spend large sums made available by legislative action.

Politically, the history of federal taxation during the period was a contest between those who favored excise taxes and those who favored high income and inheritance taxes. Income taxes not only followed the principle of ability to pay, but they furnished services for the population which it could have afforded as individuals only through a more equitable distribution of the returns from industry and services. Because all income taxes have back of them this intentional levelling process, organized wealth always has opposed them bitterly. On the other hand, neither sales taxes nor nuisance taxes have any relation to ability to pay. They bear heavily upon the poor, reduce consumption, and arouse little counter opposition to government spending because they are invisible. Income taxes, with even small assessments on a broad base, have a tendency to make the people tax conscious and critical of government spending. Federal taxes on income dropped from $4,153,000,000 in 1920 to $2,399,000,000 in 1929 and to a low of $781,000,000 in 1933. Indirect taxes, however, remained fairly constant at $1,577,000,000 in 1920, $1,142,000,000 in 1929 and $1,091,000,000 in 1933. There was, therefore, a steady increase in the relative proportion of indirect taxes to the whole: 27 per cent in 1920 and 58 per cent in 1933. It was estimated that the average family on a $3600 income paid in indirect and hidden taxes more than three times as much as they paid in direct income taxes.

Congress imposed an income tax during the Civil War and another in 1894. The latter law, taxing all incomes over $4000 at 6 per cent was invalidated by the Supreme Court. A constitutional amendment authorizing a federal income tax was submitted to the states in 1909 and became a part of the Constitution in 1913. Congress immediately wrote a levy of one per cent on incomes over $3000 for single men and $4000 for married men into the tariff act of that year. They imposed an additional surtax up to six per cent on all incomes in excess of $500,000. Taxation during the World War brought into the federal treasury only slightly more than the $10,500,000,000 loaned to European governments. Our own expenditures approximated the $21,000,000,000 secured in five loans. The $1,000,000,000 collected annually in taxes, major sums in those days, was derived from levies imposed in the tax laws of 1916, 1917 and 1918. The basic income tax was raised from one to two per cent in 1916, to four per cent in 1917 and to twelve per cent in 1918. Surtaxes were raised from a maximum of six per cent to 50 per cent in 1917 and 65 per cent in 1918. The tax of one per cent on corporation profits in excess of $5000 was raised to six per cent in 1917 and to 10 per cent in 1918 and an excess profits tax was imposed. This tax amounted to 25 per cent of all profits between 15 and 20 per cent of capital, 35 per cent between 20 and 25 per cent and 45 per cent between 25 and 33. In the field of nuisance taxes, levies were placed on railroad, Pullman, and theater tickets, telegraph and telephone messages, chewing gum, etc.

The fiscal policies of the government from 1921 to 1932 represent a victory for Secretary of the Treasury Andrew Mellon and President Coolidge over the remnants of progressivism in Congress. All the influence at Mellon's command was mustered to carry through a program of reducing taxes on incomes of persons and corporations and keeping returns from the light of day. His arguments were in accord with the principle that general welfare could be promoted best by lending every encouragement to the expansion of production with little thought to the problems of distribution or consumption. He asserted that the development of industrial enterprise was seriously restricted by high income taxes—the same argument later advanced against the Securities Act of 1933. President Coolidge lent his support with the argument that surtaxes were passed on to the consumer which, of course, they were not or the whole power of wealth would not have been thrown back of the movement for their reduction without disturbing consumption taxes such as the tariff duties. Until 1926, Congress refused to accept their program in its entirety. The Progressives predicted that the whole structure of international reparations and debt settlements was unsound; that the United States could not safely rely upon foreign debt settlements to retire its own domestic debt; and that war-time rates on incomes should be retained to reduce the debt as rapidly as possible. They were overruled, and the result was disastrous speculation instead of healthy industrial expansion, with ultimate collapse of foreign debt settlements as they had predicted.

The income tax law of 1913 had allowed exemptions of $3000 for single persons and $4000 for heads of families. The need for war revenues had caused Congress to broaden the base in 1917 by lowering exemptions to $1000 and $2000. These were not disturbed until 1926, when they were raised to $1500 and $3500. The search for revenues during the depression resulted in their reduction in 1932 to $1000 and $2500. After 1921, there was a further reduction allowed of $400 for each dependent child under 18 years of age. The excess profits tax of the war had brought into the Treasury $1,638,748,000 in 1917, $2,505,566,000 in 1918, and $988,726,000. This was repealed in 1921 and not restored until 1934 when a five per cent levy was placed on all corporate incomes of more than 12½ per cent of capital stock. At the request of the Treasury Department, Congress reduced the maximum surtax from 65 per cent to 50 per cent in 1921, to 40 per cent in 1924, and to 20 per cent in 1926. It was restored to 55 per cent in 1932 and 59 per cent in 1934. The estate tax of 1916 had been fixed at a maximum of 10 per cent with a basic exemption of $50,000. The rate was raised to a maximum of 25 per cent in 1917, 40 per cent in 1924, 45 per cent in 1932 and 60 per cent in 1934. An exemption of $100,000 was allowed by the law of 1926, but it was reduced again to $50,000 in 1932. The 1924 law also placed a tax on money gifts and distinguished between earned and unearned incomes. Incomes derived from personal effort were allowed a reduction of 25 per cent up to $10,000. This was increased to $20,000 in 1926, $30,000 in 1928, and abolished entirely in 1930.

Meanwhile, receipts from income taxes dropped to $3,228,000,000 in 1921, to $2,000,000,000 in 1922 and to $1,698,000,000 in 1923. This was, in part, due to the decision of the Supreme Court in *Towne* v. *Eisner* (1918) that stock dividends were not taxable income. There followed a veritable avalanche of stock dividends, many corporations splitting their stock as much as five to one. Over-capitalization and wild speculation were the two most noticeable results, but lessened revenues from income taxes were equally important. There was a strong suspicion, however, that evasion of income taxes was prevalent. Congress, therefore, insisted on writing a publicity clause into the tax law of 1924. What was intended to be a corrective measure for suspected dishonesty in making income tax returns, was seized upon by the yellow press, unscrupulous politicians, grass-widows and gold-diggers and wretchedly abused. Whether abuse of publicity was as great as abuse of secrecy, would be difficult to determine; but in one case the Treasury suffered, and in the other wealthy private citizens. Congress, therefore, repealed the publicity clause in 1926. The Progressives returned to the attack and, in 1934, Congress authorized the Senate Finance Committee and House Ways and Means

Committee to investigate all income tax returns at their discretion. It also provided for what was known as the "pink slip" return—a separate statement to be made out by the taxpayer and open to public inspection for three years. A storm of protest resulted in the repeal of the latter provision one year later; but publicity of all incomes over $15,000 received from corporations was required.

There were two eras of consumption taxes during the period, the war years and the depression years. Taxes on distilled spirits and malt liquors, the oldest form of internal revenue, had brought $483,000,000 into the Treasury in 1919. Abandoned by the adoption of the Eighteenth Amendment, they dropped off almost completely after that year and provided only $8,700,000 in 1932. The Twenty-first Amendment permitted their restoration and they brought into the federal Treasury $259,000,000,000 in 1934 and an estimated $430,000,000 in 1936. Tobacco taxes, on the other hand, remained a lucrative source of revenue during the twenties, producing $88,000,000 in 1916, $450,000,000 in 1930 and $425,000,000 in 1934. In the revenue act of 1932, a gasoline tax of 1½ cents per gallon was imposed by the Congress which produced $202,575,000 in 1933-1934. In addition to these federal taxes, the several states also turned to liquor, tobacco, and gasoline as attractive sources of revenue, the average combined state and federal taxes amounting to something more than five cents per gallon for gasoline, eight dollars per barrel on beer, and seven cents on a package of 20 cigarettes. Lesser items included in the 1932 federal act were two cents each on bank checks, five cents per $100 face value on stock sales, three per cent on sales of electrical energy and passenger autobiles, four cents a gallon on lubricating oil, 2¼ cents a pound on automobile tires and variable amounts on telegraph and telephone services, toilet articles, furs, matches, club dues, refrigerators and exchange produce sales. All of these items combined, produced less than either the liquors or tobacco taxes and only slightly more than the gasoline tax. The processing taxes of five cents on corn, 2¼ cents on hogs, 30 cents on wheat,

4.2 cents on cotton, etc., produced nearly $1,000,000,000 a year until declared invalid by the Supreme Court, but they were immediately expended in acreage retirement benefits and cannot be considered a part of the general tax program. Two other noticeable changes in tax systems in very recent years were the taxation of life insurance companies by thirty states and the adoption of from one to three per cent general sales taxes by almost an equal number.

Tax Evasion

That there had been widespread evasion of the income tax laws was revealed by the Senate Banking Committee's investigation of 1933-1934. It revealed, moreover, that tax evasion had come to be a respectable avocation, and furnished the legal profession with substantial revenues. Tax laws were complicated and often unintelligible to the average layman. It was necessary, in the interest of reasonable accuracy, to consult legal advice in making out tax returns; but too often the spirit of evasion, of circumventing the clear intent of the framers of the law, prevailed. The responsibility of keeping Congress informed on how its tax policies were actually working out in practice belonged to the Treasury Department. That there were loopholes in the income tax laws, both private and corporate, there can no longer be any doubt. The amazing sums of Treasury refunds finally aroused Congress to a realization that something was wrong. Whether the practice of refunds was being prostituted, as both Senator Couzens and Congressman John N. Garner charged, to the encouragement of political campaign contributions, is a moot question. Secretary Mellon certainly did not take the initiative in seeking to have necessary corrections made in the structure of the laws which permitted evasions. Instead, he took advantage of the law's infirmities in making his own personal returns. When the government finally brought proceedings before the Board of Tax Appeals for an additional $3,089,000 for the year 1931, it was revealed that he had transferred large blocks of stocks to holding companies controlled by members of his family to establish losses in that year. The tax of $647,559, which he paid, was frankly admitted to have been voluntary because he felt that, having a substantial income, he should pay something.

Not only were surtaxes in the higher brackets evaded by splitting incomes among the members of one's family, but so-called wash sales of stock were made to establish losses. The most famous case was that of Charles E. Mitchell, President of the National City Bank, who sold 10,000 shares of stock to his wife at a loss of $2,800,000, thus depriving the Treasury of $657,112 in income tax. President Albert Wiggin, of the Chase National Bank, devised the technique of organizing a small corporation in Canada, to which he sold stock at its original purchase price but which he entered on the books of that corporation at the market price as allowed by Canadian law. J. P. Morgan and his partners cancelled the profits of certain subsidiaries and affiliates against the losses and depreciation of others by making joint returns as permitted by the law. The government lost further large sums because an estimated 20 per cent of those subject to income taxes did not make returns. How general this form of evasion became is shown by the fact that between 1927 and 1933 a total of $182,000,000 was discovered by the Intelligence Unit of the Bureau of Internal Revenue. More than $100,000,000 annually was lost because, under the act of 1928, the government was allowed a maximum of two years to make its investigations. How much more was lost through evasion by gifts is difficult to determine. The law of 1924 placed gifts in the same category as inheritances for taxation purposes and made gifts within two years of death *prima facie* evidence of attempt to evade. The Supreme Court invalidated this provision and, in 1926, Congress restored all taxes collected under the law by repealing the gift tax retroactively. Gift taxes were again placed on all sums over $10,000 in 1932. Corporations evaded taxes by establishing dummy corporations which leased factories and subleased them to the parent corporations at exorbitant rentals or which acted in the same capacity for the purchase of materials. 498,110 corporations filed income tax returns in 1930, but less than 40 per cent of that number paid any tax.

Evasions under the general property taxes of subordinate units of government also became so general as to evoke concern. The exemption of property held by churches, schools and benevolent societies induced many such institutions to invest their funds in valuable real estate in anticipation of unearned increments. Large gifts of otherwise taxable city property were made to such institutions in return for guaranteed annuities over a period of years. Such property could be rented for less than other property to which an additional tax burden was shifted, the donor was assured a fixed income for himself or his heirs and the endowed institution of an eventual enlargement of revenue-producing endowment. Nearly one-fourth of all real estate in New York City in 1930 was tax exempt. More than $3,000,000,000 of that amount was government-owned property, but real estate worth $419,000,000 was owned by religious institutions and $37,000,000 by fraternal and benevolent organizations. Under the federal income tax laws, the income of labor organizations, agricultural cooperatives, religious, charitable, scientific, literary and educational institutions was exempt from taxation. Many states met the issue by placing limits on the amounts of tax exempt property such institutions might hold.

The most notorious method of tax evasion, however, was through investment in tax exempt securities. Amendments giving Congress power to tax such property were introduced into Congress numerous times but never received much support. Cordell Hull said, in support of such an amendment: "We have some 36 billion dollars of Federal, state, and local securities, largely exempt from all taxation. . . . It is unwise to create a class in the country which cannot be reached for tax purposes. Such policy is utterly inconsistent with any system of graduated income taxes, and it would ultimately destroy the latter. In event of war, it would be an unspeakable tragedy to have looked up in tax-exempt securities 40 to 70 billions of dollars, owned by a privileged class which could not be reached, even for the most urgent emergency war tax." Presidents Harding and Coolidge both recommended that tax exemption be abolished. Herbert Hoover took the same position both as Secretary of Commerce and as President. Secretaries of the Treasury Andrew Mellon and Ogden L. Mills both supported the reform. Mills said in the House of Representatives in 1923 that the government lost $240,000,000 annually because of the exemptions. He added: "A progressive income tax at high rates and tax-exempt securities can not exist side by side." As Secretary of the Treasury, he said in his report of June 30, 1932, that there were $22,536,000,000 such securities exempt from income and surtaxes. Professor Seligman of Columbia University placed the annual loss to the government at $300,000,000. Secretary Mellon argued that high income and surtaxes drove capital out of productive enterprise into tax exempt securities. It was never quite clear whether he was most concerned about having taxes lowered or tax exemption abolished. Finally, they were looked upon as the strongest influence to government extravagance, making it easy for the several units to borrow money instead of holding expenditures within general revenues.

Opposition to any action in the way of abolishing such securities was based on the theory of reciprocal balance between exemption from taxation and lower rates of interest. The government, it was contended, neither lost nor gained by the practice. Mellon, however, was always accused in Congress of keeping interest rates on government bonds too high and there was an equally pronounced agitation for refunding the national debt at lower rates. Nothing was accomplished, however, until Roosevelt's Administration. It was maintained also that ability to tax such securities would give the federal government a powerful weapon for taxing states out of existence at some future time should it decide to do so. Finally, the argument of those who sponsored a change in order to reach wealthy slackers was weakened by the assertion that less than 15 per cent of tax-exempt securities were owned by persons whose taxable incomes exceeded $10,000; that large amounts of them were owned by educational and charitable institutions whose need was for safe investments rather than large incomes; and that further large amounts were held by people of small means who did not fall within the group of 60,000 persons who paid 80 per cent of the income taxes. On the other hand, the Treasurer's report for 1932 maintained that $3,609,053,815 worth of tax-exempt securities were owned by those whose incomes exceeded $5000; that their interest return, not subject to taxation, amounted annually to $202,684,000; and that two persons whose annual incomes exceeded $4,000,000 received $4,344,491 in non-taxable income from such securities. Those who considered the matter from the point of social reform contended that non-exemption and higher interest rates would place more of such securities in the hands of the small investors who needed security but were not subject to income taxes. An amendment to the National Industrial Recovery Act, authorizing levies on federal, state and municipal securities, was introduced by Senator Bennett C. Clark of Missouri and strongly supported by Senator Ashurst of Arizona, but was eliminated in the conference committee as unconstitutional. That the committee was clearly justified in exercising its judgment in the matter was beyond question; but there was some doubt as to the correctness of its judgment. The Sixteenth Amendment gave Congress the power "to lay and collect taxes on incomes, from whatever source derived." Governor Charles Evans Hughes of New York, now Chief Justice of the Supreme Court, said at the time the amendment was under consideration that it would enable Congress to tax government securities. Justices Holmes, Brandeis, Sutherland and Stone indicated probable agreement with that interpretation when they dissented in cases invalidating laws taxing the salaries of federal judges and patent royalties. Congress showed no further disposition to bring the issue to a test although it was certain to arise perennially until some action was taken. In his tax message to Congress, 1935, President Roosevelt included, as one of his three suggestions, a constitutional amendment providing for taxation of future issues of government securities. The other two were for large inheritance and income levies in the higher brackets.

CHAPTER XII

THE LAST STAND OF RUGGED INDIVIDUALISM

The Agricultural Problem

Agriculture always has been the foremost industry in the United States. It nourished the institution of slavery and has sustained the major portion of the Negro race since emancipation. It lured millions of immigrants to American shores and on into the wilderness where the greatest timber resources any one nation ever possessed were sacrificed in men's haste to till the soil. For nearly a century, it furnished the men who assumed leading positions in every walk of life and controlled the thought and governmental policies of the nation. It still dominates the policies of most state governments. It furnished much of the labor supply for expanding industry, re-absorbing industry's unemployed from time to time. It provided the exports which were exchanged in the intricate processes of world economy for the capital resources needed to build the nation's industries. It embraced, at the close of the World War, an area of 350,000,000 acres cultivated by six and one half million farmers and sustaining directly five times that many people or about one-fourth of the total population of the country. Above all else, it served as the great shock-absorber for a mismanaged national economy, supporting its own workers and those who failed to find sustenance elsewhere, operating with profit or without, providing an ever increasing consumers market for the artifacts of manufacturing enterprise, and supplying one-half the freight traffic for the $20,000,000,000 railway system.

The agricultural population of the country was never wholly self-sufficing, though it came close to being so before the Civil

War. Within the rural areas of the North and West were hundreds of small towns whose populations were engaged in supplying the various types of services needed to supplement labor on the soil. It was, in the beginning, a simple agrarian economy, embracing 90 per cent of the population of the country. That does not imply uniformity, identity of interest, nor singleness of purpose on the part of the several types of producers. Cotton, tobacco, sugar, cereals, dairy products, meat, fruit and vegetables indicate the infinite variety of products which come from the soil. Each requires its own peculiar soil, proximity to markets, and degree of labor. They are not equally sensitive to world market conditions, nor equally adaptable to large scale production. They require various amounts of capital investments, of processing before consumption, of systematic marketing arrangements. Yet agriculture constituted a singular unity during the twenties from the points of world trade, governmental policies, soil depletion, flood control and its complete prostration.

Agriculture always has lacked stability, to an even greater degree than the manufacturing and extractive industries. If the exploiters of copper, coal and oil and the employers of human labor have roamed about over the country in search of virgin regions, so too have the farmers. The steady march of grazing herds, of cotton fields and waving cereals across the continent is as familiar as the westward movement itself. Virgin lands were so plentiful until recent years and so easily obtained by preemption or purchase that men did not hesitate even to abandon exhausted land and seek their fortunes elsewhere. So many riches were made from unearned increment that land speculation frequently became as general as the speculation in corporate stocks of the twenties. Land ownership lacked permanence. Every migration to the West and to the cities meant that countless farms passed to new owners. At any given time, therefore, land ownership represented either an actual capital investment of considerable proportions or of a small equity supported by a land mortgage. In either case, the maximum production was desired, with a minimum of cash returns expended for replacement of soil fertility. The result is that the United States today has no less than 300,000,000 acres of marginal and sub-marginal land under cultivation. One-third of that amount has been totally destroyed by erosion. Estimating 2000 years as the minimum period required for rebuilding a top soil by natural processes, one may well question if there has ever been much real wealth produced by the labor on agricultural lands in the United States.

Equally important was absentee ownership. The large landed estates in the South were broken up by the emancipation of the slaves. Thereafter, land-holdings were equally large but they were not operated as a unit. The owners, for the most part, resided in the urban centers and depended upon crop renters, both Negro and white, for their farming operations. In the North, thousands of farmers moved to the small urban centers where modern conveniences rendered life more attractive, and rented their farms on a cash or crop sharing basis. Thirty-five per cent of those who tilled the soil were renters at the close of the World War, more than fifty per cent in 1933. A large proportion of the absentee landlords at the beginning of the period were farmers in their own right and absent by choice. The increase after the war was the tragic consequence of falling prices, credit stringency and lower profits which wiped out the owner-operator's equity and transferred title to his creditors. This increase was largely in the North Central states, where diversified farming and relatively small land-holdings had provided a normally prosperous and sturdy yeomanry.

A third group in the farming industry was that of agricultural laborers. They neither owned nor rented land, but supplied the seasonal labor required in harvesting certain crops. The region of diversified agriculture, embracing the New England, Middle Atlantic and North Central states had fewer of them than the South and West. There were exceptions, such as in the cranberry marshes, the truck farms, the onion and beet fields and the orchards; but the extra help required for a short period was usually supplied in these regions by the female members of the farmers' families or by pooling neighborhood resources. In the West, transient laborers worked in the wheat fields, moving from the Texas panhandle to the Canadian prairies as the harvesting season progressed and seeking refuge from winter's blasts in Chicago and other western cities. In the South, there were between 2,000,000 and 3,000,000 men, women and children, who lived on the extreme margin of civilization and eked out an existence from a short period of labor in the fields during the cotton picking season or on the wharves and docks as the crop moved to market. Their ranks were augmented by several hundred thousand transient Mexicans who worked from Texas to California and occasionally found their way as far north as the cherry orchards of western Michigan. Agricultural laborers worked for a cash wage, something less than $500 annually on the average. Crop renters received their share of marketable produce, if any, at the end of the harvesting season. Northern renters seldom failed to produce their food as a bare minimum and normally derived some additional supplies from the barter or sale of by-products such as eggs, milk and vegetables. Southern renters, however, caught in the vicious cotton complex, relied upon the country merchant for the simplest items of their diet and surrendered the advantages of a cash economy for the convenience of a credit and crop *lien* system.

In every section—North, South, East and West—the most striking characteristic of the American farmer ever has been his unwillingness to join in cooperative regimentation. Increasing production, trusting in a beneficent Providence for the return of a better day, and relying ultimately upon the assistance of an ever generous government, he remained the victim of his own intransigence. The manufacturer, following closely the trends of business cycles, bent every effort to adjust production to fluctuating purchasing power. He established stable prices by creating monopolies or by agreement. Circumstances favored the manufacturer in this respect. The farmer could not take land out of production for less than one year. Six million farmers could not be brought into agreement so easily as a half dozen manufacturers of a particular commodity. Land ownership fluctuated more rapidly than the directorship of corporations. The farmer did not have a closed market behind tariff walls in which to operate. He could not build up capital surpluses to tide over periods of non-production. Nevertheless, the American farmer did not join in cooperative movements to eliminate the middle men as has been proved a possibility by the farmers in Scandinavian countries; and he did sabotage the government's efforts to assist in the control of crops under the Agricultural Adjustment Administration.

Much of the farmers' difficulty arose from the expectation of exorbitant returns from his labor. Farm ownership and operation had become capitalistic ventures by the second decade of the twentieth century. The average sale price of farm lands in the North Central states rose to about $125 per acre by 1920. Much of the better land was selling for $300 or more. Men who purchased at this price had a capital investment ranging from $10,000 upward on a one hundred acre farm. If part of the purchase price was represented by a first mortgage, the annual interest payment alone was a heavy fixed charge. Many farms carried additional second mortgages on which the interest plus service charges amounted to usurious sums. Periods of decreasing land values would wipe out the owner's equity faster than it accumulated. Declining prices not only reduced the margin between total income and fixed charges, representing consumer's purchasing power, but increased the initial debt in terms of what the farmer had to sell. Expensive machinery—binders, mowers, hay loaders, tractors, automobiles, and myriads of other items of the machine age—was introduced. They could not be manufactured within the rural economy, but were produced by monopolies and represented an additional capital investment. Moreover, the standard of living of farm families advanced in line with that of urban folk. New and expensive furniture, electrical appliances, education and commercial amusements added to the cost of living. The farmer did not sell his labor, nor was he ever without employment; but the products of his labor and his soil were sold and the difference between his cash returns on the one hand and fixed charges and replacements on the other represented his wages. As it grew less his ability to purchase goods declined or was maintained by abandoning the use of fertilizers, then postponing repairs on buildings, fences, drainage and the like, then by allowing taxes to accumulate, finally by increasing the mortgage if possible, otherwise defaulting on interest payments and reverting to the status of tenantry. Little of this is revealed in statistics of total farm mortgages. There is no completely accurate way of measuring the actual losses incurred or the resulting derangement in the economic life of the nation, but they assumed damaging proportions in the midst of fancied national prosperity. There was very little difference between the amount of farm produce required to purchase a given amount of consumers goods in 1914 and in 1920. Thereafter, the prices of farm products declined much more rapidly than that of the things the farmer purchased until, by 1933, his purchasing power in terms of what he produced was little more than 60 per cent of what it had been in 1920. The farmer's portion of the total national income dropped from 15 per cent in 1920 to 9 per cent in 1929 and to 7 per cent in 1933. Taxes likewise increased until tax delinquency on 40,000,000 acres of farm property forced many states to resort to general sales taxes to meet ordinary revenues of the government.

The farm mortgage problem after the World War centered in the twelve North Central states. The value of farm lands in these states decreased 40 per cent in ten years. The total amount of farm mortgages in these states increased from $4,791,000,000 to $5,496,000,000. Sixty per cent of the national total was in these states, with one-half of it in Illinois, Iowa and Nebraska. By contrast, the farm debt of the New England and Middle Atlantic states increased from $508,000,000 in 1920 to $624,000,000 in 1930, about five per cent of the national total; and that of the Mountain and Pacific Coast states from $1,178,000,000 to $1,343,000,000.

There were powerful forces beyond the control of the farmer which precipitated this revolution in agricultural economy. One was the tremendous increase in world acreage under cultivation; another, increased mechanization and the use of power. Fifty million acres of land were taken out of production in Europe during the war and, because the United States was extending loans and credits to the allied nations, 37,000,000 additional acres were put into production in this country to supply the deficiency. Sales from this country continued through 1919-1921 because of the further extension of post-war loans for rehabilitation purposes. Then cheaper land in other countries immediately came into cultivation. Approximately 42,000,000 acres of wheat in excess of 1914 were being grown in Canada, Australia, and Russia in 1930. The combined world acreage of all crops increased by more than 100,000,000 during the same period. Immediately after the war, also, tractors began to replace horses and mules in the United States until there were 800,000 more tractors and 9,000,000 less draught animals in the country and 30,000,000 acres of land formerly used to produce food for animals had been converted to other crops. Changing habits of food and dress further complicated the problem of surpluses. People ate less cereals, meat and potatoes, more sugar, milk and fruits. They wore less wool and cotton, more silk and rayon. Domestic consumption declined, production increased and the government made no effort to revive exports. Nothing short of a restoration of world trade could have accomplished much. So long as the United States expected annual payments on the war debts and raised its tariff barriers against foreign imports, European nations had nothing to send us in exchange for agricultural commodities. Every nation entered upon a program of economic self-sufficiency which reduced our agricultural exports, caused surpluses to accumulate and rendered ineffective tariff duties on any such products in so far as the domestic price was concerned. Wheat exports to Europe declined from 120,000,000 bushels to 20,000,000 bushels and the domestic price from $1.26 to 47 cents. Cotton prices fell from 18 cents per pound to 5 cents; hogs from 11 cents to 2 cents. Tariff duties benefit but a small portion of the farmers—those who produce sugar, wool, flax, and perhaps a few other minor products. They have no value to the producers of those crops in which there are exportable surpluses, estimated at no less than 85 per cent of the total production. More than one-half of the cotton produced in the United States, nearly one-half of the tobacco and one-fourth of the wheat were normally exported. It was in the twenties that the farmer, after more than a half century, finally realized how detrimental the ordinary tariff system was to his interests, and devised certain modified tariff subsidy schemes.

On August 11, 1916, President Wilson wrote to A. F. Lever, Chairman of the Committee on Agriculture, that the legislative record of Congress for the betterment of rural life was "a remarkable one." It included the Federal Reserve Act (1913), the Federal Farm Loan Act (1914), the Grain Standards Act (1916), the Bonded Warehouse Act (1916), the Federal Road Act (1916) and the Agricultural Extension Act. The Federal Reserve Act, designed to keep reserve funds available for local needs, allowed National Banks to loan on farm mortgages and Federal Reserve Banks to re-discount agricultural paper. The Federal Farm Loan Act was designed, in the words of Wilson, to "introduce business methods into farm finance . . . reduce the cost of handling farm loans, place upon the market mortgages which would be a safe investment for private funds, attract into agricultural operations a fair share of the capital of the nation and lead to a reduction of interest." It established the Federal Farm Loan Board and twelve Federal Farm Loan Banks. It authorized farmers seeking loans to form farm loan associations and interested parties to establish Joint Stock Land Banks. The Cotton Futures Act and the Grain Standards Act were designed to improve the quality of production by establishing uniformity in grading and regulation of the Cotton

Futures Exchange. The Bonded Warehouse Act was designed to promote better storage facilities and make available negotiable warehouse receipts to farmers for grain in storage. The Federal Aid Road Act made available $240,000,000 for road building, as an incentive to increased state and local appropriations for that purpose, to "stimulate larger production and better marketing, promote a fuller and more attractive rural life, add greatly to the convenience and economic welfare of all the people, and strengthen the national foundations." The Agricultural Extension Act provided for farm demonstration work by two agents in each of the 2850 rural counties through joint federal and state appropriations. In 1923, Congress passed the Federal Intermediate Credit Act, making available an initial sum of $60,000,000 for short term loans as a supplement to those available through National Banks, Farm Land Banks and Joint Stock Land Banks. The Intermediate Credit Banks were to be adjuncts of the twelve Federal Land Banks and were to rediscount agricultural paper held by banks, trust companies and credit corporations and make loans on warehouse receipts. The act authorized the establishment of agricultural credit corporations, and extended the facilities of the Federal Farm Loan Bank and Federal Reserve Banks by increasing the maximum loans permitted and the period of loans. By 1932, farmers had availed themselves of nearly $4,000,000,000 in loans from the three sources.

Congressional action in the Harding-Coolidge-Hoover Administrations centered around the question of foreign and domestic markets. The Fordney-McCumber Tariff Act of 1922 and the Hawley-Smoot Act of 1930 both raised tariff duties on agricultural products to the highest point in history. In addition special tariff acts in 1924 and 1926 raised the tariff on wheat to 42 cents per bushel and on butter to 12 cents per pound. Farmers, however, came to realize the futility of tariffs on any crop of which there continued to be an exportable surplus, because the price of that consumed in the domestic market as well as that which went for export was determined by world price conditions. They designed, therefore, two subsidy schemes to make the tariff as effective for agriculture as it was for manufacturing where exportable surpluses were non-existent. The first, known as the equalization fee program, was incorporated in the McNary-Haugen bill twice passed by Congress and twice vetoed by President Coolidge. The second, known as the export debenture system, was killed by the opposition of President Hoover. A third subsidy program, that of the domestic allotment plan, was enacted and put into operation only to be overthrown by the Supreme Court. Finally, a soil conservation program was established.

The McNary-Haugen bill was first introduced in Congress in 1924, endorsed by such men as Henry A. Wallace, Frank O. Lowden and Charles G. Dawes. It provided for the creation of a Federal Farm Marketing Board whose function was to get rid of agricultural surpluses over and above the demands of the domestic market in order that prices of farm products at home might be raised by the amount of the tariff duties. The Board was to accomplish this by contracting with exporters for the sale abroad of a sufficient quantity of each product to accomplish this and to reimburse them for losses incurred to the amount of the tariff duties. Assuming that the export of 200,000,000 bushels of wheat would be necessary to accomplish this objective and the full payment of 42 cents per bushel required, the scheme would call for an expenditure of $84,000,000 which was to be raised by a tax on the total wheat crop of about 800,000,000 bushels. The net profit to the wheat grower in higher prices would then amount to $252,000,000. The plan was vigorously opposed as a burden, in the form of higher prices for bread, upon the American workingman to the benefit of foreign labor. It was predicted that the scheme would fail because it would further stimulate production, decrease consumption, and lead to foreign retaliation. The sentiment of the country, aside from the farming population, was undoubtedly sympathetic to President Coolidge's veto. The plan disappeared from Congressional debates in 1928 after four years of bitter controversy and the export debenture proposal was substituted. This plan provided for a slightly different system of financing and a reduction of the amount of subsidy by 50 per cent. Exporters were to receive export debentures for all exports of farm products equivalent in amount to one-half the existing tariff on each unit. These debentures were negotiable and could be used in the payment of import duties. The total subsidy to the farmer, therefore, would be lower than under the McNary-Haugen proposal and the cost of the export subsidy would come from the Treasury in the form of a reduction in tariff receipts. In the end, the consumer would pay an increased price for commodities and additional taxes would be imposed to replace the Treasury deficits. President Hoover stanchly opposed the debenture scheme, insisting that "no Government Agency should engage in buying and selling and price-fixing of products." He offered as a substitute program the creation of a Federal Farm Board.

Hoover's ideas were incorporated in the Agricultural Marketing Act of June 15, 1929. It created a Federal Farm Board of eight members, which was to encourage the organization of farm cooperatives, establish stabilization corporations for buying and selling in the open market and guarantee both against losses. The Board did establish many national cooperatives such as the Farmers National Grain Corporation, the American Cotton Cooperative Association and the National Livestock Marketing Association. It loaned them a total of $165,000,000 from its revolving fund of $500,000,000 for purposes of marketing innumerable types of commodities. It loaned them money to withhold wheat and cotton from the market. It created the Grain Stabilization Corporation in February, 1930, and the Cotton Stabilization Corporation in June, 1930. It gambled in the wheat and cotton markets, losing heavily: $154,000,000 in wheat and $85,000,000 in cotton. It carried on an intensive campaign to encourage voluntary reduction of acreage. In short, it did exactly what President Hoover said no government agency should do: "engage in buying and selling and price-fixing of products." Its losses were a heavy burden upon the taxpayer without the slightest gain toward checking over-production or stabilizing prices. The export debenture and equalization fee proposals were no less sound economically and neither could have failed more completely.

In February, 1931, Congress again came to the relief of drought stricken farm areas with appropriations of $67,000,000 for direct loans to be used for seed, feed, fertilizer, food, medical supplies and voluntary crop reduction. One year later, in setting up the Reconstruction Finance Corporation, it provided for additional credit to Federal Farm Land Banks. Until 1933, therefore, the Department of Agriculture of the federal government and the several state departments continued to stimulate production by encouraging better farming methods. Otherwise, the government did nothing except provide machinery for easy credits to farmers and encourage cooperative associations to some extent. No effective action was taken to restore foreign markets, but they were further restricted by increases in the tariff and non-cancellation of the war debts. Having entered upon a narrow program of economic isolation, nothing was done to reduce crop production to the needs of the domestic market.

Industrial and Trade Cartels

Faith in competition was the dominant note in American economic philosophy. It was to preserve competition that the Sherman Anti-Trust Act of 1890 was written, the trust-busting activities of Roosevelt and Taft were conducted, and the Federal Trade Commission was established in 1913. These acts failed, however, as did the Clayton Act, to preserve competition. Integration of industrial and finanical control continued until, at the time of our entry into the World War, modern economic feudalism was well on its way to becoming an accomplished fact. The first stage of economic development, distinguished by free competition, came to an end and the middle ages were ushered in with the blessing and encouragement of the government, particularly the Department of Commerce.

The Sherman and Clayton Anti-Trust Acts remained on the statute books but the traditional method of enforcement so characteristic of the Roosevelt-Taft period—criminal prosecution by the Department of Justice—was abandoned under Harding, Coolidge and Hoover. The Federal Trade Commission remained in existence but its cease and desist orders dealt with trivialities and its investigations were ignored. Towering high in the economic system were a few absolute monopolies, secure behind the tariff walls and more powerful than the government itself. It was a significant fact that the aluminum monopoly was recognized as existing by the federal courts as early as 1912; that it was adversely reported on by the Federal Trade Commission in 1924; that shortly after Attorney-General Stone indicated intentions of moving against it, he was appointed to the Supreme Court bench; that the Federal Trade Commission filed complaints again in 1928 and 1930; that no action was taken against it in the NRA codes, nor by the Department of Justice either before or since under the anti-trust laws. More important, however, though less noticeable, was the development of trade associations. More than four hundred of these were in existence and rapidly assuming formidable stature before the beginning of the depression. Their organization was encouraged and carefully nourished by Herbert Hoover both as Secretary of Commerce and as President. Their objectives were the elimination of destructive competition, of unethical practices, in each industry. It was the practice of the Department of Justice, during the twenties, to advise these associations on the legality of their agreements under the anti-trust laws. The anti-trust laws, therefore, were unenforced except to the extent of advisory opinions of the Attorney-General to voluntary trade and industrial associations. Many such agreements violated the spirit if not the letter of the anti-trust laws. On the other hand, there were restraints by adverse opinions of the Department of Justice, but more particularly by lack of disciplinary power to bring recalcitrants within an industry into line except as the rulings of the Federal Trade Commission supported the efforts at regimentation. The limits here were set by the rulings of the Supreme Court as to how much authority Congress might delegate or had delegated to the Commission.

This movement in the direction of trade and industrial associations had its inception in the period of the World War. The individualism of business men and the Supreme Court decision in the Addystone Case had prevented more than the loosest sort of associations among independent producers and traders previous to that time. The War Industries Board and the several Commodity Administrators, particularly Hoover and Garfield, went far toward setting up temporary associations with the worst evils of such organizations, control of production and open price fixing as the primary objectives. At the end of the war, the government agencies were liquidated and, presumably, the anti-trust laws were to be enforced again by the Federal Trade Commission and the Department of Justice. The war-time machinery disbanded in the trying post-war period when industry was shifting back to peace-time production, and many independent producers were finding it difficult to survive with tumbling prices, cut-throat competition and high labor costs. It was in this situation that Herbert Hoover, former Belgian Relief Administrator, Food Administrator and organizer *par excellence*, was appointed Secretary of Commerce.

Secretary Hoover believed that industrial waste should be eliminated by cooperative action. He believed it possible to obtain the benefits of cooperation between producers in a given industry without destroying equality of opportunity and individual initiative. In his first *Annual Report*, he said: "No one would contend that there be a relaxation in the restraints against undue capital combinations, monopoly, price fixing, domination, unfair practices, and the whole category of collective action damaging to the public interest." But he believed the public interest suffered a greater loss through the restraints of the Sherman Act than it would suffer from the use of associations as a cloak for the above named activities. He requested that the Sherman Act be amended to permit cooperative organizations "to file with some appropriate governmental agency the plan of their operations, the functions they proposed to carry on, and the objectives that they proposed to reach; that upon approval, such of their functions as did not apparently contravene public interest might be proceeded with." What he proposed was that associations be formed for the following purposes: (1) the preparation of statistical abstracts from information supplied by the members as a guide to future production; (2) standardization of products along the lines of variety, grade and quality; (3) uniform credit policies; (4) settlement of trade disputes by arbitration instead of litigation; (5) elimination of unfair practices and misrepresentation of goods; (6) promoting uniform improvement of laboring conditions; (7) cooperation for economy in insurance; (8) establishment of common agencies to handle all problems of transportation; (9) cooperative research.

Early in 1923, Secretary Hoover appointed a Committee on Business Cycles and Unemployment to study the feasibility of his proposed program. This committee reported that if industrialists were provided with "more adequate information as to the tendencies in production, stocks, consumption, of commodities and unemployment," cyclical unemployment and business depressions could be eliminated. Secretary Hoover followed this by insisting that the standardization of products then being sought by legislation could be accomplished better by voluntary agreements within trade associations. More than two hundred trade and industrial conferences were held during the first four years of his incumbency in the Commerce Department. They were attended, presumably, by producers, distributors, and consumers, though the ultimate consumer was about as well represented as when the NRA codes were drawn up, which was not at all. The prevailing philosophy of government, that the general welfare could best be promoted by giving the captains of industry free reign, militates against considering government officials as representatives of the public interest. Standardization of products was but a small item on the agenda of these conferences. What was sought and ultimately accomplished was the exchange among competitors of information relatives to prices, sales, stocks and shipments sufficient to achieve open, intelligent, uniform price fixing. The Webb-Pomerene Act, which had legalized associations for export trade purposes, served as a convenient aid. In 1923, the Department of Commerce published a handbook entitled *Trade Association Activities* designed to spread the gospel of cooperative action. In four years, 1921-1925, American industry was regimented within the framework of a vast trade and industrial association structure.

This development, nourished by the Commerce Department, was directly contrary to the spirit of the Sherman Act as interpreted by the Department of Justice and the Supreme Court. Attorney-General Harry M. Daugherty insisted that the gathering and distribution of information and statistics among the members of a trade association was in violation of the law. The Supreme Court in the case of *American Column and Lumber Co.* v. *United States* (1921) held that the pooling of information, known as the Open Competitive Plan, by the American Hardwood Manufacturers' Association was in restraint of trade. Justice Clarke, rendering the majority opinion, said: "Genuine competitors do not make daily, weekly and monthly reports of minutes and details of their business to their rivals, as the defendants did; they do not contract to submit their books to the discretionary audit and their stocks to the discretionary inspection of their rivals for the purpose of successfully competing with them; and they do not submit the details of their business to the analysis of an expert, jointly employed, and obtain from him a harmonizing estimate of the market as it is; and . . . promises to be . . . if it did not stand confessed a combination to restrict production and increase prices in interstate commerce . . . the conclusion must inevitably have been inferred from the facts which were proved." Justice Brandeis, in a dissenting opinion concurred in by Justices Holmes and McKenna, denied it was in violation of the law, largely because membership was voluntary and "no information gathered under the Plan was kept secret from any producer, any buyer, or the public." But the opinion of the majority prevailed that it was "an old evil in a new dress and with a new name . . . the gentlemen's agreements of former days, skillfully devised to evade the law."

The members of the American Hardwood Manufacturers' Association produced but 30 per cent of the hardwood in the United States. Two years after the adverse opinion against them, an Association of Linseed Oil producers, twelve in number and controlling 70 per cent of the production in the industry, was held to be a combination in restraint of trade by the Supreme Court (*United States* v. *Linseed Oil Co.*). Chief Justice Taft, in rendering the majority opinion of the Court, said: "With intimate knowledge of the affairs of other producers and obligated as stated, but proclaiming themselves competitors, the subscribers went forth to deal with widely separated and unorganized customers necessarily ignorant of true conditions. Obviously they were not *bona fide* competitors. . . . Their manifest purpose was to defeat the Sherman Act without subjecting themselves to its penalties."

Secretary Hoover then took the final step in using the machinery of his department to circumvent the restraints of the Supreme Court and the Department of Justice. Voluntary committees within the industrial and trade groups sent statistical data to the department. This was combined with data furnished by the Bureau of Census and the Bureau of Foreign and Domestic Commerce, analyzed, and returned to the associations to be distributed among their members. The Federal Trade Commission denounced the practice as open price fixing through the agency of the Department of Commerce. This was followed by two Supreme Court decisions (*Maple Flooring Manufacturers' Association* v. *United States and Cement Manufacturers' Protective Association* v. *United States*) in which the Court held that associations were not combinations in restraint of trade providing they gathered and published without comment information respecting "the cost of their product, the volume of production, the actual price which the product had brought in past transactions, stocks of merchandise on hand, shipping costs," and held meetings where this information was discussed "without reaching or attempting to reach an agreement." Justice McReynolds, however, in a vigorous dissenting opinion in the latter case held that "pious protestations and smug preambles but intensify distrust when men are found busy with schemes to enrich themselves through circumvention."

These decisions opened the way to further progress in price fixing. The associations had proved profitable for purposes of combined research, advertising, insurance, regulation of traffic and lobbying. They had approached the borderline of illegal activity by gathering and disseminating statistics and by the standardization of products. They now turned to uniform accounting methods, exchange of credit information, and joint purchases. But beyond all else, they introduced what was to constitute one of the fundamental items of the NRA codes, namely, codes of ethics or trade practice agreements. These agreements were more in line with what the Federal Trade Commission had been trying to achieve. They outlawed bribery, misbranding, misrepresentation of products, refunds, rebates, discounts, freight allowances, etc. Two hundred forty-three such trade agreements were devised through the good auspices of the Department of Commerce before 1927. Secretly, there were added to the list of unfair practices such items as sales below cost, price cutting, etc. In business ethics, thereafter, lowering prices from those fixed by agreement was a crime. Standard prices became an accepted feature of the competitive system.

The final step in the movement before the NRA was the formation of institutes or incorporated trade associations. The Cotton-Textile Institute was the first to be formed and, by coincidence, the Cotton-Textile Code was the first approved under the NRA, having been handed to the President the same day that the National Industrial Recovery Act was signed. It was followed by the formation of institutes in carpet manufacturing, copper, sugar, woolen goods, industrial alcohol and rubber. The Cotton-Textile Institute cut production and raised the price level, both by 25 per cent, showing profits in 1926 for the first time in years. Carpet prices failed to fluctuate in 1928 for the first time in twenty years. Copper prices were raised from 15.4 cents per pound to 18 cents per pound and profits increased 300 per cent. The price of sugar was set at intervals by the Institute and announced over the telephone and that of alcohol at monthly meetings. The Rubber Institute failed to maintain fixed prices because the Firestone Company refused to participate in the monthly meetings. The institute of particular concern to the Secretary of Commerce was that of petroleum. Oil and coal were the two industries suffering most severely from overproduction and cut-throat competition. In oil, about one-half of the crude oil production was controlled by two interests: the Standard and the Royal Dutch Shell. Twelve thousand smaller producers accounted for the remainder. Few of the 12,000 were ever far removed from bankruptcy. Secretary Hoover first suggested voluntary curtailment of production in 1922. The task of persuading the 12,000 independents to join in a cooperative movement for curtailing production was undertaken by the Petroleum Institute. A plan was drawn up and agreed to in March, 1929. The agreement was recognized, even by some of its proponents, as an open violation of the Sherman Act, and when Attorney-General Mitchell declared it illegal the plan was abandoned without being put into operation. Four years later the question of oil was regarded seriously enough to be dealt with separately as section 9c of the National Industrial Recovery Act.

The formation of trade and industrial cartels revolutionized competition. Competition by price cutting between producers within an industry largely disappeared and in its place appeared competition between industries and commodities. In recognition of this new condition, the Department of Commerce reported: "Competition has changed from the contest of merchant with merchant to a gigantic struggle of industry with industry, for outlets, for space on the dealers' shelves, and for a place in the consumer's budget." It was no longer a contest between lumber dealers but between the lumber, brick, cement and steel men in the sale of building materials. Hoover could say: "I believe that we are, almost unnoticed, in the midst of a great revolution, or perhaps a better word, transformation of the whole super-organization of our economic life. We are passing from a period of extremely individualistic action into a period of associated activities." Thus spoke the great champion, in later days, of "rugged individualism."

The public was indifferent to the new development and business was exceedingly sympathetic. Few public officials had the courage to oppose what all knew to be illegal and contrary to national policy as defined in the anti-trust laws. The general attitude was one of waiting for Congress to decide whether to repeal the Sherman Act or silently acknowledge its demise. John Lord O'Brian, Assistant Attorney-General, said, in 1931, that more than fifty associations had been investigated and most of them found to be in violation of the law. The Federal Trade Commission discovered among the methods designed to control prices and increase profits "at the expense of the public generally," such things as "exchange of price information, prohibitions of selling below cost, weekly reports by committees as to what was considered a fair price, discussions at meetings to deter price cutting, publication of bulletins designed to prevent price cutting, exchange of price lists, and agreements to operate on a part time basis." Suit was filed by the Department of Justice against the Sugar Institute in March, 1931, but was not pressed. Attorney-General Mitchell asked for an injunction against the Wool Institute in 1930 and forced its dissolution. But these were isolated incidents in the general program of sympathetic aid to the movement which was the handiwork of Hoover as Secretary of Commerce and as President.

When President Roosevelt was inaugurated in March, 1933, amid a general stagnation of business and industry, the trade and industrial associations were legalized by suspension of the anti-trust laws and given power, by delegation of Congress, to transform their codes into federal statutes for the control of recalcitrant independents. The Cotton-Textile, Carpet, Woolen and Sugar codes and probably many more were exact copies of the association agreements drawn up during the Hoover regime. The officers of the associations, for the most part, became the Code Authorities. Industrial practices were legalized with the addition of government supervision to protect the interests of the consumer and labor; that, and nothing more.

Industrial cartelization would have been impossible under a system of unrestricted foreign trade. The tariff policies of the Harding-Hoover-Coolidge regime, therefore, were an integral part of the whole economic revolution. The Emergency Tariff Act of May, 1921, raised duties on agricultural products, virtually excluded all German chemical products, and safeguarded American industry against "dumping." The Fordney-McCumber Act of September, 1922, raised tariff rates back to pre-Wilson levels and set up a Tariff Commission for the purpose of investigating the costs of production of commodities offered for import to be followed by recommendations of rates sufficient to equalize costs of production abroad and in the United States. The President was given discretionary power to raise or lower rates on specific commodities by as much as fifty per cent in line with these recommendations. The same advocates of national self-sufficiency, economic isolation, or whatever one may choose to call it, again controlled Congress in 1929, and revised rates upward in the Hawley-Smoot Act of June, 1930. There was a great deal of opposition from the industries such as automobiles, which did not fear foreign competition, from bankers and importers, from the farmers who wanted the export debenture scheme included, and from Senators who wanted to deprive the President of the power to raise or lower rates. The Act was passed, however, by the narrow margin of two votes in the Senate and tariff duties were raised to the highest levels in the history of the country.

This tariff policy so zealously defended by President Hoover was denounced by over a thousand economists in May, 1930, as certain to raise consumers prices, foster unsound industrial practices, ruin export trade, make impossible the collection of foreign debts, lead to retaliatory tariffs in foreign nations, and bring no benefit to producers of agricultural products of which there were exportable surpluses. They were probably correct in every particular. Retaliatory tariff walls were immediately erected in more than a score of countries, foreign debts were repudiated, American manufacturers speeded the construction of branch factories in foreign lands, the merchant marine languished, and agricultural prices fell to the lowest point in many decades.

Transportation and Power

At the close of the World War, Congress was faced with the task of formulating a new transportation policy before returning the railroads to private control. The Transportation Act of 1920 or Esch-Cummins Act was passed and approved on February 28, one day previous to the termination of government operation. This Act increased the size of the Interstate Commerce Commission to eleven members and their term of service to seven years. It also created a Railroad Labor Board of nine members. Employees of the roads and the management were each to nominate six men for membership on the Board. The President and Senate were to appoint three from each of these groups and an additional three representing the public. This Board was to hear and settle all disputes with respect to wages, taking into consideration "the scale of wages paid for similar kinds of work in other industries; the relation between wages and the cost of living; the hazards of the employment; the training; the skill required; the degree of responsibility; the character and regularity of employment; and inequalities of increases in wages or of treatment, the result of previous wage orders or adjustments." The Board was not given authority to enforce its decisions and was replaced by a

Federal Board of Mediation in 1926, with authority only to serve upon the voluntary request of the management or employees.

The second important feature of the Act was the Recapture Clause. The Commission was given the power to establish rates, including the prescription of minimum rates on the basis of "a fair return upon the aggregate value" of the railway property of the country, which the Supreme Court later defined to mean reproduction cost new. The act said, however, that since it was impossible to establish uniform rates on that basis without allowing some roads more than a fair return on the value of their property, all roads receiving more than a 6 per cent return should place one half of the excess in a reserve fund and the other half in a contingent fund to be used by the Commission in making loans for capital expenditures to less prosperous roads. The third important departure from precedent gave the Commission the power to consolidate the four express companies into one and to consolidate the railway lines into a few systems on an economic rather than geographical basis. These combinations were to be exempt from the force of the anti-trust laws. The pooling of traffic for economy in operation was permitted. Interlocking directorates were prohibited. The sale of securities and expenditures of funds received therefrom were placed under control of the Commission. Finally, the control of the Commission was extended sufficiently to eliminate discriminations between intra-state carriers and inter-state carriers.

In 1926, the Interstate Commerce Commission published a plan to consolidate all railroads into nineteen systems. It was abandoned as a result of the opposition of the roads and management itself was requested to offer a substitute plan. In 1930, in accordance with their own request, all of the roads in the North Central States and west of the Hudson were consolidated into the Baltimore and Ohio, the Chesapeake and Ohio, the New York Central and the Pennsylvania.

The year 1920 marked the end of an era in railroad history.

For a quarter of a century, the railroads had enjoyed a monopoly of transportation. They had bitterly opposed and, for the most part, successfully resisted regulation. Whether the Esch-Cummins Act represented the final triumph of government over the unsocial practices of a great monopoly or the first acknowledgment by railway management that there was nothing more to gain by further opposition is difficult to say. In any case, the railroad barons were reduced to humble petitioners of the government they had so long defied not by the majesty of the law and the Courts but by competition. The railroads were the leading American industry before the World War with a capitalization of approximately $20,000,000,000. Then, in slightly more than a decade, the government and technology created a great competitive transportation system of inland waterways, the Panama Canal, pipe lines, air transport and 900,000 miles of paved highways. Passenger automobiles, buses, and trucks robbed the railroads of more than 50 per cent of their business. There were 24,000,000 automobiles on the highways in 1930, and local freight and passenger traffic on the railroads had ceased to exist. Nearly six times as much traffic passed through the Panama Canal in 1930 as in 1920, and the Inland Waterways Corporation, established by the government in 1924, was doing a business of $6,000,000 annually with its barge lines. Beginning in 1926, commercial aviation forged to the front, increasing its passengers carried from less than 6,000 in that year to 165,000 in 1929 and to 450,000 in 1933. All-daylight flying schedules were introduced from New York to San Francisco, Trans-Pacific service was inaugurated and service across the North Atlantic was being planned.

Air and motor transport were to the railroads what railroads had been to prairie schooners and stage coaches before them. Flexible, fast and relatively inexpensive, they rapidly became indispensable to modern society; and their growth created problems for the railroads and the government alike. The railroads were caught in the worst possible condition to meet the new competition. They had been plundered by speculative promotion and banker control and over-capitalized to the point where rate reduction, though absolutely essential, was difficult. Notoriously lax in creating capital reserve funds, they were in no position to replace outmoded equipment with lighter and faster rolling stock or to eliminate the grade crossings which were a prerequisite to faster service. They were prohibited by law from reducing their labor costs and from abating their services to the public. Their capital structures were so integrated with the savings of the people as to eliminate almost automatically the hope of wringing out the water. Of the $11,000,000,000 of outstanding bonds in 1933, $5,000,000,000 were owned by insurance companies and savings banks and $2,000,000,000 by endowed churches, colleges and hospitals. Railroad stocks were owned by thousands of individual investors, privately or in trust funds. Finally, the strict regulation exercised by the Interstate Commerce Commission had not been extended to their competitors.

About the time railroading had ceased to be a profitable field of adventure for private capital and adequate regulation in the public interest became a possibility, a new industry emerged, second only to railroads from point of investment: the electric utility industry. It, too, was a natural monopoly; and, for the most part, free from state regulation because it moved in interstate commerce. It developed as rapidly as had the railroads, under the same driving force of reckless search for private gain. Its management fought as bitterly as had railroad management against federal regulation. New techniques in propaganda and in finance greatly complicated the problem. There were, however, two aspects of the problem of regulation which did not enter into the long controversy over railroad regulation. The first was the existence of the holding company. Like holding companies in every field of industrial and commercial enterprise, many served a useful function in economical financing, engineering, management and mass production: but many, too, when pyramided one above another, were prostituted to the purpose of defrauding investors, increasing rates unnecessarily to consumers, making capital structures so complex as to defy reasonable accuracy in rate regulation. Above all else, the system served as a device by which economic power was concentrated in a few hands, giving to a few men control over the honest savings of thousands of small investors in operating companies. The second new element was the possibility of public competition, which was far more effective in eliminating abuses than any amount of regulation could possibly be, and which the utility magnates feared far more than they feared regulatory agencies. The history of the struggle for power control extending over two decades centers about the holding company and public ownership. The fight for federal regulation was led by Senators Walsh, Wheeler and Couzens and its history includes the Federal Water Power Act of 1920, an extended investigation by the Federal Trade Commission during the late twenties and the Wheeler-Rayburn Act. The fight for public ownership and operation, so far as the federal government was concerned, began with the building of nitrate plants at Muscle Shoals during the World War, and included the Norris Resolutions vetoed by Presidents Coolidge and Hoover and the creation of the Tennessee Valley Authority.

The Federal Water Power Act of 1920 created a makeshift Federal Power Commission consisting of the Secretaries of War, Interior and Agriculture. This Commission was authorized to issue licenses for power projects on navigable waters, public lands and Indian reservations of the United States. These licenses were to run for a period of fifty years, at which time they might be revoked by payment of the amount invested. The Commission could regulate rates on all power moved across state lines by the licensed companies or their subsidiaries, and was given full access to books and records of such companies with authority to regulate accounting practices. Public ownership for sale without profit was encouraged by exempting state and municipally owned projects from license fees. This system of control proved to be wholly insufficient to cope with an increasingly complex problem. Not more than one fourth of the power being generated was from hydro-plants and, of those, not more than one fourth were under federal license. Moreover, the complex structure of holding companies was free from any regulation whatsoever.

In 1928, Senator Thomas Walsh of Montana introduced a resolution into the Senate providing for a committee investigation of the power and light industries financial and propaganda practices. One of the most powerful lobbies ever assembled in Washington succeeded in assigning the task to the Federal Trade Commission in order to keep it out of the hands of Walsh whose relentless investigations had ferreted out the oil scandals. The Federal Trade Commission's report of 7,000,000 words was the most sensational since that of the Pujo committee. It revealed, by the admissions of the industry's own propaganda agents (1) that the National Electric Light Association was spending millions of dollars annually for propaganda; (2) that unlimited quantities of printed material were placed in the hands of newspaper editors, business men, professional men and labor leaders; (3) that the tentacles of this vast propaganda machine had reached into every department of the educational system, including the kindergartens; (4) that professors in universities and the President of the General Federation of Women's Clubs were on its pay-roll; and (5) that pressure of advertising was brought to bear upon the press for friendly publicity.

The revelations of the committee's report furnished material for wide discussion in news articles, editorials and monographs, among the latter being Ernest Gruening's *The Public Pays*, Stephen Raushenbush's *The Power Fight* and Ernest M. Patterson's *Power and the Public*. A wave of popular indignation swept over the country, culminating in a demand for lower utility rates, strengthening the Senate group's demands for strict regulation of the power companies and discrediting the negative attitude of Presidents Coolidge and Hoover. The collapse of the Insull utility empire came as a dramatic climax to ten years of bitter controversy and paved the way for a sweeping reform.

Meanwhile, Senator Norris carried on a persistent crusade for government operation of the Muscle Shoals power and nitrate plant. The two nitrate plants, with an estimated annual output of approximately 50,000 tons of fixed nitrogen, were constructed by the government during the war. The cost of these plants and of the Wilson Dam, which was to supply the electric power, was about $150,000,000. The nitrate plants were not used after the war and the power generated at Wilson Dam was sold to the Alabama Power Company. Senator Norris, marshaling an array of facts and figures to prove that public owned hydro-plants in Canada were furnishing power to consumers at less than half the average American price, succeeded in getting, in 1928, Congressional approval to his resolution providing for the completion and operation of the Muscle Shoals properties; but it was pocket vetoed by President Coolidge. Numerous studies were published supporting the demand for reduction of rates, one in particular, by Morris Llewellyn Cooke of the New York Power Authority, estimating excess rates to the American domestic consumer at more than $300,000,000 annually. It was from the standpoint of the small consumer, principally, that the production of electric power was a monopoly. Large consumers, who might produce their own power, enjoyed drastically reduced rates in comparison to the average householder.

Senator Norris's resolution again passed Congress in 1930. This revised program provided for the building of another dam on the Tennessee River, the construction of transmission lines and government manufacture and sale of both power and fertilizers. Coolidge had vetoed the original act in silence. Hoover, on the other hand, condemned it with visible emotion, (1) because private interests were now able to furnish all requirements of nitrogen for war purposes; and (2) because he was opposed to government competition with private enterprise. Nothing reveals more clearly than his veto message how much the operation of the government plant was regarded as an effectual corrective of public utility abuses. On that point, he said: "Involved in this question is the agitation against the conduct of the power industry. . . . The remedy for abuses in the conduct of that industry lies in regulation and not by the Federal Government entering upon the business itself. . . . I hesitate to contemplate the future of our institutions, of our country if the preoccupation of its officials is to be no longer the promotion of justice and equal opportunity but is to be devoted to barter in the markets. . . . Muscle Shoals can only be administered by the people upon the ground, responsible to their own communities and not for purposes of pursuit of social theories or national politics."

It was this avowed purpose of the sponsors of government operation to make of the Muscle Shoals plant a laboratory to determine the actual cost of the manufacture and distribution of electricity which the power interests fought so bitterly. For ten years, it stood idle as the cost of a universal public service soared and the architects of utility holding companies peddled their worthless stocks. Concerning these companies Chairman McNinch of the New Federal Power Commission created in 1930, said: "The holding company dynasty, with its absentee ownership and management, its sovereignty over far-flung dominions in many states, but subject to the direct jurisdiction of none, its fees being taxation without representation of the operating companies, is a grave economic and social peril."

Governor Roosevelt of New York had said, meanwhile, that control of holding companies and super-utilities had proved so difficult as to be impracticable and had advocated federal control. His candidacy was opposed by the power interest, which went so far as to deluge the Chicago Convention with telegrams in an effort to secure Newton D. Baker or Albert Ritchie as the candidate of the Democratic party. In his campaign speeches, he advocated government development of water power sites with control of distribution costs and services through contracts with private companies, control of security issues, and the regulation of holding companies. He was known to be favorable to the Norris resolution, to regulation of all power entering into interstate commerce and to rigid enforcement of the Federal Water Power Act. Few people, however, expected the devastating attack about to be made upon the power utility monopoly from at least five directions. They were (1) the Tennessee Valley Authority Act (May 18, 1933), (2) the Public Works Program, (3) the creation of the Electric Home and Farm Authority, (4) the Electric Rate Investigation Resolution and (5) the Wheeler-Rayburn Act.

CHAPTER XIII

MILITANT LABOR

Craft and Company Unions

The history of American labor in the twenties did not center around the American Federation of Labor. That organization appeared to be going the way of the Knights of Labor which had ceased to be of practical importance after 1900. Craft organization became more antiquated with each passing year. Its utility lessened with the introduction of machinery. It became a positive hindrance and source of constant irritation with the growth of modern industrial systems. Machinery freed the employer from dependence upon workmen skilled in the handicrafts. It struck a body-blow at apprenticeship and opened wide the doors of the factory to labor fresh from the fields of agriculture. It brought into a single factory the members of a dozen crafts who dissipated their strength in petty quarrels and confounded the wisdom of the best intentioned employers to devise a program of operation suitable to the demands of so many minds. The fundamental principle of industrial relations, recognized by goverment, capital and labor alike, was the pitting of economic strength of employers against the economic strength of labor; but employers were organized on an industrial basis while organized laborers remained wedded to the decentralized craft unions. The reason for this was their secure status relative to the great mass of wage-earners. They were an aristocracy within their economic group. Too often, their gains in the form of wages were at the expense of the unorganized and unskilled. Any extension of the privileges of membership would entail a levelling down of their share of the returns from production; and abandonment of craft structure would require the surrender of lucrative positions by those who guide their destinies. The naked truth cannot be ignored that the members of unions as organized in the last three decades had little vision and nothing to gain by interesting themselves in the broader problems of labor as a whole. They failed to make any progress in the basic industries such as steel, rubber, and oil. They wasted their strength in petty quarrels among themselves. Their members could not escape because of the union's being institutionalized.

The weakness of this position over the long view became apparent after the World War because of (1) the increased employment of women; (2) the migration from agriculture to manufacturing; (3) the entrance of the Negro into manufacturing; (4) the greater productivity of labor as a result of mechanization; (5) the slackening rate of population increase; and (6) the decline in immigration. It would be difficult to determine the total net influence of these things upon wages, unemployment, standards of living, and general cultural advantages after each had been balanced against the other; but they did promote sweeping changes in human relationships which cannot be ignored in reconstructing the history of the period.

Negro migration away from the black belt set in strongly in 1918. The depression of 1929 virtually halted its northward movement; but there were three million Negroes outside the South by that time, including a million in the North Central States, nearly two hundred thousand in the Mountain and Pacific Coast States, and more than two hundred thousand each in New York, Philadelphia and Chicago. Negro men took over the disagreeable types of labor formerly monopolized by the most recent arrivals among the immigrants. They worked in the fertilizer factories and the stock yards, as longshoremen and hod-carriers, in the furnace rooms of the steel mills. Negro men and women alike became marginal laborers in the North. A million Mexicans moved in to take their places in the South, some 300,000 going to the sugar beet fields in the Platte River counties of Colorado and to the cantaloupe plantations of the Imperial Valley in California. Native whites entered the services long monopolized by Negroes in the Southern States. Negro women and children who migrated to the North dropped out of the class of agricultural laborers. The children went into the schools and some of the women into domestic service. The race developed its own economy in the northern cities, with its many services and skills. There always had been many aliens at the North who did not enjoy the franchise. Negroes were disfranchised at the South; but they voted at the North. Thus the lowliest of the low among laboring men became a force to be reckoned with in politics. Because organized labor excluded them from its ranks and did nothing to alleviate their sordid condition either in northern industries or southern agriculture, they constituted a fertile soil for the seeds of communism; and among the devotees of capitalism, fear of violence from alien workers was supplanted by fear of radical labor ballots. The Communist party platform of 1932 demanded for the Negro: political and social equality; abolition of Jim Crow laws, disfranchising laws, segregation ordinances, and the convict lease and chain gang systems in penal institutions; abandonment of separate educational institutions; freedom for interracial marriages; Negro jury service; a federal anti-lynching law; admission to labor unions; and equal pay for equal service.

The number of women classed as wage-earners increased more than 2,000,000 between 1914 and 1930, reaching a total variously estimated between 10,000,000 and 11,500,000. This was nearly one-fifth of all persons gainfully employed. About 100,000 moved into managerial positions and can not be classed as laborers. Another 1,500,000 entered the professions. Domestic and personal service, including the restaurants, hotels and laundries, required the services of 3,000,000, an increase of one-third in twenty years. The number in agriculture decreased, standing at about 1,000,000 in 1930. There were about 1,000,000 in the trades, and 2,000,000 each in clerical positions and factories. In manufacturing, they furnished about one-half of all workers in the rayon mills, 50,000 each in automobile factories and rubber factories, and about 100,000 each in electrical supplies and chemicals. Of all women wage-earners at the close of the period, 2,000,000 were Negro women. Forty per cent of all women wage-earners were under twenty-five years of age, including more than 200,000 under sixteen and 1,000,000 between the ages of sixteen and twenty. The nation was putting its young women to work even in the teaching profession. The National Educational Association reported in 1931 that more than three-fourths of all cities in the country were refusing to employ married women. The result was a more rapid turnover in the teaching profession. It was a retarding influence against the early marriage of young women teachers, and it deprived children of guidance by those best qualified to understand their emotions. Only about three per cent of women wage-earners were organized. Their competition kept the wages of men low; but minimum wage laws too often served to level off all wages in an industry and make a maximum wage of the minimum fixed by statute.

There was a steady decline in the labor of children under fifteen years of age; but 650,000 children between the ages of ten and fifteen were working in 1930, with one-third of that number under fourteen. Agriculture engaged twice the number of child laborers as all other industries combined. They worked on the truck farms of New York and New Jersey, in the fruit and hop vineyards of the Pacific Coast, in the beet fields of Colorado and in the cotton fields of the Southern States. Every year, however, the average age of the working class declined as women workers became "old" at thirty and men at forty. The American Federation of Labor insisted that labor was not a commodity; that employers must recognize the right of collective bargaining; and that government must throw no legal obstacles in the way of labor's use of its only effective weapon, the strike. Capital insisted upon the right to purchase labor in a competitive market and to maintain the open shop. Labor succeeded in shutting off competition from foreign labor markets, but only after capital and 100 per cent Americanism lent their assistance; and it steadfastly refused to interest itself in its three great sources of competition: women and children, Negroes and agricultural laborers. Capital bargained women against men, Negroes against whites and children against the whole.

Capital, to counteract the strength of craft organizations, began to organize company unions. The company union takes second place only to craft unions as an archaic institution. Every company union was an entity unto itself. The employees in a factory lacked cohesion in dealing with their employers under the craft system, but they did have some contact with similar craftsmen in other factories and other industries and the advice, leadership and financial support of men whose sustenance emanated from some other source than their own. Company unions made for cohesion within the factory unit but severed all connection between its members in other factories of the same industry and from those in other industries. One of the great weaknesses of the labor movement during the twenties, particularly in the South, was the constant draining away from labor into managerial positions of its natural leaders. Company unions accentuated this process. It enabled the employer to dictate the appointment of its employees' representatives. Labor's representatives, however free from employer influence their choice might be, were still employees of the men with whom they were supposed to bargain. All manner of subtle coercion was employed to destroy labor's bargaining power under the company union. The company town of the textile mills and the coal mines presented a mode of life little removed from feudalism. Families lived in company houses, bought at company stores, worshipped in company churches and sent their children to company schools. If the companies did not own and operate these agencies outright, they controlled them. They ruled the sheriffs, the deputies and, too often, the courts. Workers were ofttimes in arrears on house rent or for food supplies just as were the crop renters of the cotton belt. The vast majority of agricultural laborers, including crop renters, of coal miners and textile workers never really have been on a money economy. They labored, year in and year out, for a meager subsistence wage which came to them through the crop *lien* and credit system, company stores and welfare projects of the company towns. In agriculture and in the textile industry, it approached serfdom, because the labor of women and children was a requisite to employment. One would have to be naïve indeed to suppose that workers possessed freedom of action under such a system of economic subserviency. The companies could shut down their plants or discharge recalcitrant employees, and did so in many places after the NRA went into effect, to force their will upon the workers. Elaborate spy systems in many plants kept employers fully informed of any contacts between employees and outlanders and strict rules against fraternizing, even in private life, between supervisors and workers completed the isolation. Nowhere was this more true than in the textile districts and coal fields of the South where to get within the zone of possible communication entailed trespass upon company property; where the workers' distrust of outside leadership and public resentment of northern interference robbed labor of all outside support.

Militant Labor Movement

Opposed to the structure, aims and methods of craft and company unions was an entirely different type of labor movement. Its supporters, regardless of the particular organization with which they might be affiliated, lacked the stabilizing influence of homes, permanent employment and relative security so characteristic of the craft union membership. They organized along industrial lines, rejected capitalism and the idea of trade agreements, and proceeded by militant direct action. They belonged to the most oppressed and underprivileged working groups, particularly the Negro and the women in the textile mills and garment factories.

The philosophy of Samuel Gompers, President of the American Federation of Labor until 1924, embraced the idea that there was an essential harmony between capital and labor directly contrary to the Marxian theory of class conflict. He placed emphasis upon the opportunist policy of achieving, from day to day, specific gains such as shorter hours and higher wages to the end of increasing labor's share of the industrial product. His technique was that of high membership fees, large strike funds and benefit payments but a limited use of strikes and boycotts and repudiation of the sympathetic strike. Above all else, he was opposed to bringing the labor unions into politics, preferring to act as a pressure group upon both political parties. It was this attitude which resulted in the withdrawal of the socialists from any connection with the American Federation of Labor in 1895 and the formation of the Socialist Trade and Labor Alliance under the leadership of Daniel De Leon. Thenceforth, Gompers regarded the socialists as the most dangerous enemies of the laboring class. This was essentially the attitude of other Federation leaders, including Peter McGuire, James Duncan, James O'Connell, John Mitchell and Frank Morrison. They were practical men who became, as time passed, more and more conservative, interested in promoting harmony between capital and labor, and in defeating the aims of "radicals" who believed in class conflict.

The Socialist Trade and Labor Alliance rose and fell within the short space of three years, but its principle of dual unionism became an important issue in the labor movement. Sceptical of any possibility of changing the philosophy of the American Federation of Labor, it sought to withdraw the radical elements and establish industrial unions dedicated to the task of overthrowing the capitalistic system. Its technique included the general strike, and its objectives those of syndicalism. Its political support was given to the Socialist Labor party. De Leon has been called the "intellectual father of American syndicalism," though probably without justification. Nevertheless, Lenin spoke of him in 1917 as the only socialist who had added anything to the Marxian thought and as the progenitor of the Soviet idea. His contributions to the American labor movement were those of dual unionism and revolutionary industrial unionism, but his organization failed because it was dogmatic, sectarian and produced no immediate benefits to its members.

The decline of the Socialist Trade and Labor Alliance led to the formation of the Socialist party in 1901, and the Industrial Workers of the World in June, 1905. The latter organization was formed at Chicago by Eugene V. Debs, De Leon and William D. Haywood, all supporters of industrial, revolutionary, class-conscious unionism. Delegates were said to represent 27,000 members of the Western Federation of Miners, 16,750 members of the American Labor Union, 3000 United Metal Workers, 2000 United Brotherhood of Railway employees and 1450 members of the Socialist Trade and Labor Alliance. Among the delegates were William E. Trautman, editor of the *Brauer Zeitung*, the official organ of the United Brewery workmen; Charles O. Sherman, General Secretary of the United Metal Workers International Union; A. M. Simons, editor of the *International Socialist Review;* and Thomas J. Hagerty, a Catholic priest and editor of the *Voice of Labor*. The preamble of the constitution drawn up by the convention was as follows:

"The working class and the employing class have nothing in common. There can be no peace so long as hunger and want are found among millions of working people and the few, who make up the employing class, have all the good things of life.

"Between these two classes a struggle must go on until all the toilers come together on the political, as well as on the industrial field, and take and hold that which they produce by their labor through an economic organization of the working class, without affiliation with any political party.

"The rapid gathering of wealth and the centering of the management of industries into fewer and fewer hands make the trade unions unable to compete with the ever-growing power of the employing class, because the trade unions foster a state of things which allows one set of workers to be pitted against another set of workers in the same industry, thereby helping defeat one another in wage wars. The trade unions aid the employing class to mislead the workers into the belief that the working class have interests in common with their employers.

"These sad conditions can be changed and the interests of the working class upheld only by an organization formed in such a way that all its members in any one industry, or in all industries, if necessary, cease work whenever a strike or lockout is on in any department thereof, thus making an injury to one an injury to all."

Following the organization of the I.W.W., the American Federation of Labor launched a bitter attack upon both it and the Socialist party and in May, 1906, a factional fight led to the secession of the Western Federation of Miners. All three groups, however, rallied to the defense of the leaders of the W. F. of M., Moyer, Haywood and Pettibone, who were accused of the murder of ex-Governor Steunenberg of Idaho in February, 1907. Defense funds poured in from all classes of labor throughout the country and Eugene V. Debs wrote his famous "Call to Arms" editorial asking for a million armed revolutionists to free the accused men if they were convicted. They were acquitted in July, 1907, leaving the Western Federation of Miners a strong organization and the Industrial Workers of the World financially bankrupt. The following year, the latter organization was purged of the Social Laborites under De Leon, and control passed into the hands of the "industrial actionists," St. John and Trautman. The followers of De Leon set up their own headquarters in Detroit and posed as the true I.W.W. but in 1915 changed the name of their organization to Workers International Industrial Union. They carried on a series of textile strikes in 1911-1912 with little permanent gain and officially dissolved their organization in 1924.

The Industrial Workers of the World, after purging their

organization of the De Leon group, added the two following paragraphs to their declaration of principles:

"Instead of the conservative motto, 'A fair day's wages for a fair day's work,' we must inscribe on our banner the revolutionary watchword, 'Abolition of the wage system!'

"It is the historical mission of the working class to do away with capitalism. The army of production must be organized, not only for the every-day struggle with capitalists, but also to carry on production when capitalism shall have been overthrown. By organizing industrially we are forming the structure of the new society within the shell of the old."

Thereafter, it remained bitterly opposed to participation in politics. The majority of its members were migratory workers from the West who could seldom vote because of residence requirements—men who were, from the nature of their existence, distrustful of small-town politicians and law enforcement agencies. Their philosophy of life was that of the anarchist rather than of the socialist. Alien members, likewise, were not interested in politics. Eternal warfare against capitalism and ultimate control of industry by the working class was their motto. Having nothing to lose and being migratory workers, they struck hard and fast, winning quickly or not at all. If they lost, they moved on to another job. There were no strike funds, no strike benefits, no long strikes and no binding agreements with the employer. When the strike failed, they resorted to sabotage. Industrial peace under the wage system was, to them, impossible. Year by year, they increased their strength among the migratory harvest hands, the foreign born steel workers, the lumber camp workers and the textile workers—all groups which were unskilled, poorly paid, and ignored by the American Federation of Labor.

Meanwhile, the Socialist party spread its gospel of "striking at the ballot box" among all classes of workers. Maintaining a neutral position on the question of craft versus industrial unionism, though sympathetic to the latter, it adopted the following rule in 1912:

"Any member of the party who opposes political action or advocates crime, sabotage, or other methods of violence as a weapon of the working class to aid in its emancipation shall be expelled from membership in the party. Political action shall be construed to mean participation in elections for public office and practical legislative work along the lines of the Socialist Party platform."

War and Post-War Readjustment

Of the three organizations, only the American Federation of Labor came through the war period unscathed. Gompers dropped all pretense of pacifism, even of neutrality, as early as 1915. Peace sentiment in the Middle Western and Pacific Coast states had led to the organization of Labor's National Peace Council supported by the American Neutrality League and the American League to Limit Armaments, and having strong trade union backing. Gompers took the field against the new peace movement with the charge that it was inspired by German agents and succeeded in weakening it to the point where its maximum demands were for continued neutrality without an embargo on the sale of munitions. Gompers also joined in the preparedness for national defense campaign being waged in 1914 and 1915, became a member of the Advisory Commission of the Council of National Defense in 1916 and supported the ruthless suppression of the International Workers of the World. He was, in fact, so subservient to the wishes of the Administration, that President John P. White of the United Mine Workers was forced to assume leadership to secure adequate representation for labor on the committee machinery for the settlement of labor disputes. Membership in the American Federation of Labor increased steadily during the period with applicants for membership almost having to beg admittance. The Federation refused to recognize the Amalgamated Clothing Workers of America following a split in the ranks of the United Garment Workers and the new organization went on as an independent, progressive, industrial union to gain a membership of 200,000 by 1920. The American Federation of Labor, however, increased its membership from 2,000,000 in 1914 to 3,045,000.

The Socialist party, August 12, 1914, condemned the war in strong terms as a war of imperialism and called upon labor to recognize it as such. Within a year, it amended its constitution to provide for the expulsion of any member lending support to military or naval credits. Its presidential campaign in 1916 was little more than an appeal for labor to unite in opposition to war. On April 7, 1917, members of the party met at St. Louis, denounced our entry into the war and pledged themselves to oppose it by every means within their power. Only a few, however, had courage to go through the ordeal, Max Eastman, Victor Berger and Eugene V. Debs among them, and the period of official persecution, already mentioned, together with the recusancy of most of the leaders destroyed the party as an effective agency in the labor movement. Its impotency began with the defection of two left-wing groups at the Convention of 1919.

It was the Industrial Workers of the World who bore the brunt of the war hysteria. Three acts of violence marked the year 1916. On July 22 a bomb killed many people participating in a preparedness day parade in San Francisco. Thomas Mooney and Warren K. Billings were indicted, tried and convicted. The death sentence was later commuted to imprisonment for life. Substantial proof was later presented to show that they had been convicted on perjured testimony, but all efforts to secure a new trial or release for the convicted men have proved unavailing. The second event was the death of several persons during a "free speech" fight between Industrial Workers of the World and a "citizens' committee" at Everett, Washington, on November 6. The third was a violent contest between 15,000 striking iron miners led by Industrial Workers of the World in the Mesaba Range and imported gunmen. The entry of the United States into the war inaugurated a terrific official drive against the organization. More than 1,000 members were imprisoned in the course of two years, many being given long-term sentences and others being deported. The nature of the suppression may be judged from the fact that indictments were drawn up against men who had been dead for years, but who had been active at one time in the organization. Fifty thousand lumber camp workers in the Northwest struck for and won the eight hour day on June 1, 1917. This was the signal for an outburst of terrorism. Frank Little, a member of the general executive board, was kidnapped and hung to a railroad trestle outside Butte, Montana, on the night of August 1. Twelve hundred strikers at Bisbee, Arizona, were shipped to Columbus, New Mexico, and detained in military prison camps for three months. The result was increased rather than decreased labor unrest—4,233 strikes occurring during the year—and the setting up of the President's Mediation Commission and the War Labor Board on May 7, 1918. These Boards were largely ineffective and were dispersed shortly after the signing of the Armistice.

Under pressure from Criminal Syndicalism laws and government prosecution, the I.W.W. declared in 1920 that their organization "does not now, and never has, believed in or advocated either destruction or violence as a means of accomplishing industrial reform." Within two years, factional disputes, imprisonment of its leaders, conflict with the Communists and the decline of the importance of migratory workers completely disrupted the organization. Remnants of the group lingered on and, in October, 1927, led a strike of 6,000 Colorado miners. Failure of the strike finally eliminated the I.W.W. from the labor movement.

The post-war period began in December, 1918, with the adoption of a program by the Executive Council of the American Federation of Labor calling for government ownership of public utilities, public employment agencies, freedom of speech, etc. Unions affiliated with the Federation then undertook a series of strikes. Thirty-two thousand members of the United Textile Workers Union at Lawrence, Massachusetts, struck against a reduction of wages and for a 48 hour week on February 3. Ten thousand Irish-American and French-Canadian workers deserted but the remainder, made up of Italians, Lithuanians, Russians, Ukrainians, Syrians, Germans and Jews, continued the strike and won their demands on May 20. One hundred and ten American Federation of Labor unions struck in Seattle on February 6 in support of 32,000 shipyard workers. It was, in reality, a test of workers' solidarity and the strike was abandoned on February 11 after every important function in the life of the city, including the police service, had been in the control of the strikers' committee for seven days. There was no violence during the strike, but the demonstration served to solidify the ranks of both capital and labor for a major test of strength. It came in the steel industry. The American Federation of Labor authorized an attempt to unionize that industry at its 1918 convention. William Z. Foster directed the project, presenting labor's demands to the United States Steel Corporation on July 20, 1919. The corporation, as was expected, refused to negotiate and a strike was called for September 22. This was the third time in twenty years that an attempt was made to organize the steel workers, the others being in 1901 and 1909. It was, without question, the most terrific battle between capital and labor and the most disastrous defeat for organized labor in the twentieth century. The Amalgamated Clothing Workers alone contributed $100,000 to the strike fund. Three hundred and sixty-five thousand workers were out by October 9, but the Amalgamated Association of Iron and Steel Workers indicated a willingness to negotiate separately, the American Federation of Labor withheld its full support, 40,000 Negro strike-breakers were imported, charges of communism were injected into the controversy and the strike was broken on January 8, 1920. Meanwhile the United Mine Workers called a strike on October 31, 1919, asking for a 60 per cent wage increase and a thirty hour week. Four hundred and twenty-five thousand miners left the mines. On October 24, President Wilson declared the strike to be illegal on the ground that the country was still at war. Attorney-General A. Mitchell Palmer secured injunctions against the Union and, on November 10, John L. Lewis called off the strike with the words, "We cannot fight our government." Many miners refused to return to work, however, until the Fuel Administration negotitated a 14 per cent wage increase on December 9. In spite of these losses, membership in the American Federation of Labor increased to 4,078,740 by 1920.

The Rise of Communism

In 1919, two radical groups seceded or were expelled from the Socialist party. Membership in the party thereupon declined from 104,000 in 1919 to 11,000 in 1922. The first of the radical groups formed the Communist Labor party on August 31 and the second group formed the Communist party of America on September 1. Both groups were hostile to the political program of the Socialists and in favor of a militant struggle against capitalism. By 1920, they had abandoned the idea of dual unionism followed by the Industrial Workers of the World, and decided to build up revolutionary groups within the ranks of the American Federation of Labor. Under the leadership of William Z. Foster, the militant and communist trade unionists were united in the Trade Union Educational League which, in 1922, announced that it was not a trade union, but "an informal grouping of the progressive and revolutionary elements throughout the entire trade union movement . . . to develop the trade unions from their present antiquated and stagnant condition into modern, powerful labor organizations." Meanwhile, the Communist Labor party had become the United Communist party and a united program had been forced upon it and the Communist party of America by the Communist International.

Then began the modern contest betwcen the American Federation of Labor and the Trade Union Educational League at a time when cessation of war activities had inaugurated relaxation of government control of industrial relations and a widespread open shop drive by employers. A general wage-reduction followed and the American Federation of Labor lost 700,000 members in a single year. The tide against the unions was stemmed by a two-year strike of the International Typographical Union which began on May 1, 1921, and cost the Union $15,000,000. Six hundred thousand United Mine Workers struck against a 35 per cent wage reduction and for a single agreement covering the anthracite and bituminous fields on April 1, 1922. Violence was prevalent, reaching the point of pitched battles in southern Illinois. An agreement was signed with the bituminous operators on August 15 and the anthracite operators on September 3. There was no change in the wage scale, but contracts of the two classes were to expire at different times and the miners of West Virginia and western Pennsylvania were left out of the settlement entirely. Six crafts of the railway shopmen, representing 400,000 men, struck on July 1, 1922, against wage cuts and the abrogation of agreements made under the jurisdiction of the United States Railway Labor Board. Attorney-General Daugherty, at the instance of President Harding, secured an injunction against the unions under the Sherman Act and the Transportation Act of 1920. The strike was broken and the men returned to work on September 15.

Meanwhile, the Trade Union Educational League was pushing its program of amalgamation with the purpose of transforming craft unions into industrial or so-called "vertical" unions and the officials of the American Federation of Labor were resisting the trend with every means at their disposal. After losing the shopmen's strike, the railway unions undertook to organize a Conference for Progressive Political Action with the support of many state and city federations of labor, international unions, the Socialist and Farm Labor parties, farm organizations, and church groups. After the congressional campaign of 1922, an effort was made to crystallize the movement through the organization of an independent labor party, but extension of an invitation to attend the 1923 conference to the official communist organization, the Workers party, led to the disruption of the movement. It was later revived as the American Workers party by A. J. Muste of Brookwood Labor College but, in 1935, was absorbed by the Socialist party to the disappointment of those who had hoped for a militant labor party based on communist principles. The loss of an additional 269,000 members in 1923 by the American Federation of Labor forced it to undertake a more aggressive program at its Portland convention. Delegates suspected of communist leanings were expelled, a news service and a legal information bureau were authorized, and a union lobbying agency was planned. The entire support of the Federation was thrown behind La Follette and Wheeler in the presidential campaign. Injection of radicalism into the campaign, followed by the failure of La Follette to secure any electoral votes except those of Wisconsin, caused the Federation to return to its old non-partisan policy and to inaugurate a rigorous drive against the Trade Union Educational League members of the garment workers' unions. Sixty thousand more members were lost during the year and President Gompers died on December 13, 1924, on his return trip from the San Antonio convention.

While the American Federation of Labor was attempting to formulate a new policy under the leadership of its new President, William Green, the communists organized anew under the name of Workers (Communist) party which openly proclaimed itself the American section of the Communist International. A strike in the Botany textile mills of Passaic, New Jersey, on January 25, 1926, was the first in the history of the country under communist leadership. The workers were quickly organized into a union and affiliation with the American Federation of Labor was requested. This request was granted only after Albert Weisbord, communist leader of the strike, agreed to withdraw. The workers were admitted to the United Textile Workers Union and the American Federation of Labor backed their demands for a 10 per cent wage increase, a 40 hour week, and recognition of the union. A compromise was reached on

December 13 and the strike came to an end. The interesting feature of the strike was that a group of workers, formerly ignored by organized labor and revolting against intolerable conditions, were organized on an industrial basis by communist leaders and then admitted into an affiliate of the American Federation of Labor after those leaders voluntarily withdrew. It was the beginning of a new chapter in labor union history. The Trade Union Educational League, discouraged by consistent action against it by trade union leaders, and encouraged by a partial sanctioning of "revolutionary unions" by the Communist International, began to look favorably upon the idea of dual unionism. They began with the organization of the National Miners Union, the Needle Trades Workers Industrial Union, and the National Textile Workers Union. They insisted that none of these were dual unions; that they were simply organizing workers not acceptable to the American Federation of Labor. Actually, they were withdrawing the militants from the conservative trade unions and were rightfully called disrupters by the union officials. They reorganized the Trade Union Educational League into the Trade Union Unity League on September 1, 1925, and it became, in spite of consistent denials, a dual union center. By 1932, the communists had eleven independent unions.

Craft Versus Industrial Unionism

The rapid gains of the communists caused the American Federation of Labor, for the first time, to turn its attention to the new industrial South. Here was a region with a rather primitive economic structure and an agricultural philosophy—a philosophy of individualism and a traditional paternalism. Craft unionism existed in the skilled trades of the urban centers, but the factory workers of the Piedmont Crescent and the miners of the mountains were unorganized, isolated, subject to fluctuating economic conditions and under constant pressure from a tremendous surplus of labor. Besides these there were the Negro laborers, the agricultural laborers, the common laborers in untold numbers with only seasonal and intermittent employment. All of this vast conglomeration of wage earners constituted a wide open and fertile field for the collective philosophy of the communists. The autocratic control exercised by the mill owners, tempered at first by a fine sense of responsibility for the welfare of the dependent worker, had become, in the second generation, an intolerable despotism over every phase of human existence. The mill workers were ripe for revolt, not necessarily against prevailing wages and hours and working conditions, but for social and spiritual freedom—for the right to order their own lives, earn an honest wage and spend it according to the dictates of their own consciences. Unionization had been delayed far beyond the normal period by the surplus of cheap labor, the lack of leadership, the prevailing distrust of outsiders and the ever-present race prejudice.

The communists led the way. The National Textile Workers Union organized and called a strike in the mills of Gastonia, North Carolina, on April 2, 1929. The strike was primarily for union recognition, though the workers had plenty of other grievances, including the introduction of the stretch-out system, low wages, etc. Nothing but a deep sense of oppression and unrest could have inspired the zeal with which the workers followed the lead of a handful of avowed communist agitators. National guard, imported gunmen, injunctions, kidnapping, wholesale arrests on trumped-up charges—all the brutal methods known to labor controversies were used to break the strike and force the union underground. Meanwhile the American Federation of Labor organized the workers at Elizabethtown, Tennessee, and called a strike in those mills on March 12. The same methods were used by the authorities there with the same results. The United Textile Workers of the A. F. of L. then turned their attention to the mills of Danville, Virginia, where a strike was called in September, 1930. It failed as miserably as the others. In many ways, these were the most important contests of the decade. Employers became more cautious. The prestige of the American Federation of Labor received a damaging blow. The workers became group conscious and aware of the necessity of relying upon leaders from among themselves. They learned that outside leadership, in part at least, cost them the support of public opinion. The brutality used in suppressing the strikes aroused liberal sentiment all over the country in a way that no other strikes had ever done. The southern people, and particularly the newspapers, became conscious of existing social and economic evils. Social legislation received renewed support in an effort to eliminate the causes of labor's unrest. Economic fundamentalism suffered most over the long view.

Craft and industrial unionism met their first test of strength in the coal fields. In 1931, the Conference for Progressive Labor Action, an organization favoring dual unionism and centered at Brookwood Labor College, fostered the formation of the National Progressive Miners Union in the Illinois District of the United Mine Workers. In June, 1931, twenty thousand members of the new organization went out on strike during which the United Mine Workers signed contracts with the operators. Further conflict between the two groups was avoided by events of the depression. When the depression set in, the communists began the organization of Unemployed Councils in every city of the country. Demonstrations, supported by the Communist party, the Trade Union Unity League and the Unemployed Councils, were held on March 6, 1930, with more than 100,000 participating in New York and Detroit. Fifteen hundred delegates of the unemployed staged a National Hunger March to Washington in December, 1931. On March 12, 1932, 40,000 marched in the funeral procession of four men killed in the demonstration before the Ford plant at Dearborn on March 7. A second National Hunger March was sent to Washington. Finally, 20,000 unemployed veterans commandeered freight trains and went to Washington to demand payment of the Adjusted Service Certificates. Continuation of these conditions would certainly have led to tremendous gains by the communist group, but the creation of the National Recovery Administration on July 16, 1933, changed the entire situation. Strikes did not cease; in fact, a new wave of strikes swept the country; but the sudden rush of organization under the NRA swept all the militants, including the communists, back into the unions. Union after union of the Trade Union Unity League was dissolved and, finally, the League itself passed out of existence. This meant that the opponents of American Federation of Labor conservatism were now within the ranks of the organization. The questions of industrial unionism and the organization of the unskilled industrial workers arose in the national convention at Atlantic City in October, 1935. John L. Lewis, President of the United Mine Workers, sponsored industrial unionism with the support of Francis Gorman of the United Textile Workers, Sidney Hillman of the Amalgamated Clothing Workers, David Dubinsky of the International Garment Workers Union, and Charles Howard of the International Typographical Union. Losing their fight for endorsement in the convention, they formed the Committee for Industrial Organization. Since William Green's term as President of the American Federation of Labor was to expire before the next national convention and the rebels controlled enough votes to defeat his re-election, he could do nothing else but capitulate or fight. In June, 1936, he ordered the Committee for Industrial Organization to disband within two weeks. They took no action and were ordered before the Executive Council of the Federation for trial. They failed to appear for the trial and an *impasse* was reached. Meanwhile, Lewis went ahead with plans to organize the steel industry with indications that the greatest battle in industrial history was in the making. It was to decide whether Lewis, Green, or the Steel Institute was to control the foremost open shop industry of the country. With a presidential campaign in progress, it could scarcely avoid having wide repercussions on the political front.

The one legislative achievement of organized labor before the Roosevelt Administration was passage of the Norris-La Guardia Act, outlawing injunctions and yellow-dog contracts, on March 20, 1932. This act placed government approval upon the principle of collective bargaining and declared illegal all infringements upon its exercise. Specifically, it named yellow-dog contracts and forbade the issuance of injunctions against laborers ceasing to work, joining a union, paying strike benefits, giving full publicity to any facts pertaining to a strike, assembling peaceably, or persuading others to do these things. No officer or member of a union could be held responsible for unlawful acts of other officers or members unless they had authorized or ratified such acts. Section 7 of the act said that no federal court might issue even a temporary injunction "except after hearing the testimony of witnesses in open court (with opportunity for cross examination) in support of the allegations of a complaint made under oath, and testimony in opposition thereto, if offered, and except after findings of fact by the court, to the effect" (1) that unlawful acts had been threatened or would be committed; (2) that substantial or irreparable injury to property would ensue without the restraining order; (3) that the complaining party would suffer greater injury by the denial of an injunction than the defendants by its issuance; (4) that the complaining party had no adequate remedy at law; and (5) that law enforcement agencies were unable or unwilling to protect the property of the complainant. Furthermore, contempt cases, unless involving contempt committed in the presence of the court, were to be conducted on the basis of "speedy and public trial by an impartial jury of the state and district wherein the contempt shall have been committed."

CHAPTER XIV

POLITICAL DECADENCE

The Philosophy of Inaction

The Harding-Coolidge-Hoover administrations constitute an epoch in American history. It began with the precipitate collapse of the great reform movement. It ended in disillusionment and despair. In one short decade the moral tone of public life sank to the lowest depths possible without losing every semblance of responsibility for the public welfare. Warren G. Harding's election was heralded as a return to "normalcy," meaning an abandonment of Wilsonian idealism in international relations, of the honest effort to regulate business practices in the common interest at home. Long the servant of special interests, President Harding inaugurated a philosophy of government which his successor, President Coolidge, cryptically defined with the words: "The business of the United States is business." The deep concern of the three preceding Presidents—Roosevelt, Taft and Wilson—about the rapid development of an industrial and financial feudalism in the country was scorned. The system of controls, which had been so painfully constructed, was allowed to fall into disuse. Financiers and industrialists were given free reign and the government adjusted its policies to theirs.

The Federal Reserve System was so loosely controlled as to contribute heavily to wild speculation on the stock market, but President Coolidge refused to interfere, with the statement: "Everything is fundamentally sound." Millions in foreign government bonds were peddled to private investors by men who knew they were worthless, but the Department of State, which also knew it, was restrained from making the information public. Millions in income taxes were evaded because the law was poorly written, but Andrew Mellon, Secretary of the Treasury for 11 years, failed to inform Congress of what was taking place. Of the four Attorney-Generals—Harry M. Daugherty, Harlan F. Stone, John G. Sargent and William D. Mitchell—only Stone was distinguished enough to justify the conclusion that he measured up to the important functions of his office. Daugherty was driven from office by outraged public sentiment following disclosures by the Brookhart investigating committee, but his resignation was accepted by President Coolidge with a statement of confidence and regret. The Director of the Veterans Bureau, Charles R. Forbes, was found by a Senate Committee to have been guilty of such flagrant corruption that he was brought to trial in the courts and convicted of conspiracy to defraud. Great naval oil reserves were bartered away by the Secretary of the Interior, Albert B. Fall, without a protest from the members of the Cabinet. Secretary of the Navy, Denby, agreed to the transfer of the reserves to the Department of the Interior. His assistant secretary carried the orders for the transfer to President Harding for his signature. Calvin Coolidge, Vice-President when the leases were granted and President when the transaction was bared, did not lift his voice in protest nor offer the slightest assistance to the Senate investigating committee. The anti-trust laws went unenforced. The Federal Trade Commission became moribund. The Tariff Commission ceased to function except to justify increased rates on the products of special industries. The growth of monopolies was smiled upon. Tariff rates were increased until they assumed the proportions of an embargo. Income and corporation taxes were reduced again and again under the prodding of the Secretary of the Treasury. All these facts, and more, reveal the complete reversal of those policies which men in public life sponsored and fought for in the first two decades of the century. They leave no escape from the conclusion that the prevailing philosophy of government in this period had no precedents in one hundred fifty years of national development.

The Harding-Coolidge Regime

In selecting Warren G. Harding at Chicago, June 11, 1920, as its choice for the Presidency, the Republican party rejected the claims of three prominent men for the honor: Major-General Leonard E. Wood, Governor Frank O. Lowden of Illinois and Senator Hiram Johnson of California. Wood, who had not been permitted to go over-seas during the war, had some following among the war veterans; but his availability received a severe blow when it was revealed by a Senate Committee that his campaign fund amounted to $1,252,000, about half of which had been contributed by W. C. Procter, an Ohio soap manufacturer. He was, moreover, reported to be in sympathy with Palmer's anti-radical activities and was totally ignorant of social and economic questions. His campaign faded rapidly after he failed to secure more than 96,000 votes of 335,000 cast in the Michigan primary early in April. Lowden, a very capable governor, was the most prominent representative of mid-western agricultural interests during the decade of the twenties. When the Senate Committee discovered that he had spent $379,000 of his own money in a campaign fund of $414,000, his position was little better than that of Wood. Senator Borah of Idaho carried the fight against both men on the grounds of excessive campaign expenditures and threatened to bolt the party if either was nominated. Hiram Johnson was the most liberal of the three, but his campaign was poorly managed in the face of strong eastern opposition. Political expediency demanded the nomination of an inconspicuous candidate on a platform of negation. The Old Guard had been in favor of Harding for several months before the convention and, when neither Lowden nor Johnson showed winning strength in the balloting, Senators Brandegee, Smoot, and Lodge and Harry M. Daugherty, national committeeman from Ohio, engineered his nomination. Calvin Coolidge, an equally unknown machine politician, was chosen for the Vice-Presidency. Harding's nomination was received in the convention without enthusiasm, that of Coolidge with facetious observations about his luck.

Harding was owner of the *Marion Star*, a good small town newspaper. He had served in the state Senate, as Attorney-General of Ohio and as United States Senator. His record was negligible except as the servant of the steel interests. He was a reactionary, narrowly partisan, in favor of high tariffs and universal military training. Calvin Coolidge also had served in his state legislature, as mayor of Northampton, as lieutenant-governor of Massachusetts and, finally, as governor. Nine months before the Republican convention met, he suddenly attained notoriety by virtue of the Boston police strike. Refraining from intervention until Mayor Andrew J. Peters had the situation well in hand, he wired to Samuel Gompers, President of the American Federation of Labor: "There is no right to strike against the public safety by anybody, anywhere, any time." In normal times, the incident would scarcely have made the front page of the newspapers; but coming, as it did, during the worst period of industrial unrest in two decades, while the red hunt and deportation delirium were rampant, it gave him an availability not possessed by a half-dozen statesmen in the party. Another possible candidate was Herbert Hoover who, though looked upon with mistrust by the farmers and organized labor, was believed to be a good economist, to possess great administrative ability and an acquaintance with the European situation. A vigorous campaign early in the year probably would have placed him at the head of the liberal forces in the country, but he refused to state in February whether he was a Democrat or a Republican until the parties had announced their principles. On March 11, he classed himself as an independent Progressive and by April 3 he was definitely identified as a Republican. By then, there was no time to organize an effective campaign for his nomination.

The Democratic convention met in San Francisco on June 28. The party had no recognized leadership and precious little talent. Like the Republican convention, it met in an atmosphere of uncertainty and confusion with a membership made up largely of office holders. John W. Davis, Ambassador to the Court of St. James and former Solicitor-General, was the most able candidate but little known. William G. McAdoo's weakness was his relationship, as a son-in-law, to President Wilson. James M. Cox, the mildly progressive Governor of Ohio, was opposed by William Jennings Bryan. A. Mitchell Palmer of Pennsylvania had shown almost no strength at all in the primaries and was wholly discredited as a result of his anti-radical activities. Alfred E. Smith, Governor of New York, was honest, capable, liberal and had a large personal following. In his message to the state legislature in January, 1920, he had recommended a minimum wage law; an eight hour day for women in industry; maternity insurance; state medical service; state ownership and operation of water power; state-operated grain elevators; municipal ownership of public utilities; and classification of the production and distribution of milk as a public utility service. No other man in either party was as well qualified to take up the leadership of the progressive movement where Wilson had dropped it; but he was a wet, a member of Tammany Hall, and a Catholic. The ascendancy of the Ku Klux Klan at the time ruled Smith out as an available candidate. Franklin D. Roosevelt, Assistant Secretary of the Navy under Daniels, a foe of Tammany, an old school liberal, more independent than Theodore Roosevelt but with the same leanings toward imperialism, was only thirty-eight years of age. Cox was chosen for the Presidency on the forty-fourth ballot and Roosevelt was nominated for the Vice-Presidency. The country was presented with a choice between two mediocre newspaper editors from Ohio. Eugene V. Debs, a prisoner in Atlanta penitentiary, was nominated by the Socialists at New York on May 8. Another mildly socialist group, known as the Farmer-Labor party and made up of intellectuals, farmers and trade-unionists, nominated Parlay P. Christensen of Utah for the Presidency.

The platforms of the two major parties offered the voters

little inspiration, the speeches of the two contestants even less. Both platforms endorsed a federal child labor law and the right of collective bargaining for labor. The Republicans denounced the Treaty of Versailles without repudiating the idea of international cooperation. The Democrats endorsed the League Covenant, the anti-sedition activities of Palmer and Burleson, independence for the Philippines and territorial status for Puerto Rico, tariff for revenue, and Wilson's Mexican policy. The Republicans favored privately owned and operated railroads and merchant marine, restriction of immigration and a protective tariff. The Farmer-Labor platform endorsed a broad program of social legislation, government ownership of transportation and natural resources, and opposed the League of Nations. Cox made an extended tour of the country in support of our entry into the League. Harding was kept at home by his campaign managers and spoke to visiting delegations from his front porch in Marion, Ohio. The real issue in the campaign was Woodrow Wilson, not the League of Nations. Social and economic questions were scarcely touched. The League was a dead issue. Living costs, relations between capital and labor, civil rights and transportation, each worthy of vigorous discussion, were evaded. Wilson had progressively ignored his Cabinet with the result that his administration had been distinguished by a lack of coordination between its several units. This emerged as a glaring weakness after his return from Paris and during his incapacity. He had taken the United States into the war almost immediately after being re-elected on the platform "He kept us out of war." He insisted upon our ratification of the League Covenant without reservations, when millions of people believed that he had bartered away the aspirations of struggling humanity at Paris and that the League would be an agency for war rather than for peace. He had permitted Palmer and Burleson to carry out a program utterly foreign to traditional American principles. Living costs were steadily mounting, but no action had been taken against the profiteers. Economic unrest was acute. All of these things created currents and cross currents of hostility to

Wilsonianism, which came to mean insincerity, inefficiency, needless entry into the war, dishonored Americanism. Men did not vote for Harding's cause. There was no enthusiasm for it or for him. His campaign was negative. They did not vote for reaction and a return of government to the control of the invisible forces Wilson had denounced in his New Freedom. They voted for a change without thought of where it would lead. Harding received 404 electoral votes to 127 for Cox. The popular vote gave the Republicans 16,152,200, the Democrats 9,147,353, the Socialists 919,799 and the Farmer-Labor Coalition 265,411. The Republicans were given majorities in the Sixty-seventh Congress of 22 Senators and 167 Representatives.

Harding's Cabinet was the dismay of every intellectual liberal in the country, the most competent appointments being those of Charles Evans Hughes as Secretary of State and Herbert Hoover as Secretary of Commerce. Andrew Mellon, wealthy Pittsburgh banker and reputed head of the aluminum trust, was Secretary of the Treasury. Will Hays, who had discovered ways and means to fill the campaign chest, was Postmaster-General. Albert B. Fall, who made his position an easy road from cattle ranch to federal penitentiary, was Secretary of the Interior. Harry M. Daugherty, Harding's pre-convention campaign manager, who later barely escaped going to the penitentiary, was Attorney-General. Edwin Denby, undistinguished and incapable, was Secretary of the Navy.

The short period of Harding's Administration turned out a sordid record of corruption and inefficiency. His policy was one of absolute reliance upon the members of his Cabinet for the fulfillment of their respective duties. His vision embraced his party, not the nation, and he served his party, not the people. He was a local politician and of all the people he gathered together in public office, few could be classed as capable public servants. The Navy Department, the Department of Interior and the Justice Department were all involved in investigations by courageous action on the part of Senators Thomas J. Walsh of Montana, Senator Smith Brookhart of Iowa, and Senator Burton K. Wheeler. The complete corruption of the Attorney-General's Department necessitated the prosecution of the investigations by outside legal talent. Over $250,000,000 of veterans' appropriations had been diverted from proper channels and Charles R. Forbes, the Director of the Veterans Bureau, was driven from office. A federal court declared him guilty of conspiracy to defraud. Attorney-General Daugherty's friends were enriched by illegally withdrawing alcohol from government warehouses. One of them, Thomas W. Miller, Alien Property Custodian, was involved in theft from the proceeds of sales in his department, fined $5000 and given eighteen months in jail. Secretary of the Navy Denby transferred to the Department of the Interior three naval oil reserves in California and Wyoming. The transfer was carried out by executive order of President Harding. Harding had been an intimate friend of Albert B. Fall when both were in the Senate. It was impossible for him or any one else who knew of the transfer to have been unaware of what was behind the transaction because Fall's hostility to conservation was an open record. That alone should have disbarred him from his office. After the transfer, Fall secretly leased the Teapot Dome Reserve to Harry F. Sinclair and the Elk Hills Reserve to Edwin M. Doheny. These men stood to make a profit of $100,000,000 from the transaction. In return, the government was to receive a few thousand barrels of oil in storage tanks at Pearl Harbor, Hawaii. Fall had already received $100,000 from Doheny and the Republican campaign fund considerable contributions from Sinclair. In the end, Fall was fined $100,000 and sent to prison for one year. The oil reserves were recaptured for the nation. Many generations will pass before the entire extent of malfeasance in office during the months before Harding's death, August 2, 1923, is known. Historians are not likely to touch the mysteries of those last days for a long time. Their importance here lies in the fact that most of the disclosures came after the death of President Harding and just as the next presidential campaign approached. The energies of every one except a small group of Senators were bent to the task of minimizing the enormity of the crimes, casting the entire blame for what had happened upon the dead President and convincing the electorate that the Republic was in grave danger from radicalism stalking through the land. The nomination went to Coolidge at the Republican convention by default. No one else really wanted it and Lowden of Illinois even refused the nomination for Vice-President. Charles G. Dawes then was given the second place on the ticket.

The Democratic convention at Madison Square Garden lasted from June 24 to July 10. There were deep cleavages in the party. The South with its rapidly growing industries and primitive exploitation of labor in the Piedmont Crescent and its racial problem in the Black Belt was hostile to an endorsement of social and economic reform. There were Catholic Democrats in the North and East, Protestant fundamentalists in the Midwest and South. There were wet Democrats in the urban centers and dry Democratic agrarians. The encroaching industrialism in the South militated against a revival of the tariff issue. The party lacked leadership capable of holding the divergent elements together and it lacked real issues for an appeal to the people. McAdoo's services to the oil interests as charged in testimony before the Lenroot Senate Committee injured his chances for the nomination; yet McAdoo, the choice of the Ku Klux Klan and the political lawyer of Doheny, appeared in the convention as the leader of reform against big business and the liquor interests. Smith was the most progressive man in the list of possible candidates but the Klan and prohibition were still too strong to permit his nomination. Nevertheless, the Democratic convention presented the first and only open debate of the Klan issue by a political party. The convention finally faltered on the question of denouncing it by name, refusing to do so by a vote of 541 to 546; but no one could have listened to the proceedings without realizing that men in public life had finally found courage to fight it even at the risk of political oblivion or worse. The rapid decline of its power dates from those July days of 1924. John W. Davis of West Virginia was nominated after a bitter contest between the Smith and McAdoo forces and Governor Charles W. Bryan of Nebraska, brother of William Jennings Bryan, was named for the Vice-Presidency.

A third party, organized originally in February, 1922, as the Conference for Progressive Political Action, nominated Robert La Follette and Burton K. Wheeler of Montana. It was the only party which offered a clear-cut program. It favored higher inheritance taxes, excess profits taxes, government ownership of the railroads, reduction of the tariff, abolition of child labor and the use of injunctions in labor disputes, the direct election of Presidents, a federal initiative and referendum, the power of Congress to override Supreme Court decisions by the two-thirds vote of each House and a reduction of armaments. As against this definition of principles the Democrats favored a government-owned merchant marine, disarmament by negotiation, independence for the Philippines, and submission to popular referendum of the question of joining the League of Nations. The Republicans favored economy, tax reduction, and membership in the World Court. All other planks in the two old party platforms were so ambiguous as to be meaningless.

The nomination of Davis by the Democrats cast the dark shadow of the League of Nations over the party again. Moreover, he was properly looked upon as a conservative. He had been Solicitor-General in Wilson's first term and was known to be a brilliant lawyer. He had been Ambassador to Great Britain from 1918 to 1921. Upon his return, he entered the private practice of law, representing the House of Morgan, the Erie Railroad, the Guaranty Trust Company and Standard Oil. His own private fortune, his close association with large corporations, and his hostility to the release of dissenting opinions by the Supreme Court, all raised grave doubts as to his liberalism on social and economic questions. Many Democrats deserted the party because it did not denounce the Klan by name, many because Smith had been defeated for the nomination. La Follette was supported by the railway brotherhoods and the American Federation of Labor, both representative of the most conservative labor groups in the world; by the northwestern wheat farmers; and by the Debs Socialists. La Follette's strong denunciation of the Klan, and Wheeler's long record of service to the underprivileged, plus his indefatigable labors in uncovering corruption in the Attorney-General's department, won them many votes.

Coolidge received 15,725,000 popular votes; Davis, 8,386,500; and La Follette, 4,822,000. The popular vote in this election, however, is an unsatisfactory criterion by which to judge the strength of the party candidates. Only 52 per cent of the qualified voters of the country went to the polls, as compared to 49 per cent in 1920; 62 per cent in 1912; 73 per cent in 1900; and 80 per cent in 1896. Figures compiled by the National Association of Manufacturers showed that only 8 per cent of the qualified voters cast their ballots in South Carolina, 10 per cent in Georgia and Mississippi, and less than 20 per cent in Alabama, Arkansas, Florida, Louisiana, Tennessee, and Virginia —all solidly Democratic states. La Follette received the 13 electoral votes of Wisconsin, not more than 100,000 votes in the entire South, but four times as many as Davis in California and twice as many in seventeen states west of the Mississippi. In only nine small states did Coolidge's vote fail to exceed the combined support of his two opponents. Republican majorities in Congress were cut to 12 in the Senate and 60 in the House of Representatives.

The Promise of a New Era

The campaign of 1924 missed being a complete sacrifice to intellectual sterility because of the ferment injected into it by the La Follette-Wheeler campaign. The campaign of 1928 lacked even that saving quality and degenerated into the most shameful political depravity since the days of Know-Nothingism. The Democrats had several possible candidates. Governor

Albert C. Ritchie of Maryland was probably the most available. He had proved equal to the task of reorganizing a state government in much the same fashion of Smith of New York and Lowden of Illinois, introducing a state budget system, a civil service, a reformed prison system and modern educational facilities. He was an old-line champion of state rights who had earned the right to be so by making his state government function. He stood by his state rights principles to the point of opposing the federal child labor amendment, federal inheritance taxes and prohibition, and favoring a popular referendum in the states on federal constitutional amendments. He steadfastly refused to use troops to suppress strikes; and he flatly refused to participate in the preparedness day mobilization Coolidge had sponsored. Economically he was opposed to government intereference with business other than public utilities or to its entering into competition with private enterprise. Thomas Walsh of Montana was the most liberal man in the party with a splendid record; but he was a Catholic and from the state of Montana which was not a pivotal state. He had uncovered the oil scandals by relentless digging against tremendous opposition; had led the fight against seating Truman H. Newberry of Michigan, for the seating of Louis D. Brandeis on the Supreme Bench, and for an investigation of the propaganda activities of public utilities; and favored the child labor amendment and woman's suffrage. He had helped draft the Federal Reserve Act. He was opposed to the use of the anti-trust laws against labor. He was a dry. Governor Vic Donahey of Ohio was much the same type as Smith as to origins and human interests. He was, moreover, from a pivotal state of which he was the only governor who had ever served three terms. He was for economy in government, a Methodist, an ardent prohibitionist, an opponent of the Klan, and sympathetic to labor.

The Republicans had Frank O. Lowden of Illinois, a wealthy business man and gentleman farmer with farms in Illinois and plantations in Arkansas and Texas. He had proved to be a capable governor, had favored the McNary-Haugen farm bill, and was in sympathy with high income taxes. He had three weaknesses: unusual intolerance during the war, the unethical use of money by his supporters in the pre-convention campaign of 1920, and his age of sixty-eight years. Vice-President Charles G. Dawes, many things to different people, was known to be vindictive toward opposition, bitterly opposed to labor unions, fascist in his tendencies and demagogic in his attacks upon liberals. William E. Borah of Idaho was the most unique personality in public life. He was a resourceful debater, an authority on constitutional law, and a master of detailed facts. He was an opponent of monopoly with a curious idea that economic competition could be restored, of imperialism in Central America, and of the Lily White movement in the Republican Party South. He was the great champion of civil rights and of Russian recognition; but never concerned about the question of the tariff. Herbert Hoover was the most sensitive to criticism of any man in public life. He probably would have heartily endorsed the peculiar idea then prevalent in the land that it was unpatriotic to criticize the President. In those two respects, and in his rapid assumption of an air of self-importance, he was remarkably like Woodrow Wilson. He held to the theory of self-government in industry, professing to believe that voluntary cooperation within the several units of industrial life could more effectively eliminate abuses than any degree of government compulsion. That idea put into practice by the many conferences initiated during his incumbency in the Department of Commerce laid the basis for the experiment tried under the National Industrial Recovery Act in Roosevelt's Administration.

There was less contest in the pre-convention stages of the campaign than in any other in three decades. Smith's nomination became a certainty at an early date as a result of his splendid showing in the primaries, and he was nominated on the first ballot at Houston with Senator Joseph T. Robinson of Arkansas as his running mate. Thus was the attempt made to bridge the deep chasm between the several divergent elements in the party. When Hoover announced his entry into the Ohio primaries, he said, "If the greatest trust which can be given by our people should come to me, I should consider it my duty to carry forward the principles of the Republican party and the great objective of President Coolidge's policies—all of which have brought to our country such a high degree of happiness, progress and security." It is true that pronouncements of this nature and his approval of Coolidge's McNary-Haugen veto were calculated to win him the support of the President in the contest for nomination. It is, however, doubtful if that had very much to do with the nomination. It was the sequel to years of planning and skillful publicity. The Hoover myth is one of the most firmly established in American history. Whatever may be the final judgment as to his work in the Department of Commerce, it is certain that it gave him more intimate contact with more people in the country than was true of any other man in public life. Time after time he wrested the front page from President Coolidge. That, plus his career as Director of Belgian Relief and as Food Administrator were sufficient in themselves to have made him President. He early had the support of such newspapers as the *Chicago Tribune* and, when the Scripps-Howard papers declared for him in January, 1928, in preference to Dawes and Lowden, there was no question about his nomination. The Republican convention at Kansas City nominated him on the first ballot and named Senator Charles Curtis of Kansas, the majority leader who spoke in monosyllables, for the Vice-Presidency. The platforms of both parties were a collection of platitudes and ambiguities. There was nothing in them except the Republican endorsement of a protective tariff and Coolidge imperialism in the Caribbean and the pledge of both parties to enforce the Eighteenth Amendment.

The campaign which followed is indescribable. The nation was in the grip of a fictitious stock-market prosperity; but there were not less than four million unemployed, and hunger and privation were already abroad in the land. The coal industry was in a state of chaos. The oil industry was engaged in a destructive and wasteful competitive warfare. Agriculture was bordering on a state of collapse. The railroads were facing the inevitable consequences of speculative banker control. Economic experts were privately warning their friends to get out of the market before the crash came. There were great problems like prohibition, the increasing crime wave, the disposition of Muscle Shoals, flood control, veterans' benefits, and international debts crying for solution. It was a situation which called for vigorous discussion of governmental policies touching social and economic questions; yet the most important topics in the world seemed to be Smith's grammatical errors, the exact degree of culture possessed by his family and the depravity of the Catholic Church. Hoover and Curtis did not say very much about anything. It was not necessary. They simply remained silent and rode into office on the most powerful whispering campaign ever set in motion. It was the final flare-back of a dying post-war intolerance which gathered race, religious and moral prejudices into a torrent of opposition to Alfred E. Smith, the Catholic, anti-prohibition representative of Tammany Hall. Hoover carried forty states, five in the traditionally Democratic South: Virginia, North Carolina, Florida, Tennessee, and Texas. His popular vote was twenty-one million to fifteen million for Smith. Their electoral votes were 444 to 87 respectively. It had the appearance of a great victory for the candidates of the Republican party; but never were statistics more deceiving. Smith received six million more votes than any candidate of the Democratic party had ever received previously. He received 40 per cent of the total vote cast, whereas Cox had received but 34 per cent in 1920 and Davis 30 per cent in 1924. Moreover, the results of the elections in Minnesota, Wisconsin, Nebraska, North Dakota, Washington and Arizona were pregnant with meaning; because in all of those states independent progressives who openly opposed the Republican candidates and policies were elected by tremendous majorities while Smith was being repudiated. Smith lost Minnesota by only 100,000 votes and Shipstead, Farmer-Laborite, carried the state against the Republican candidate by 400,000. It is certain that, despite the association of Republicanism and prosperity as synonymous terms in the minds of many people, Smith would have come close to winning had he not been a Catholic and Tammanyite. Republican majorities in Congress were increased to 15 in the Senate and 101 in the House of Representatives.

Thus was the stage set for the crucial test of an ingenious theory of political economy—the omniscience of the modern industrialist as a determining influence in governmental policies. For twelve years nothing had been done about the vast concentration of economic power into a few hands which had so greatly disturbed Roosevelt, Taft, and Wilson and had been so ably demonstrated by Brandeis and the Pujo Committee. Taft's pleas for a curb on over-capitalization, for publicity of corporate affairs and for federal incorporation had gone unheeded. The consequence was nefarious holding companies, gambling on the stock market by the directors of corporate management, an alliance between investment and commercial banking, and a tremendous distribution of stocks to the investing public at fictitious values. Nothing had been done about reducing foreign debts on the principle of capacity to pay. Nothing had been done about the tariff except to increase it to the point where foreign nations were forced to repudiate their debts and enact retaliatory tariffs, and American manufacturers, in turn, were forced to establish their branch factories in foreign lands. Nothing had been done to relieve the unequal tax burden either by drastically reducing the debt through high income and inheritance taxes or abolishing tax exempt securities. Nothing had been done to counteract technological unemployment. Nothing had been done to maintain an even economic balance between industry and agriculture. Nothing had been done to relieve the railroads from the burden of destructive competition, to promote flood control or soil conservation.

This policy of inaction was no more the fault of President Hoover than of countless other men in public life or of the millions of people of all parties who believed, like they, that business had found the secret of a modern economic utopia. But Hoover did more than any other man to popularize the idea that prosperity would go on and on if the policies of his predecessors were adhered to. He pledged himself to continue those policies if elected to the Presidency. He fulfilled his promise even to the point of increasing the tariff by signing the Hawley-Smoot Act against the advice of the trained economists of the country. He refused to admit that it was a mistake and permitted his campaign headquarters to denounce the economists as radicals; and he continued to issue optimistic statements of imminent recovery when the collapse of the economic system had scarcely begun. He had been elected as the representative of industrial efficiency—as one whose peculiar equipment, by his own admission, would guide the nation to yet undreamed-of abundance. In his acceptance speech, he said: "We have not yet reached the goal, but given a chance to go forward with the policies of the last eight years, and we shall soon with the help of God be within sight of the day when poverty will be banished from the nation." Business prostration followed shortly thereafter. Millions of people lost savings invested in gilt-edged securities. Millions more were reduced to beggary. Private charity proved incapable of sustaining the destitute. Little by little the totality of the collapse dawned upon an incredulous people. Destitution, despair and divided counsels prevailed. No man of vision came forward with a program of relief. It was the price a people paid for sixteen years of political stagnation; for the proscription of dissent, the suppression of ideas. It was then that the fundamental weakness of the President appeared: an inability to see the possibility of a better way of life than that which permitted any man to accumulate great wealth. It is doubtful if he had any appreciation of the extent of suffering in the land or of its import. He set himself inflexibly against federal expenditures to feed the starving. His recovery program consisted of passing out millions to save from bankruptcy corporations which had turned out millions of men to starve until they could be reemployed at a profit. In

July, 1932, a great army of veterans went to Washington and encamped on government property. They were there because they were unemployed, not primarily because they were veterans. They were well-behaved and well-disciplined; but they were driven out with cavalry, infantry, tanks, and machine gun troops. Two men were shot, 1000 men, women and children were gassed. Whatever hope of re-election remained was effectively destroyed on this July 28 by one of the worst exhibitions of official blundering and cruel oppression the country had ever witnessed. The country has long since forgotten the dark forebodings of disaster everywhere; but people were almost driven to strike out blindly for relief and the danger was real. Under the pressure of the impending nominating conventions, President Hoover announced his unemployment relief program: an increase in funds to be loaned by the Reconstruction Finance Corporation to the states for self-liquidating projects of public works.

1932 and Party Chaos

There was no effective opposition to Hoover's nomination. In the Democratic party, there was a real contest. Franklin D. Roosevelt had emerged from the election of 1928 as the most available man in the party. He had been Assistant Secretary of the Navy in Wilson's Administration and Vice Presidential candidate on the ticket with Cox in 1920. He had attracted a great deal of attention with his speech placing Smith in nomination in 1924, and in 1928 Smith had prevailed upon him to run for the governorship of New York. He did so, being elected by a substantial majority while Smith failed to carry the state. He was reelected in 1930 by a very large majority. During these four years, he proved a capable governor and a very shrewd politician. He met the depression in the state by increasing income taxes 100 per cent and using the money for direct relief. There was much doubt, however, about his being classed as a liberal and, also, about his ability to formulate a definite program of action. His strongest opponent for the nomination was John N. Garner of Texas, who had been sponsoring a sales tax to balance the budget in the last Hoover Congress. He had been in Congress since 1903 and no one questioned his ability, least of all Andrew Mellon whose tax proposals had more than once been defeated by Garner's opposition. The Hearst newspapers and William G. McAdoo both favored his nomination. The third prominent candidate was Alfred E. Smith who had broken with Roosevelt and had the support of the Scripps-Howard newspapers. Albert Ritchie and Newton D. Baker were considered possible compromise candidates. Roosevelt's managers made a tactical blunder in seeking to repeal the ancient two-thirds rule for nomination in the convention and failed. A deal was then consummated whereby the Garner votes from Texas and California were thrown to Roosevelt and Garner given the Vice Presidency. The resulting bitterness of the Smith forces was to remain a source of annoyance even in the next campaign.

Hoover's renomination drove the Progressives out of the party. No one among them attempted to lead a third party movement as Roosevelt had done in 1912 and La Follette in 1924. Five million people had voted for La Follette and Wheeler in 1924 because theirs was the only platform that an intellectually honest man could support. There had been no La Follette party in 1928 in fact, but in reality there was just that. How many votes went to Hoover instead of Smith as the lesser of two evils but at the same time were given to dissenters like Shipstead, Norris, Ashurst, Dill, Norbeck and others, one may only guess; but it is safe to say more than 5,000,000. In short, if the Democratic party or any other party had presented a platform in 1928 like the La Follette platform of 1924 or the Democratic platform of 1932, Hoover would have gone into office, if at all, with far less than a 6,000,000 majority of the popular vote. It was the Democratic platform which made it possible for the Progressive Republican leaders to support Franklin D. Roosevelt—in fact made it impossible for them to do otherwise and remain true to their political philosophy. Norris of Nebraska took the lead and was followed by Robert

La Follette of Wisconsin, Bronson Cutting of New Mexico and Hiram Johnson of California. They were denounced by Hoover as dangerous radicals, but in public opinion they were spokesmen of great constituencies and, as a group, the most consistently honest men in public life. They came from the great agricultural states. Their people had voted Republican since the days of Abraham Lincoln; but their economy had nothing in common with that of the industrial East; their philosophy could not be reconciled with that of the Republican hierarchy; they had been Republican in nothing but name; they did not become Democrats.

The Republican platform was conservative and conventionally non-committal. The Democratic platform was concise, understandable and liberal. The Socialist platform was, as usual, radical. The Republicans had successfully sounded the alarm of radicalism so often that it had become habitual and again found its way into the platform. They promised to balance the budget, but said nothing about the tax program for doing it. They endorsed pensions for veterans suffering both from service and non-service disabilities, the gold standard, restriction of immigration, and the removal of submarginal land from production. They promised to maintain and extend the tariff schedules, and to submit a modified prohibition amendment. The Democratic platform would reduce government expenses 25 per cent; tax on the basis of ability to pay; pay pensions only to those disabled in service; divorce investment banking from commercial banking; extend public works and federal credit for unemployment relief; enact state unemployment and old age pension laws; control crop surpluses; collect the war debts; repeal the Eighteenth Amendment; and seek tariff reduction by negotiation. The Socialists demanded social ownership of principal industries; increased income and inheritance taxes; abolition of tax-exempt securities; a national banking system; ten billion dollars for direct relief and public works; abolition of the R.O.T.C., of conscription, and of munition sales; the recognition of Russia; entrance into the League of Nations; cancellation of war debts; disarmament by example; minimum wage laws; social insurance; the direct election of the presidents, proportional representation and abolition of judicial review.

In the campaign, Hoover stanchly defended the Hawley-Smoot Tariff, and the National Committee denounced the economists who had protested against it as radicals, socialists and communists. Ogden L. Mills defended the policies of the Administration as one hundred per cent perfect. Hoover assumed the role of savior of the country by hinting with an air of secrecy at grave dangers which the Administration had overcome. Ex-President Coolidge wrote in the *Saturday Evening Post* of the great wisdom of President Hoover in avoiding the dole, although millions were receiving local and state relief at the time. He and others repeatedly asserted that the standard of health in the country had been raised under Republican Administrations—even during the depression. The prohibition forces threw their support to the Republican party, which redounded to the benefit of their opponents. The efforts of the Republicans to disclaim responsibility for the economic catastrophe were futile. They had claimed the benefits of prosperity too long to evade the consequences of the depression. That and prohibition were the deciding factors. Prohibition had been a dismal failure. Moreover, it had been dragged into every campaign to the confusion of other and more important issues. It had to be settled before there could be any rational consideration of pressing economic questions. Millions voted for the party which promised outright submission of an amendment for repeal. The general accumulation of dissatisfaction with three Republican Administrations, the failure of the party in power to arrest the deflation, and its refusal to face squarely the failure of the prohibition experiment combined to deprive the party of all but regular votes. The independent vote went to Roosevelt instead of Norman Thomas. Roosevelt received 472 electoral votes. It was more than an election. It was a veritable political revolution. Only eight Republican governors were elected and such stalwarts as Senators George H. Moses of

New Hampshire and Hiram Bingham of Connecticut went down to defeat. The House of Representatives was Democratic by almost three to one.

March, 1933, marked the end of an era, but the weeks between the election in November and the inauguration in March were the most depressing the nation had witnessed since the winter of 1860-1861. Deflation had been running for more than three years. Unemployment had reached an estimated peak of 15,000,000. More than 200 cities were facing imminent bankruptcy. There was no way under the law by which fixed charges on bonded indebtedness might be reduced. Retrenchments, therefore, were being made at the expense of essential public services: schools, fire and police protection, garbage disposal, maintenance of streets, public buildings and playgrounds. Farm and city home owners were unable, under the law, to reduce debts in proportion to the decline in prices and wages. Property was forfeited and millions of people had lost their hard-earned equities. Home building had long since ceased; but there was actually a surplus of homes as families doubled up or returned to rural communities. Private and local relief could no longer bear the burden of these unprecedented conditions. Several hundred thousand boys, many scarcely out of their teens, were roaming the country without purpose and in hopeless despair. Millions had reached maturity without prospect of honest labor. The situation was not only acute; it was desperate. Prime Minister Ramsay MacDonald said at the London Economic Conference in 1933: "This can not go on. The world is being driven upon a state of things which may well bring it face to face again with a time in which life revolts against hardship and the gains of the past are swept away by the forces of despair." He was not indulging in mere rhetorical bombast. The danger was as real in the United States as in Europe and more ominous because it was more silent.

It is not to be implied that the Hoover Administration had no recovery program. It did have; but the agencies set up will be considered later because they were incorporated in the program of the Roosevelt Administration. The point is that the Hoover Administration was restrained by its basic philosophy from coming to grips, in a realistic way, with the problem of human distress. Every item in the Roosevelt program was destined to be bitterly contested because they were of such a nature as to sorely trouble the minds and hearts of men. Human compassion and the generosity of a people distinguished for generosity were, from the first, confounded by real concern over justice, the security of their institutions and of their basic social philosophy. Men who had no work, whose families lacked the barest necessities of food, shelter and clothing, were not much given to reflection on the blessings of decentralized government, the doctrine of judicial review, or of any other philosophical theory or institution. More than 15,000,000 men lived through the nightmare of unemployment during the depression. Their dependents numbered as many more. Liberty, to them, meant something quite different from what it meant to the men who later sponsored the American Liberty League. The latter might stoutly deny that liberty had changed its meaning; but the fact remained that it was given a new connotation by millions of people. Economic justice was as fundamental to liberty in 1932 as the Bill of Rights had been in 1787. Economic justice meant some relief for debtors at the expense of creditors. Existing law provided none. It meant that any man who was willing and able to work should not be denied the privilege. Tradition decreed that production would be resumed only when private capital was assured a return in the form of profits. Capital, unlike labor, did not work for wages. Both were essential to productive enterprise; but idle capital seldom meant distress in the owner's family as did idle labor. Economic justice meant, too, that none should suffer for lack of life's necessities. If the breadwinner of the family could find no labor, and the wells of private charity were dry, then government must supply the deficiency. If local and state governments were unable, unwilling or forbidden by state constitutions to do so, then the general government must assume the responsibility. None of this involved the demand for future security. That was a fundamental phase of the reform movement; but unemployment was a present fact—a condition and not a theory. The demand for future security would be a determining factor in politics; it might alter the nation's economic thought; it might even alter its political institutions; but relief was imperative and, upon the degree to which it was furnished and upon the ways and means by which it was financed might well depend the permanence of democratic institutions.

It was this which sorely troubled so many men. That there should have been bitter accusations, misunderstanding and fear was inevitable. Men who walked the streets in vain search for work with the cries of hungry children ringing in their ears could hardly have been expected to be philosophical about it. Men who had lost their savings and had seen the homes around which clustered the memories of a lifetime sold to satisfy the claims of distant creditors could not refrain from occasional violence. All of these people looked out of their barren lives in bitterness toward those who sat complacently with the nation's wealth in their grasp and condemned heavy governmental expenditures for the relief of human distress. They lent ready support to the epic plan of Upton Sinclair, to the Union for Social Justice of Father Charles E. Coughlin, to the Share the Wealth clubs of Senator Huey Long, and to the Old Age Pension plan of Dr. Francis Townsend. Opposed to them was the rugged individualism of an earlier day: a philosophy which denied that the government could spend the nation into prosperity; which saw government budgets unbalanced, government debts accumulating, and wondered if they would be paid without a capital levy, repudiation or worse. One can no more charge this group with insincerity, than one can pin the badge of demagoguery on their critics. That there was greed, selfishness and deceit in all quarters is perfectly plain; but there was a respectable body of economic thought in the country which maintained that prolonged and excessive governmental spending would lead to the control of capital and labor by the state;

and that higher taxes meant increased costs of production, lower returns to labor and decreased consumption. This seems to have been apparent to the Roosevelt Administration and responsible for its efforts (1) to secure, by persuasion or compulsion, a greater return to labor at the expense of dividends, and (2) to finance recovery measures by borrowing instead of taxation that the immediate trend toward recovery might not be retarded. How much the fear expressed in many quarters over the dangers which threatened the Constitution were sincere and how much they were a cloak for partisanship, is difficult to say. These things were fundamental. Out of the turmoil and intellectual ferment they produced came impulses for the reform of human institutions. Recovery and reform were inseparable. The history of both began in 1932.

Reform was long overdue, for not every one in the country was hypnotized by the glitter of gold, nor satisfied that the American way of life was the best way. Newspapers, for the most part, and magazines too, had become enormous business enterprises and bowed to the slightest whims of materialistic advertisers, to the prejudices of their sections and to the taboos of their age; but there were exceptions. Mention has already been made of the newspapers of the South which fought the Klan. The *New York World* until its demise and the *St. Louis Post Dispatch* kept alive the spirit of their founder, Joseph Pulitzer, as tribunes of the people. The *New York Times*, fearing no one, devoted its widely read pages to a faithful exposé of conditions as they were in a hundred regions as widely separated as the Kentucky coal fields, the Piedmont Crescent, and far distant Soviet Russia. Louis B. Seltzer and Carlton K. Matson of the *Cleveland Press* were willing to go to jail to preserve the freedom of the press from censorship by injunction. The *Nation*, among other innumerable services to truth and justice, rose to new heights of journalistic performance in exposing the American government's imperialistic venture in Nicaragua. The *Outlook* wrote a new chapter in service to humanity, with a revelation of the facts about Vanzetti's innocence.

D. H. Mellett of the Canton *Daily News* gave his life to purge his city of crime and official corruption. The *New Republic* labored ceaselessly to create an intelligent attitude toward Russia and presented to the reading public the excellent interpretations by John Dewey, dean of American educators, on that subject. Ernest Gruening, editor of the *Portland Evening News*, took the leading rôle in freeing a long suffering nation from exploitation by the power interests. *Fortune* magazine and Dorothy Detzer, Executive Secretary of the Women's International League for Peace, share honors equally for precipitating an investigation into the munitions industry which produced repercussions even beyond the limits of the United States. Edgar A. Mowrer of the *Chicago Daily News*, author of *Germany Sets the Clock Back*, exposed Nazi outrages against submerged racial groups; and the *New Masses* revealed the astounding nature of their propaganda in this country. Walter Lippmann rounded out a quarter of a century of brilliant journalistic writing with continued sane, yet penetrating, discussions of every phase of public life. Robert S. Allen, the modern Suetonius, sacrificed his position to strip official Washington of its cloak of mystery in *Washington Merry-Go-Round*. H. L. Mencken dedicated his *American Mercury* to the task of keeping America sane.

The liberal journals and the press were ably assisted in their task by a group of novelists who undertook to reveal the pattern of national life to the people. Sinclair Lewis with his *Main Street*, *Babbitt*, *Elmer Gantry*, *Arrowsmith*, and *Dodsworth*, satirized life in the machine age in such a thought-provoking manner as to cause countless thousands to take stock of themselves, their prejudices, their taboos and their fetishes. Finally, he wielded his gifted pen in much the manner of a meat-axe and revealed to startled Americans, in *It Can't Happen Here*, a perfect setting for the rise of a dictatorship. Theodore Dreiser, realist *par excellence*, shocked middle-class America with his brutally frank portrayal of conventional hyprocrisy in *The Financier*, *The Titan* and *An American Tragedy*, and gave solace only to those who found difficult the task of adjusting themselves to modern life. Louis Adamic combined literary art and propaganda in his *The Native's Return;* while Maxwell Anderson and Harold Hickerson in *Gods of Lightning* and Upton Sinclair in *Boston* brought drama into the realm of reality with their interpretations of the story of Sacco and Vanzetti. John Dos Passos stripped war of its fictitious glamor, until it stood revealed in the stark reality of sordidness with his *Three Soldiers*, and made his reputation doubly secure with the trilogy beginning with *The Forty-Second Parallel.* Margaret Sanger crowned a lifetime of service to the betterment of the human race with her *Motherhood in Bondage.* Morris L. Ernst and William Seagle shook the foundations of prudishness and unintelligent censorship with *To the Pure.* Finally, dozens of men and women, in as many different ways, approached the problems of the New South, where the racial antagonisms and a rising industrialism combined to create the most difficult problem of social adjustment ever encountered by the nation. Du Bose Heyward's *Porgy;* Paul Green's *In Abraham's Bosom;* Stribling's *The Store*, *The Forge* and *The Unfinished Cathedral;* Robert Moton's *What the Negro Thinks;* Charles S. Johnson's *The Negro in American Civilization;* Howard Odum's series of brilliant sociological studies including *Rainbow Round My Shoulder* and *Southern Regions;* Julia Peterkin's and Doris Ulmann's *Roll, Jordan, Roll;* the work of the Southern Commission on the Study of Lynching under the chairmanship of the brilliant and versatile editor of the *Chattanooga News*, George Fort Milton; and *I'll Take My Stand* by Twelve Southerners, stand as evidence of the divers literary and scientific approaches to the problems of the section.

If the public service was cluttered up with time-serving politicians who sought to avoid commitments on important questions of public policy, it also had its men who sacrified the possibility of advancement and jeopardized their present positions by forthrightly championing unpopular causes: William E. Borah with his unceasing demand for the recognition of Russia and abandonment of imperialist ventures in Central America and the Caribbean; Alfred E. Smith with his outspoken denunciation of the Ku Klux Klan and the evils of the experiment in national prohibition; George W. Norris with his opposition to our entry into the World War and his fight to save Muscle Shoals for the people; Bennett Clark with his denunciation of the nation's tariff policies; and Brigadier-General P. D. Glassford with his stanch defense of the bonus army. Dwight W. Morrow abandoned his high position in the world of finance to write a brilliant chapter in foreign diplomacy and bring to an end a century of mutual misunderstanding and distrust between Mexico and the United States. Mary Van Kleeck laid the basis for an intelligent approach to the problem of social security by years of scientific study. Clarence Darrow, Arthur Garfield Hayes and Dudley Field Malone, sometimes singly, ofttimes together, championed the cause of justice for the underprivileged and for the victims of racial and class and religious prejudice throughout the nation. A group of public-spirited scientists, led by E. J. Schlink and Stuart Chase, established the organization known as Consumers Research and engaged in the stupendous task of exposing the fraudulent and misleading advertising so prevalent in the business practices of the decade. Hundreds of men of prominence in every branch of the professional world lent their prestige to the support of the American Civil Liberties Union. George W. Wickersham brought to a close a distinctly honorable career in the public service by directing the work of the Commission on Law Enforcement which exposed intolerable conditions in the treatment of prisoners and in disregard for the law by law-enforcement officials. Norman Thomas brought sanity into public discussions of the question of socialism by the intelligent and dignified manner in which he analyzed existing institutions.

In the field of science and discovery, scores of men, in and out of research laboratories, added to man's knowledge of his environment. The scope of their work may be indicated by the mere mention of Commander Richard E. Byrd's search of the

South Pole Regions for new secrets of atmospheric changes; C. V. McCauley's and J. C. Hostetter's skillful casting, at the Corning Glass Works, of a 200-inch lens for astronomers to use in penetrating the mysteries of an unseen universe; Harold C. Urey's challenge to the genius of science and medicine with his discovery of "heavy water"; the discovery of the hydrogen isotrope by Harold C. Urey and G. M. Murphy of Columbia University and F. G. Brickmedde of the United States Bureau of Standards; and the lessening of the pressure for economic imperialism through the discovery of synthetic rubber, known as duprene, by F. B. Downing, W. H. Carothers and Ira Williams.

Other men and women made their contributions to the more abundant life in many different ways. John Carpenter and Robert Edmond Jones created a striking new form of art with their presentation of the ballet *Skyscrapers*. Walt Disney reached a far wider group with his even more unique and entertaining Silly Symphony Series. Walter Damrosch labored indefatigably to educate the public, especially through the medium of the radio, to an appreciation of fine music. Deems Taylor and Edna St. Vincent Millay made American opera a reality with their *King's Henchman*. Paul Whiteman and George Gershwin harnessed riotous jazz and gave it dignity. Eliel Saarenen created a permanent monument to combined utility and art in the buildings of Cranbrook School in Detroit. Cass Gilbert and Robert T. Walker did likewise in the New York Life Insurance Building. The American Council of Learned Societies and the *New York Times*, together with the editors Allan Johnson and Dumas Malone, gave to America its finest historical publication from the standpoints of utility and consistently good scholarship in the *Dictionary of American Biography*.

One might go on to fill a volume with references to the work of those who looked upon life as something more important than making a livelihood—men and women given to the contemplation of ideas and ideals, loving freedom and justice, and striving to give America a cultural pattern above the mere plane of existence. Their lives and works constituted a formidable, though often unnoticed, barrier to the crass materialism fostered by the prurient standards of middle class America. They were the link between Wilson's New Freedom and Roosevelt's New Deal.

CHAPTER XV

BOURBONS TO CRACK-POTS: A MEDLEY OF IDEAS

THE wild orgy of war and post-war days having come to a tragic end on that Black Thursday in October, 1929, America turned sadly to the task of studying the three R's: Relief, Recovery and Reform. The economic collapse was so complete that virtually every one wanted relief, as much and as quickly as possible. Every one, too, hoped for recovery; some for the recovery of their lost paradise; others for the recovery of the sanity and stability of pre-war days. Few wanted reform, if reform interfered with their own particular interests. Men knew that there was a surplus of consumers' goods, both of agricultural and of manufactured products, in terms of what the people could buy. They knew that there was a surplus of capital in the control of a relatively few people who could use it only for investment purposes. They knew that the purchasing power of the farmers had been destroyed by low prices. They knew that purchasing power of consumers must be restored by increasing the price of agricultural products and by reemployment of idle wage earners before recovery could be accomplished; but they disagreed as to the cause of the condition and the remedial measures required. Did tariff barriers, foreign debts and reparations payments destroy world trade? Did the cartels so assiduously promoted by Hoover and the monopolies three administrations had tolerated foster artificially high prices and result in an unbalanced economy? Was the collapse due to over-speculation and, if so, were the banking policies or the tax policies at fault? Had the increased productivity of the machine age produced a permanent technological unemployment which could only be remedied by shorter working hours? Had the take of capital out of industrial profits been too great as compared with that of labor? On these questions, there was a sharp division of opinion which cut squarely across party lines and called for courageous leadership. No one will ever understand the events from 1929 to 1936 who thinks in terms of politics. The problem must be approached from the viewpoint of conflicting social and economic philosophies.

The Bourbon Philosophy

The country was deep in the mire of depression and unemployment mounted to staggering totals between 1929 and 1930 because producers of goods could no longer sell their products at a price which would permit continued operation. Recovery required not only that consumers' purchasing power be restored by placing money in their hands through government largess or reemployment, either private or public; but that prices be restored to such levels that profits from production were once more a possibility. Restoration of economic stability on the basis of low prices and low wages was impossible because of the tremendous burden of private and public debt which could only be reduced by wholesale bankruptcy or default and dangerous curtailment of essential public services. Restoration on the basis of high prices and low wages was impossible because it was the very thing which added momentum to the deflation process at the outset.

The Hoover Administration proceeded from the first on the theory that the economic structure of the country was fundamentally sound and that the period of deflation must necessarily be short if confidence could be restored. It brought pressure to bear, without success, upon industrialists to check the discharge of employees and wage cutting; issued optimistic statements from time to time about the imminence of recovery; and refused to resort to direct federal relief for the unemployed. Long after he had been relieved of responsibility and the nation was well along the way to recovery, Hoover kept insisting that it was lack of confidence, fear of what the Roosevelt monetary policies would be, which delayed rapid recovery in 1932-1933. Wherever one touches the controversy in its early stages, one inevitably comes back to this question of monetary policies. The dark shadow of 1896 and the darker shadow of post-war Europe hung like a pall over the White House.

The Constitution gives to Congress complete power to establish a monetary system and regulate the currency of the country. During the Civil War, it taxed the paper currency issued by state banks out of existence. In 1873, it demonetized silver. Great Britain had been on the gold standard since early in the nineteenth century. Every leading nation except China followed the example of the United States and Great Britain before the turn of the century. Thereafter, the world price level of commodities rose or fell in terms of gold as the supply of gold and the demand for it fluctuated. Gold did not increase in amount between the action of 1873 and 1896, but business and trade did expand and prices declined sharply. The demand for remonetization of silver emerged, and the battle for the restoration of free coinage at a ratio of 16 to 1 was fought to a conclusion in the United States in 1896. The silver forces were defeated and from that time forward the position of the country remained substantially one of opposition to bimetallism except by international cooperation. The fundamental principle for which the free-silver forces were contending in 1896, however, was written into the monetary system of the country by the Federal Reserve Act of 1914. It was that of a greatly expanded and flexible currency system. That act made commercial and agricultural paper instead of government bonds the basis of the paper circulating medium. Any member bank could take such paper to the Reserve bank for rediscount or it could take government bonds as collateral for loans and receive Federal Reserve notes in exchange. The amount of paper notes in circulation, then, and the aggregate amount of deposits subject to check, depended upon the willingness of people to borrow and spend and upon the willingness of bankers to loan and rediscount or borrow from the Federal Reserve banks, subject only to the following limitations: a 40 per cent gold coverage for Federal Reserve notes must be maintained, and banks must keep cash reserves for demand deposits of 15 and 12 per cent, depending upon their location, and 5 per cent for time deposits. These ratios were reduced in 1917 to 13, 10 and 7 for demand deposits and 3 for time deposits. The amount of gold, thereafter, operated only as a check upon the expansion of credit beyond certain limits. If business languished, credit stringency ensued and the percentage of gold coverage and cash reserves rose, then gold ceased to be a vital force in the general price situation. Within the limits of the rates of cash reserves set by Congress, the Federal Reserve System could control the volume of credit available by raising or lowering rediscount rates and by the indirect method of the purchase and sale of securities.

The World War which followed laid the basis for a tremendous expansion of credit in the United States by transferring to this country an extraordinary proportion of the world's supply of gold, and by the issue of more than $25,000,000,000 worth of government bonds. At the same time, however, the gold stocks of other nations were depleted to the point where they did not have enough gold with which to do business. They continued to buy from us only so long as we were willing to extend public or private credit for what we sold abroad and then world trade collapsed. Economists saw what was coming and warned of the danger of too much gold being concentrated in France and the United States while other nations remained on the gold standard. European nations had staggering internal and foreign debts. We had a large domestic debt but, with respect to the rest of the world, were a creditor nation. They had depleted gold stocks. We had more than we needed. Foreign trade balances were running heavily against them and in our favor. Government deficits faced them year after year. We had government surpluses to be applied to our debt all through the twenties. Because of the intricate nature of world trade, it was impossible for the United States to prosper, in spite of its 40 per cent of the world's gold supply, when other nations were impoverished. The abnormal business conditions of the war and immediate post-war period merged into the speculation boom in the late twenties which carried the country to the dizzy heights of an economic fool's paradise and served to compound the calamity of deflation when it came. Year after year, larger amounts of money flowed out of the channels of consumers' trade and into the savings deposits of the relatively well-to-do. Ever larger amounts of bank loans went into the speculative markets instead of into legitimate business channels. Banks were weighted down with government bonds, real estate mortgages based on greatly appreciated valuations, and speculative securities. Over-production in terms of what the domestic market could consume with the money people had or were willing to spend precipitated the first signs of retrenchment in 1928. Bank failures throughout the agricultural belt of the South and North Central States were exceptionally numerous throughout the twenties. In October, 1929, the stock market crashed, wiping out an average of more than a billion dollars' worth of paper values a day. The frenzy of speculation gave way to a mad scramble on the part of every one to get liquid. Every transaction drove down the market value of what had been considered gilt-edged securities. Gold flowed out of the country and both gold and Federal Reserve notes into the safety deposit boxes of private citizens. Unemployment mounted to more than seven million within a year and those who continued to work did so under drastically reduced wage scales. For three and one-half years ruinous deflation continued and its paralyzing effects spread to all parts of the world.

Meanwhile, European nations had bowed to the inevitable and inflated their currencies. France inflated her currency 80 per cent, Great Britain 30 per cent, Italy 66⅔ per cent, Belgium 40 per cent and Austria 44 per cent. Germany and Russia went all the way to uncontrolled inflation and printed fiat money until their currencies were depreciated to utter worthlessness. The fear of such uncontrolled inflation with its destruction of all savings, and the feeling that such methods are little more than legalized robbery for the benefit of improvident debtors, restrained the United States from action of any kind for some time. At length, the pressure from large industries, banks and service companies became so great that Hoover resorted to relief from the credit stringency by recommending the establishment of the Reconstruction Finance Corporation. The purpose of the move was to make available to hard-pressed key organizations the credit which the crumbling banking structure was unable or unwilling to extend.

The act, as passed in January, 1932, created a corporation under a board of seven directors, including the Secretary of the Treasury, the Governor of the Federal Reserve Board and the Farm Loan Commissioner. It was capitalized at $500,000,000 and authorized to sell a maximum of $1,500,000,000 worth of five-year notes or bonds to the public or the United States Treasury. Regional offices were established for the most part in conjunction with the Federal Reserve banks, for the purpose of making loans. These loans could be made directly to banks and railroads, to agriculture through the Department of Agriculture and to industry by acceptance of bills of exchange. Loans were limited to five years and a maximum of $100,000,000. Not even Congress was to be allowed information as to what loans were made, except the aggregate amount in each class and state. In July, 1932, the capital funds of the corporation were increased to $3,800,000,000: $500,000,000 for initial capital, $1,500,000,000 for loans to corporations, $1,500,000,000 for loans on self-liquidating projects, and $300,000,000 for relief loans to states. An additional $125,000,000 was appropriated for the establishment of a Federal Home Loan banking system. Further, Congress had passed an amendment to the Federal Reserve Act, February 27, 1932, permitting the use of Government bonds instead of commercial paper as collateral for the issuance of Federal Reserve notes, the lending of money to member banks without collateral under certain conditions, and to individuals. The corporation was transferred from the status of a relief to a recovery agency by permitting construction loans for self-liquidating projects. Loans to subordinate units of government for relief work, to agricultural export agencies, and to farmers through agricultural credit corporations were also authorized. The secrecy provision was also dropped, and monthly reports to the President and to Congress, including the names of borrowers and amounts of loans, was required. This action was taken because the former chairman of the Board of Directors, former Vice President Charles G. Dawes, had secured a $90,000,000 loan for his Chicago bank shortly after resigning. The amendment prohibited such loans in the future and Dawes' bank filed court proceedings to keep from repaying $60,000,000 which had been authorized but not transferred until after the amendment was passed by Congress. The corporation eventually became a banking institution for short term loans to banks, railroads, agriculture and local relief, loans to banks and railroads constituting a substantial majority of the total amount. During the first year of its existence, which was the critical period before all banks were closed, nearly $1,000,000,000 was loaned to banks and about one-third that amount to railroads. Nothing was accomplished toward thwarting a banking panic. Withdrawals continued, bankers refused to borrow and lend, and confidence was not restored. It became increasingly evident that the banks must close and, in well-informed financial circles, that the gold standard in all probability would have to be abandoned. As goverment revenues declined, business stagnated and unemployment increased, it became perfectly apparent that neither income taxes nor sales taxes could go far toward balancing the budget, nor could continued spending with increasing deficits do much more than equalize poverty until production, consumption and normal price levels were restored. It was inevitable that inflation of credit begun with the creation of the Reconstruction Finance Corporation should be followed by demands for inflation of the currency through devaluation of the dollar in terms of gold, restoration of silver to the status of money, or the issue of greenbacks. Confusion and heated controversy, therefore, arose out of the government's monetary policies. They are the inevitable concomitants of any tinkering with monetary systems because the layman does not understand the principles of exchange, is easily frightened by propaganda, and receives little help from disagreements among economists.

The banking crisis came precisely at the close of Hoover's Administration. Nearly 7000 banks had closed during the twenties, more than 2000 in 1931. The Reconstruction Finance Corporation had temporarily halted the general collapse by loaning nearly $1,000,000,000 to shaky institutions in 1932. Banks were temporarily closed by governors' proclamations in Nevada in January and in Louisiana the following month. Governor Comstock of Michigan closed the banks of that state on February 14. By March, the holiday had been extended to more than half of the states and, three days later, was decided upon in New York City. Almost the entire country was without banking facilities and without currency except for that which was being hoarded. On March 5, President Roosevelt by proclamation closed every bank in the country and ordered all movements of gold and silver stopped.

Business and industrial management, meanwhile, adopted an attitude of watchful waiting for the deflation to run its course. The first thought of the Chamber of Commerce and other business men's organizations was for economy in government and retrenchment in education. No other nation in the world ever undertook to educate its masses to the same degree as the United States. No other nation ever built an economic and political system so dependent upon the literacy of its people. No other nation so large and with a population so diverse in its origins and social backgrounds ever relied upon its educational system so heavily to train its people in the art of living harmoniously together. If ever there was a time when huge expenditures for education by past generations justified themselves, it was in 1929-1933 when everyone was in trouble, everyone needed to be tolerant, every one needed to be thoughtful yet critical that the nation's political and social solidarity might not perish. If there was one institution which measures of economy should have passed by, it was the educational system. Yet the United States Chamber of Commerce and business men's organizations inaugurated a nation-wide drive against the cost of education which, before it was stopped, all but ruined the school system. They followed it with a bitter and concerted drive, which never ceased, against expenditures of public funds for the relief of the unemployed and for sales taxes to balance government budgets. They were determined that wealth should not be made to bear the burden either of relief or recovery. President Hoover's repeated appeals to prevent wage-cutting and discharge of employees by industry were utterly futile. The lodestar of industrial management was profits. From 1929 to 1933, the basic industries continued to reduce their labor forces and to pay dividends out of accumulated surpluses. The *Wall Street Journal* reported that earnings of 83 corporations decreased 19.8 per cent and dividends on common stock increased 5.9 per cent during the first year of the depression. Many corporations continued to pay the usual dividend rates after their earnings dropped to zero. At the same time, they were making wage cuts, laying off men and reducing others to part time. Wages dropped 60 per cent in three years, with an inconsiderable decline in total dividend payments before 1932. In short, industrialists refused to admit, or at least to act, upon the basic principle, now recognized by all competent economists, that recovery depended upon restoration of the purchasing power of the masses. However much they might give lip service to the theory that economic stability in a highly mechanized civilization required widespread economic equality among the people, they denied that there was anything fundamentally wrong with a system which ultimately placed 60 per cent of the nation's wealth in the hands of two per cent of the people. They believed and acted upon the thesis that recovery could be accomplished without reform; and they opposed all recovery measures which involved or were likely to lead to changes in the economic structure of the nation.

Two plans for recovery, slightly different from that of the Reconstruction Finance Corporation, were proposed and widely discussed in business circles. In the spring of 1931, Albert L. Deane, former head of the General Motors Acceptance Corporation and later Deputy Administrator of the Federal Housing Administration, published his Mutual Security Plan. It included the three principles of work spreading, permanent public works and a tax system to sustain purchasing power. Its object was to control purchasing power by 100 per cent employment and stability in wages and consumers' demand. The plan itself called for a revolving reserve fund from which to supplement the wages of all workers whose hours of employment in a given month fell below a long term average. The long term average, to be computed over a ten year period, and the average hours of employment for each preceding month were both to be derived by dividing the total man hours of employment by the total number of employees. If the monthly average fell below the all time average, every man's pay was to be supplemented with a government check on the reserve fund to the amount of one per cent per man hour of deficiency. The fund was to be sustained by a tax on the payrolls of employers who worked their employees more hours in any given month than the long term average. The tax was to amount to 1¼ per cent on the total pay for each excess hour. The government should also provide a permanent public works program for all eligible workers unable to find employment in private industry. The program was to be carried out by a National Employment Reserve Corporation with an initial capital of $500,000,000 and authority to borrow $5,000,000,000. It was offered as a substitute in Congress for the NRA in March, 1933, and was again presented by Representative Frank W. Baykin of Alabama on April, 1935.

A somewhat similar program, known as the Kent Plan, was submitted to the Senate Committee on Manufacturing by

Charles A. Miller of the Reconstruction Finance Corporation. As a substitute for paying men on relief for doing nothing, he proposed that the RFC conclude a survey to determine the extent of employment, amount and kinds of raw materials used, etc., in normal times, and the amount of capital required by each unit of the industrial system to immediately restore normal operations. Banks would then be authorized to lend this required capital with a guarantee against loss by the RFC and with 50 per cent of any increased profits accruing to an industry going to the government.

Technocracy and Share the Wealth

Precisely at the time when unemployment had reached its peak and when the banking crisis was approaching an acute stage, a dire prophecy of impending disaster coupled with a most amazing revolutionary scheme was thrust before the people. At exactly the same time Senator Huey P. Long appeared in the Senate with his idea for making every man a king. It is only necessary to recall, at this point (1) that the traditional policy of the nation, as written into the anti-trust laws, was based upon faith in competition to maintain economic stability; (2) that the Hoover philosophy envisioned not only stability but an economic utopia arising from an era of self-government of industry through trade associations or cartels; (3) that fundamentally opposed to these ideas were the socialists' doctrines of public ownership and control of all instruments of production in a democratic political system and the soviet theories of the communists. In the winter of 1932-1933, from September to February, the most widely discussed subject in the United States was a new plan for remaking the state known as Technocracy. The term was originally applied to an organization for research, but later was used in the sense of applying science to remaking the social order. It began in 1919 with the publication of Thorstein Veblen's *The Engineers and the Price System,* in which he condemned the restraints placed upon technical achievements by industrial management for the purpose of securing maximum profits. Veblen's suggestion was for industrial control by technicians to the end of securing maximum production at minimum cost. Shortly afterward, a group of men including Howard Scott, Charles Steinmetz and Stuart Chase were associated in an endeavor to test Veblen's thesis. In September, 1920, Scott entered the services of the Industrial Workers of the World and published an article in their magazine, *One Big Union Monthly*, in which he said: "It is possible under a system of scientific administration to increase the present standard of living 800 per cent. Given a plan or design of industrial administration, the movement of the mass can be directed into constructive channels, but without such the country shall be plunged into a maelstrom beside which the Russian Revolution is but a tempest in a teapot." Controversy between Scott and Ralph Chaplin caused the former to sever his connections with the I.W.W. and, until the depression, he receded from public notice. In 1931, he became acquainted with certain men in Physics and Industrial Engineering at Columbia University and was allowed to use office space in the University to carry on the old Technical Alliance's Energy Survey of North America, 1830-1930. This study included what he called 3000 basic industries. Unemployed architects and engineers were put to work and an announcement was made that the Department of Industrial Engineering and the Architect's Emergency Committee of New York City were jointly sponsoring the survey. A report of the Department of Public Information of Columbia University drew attention to the survey in September, 1932. The amazing audacity of the survey's conclusions riveted the attention of the world upon them for six months.

Technocracy rested upon the thesis that technological unemployment was permanent and destined to increase. Man power had ceased to be of importance in production. Employment had reached its peak in the United States in 1918 and had steadily declined as production increased to its peak in 1929. Consumers' labor no longer being necessary to production, money no longer flowed into their hands to purchase the production output. Under the price and profit system debt increases faster than production. Debt must give way to machinery. The price system, private enterprise, money, banking, securities, the political system—all such institutions must be discarded and a new ecomonic utopia known as Technocracy set up. In this Technocracy, which should embrace a self-contained American continent, each individual would be required to fulfill a period of service to the state known as an energy contract. This period need be only for four hours per day, 165 days per year, between the ages of twenty-five and forty-five. Relative costs of all consumers' goods were to be determined by the relative amount of energy required to produce and deliver them. Every individual in the state would receive periodically an energy certificate from which would be deducted the amount of each purchase. There would be no profits under this scheme of complete social ownership and every one would have an equal income through life. Scott predicted absolute chaos in eighteen months unless his plan were adopted, on the grounds that 45 per cent of the unemployed could never be reabsorbed in industry. The plan was so unintelligible in parts as to appear profound to many people. It was completely rejected after a short period of hysteria arising from fear of the total collapse of the economic system; but not until it had been presented in all seriousness before the American Association for the Advancement of Science at Atlantic City, December 29, 1932, and Scott had presented it in a national broadcast on January 13, 1933. Devastating articles by Walter Lippmann, Norman Thomas, Paul Blanshard, Stuart Chase and the Vatican newspaper *Osservatore Romano* did much to bring the nation out of the hysteria. All connections between Scott and Columbia University were disavowed on January 23, 1933. Scott then organized Technocracy Incorporated, called the Technological Army of New America. A separate organization known as the Continental Committee claimed 250,000 members by May, 1933.

Senator Long's Share the Wealth program was not so easily

laughed away as was that of the Technocrats. For one thing, Long was no fly-by-night adventurer in the realm of economic philosophy. He was a practical politician and the absolute dictator of the sovereign state of Louisiana. Moreover, he had demonstrated a capacity to translate his proposals into practical realities to the utter discomfiture of business interests. He had lifted himself out of a backwoods environment into the governorship of his state as the champion of the underprivileged. He had wrested control of the state government out of the hands of a Bourbon oligarchy and centralized it; shifted the burden of taxation onto the wealthy; built a magnificent system of state highways; remodeled the school system by providing an eight month term, free textbooks, and an outstanding state university; stamped out illiteracy; and curbed the power of utility monopolies. He took his seat in the United States Senate in January, 1932, and immediately launched a campaign to save the country by redistributing its wealth. The favorite quotation by which he later justified his program was from Governor Roosevelt's speech at Atlanta, May 22, 1932: "Our basic trouble was not an insufficiency of capital, it was an insufficient distribution of buying power coupled with an oversufficient speculation in production"; and his favorite admonition was "Ye rich men, weep and howl, for your miseries that shall come upon you." On April 1, 1932, he introduced *Senate Resolution No. 204* instructing the Senate Finance Committee to reform the revenue act under consideration "so that no person shall have an annual income in excess of $1,000,000, so that no person during his or her life time shall receive by gifts, inheritance or other bequests more than $5,000,000." On April 21, 1932, he first explained in the Senate his philosophy of redistributing wealth by a capital levy. His plan was for a capital tax of 1 per cent on fortunes between $1,000,000 and $2,000,000, 2 per cent on fortunes between $2,000,000 and $3,000,000, 4 per cent on fortunes between $3,000,000 and $4,000,000, etc., doubling the rate on each successive million with a tax of 99 per cent on everything in excess of $8,000,000.

His plan was further developed in two radio addresses: "Decentralization of Wealth" on March 17, 1933, and "Currency Inflation" on April 21, 1933. On January 4, 1934, he introduced *Senate Resolution No. 65* providing for old age pensions of $30 per month for all persons over sixty years of age with less than $10,000 worth of property or net incomes of less than $1,000 per year. His complete program, which he called a "Plan to Carry Out the Command of the Lord," was presented in the Senate February 5, 1934. It was the program of his Share Our Wealth Society, the motto of which was "Every Man a King." The principles of his program, in addition to old age pensions, were:

(1) "To limit poverty by providing that every deserving family should . . . possess not less than $5,000.

(2) "To limit the hours of work to such an extent as to prevent over-production and to give the workers of America some share in recreations, conveniences, and luxuries of life.

(3) "To balance agricultural production with what can be sold and consumed according to the laws of God, which have never failed.

(4) "To care for the veterans of our wars.

(5) "Taxation . . . by reducing big fortunes from the top . . . to provide employment in public works wherever agricultural surplus is such as to render unnecessary in whole or in part one particular crop.

(6) "There shall be guaranteed a homestead to every family in the United States of America . . . which said homestead shall not be less than one-third the wealth of the average family in the United States of America.

(7) "The income of every family of America shall not be less than from one-third to one-half the average family income of the particular year. The income of no one person shall be more than 100 times the income of the average family for that year."

The nearest Long ever came to explaining how the wealth of the country could be redistributed short of the complete nationalization of property was to say: "We are going to take into the ownership of the United States of America every dollar, every bit of property that anybody owns above a few million dollars, and we are going to distribute that property, either by selling it and distributing it or otherwise, to those who have less than a homestead, of around $5,000. That is how we are going to get it." He continued to popularize his dream of a debt-free home, a motor car, an electric refrigerator, and a college education for everybody until his assassination in the late summer of 1935. It was his ambition to defeat the Administration Senate leaders Pat Harrison of Mississippi and Joseph Robinson of Arkansas and to prevent President Roosevelt's re-election by shifting five million votes to some other candidate. After his death, the burden of accomplishing this was carried by his lieutenant Gerald L. K. Smith of Shreveport who claimed the support of six million people by the summer of 1936.

Industrial Democracy

Midway between the ideas or lack of ideas of the radical and conservative extremists was the basic principle on which "New Deal" legislation was to rest. It was that the consumers' market could be recovered and retained only by raising the real income of farmers to pre-war levels and by giving wage-earners a larger share of what they produced; in short, by increasing the return from production going to consumers and decreasing the returns going to investors and speculators. It was an approach to, though not an open endorsement of the idea, that our industrial system had developed to the point where a smooth functioning could be achieved only by putting capital instead of labor on a wage basis.

Edward A. Filene, a Boston merchant and philanthropist, proposed in January, 1933, that business and industry as a whole immediately adopt a thirty-hour week without any reduction in weekly wages and that thereafter workers be regarded entirely in the light of consumers with minimum wages based on unit cost of production. A. B. Lambert, a practical business man of St. Louis, suggested a 100 per cent Profits Tax Plan similar to the excess profits tax of World War days. His argument was that any industry which utilized machinery to the exclusion of man power and made large profits was a parasite on other industries, selling its products to their workers and providing no market in turn for their products. He proposed placing a 100 per cent profits tax on all profits above 6 per cent of the actual working capital and the use of the money so derived for the support of the unemployed.

It is only when the theory behind these suggestions is set over against the prevailing attitude of business men and industrialists from 1929 to 1933 that one begins to realize the tremendous difficulty of trying to solve the problem with reason rather than rhetoric, with intelligence rather than passion. The theory was that the country was dealing with a social revolution rather than an economic depression; that, in the new industrial age, the buying power of the masses must be increased by raising wages and lowering prices. Business men who had always been accustomed to think in terms of stabilizing prices at the highest possible levels and bargaining for the cheapest possible labor in order to increase the margin of profits, naturally found it difficult to change their attitude or to believe that economic changes had made it necessary for them to do so. The fact that there was a distinct moral tone to the reform movement—and the recovery measures were predicated upon the thesis that industrial relations were matters of social justice, of ethics, of morality as much as they were matters of economic expediency, did not make their endorsement by hard-headed business men any easier. This idea that recovery required a larger share of returns to labor was stressed by President Roosevelt when he signed the National Industrial Recovery Act. We shall see how the refusal of business men to accept the thesis caused that experiment to fail. It was back of Huey Long's Share the Wealth program and, later, of Father Charles E. Coughlin's Union for Social Justice. On the other hand, it was significantly absent from the programs of the industrialists. It was the point at which men separated into new political alignments.

The man who, more than any other, presented a plan by which both economic liberty and economic prosperity might be retained was Monsignor J. A. Ryan, Professor of Moral Theology and Industrial Ethics at the Catholic University. Ryan's program for an industrial democracy is important to the historian not only because he belongs among the really great leaders of social reform, but because his philosophy represents that of so many men whose business it is to analyze social forces and because of the tremendous influence it had on the Roosevelt Administration. Ryan's program was unique among the many because it was not suggestive of a quick cure-all for existing difficulties but consisted of proposed modifications in the economic system. Recovery depended upon increasing the purchasing power of those who buy consumption goods. The new demand for consumers' goods and services would be followed by a demand for capital goods. The real income of farmers and wage-earners should be increased, because they purchase consumers' goods; and increased at the expense of those who invest and speculate with their incomes. This can be accomplished first by raising money wages through the agency of strong labor unions and minimum wage laws. The increase in money wages could then be transformed into an increase in real wages by indirect action such as forcing down interest rates by offering low rates on government securities and bank deposits and government competition with those private industries which insist upon maintaining high prices and low wages. It could be accomplished directly by establishing a thirty-hour week by law with no reduction in weekly wages. In so far as this would destroy marginal and inefficient producers artificially kept alive by the tariff, it would benefit society. Finally, purchasing power could be increased by large governmental expenditures for public works until the unemployed were reabsorbed into private business, the money to be derived from high income, inheritance and excess profits taxes. Public works should be of those types unattractive to private capital, such as the elimination of grade crossings and construction of low cost housing. There should be a restriction on the production of those agricultural commodities which would not be absorbed by the market if consumers were fully able to purchase, but not otherwise. Recovery should envision an increase in small farms and subsistence homesteads with the cooperative use of farm machinery and community industries. Finally, there should be a distinct reform in the ethical standards which governed economic relations.

Rejecting collectivism of every sort, whether it be socialism, communism or fascism, Ryan evinced a sublime faith in the democratic system by advocating its extension to the industrial order. The objective should be an industrial democracy embracing living wages, social insurance and a division of surplus profits between labor and management with a guaranteed fixed wage to capital. Such a system would necessitate the abandonment of individualism and bring the managers, the owners and the employees of an industry into a single unit for the control of wages, dividends, prices and working conditions. These occupational groups might be federated in a national council for the industry and all of them brought under the restraining influence of the state. It would place in the hands of wage-earners some influence over their environment, curb the power of the unscrupulous individualists, and eliminate conflict between classes. It was, in reality, a compromise program between socialism and individualism, between capitalism and communism.

Unemployment Relief

The United States was as completely without a plan for the relief of the unemployed in January, 1933, as it had been at the beginning of the depression. One of the important aspects of our economic system had been that society must bear the burden of supporting, in times of depression, the surplus labor supply of industry. Labor was recruited in the open market when needed, discharged when no longer required. During the twenties this recruitment of labor had been in the agricultural region of the South. Thousands of families were moved long distances by industry and given employment for a time, then dismissed. The determining factor was the ability of industry to sell at a profit the artifacts it produced. When the demand for its products slackened, whether it be for a few days or, as in this case, for months without end, labor was turned out to shift for itself. Families lived, during these periods, from savings, if any, returned to the comparative security of their former homes to live by the generosity of relatives or friends, did odd jobs for a meager wage, or depended upon private and public relief agencies. The same was true when wage-earners were discharged because of physical disability, old age, or technological improvements. County poor farms, public hospitals, clinics, etc., bear witness to the efforts of society to care for the derelicts of the industrial system. Organizations of private charity were spending $100,000,000 a year before the depression, probably 20 per cent of which was contributed by industrial and business institutions. There were no expenditures of federal funds for the purpose and little, if any, of state funds. The problem was regarded as a purely local responsibility and, for the most part, a service of charity. There is no escaping the fact that the United States had been dilatory about setting up safeguards against the hazards of unemployment. Few people thought in terms of the insecurity of labor.

No one knows how many wage-earners were unemployed at any time during the depression because no census was ever taken. It was variously estimated between 12,000,000 and 15,000,000 at the peak. The National Industrial Conference Board said it was 13,203,000 and the American Federation of Labor said 13,689,000 in March, 1933. In May, 1934, the two agencies placed it at 7,899,000 and 9,807,000 respectively; but some authorities maintained it was no less than 10,500,000 as late as the spring of 1936. Two facts became increasingly clear as the years came and went after 1929. The first was that shrinkage in the relief rolls was not keeping pace with industrial recovery. President Roosevelt professed to believe it was due to the increased use of machinery during the depression. His political opponents said people were being retained on the relief rolls unnecessarily for political reasons. There was probably some truth in both observations. A less partisan approach to the problem would have revealed (1) that as some persons left the relief rolls because of finding work others were added whose private savings had finally become exhausted; and (2) that several million young men and women had reached the status of wage-earners with no opportunity to work. The second fact was that restoration of complete normality in business and industry would leave 5,000,000 persons and their dependents a permanent liability against society. Most of them were unemployables: persons who because of advanced age or physical disabilities, or because of the loss of means of support at an advanced age, must depend on charity. Others were marginal laborers who could be reabsorbed into productive enterprises only by a restoration of world trade and the recovery of foreign markets.

Not only, then, was there no preconceived plan for relief but the problem constantly became more complicated as time went on. From the very first, there were two schools of thought as to how the relief problem should be handled. President Hoover was inflexibly opposed to the use of federal funds, insisting that the responsibility belonged to state and local governments and, for the purpose of maintaining public morale, to private charity. Needless to say, his position was untenable and received little support. Local and state funds were soon exhausted and appeals were made on every hand for aid from the inexhaustible resources of the federal treasury. Those who insisted that the federal government assume the burden were not without reason. The relief burden centered, at first, in the industrial centers. Municipalities simply could not maintain essential public services with decreased revenues and, at the same time, provide relief to thousands of unemployed adequate enough to maintain health and decency and counteract the appeals of radical revolutionary groups. The destitution wrought by the ensuing droughts throughout whole groups of agricultural states ably supported their contention. Unemployment was so general as to be a national problem and only the federal government could reach the resources of accumulated wealth concentrated in the industrial North and East. The southern states which had, for more than a decade, been wrestling with the problem of caring for the non-productive people left behind as young men and women migrated to the northern industrial centers, now suddenly found those same persons returning in a state of destitution. It was no simple affair when a state like South Carolina suddenly found its population increasing 16 per cent during the depression and Georgia 15 per cent. Some of the western states even resorted to border patrols to prevent destitute persons from entering the state. State and municipal funds, if forthcoming at all, must be derived from sales taxes which were an added burden upon the poor. On the other hand, those who opposed federal relief and continued to insist upon its abandonment at the earliest possible moment were equally sound in their position. Relief was, after all, a matter of individual adjustment. Local officials and existing welfare agencies were in a position to know how much assistance was necessary in a particular case and when it might properly be withdrawn. Local politicians were inclined to shirk their own responsibility for political reasons under a federal dole. They could be lenient in dispersing federal funds without offending local taxpayers and, on occasion, turn that leniency to good political purposes. Long-continued government support had a demoralizing effect upon the individual. It fostered pressure politics instead of self-reliance and had a demoralizing effect upon the recipient's family.

Men were equally torn between their real fears of excessive public expenditures and their human sympathy for those in distress. It was said, and was probably true, that continued deficits would lead to uncontrolled inflation; and that fear of inflation was retarding recovery. Generous relief for the unemployed, therefore, was simply preventing the reemployment of the recipients into private industry. This was the difficulty in making a decision between work relief and direct relief. Work relief was expensive and meant larger capital expenditures or aid for fewer people. Direct relief was cheaper, and could be extended to a larger number, but it carried a stigma that destroyed self-respect. Moreover, a minimum dole was of no assistance in restoring the consumers' market. Unless sufficient funds could be placed in the hands of the unemployed to stimulate buying, it was purely a relief and not a recovery measure.

The problem of working out a formula for the care of the unemployed was quickly complicated by the existence of such a large number of unemployables, particularly of the aged. It is a significant fact that Dr. Francis E. Townsend, promoter of the Old Age Pension Plan which bears his name, was nearly seventy years of age when he lost his savings and his position at the beginning of the depression; and he is said to have evolved his plan after seeing three old women searching garbage cans for food. The plan, originating in 1933 and printed in the form of a petition to Congress, provided that every worthy citizen over sixty years of age who was willing to cease work should receive $200 per month from the federal government. The money was to be raised by a 10 per cent sales tax and each pensioner was to be required to spend his $200 within thirty days. The economic aspects of the plan, first presented as a recovery measure, were obscured by the sentimental appeal of caring for the aged. It was reduced to a concrete formula by Robert Clements and finally introduced in Congress by Representative John S. McGroarty of California on January 16, 1935. Meanwhile, an organization, known as the Old Age Revolving Pensions, Ltd., was formed and incorporated in California and a magazine, *The Official Townsend Weekly*, was established. By February, 1934, clubs were being organized at the rate of 100 per day. The membership fee was twenty-five cents and the charter fee for local clubs twenty-five dollars. By 1936, there were 6500 local clubs with 5,000,000 members and regional offices in Washington, New York, Chicago and Los Angeles. Every club meeting was opened with prayer and a religious fervor soon permeated the whole movement. Its strength was among the ne'er-do-well groups of the small towns and rural districts which were unfamiliar with or unaffected by the philosophy of the labor movements; but it was viewed with favor by an amazing number of people from all walks of life. The plan was supported as an immediate stimulus to business recovery and as a solution to the problem of caring for the aged. Its economic fallacies were painstakingly exposed by so many people so many times that it should have disappeared as quickly as Technocracy; but recovery and not reason soon appeared to be the only antidote. Speaking to the first national convention of the organization at Chicago, 1935, Townsend said:

"For every hundred delegates assembled here today, a million prayers go up to the God of Justice that our efforts in this Convention may not fail. Our plan is the only hope of a confused and distracted nation. . . . We have become an avalanche of political power that no derision, no ridicule, no conspiracy of silence can stem."

Making allowance for over-enthusiasm, it is true, nevertheless, that pressure politics put many Congressmen in an uneasy state of mind. Memorials from local clubs and the legislatures of Arizona, California, Colorado, Idaho and North Dakota in favor of it, finally forced Congress to appoint a special committee in the House of Representatives to investigate the financial transactions of the organization as violating the Corrupt Practices Act. Fear of the political strength of the organization prevented the committee from citing Townsend for contempt when he refused to complete his testimony after three days of questioning. No one was quite certain how much truth there was to his claim of controlling the votes of 30,000,000 people; nor will any one ever know because of the rapid progress of recovery before the presidential election.

Politics and Policies

The most annoying aspect of the national situation in 1933 was the lack of a group devoted to a principle and strong enough to over-awe the extremists and formulate a policy. The country was essentially conservative. The menace of the Technocrats, the Townsendites, the Share the Wealthers, the Communists, or any of the other minority groups was not in the programs they offered. Eventually, those programs would be analyzed, discussed, refined and out of the ferment would come a modified national policy. The real danger was in the lack of an intelligent organized minority. The party in power was the traditional minority party faced with the task of consolidating its position. The Republican party was hopelessly disorganized and groping for issues. President Roosevelt attacked the problems which faced his administration in a way that cut squarely across party lines. The task which faced the Administration was both immense and complex. It was made more difficult by the great popularity of Roosevelt and the absence of a vocal opposition. Every one hesitated to criticize, partly from habit and partly through fear of hindering the process of recovery. No government can function properly without an intelligent minority and this was no exception. Every one wanted recovery, none wanted reform if reform invaded his own realm of privilege—yet sound recovery demanded drastic reform on many fronts. Liberalism requires experimentation, reason and ofttimes compromise; but the open-mindedness President Roosevelt professed was difficult to maintain in the face of attack from both extremes. He turned out to be more of a liberal than was expected. The conservative forces of privilege and power, which had long been entrenched in both old parties to the despair of the independent voters, had not feared greatly the consequences of his nomination and election. The one exception was the power interests which deluged the convention with telegrams in an effort to prevent his nomination. The National Industrial Recovery Act, with its prohibition of child labor, the right of labor to organize, its minimum wage provisions and outlawing of unethical practices in competition, awakened them to a realization of what had happened. The laws regulating the sale of securities, etc., struck dismay in the hearts of industrialists and financiers who had known no restraints other than their own conscience. The Economy Act, under the provisions of which President Roosevelt immediately cut off half the burden of veterans' benefits, added another powerful lobby to the opposition. The immediate disposition of the prohibition question alienated the die-hard drys. The inauguration of the Tennessee Valley Authority further incensed the already hostile power interests. The Agricultural Adjustment Act, designed to apply to agriculture the same control over volume of output which industry had always used, not only alienated the processors but touched the pockets of every consumer. These and every other act of the Administration added to the list of dissenters. In every case they cut across the unrealistic party alignments. People no longer thought of themselves as Democrats or Republicans. They were for the Roosevelt Administration or against it. Nothing showed the trend more clearly than one of the famous *Literary Digest* polls in which people were asked if they approved the policies of the Roosevelt Administration. The returns showed a slightly adverse sentiment; but in them were grouped all degrees of opposition—Socialists, Wall Street conservatives, Free Silverites, Share the Wealthers, etc.—groups which were as far apart as the poles on any substitute program for the one they condemned.

The second important aspect of the new situation was the lack of intelligent leadership in the opposition. Hoover remained the one opponent of the Administration with a respectable following. He waited two years before saying anything critical and then did so with the utmost dignity and propriety. His book *The Challenge to Liberty* included his first major indictment: that the policies of the Administration were totally and without reservation un-American, a repudiation of democratic institutions for a system of bureaucratic controls. From that point the same sensitiveness to personal criticism which had militated against his success as President destroyed his utmost usefulness as a minority leader. He made innumerable addresses in which he sought to prove that his administration had succeeded in turning the tide against deflation and would have succeeded but for the lack of confidence growing out of Roosevelt's election. The second source of opposition centered in the activities of the financial and industrial leaders, Democrats as well as Republicans. Their tactics were not to discuss the merits of any particular measure, but rather to create fear of the whole. Personal liberty, the safeguards of the Constitution, all the beautiful and beneficent institutions of another day were being destroyed by an administration whose philosophy emanated from Russia rather than from the Fathers of the Constitution. In the whole of the millions of words which went out over the radio, through the press and in private conversation there was little of practical value. It was the traditional tactics of a discredited leadership.

For seventy-five years, the Republican party had neglected the best interests of agriculture and labor, never consulting them and making concession grudgingly when forced to do so. The Roosevelt policies were dictated by the agrarians and labor, with strong support from an important group of industrialists. It was the first time such an alignment had materialized since before the Civil War. The Republican party was faced with the task of formulating a program which would regain for it the confidence of the people. It failed to do so for two years and, in the Congressional elections of 1934, party stalwarts such as David A. Reed of Pennsylvania and Simeon D. Fess of Ohio were retired to private life.

In the third place, there was an important issue involved in the question of emergency legislation. It centered in the delegation of power to the executive by Congress. The most important example was the Economy Act which gave the President power to do what Congress had found itself incapable of doing: reduce expenditures for veterans in the face of a powerful veterans' organization. The same thing was done in the case of the tariff, in fact, in nearly all the emergency legislation, because the innumerable pressure groups, temporarily at least, threatened to destroy the usefulness of the legislative body. Senator Borah led the attack against this departure from traditional procedure and the Supreme Court soon placed restraints upon it in the NRA and AAA decisions. There was a very real danger that emergency powers would be continued, at least sought, as permanent powers. Unless that tendency could be restrained and traditional limitations on the powers of government long considered an essential part of the American system restored, democratic government might well be lost. It was this phase of events which embodied the real promise of an opposition party, perhaps a realignment of parties on new and more realistic lines. The American Liberty League appeared to be about to fulfill the requisite task of crystallizing sentiment along these lines when it suddenly veered off on a tangent and began talking about communism. The President almost precipitated the issue when, after the NRA decision, he momentarily lost his political acumen and intimated he might incline toward abolishing the power of Judicial Review; but he did not return to the issue, probably because of the immediate wave of criticism over the country, and again the possibility of a new alignment along those lines receded into the background.

CHAPTER XVI

RESTORING THE NATION'S MORALE

Currency and Credit Inflation

Those measures of the Roosevelt Administration known at the time as relief measures proved to be recovery measures and those spoken of as recovery measures, when subjected to close scrutiny, proved to be the most far-reaching social and economic reforms ever attempted in the nation's history. On the basis of what we now know, the history of recovery began with financial relief. It was inflation of currency and credit and financial aid to debtors and the unemployed which, after three years, appear to have been responsible for whatever degree of recovery has been achieved. Recovery by deflation, government economy, wage cutting and bankruptcy had failed. Deflation apparently had no bottom and all values were in danger of being swept away when the banking crisis forced drastic action upon the incoming administration. President Roosevelt issued his proclamation closing all banks within twenty-four hours after taking the oath of office. Four days later (March 9), Congress passed the Banking and Gold Control Act sent to it by the President and, on March 16, the Agricultural Adjustment Act which included certain financial provisions. In his message submitting the Banking and Gold Control Act Roosevelt said: "In order that the first objective—the opening of banks for the resumption of business—may be accomplished, I ask of the Congress the immediate enactment of legislation giving to the executive branch of the government control over banks for the protection of depositors; authority forthwith to open such banks as rapidly as possible; and authority to reorganize and re-open such banks as may be found to require reorganization to put them on a sound basis. I ask amendments to the Federal Reserve Act to provide for such additional currency, adequately secured, as it may become necessary to issue to meet all demands for currency and at the same time to achieve this end without increasing the unsecured indebtedness of the government of the United States."

The Emergency Banking and Gold Control Act provided that all banks belonging to the Federal Reserve System could reopen when their condition had been determined and licenses issued by the Treasury Department. Any deemed insolvent were to be placed under "conservators" for restricted operation or liquidation. The Treasury was authorized to capture all gold and gold certificates, the Reconstruction Finance Corporation to subscribe to the capital stock of banks and trust companies, the Federal Reserve banks to issue notes to member banks to a maximum of 100 per cent on government bonds and 90 per cent on other assets and to make private loans on government bonds as collateral. Under this act many banks were allowed to open which later on were forced to close again. The reason was probably not one of haste or laxity in judging their financial condition, but rather leniency upon the assumption that the general price level could be raised by other anticipated measures—something which the Administration failed to accomplish.

Congress then undertook to frame a new banking reform act which emerged near the close of the session as the Glass-Stegall Act or Banking Act of 1933. This act permitted branch banking, divorced commercial and investment banking, provided for deposit insurance and gave the Federal Reserve Board power to prevent loans for speculation. The separation of commercial and investment banking was provided by forbidding commercial banks to sell securities directly or through affiliates and investment banks to accept deposits. The deposit insurance provision created a Federal Bank Deposit Insurance Corporation with capital stock consisting of an initial subsidy of $150,000,000 from the Treasury, 50 per cent of the surplus of Federal Reserve banks and .5 per cent of the deposits of participating banks. The entire Federal Reserve System was brought into the system and non-member banks were allowed temporary participation until July 1, 1936. This time limit was extended one year by amendment on June 19, 1934. All deposits up to $10,000 were fully insured, those from $10,000 to $50,000 seventy-five per cent, and those over $50,000 fifty per cent. On March 9, 1934, Congress passed the Collateral Security Act allowing Federal Reserve banks to issue notes against government bonds until March 3, 1935, and, on March 24, 1934, an act permitting non-member banks to borrow from the Federal Reserve for one year. It was perfectly apparent to every one that the banking structure was still far from satisfactory, particularly in those respects which had to do with the control of credit which determined the amount of bank deposits and, consequently, the volume of that part of the monetary system consisting of checks. Interest centered about the Eccles bill which sought to fix responsibility upon the Federal Reserve Board. The economic fundamentalists, led by Senator Carter Glass, did not want regulation. The American Bankers Association, fearing political control of the Federal Reserve Board, wanted responsibility decentralized in the District Boards. Others, who felt that a golden opportunity for a national banking system had been missed in March, 1933, wanted government ownership of the entire Federal Reserve System. Little progress was made because of the charge that what the Administration was seeking was sufficient control over the banking system to permit unlimited spending.

The first of the Administration measures designed to raise prices to 1926 levels was the Agricultural Adjustment Act which passed Congress after two months of debate and was approved by the President on May 12, 1933. By successive proclamations on March 10, April 5 and April 19, President Roosevelt had taken the country off the gold standard and ordered all private holdings surrendered to the Federal Reserve Banks. The controlled inflation clauses of the Agricultural Adjustment Act gave the President discretionary power to do one or all of five things: (1) to replace government bonds worth $3,000,000,000 with paper currency having only the government credit as security; (2) reduce the gold content of the dollar to a minimum of 50 per cent; (3) accept a maximum of $200,000,000 worth of silver in war debt payments at not more than 50 cents an ounce; (4) reestablish bimetallism at whatever ratio seemed desirable; and (5) compel the Federal Reserve System to put $3,000,000,000 of government securities in the open market.

This discretionary power placed in the hands of President Roosevelt, prevented Congress from taking positive compulsory action for currency inflation. It also enabled Roosevelt's financial advisors to try an entirely new experiment in government finance: that of raising prices by forcing down the value of the dollar in terms of gold and then keeping the dollar at a fixed exchange value by maintaining a fluctuating gold content. It was this idea, championed by Professors Irving Fisher and George F. Warren, that led critics to coin the phrases "baloney dollar" and "rubber dollar." As Professor Warren explained it: "The dollar has to be rubber either as to weight or value. It can not have a fixed weight and a fixed value. This proposal would give it a fixed value and a rubber weight." There was much opposition to this experiment between the closing of Congress in June and the next regular session, January 1, 1934. Before adjourning, Congress passed (June 5, 1933) a joint resolution invalidating the gold contracts in all public and private contracts, amounting to an estimated $125,000,000,000, of which $14,565,727,180 were United States government bonds.

The last half of 1933 was a period of great uncertainty. Devaluation of the dollar was accomplished gradually by decreeing a higher price for gold than the old $20.67 per ounce. The purpose was twofold: (1) to aim finally at a fluctuating value within limits, and (2) to wait until all gold was in the Federal Reserve banks before seizing it under the right of eminent domain and thus giving to the government the profits accruing from re-valuation. Critics of the government maintained that business could not resume operations through refinancing and expansion until the value of the dollar was fixed. There was fear that inflation would become uncontrolled; but informed circles never seriously believed that a creditor nation, with 40 per cent of the world's gold supply and a lower national debt than any other leading nation in the world, would seriously consider printing-press money. The chief source of annoyance was the activities of the silver *bloc* backed by the agitation of speculating propagandists. As the opening of Congress approached, President Roosevelt exercised the power given him under the inflationary amendment to purchase silver. He ordered the Treasury to purchase at 64½ cents an ounce 24,412,410 ounces of silver annually which meant remonetization on the ratio of 53 to 1. This price was 21½ cents above the current market price and indicated an extra profit to the silver mine owners of something over $5,000,000 annually. This action divorced the silver *bloc* from the greenback inflation group and lessened the possibility of mandatory action on the part of Congress.

On January 15, President Roosevelt asked Congress for authority to impound the gold held by the Federal Reserve banks, fix the upper limits of the dollar's gold content at 60 per cent, give him discretionary power to regulate its value between 50 and 60 per cent, and create a $2,000,000,000 stabilization fund from gold profits. This authority was granted by Congress on January 27, 1934. Four days later, President Roosevelt abandoned the idea of a commodity dollar and fixed its value at 59.06 per cent of what it had originally been. The gold thus impounded in the Treasury was paid for with gold certificates. From the profit of approximately $3,500,000,000, a stabilization fund of $2,000,000,000 was created for the purchase and sale of gold, foreign exchange, and government securities to protect the credit and regulate the currency of the nation. Presumably the country was back on a gold bullion standard and, certainly, all doubt about the future value of the dollar was removed. The gold stock of the country, after devaluation, amounted to about $7,250,000,000, much more than all currency in circulation. The gold notes in the Federal

Reserve banks amounted to more than 80 per cent of all outstanding Federal Reserve notes, and the Treasury had a surplus of nearly $1,500,000,000 in gold bullion, over and above the stabilization fund, against which to issue paper currency if it so desired.

The period of uncertainty was ended but not agitation for further inflation, nor criticism of devaluation. The latter was denounced as confiscation and repudiation. The question of gold contracts inevitably came before the Supreme Court which handed down its decision on February 18, 1935. In what was regarded by many as the most famous decision since the Civil War, the Court refused the claims of those who held gold clause securities to payment at the rate of $1.69 for each dollar of valuation, confirmed the absolute power of Congress to regulate the currency, and ended forever gold contracts in the United States.

Meanwhile, the general price level having failed to rise as was expected, there were increasing demands for further inflation. President Roosevelt then asked Congress for authority, which it granted in the Silver Purchase Act (June 19, 1934), (1) to increase the monetary value of silver stocks in the Treasury to 33⅓ per cent of the value of gold stocks; (2) to nationalize silver and regulate its movements in trade; (3) to place a 50 per cent profits tax on all silver exchange. The leaders of the silver *bloc* in Congress were Senators Thomas of Oklahoma and Burton K. Wheeler of Montana. Wheeler wanted the Treasury to buy silver until the world price rose to $2.19 an ounce, Thomas until it reached $1.29 which was the ratio prevailing in 1837. The theory was, in part, that the depression was due to a lack of money. It ignored the fact that 90 per cent of all business transactions were handled by check and that it was bank credit, not currency, which had declined in volume during the depression. More important than the domestic situation, however, was the world price levels. A world economic conference was held at London during the summer after Roosevelt's inauguration. Secretary Cordell Hull and Senator Key Pittman labored at that conference to reestablish world trade by a lowering of trade barriers and restoration of silver. Little was accomplished except an interchange of opinion; but the silver policies of the Roosevelt Administration were aimed at an eventual reestablishment of silver throughout the world. On August 9, 1934, President Roosevelt ordered the Treasury to purchase all silver in the United States at 50.01 cents an ounce, all new silver mined at 64.64 cents an ounce and to pay for it with silver certificates at the rate of $1.29 an ounce. The difference represented silver profits corresponding to the profits of the gold transactions and the law permitted, but did not require, the issuance of certificates against these profits. This action raised silver from the status of a commodity like potatoes and pianos, gave it an artificial value in terms of gold and placed it along with gold as the metallic basis of the currency. At $1.29 an ounce, it represented the reestablishment of a bimetallic standard on the ratio of 27 to 1.

Relief to Debtors

The total mortgage debt of the nation in 1933 has been estimated as high as $250,000,000,000. That part of it consisting of mortgages on farms and city real estate and of bonded indebtedness of corporations and municipalities involved a common situation: debts contracted at a time of appreciated values had to be paid with incomes derived from depression prices and wages. One fifth of the national income in 1933 went to pay interest on debts. There was no legal escape for the debtor, no orderly procedure by which any portion of this indebtedness could be cancelled. There were the bankruptcy laws under which individuals and corporations surrendered all available assets to be liquidated at prevailing prices for the satisfaction of creditors. Corporations might go into receivership; but receiverships were, as a rule, only a more tedious route to the same destination. If there were a reorganization, the consent of all creditors must first be obtained. In such situations, real estate owners usually lost everything and the holders of mortgages frequently lost something. The same was true in the case of corporate bankruptcy. Always, however, the basis of other fortunes was laid by men who had available resources to acquire this real property at depression and forced sale prices. Municipal bond-holders reaped a harvest because the real value of their interest returns rose by more than 50 per cent. This inviolability of creditors' claims made it impossible to bring wages, prices and values into proper balance at lower levels without terrific losses and widespread injustice. It accounts for the resort to currency and credit inflation as an indirect method of raising prices.

The Hoover Administration had sought to prevent wholesale bankruptcy and receiverships by bolstering the tottering credit structure with government funds. The Roosevelt Administration continued the Reconstruction Finance Corporation as an integral part of its relief agencies. The original act had permitted loans to financial institutions such as banks, trust companies and building and loan companies, and to insurance companies and railroads. Industrial corporations could secure assistance only through the medium of a recognized, private lending agency. Something less than four billion dollars thus found its way from the Reconstruction Finance Corporation to private borrowers before the end of the fiscal year 1933-1934. On June 19, 1934, a Loans-to-Industry Act was approved extending direct aid to the amount of $500,000 to any one corporation existing before January 1, 1934, and operating under the NRA codes. These loans were not to run for more than five years, the borrowing corporations must be financially sound and must show reasonable assurance of being able to bolster the labor market by virtue of the loans. The loans were to be made by the Reconstruction Finance Corporation from a revolving fund consisting of $300,000,000 of its own funds and $280,000,000 supplied by the Federal Reserve banks. First mortgages on real property, chattels and accounts receivable were to constitute acceptable collateral.

Meanwhile, among the first measures of the Roosevelt Administration were those extending aid to harassed owners of farms and city real estate. The Agricultural Adjustment Act, approved on May 12, 1933, included an amendment to the original Farm Loan Act, authorizing the Federal Land Banks to issue 4 per cent farm-loan bonds worth $2,000,000,000, and to use them in refinancing farm mortgages up to 50 per cent of the value of the land and 20 per cent of the value of permanent improvements. The government guaranteed the payment of interest on these bonds. Under the provisions of the law foreclosure proceedings could be suspended, by appeals to the Courts, while negotiations were pending. The law failed because of the disinclination of mortgage holders to accept bonds on which the government had not guaranteed the payment of principal and, one year later, in the face of incipient revolution in the farm belt, Congress rushed through the Frazier-Lemke Farm Bankruptcy Act. On June 13, 1933, President Roosevelt approved the Home Owners Refinancing Act. This act established the Home Owners Loan Corporation with a capital of $200,000,000 and authority to issue bonds worth $2,000,000,000. The home owner might liquidate outstanding indebtedness, even if in default for two years, borrowing on a first mortgage from the corporation at five per cent, the principal and interest to be amortized over a fifteen year period. The act made it possible for banks, loaded with unsaleable real estate, to exchange defaulted mortgages for government-guaranteed bonds. More than 1,000,000 homes were thus saved to their owners, and $225,000,000 in previously uncollectable taxes poured into the depleted treasuries of local government units for the maintenance of essential public services.

In the spring of 1934, in addition to the Loans-to-Industry Act mentioned above, Congress passed the Municipal Bankruptcy Act, the Corporate Bankruptcy Act and the Frazier-Lemke Farm Bankruptcy Act. The Municipal Bankruptcy Act, approved May 24, 1934, made it possible for local government units to go into the federal courts on approval of the owners of

51 per cent of their bonds with a petition for re-adjustment of their debts. The courts might approve any plan thus devised with the consent of only two-thirds of the bondholders, providing they held 75 per cent of the outstanding obligations. The Corporate Bankruptcy Act, approved June 7, 1934, permitted a corporation to go into court and petition for a reorganization under the jurisdiction of the Court. Such reorganization could be completed with the consent of only two-thirds of the creditors. It eliminated costly receivers' fees by limiting them to the amount received by Federal Referees in Bankruptcy. These two acts were similar to the original farm bankruptcy act of 1933 which failed because creditors preferred to take a chance on recovery. Of the three 1934 acts setting up machinery for the partial cancellation of domestic debts, the Frazier-Lemke Act of June 28 was the only one containing the element of compulsion. Under its provisions, a Federal District Judge could provide for an appraisal of a mortgaged farm. The owner then had to pay the principal of the newly appraised valuation within six years, meanwhile taking care of the taxes and making a one per cent annual payment on the principal. If the creditors did not unanimously agree to this procedure, the court could order a five year suspension of foreclosure proceedings, during which time the debtor was to pay a fair rental on the appraised valuation. This appraised valuation had to be liquidated by the debtor within the five year period. At the end of that time, a new appraisal could be demanded by any creditor and the debtor was to be compelled to pay any additional amount represented by a raise in the appraised valuation. The purpose of the act was to stop foreclosures until government action or a return to normal conditions had provided a permanent solution of the mortgage problem.

Neither the Municipal Bankruptcy Act nor the Frazier-Lemke Act stood the test of constitutionality. The Municipal Bankruptcy Law was invalidated by the Supreme Court on May 25, 1936 (*Ashton* v. *Cameron County Water Improvement District No. One*), with Justices Cardozo, Brandeis and Stone dissenting. The decision of the Court, written by Justice McReynolds, was that "if obligations of states or their political subdivisions may be subjected to the interference here attempted, they are no longer free to manage their own affairs . . . and the sovereignty of the states . . . does not exist." The minority opinion, written by Justice Cardozo, pointed out that by virtue of the decision neither the state government nor the federal government could give relief to municipalities, since the Constitution forbade state laws impairing the obligations of contracts. The Frazier-Lemke Act had been declared unconstitutional by a unanimous court on May 27, 1935.

In his presidential campaign, Roosevelt had advocated financial support to the railroads by the government, regulation of commercial motor transportation, further consolidation of railway lines, the regulation of railway holding companies and a revision of laws governing railroad receiverships. On June 16, 1933, Congress passed the Emergency Railroad Transportation Act. It repealed the Recapture Clause of the Transportation Act of 1920, and placed railroad holding companies under the jurisdiction of the Interstate Commerce Commission. It set up a Federal Coordinator of Transportation who was to be assisted by three regional committees—Eastern, Western and Southern—of five members each to be named by railroad management. The Coordinator was given broad powers to simplify service by cooperation, eliminate waste and rebuild the capital structures of the roads. He was given power to suspend all state and federal laws, including the anti-trust laws, which hampered his program, except health and safety codes and the Railroad Labor Act. The Interstate Commerce Commission was forbidden to approve loans by the Reconstruction Finance Corporation to hopelessly bankrupt roads or security issues by such roads. Joseph B. Eastman, a member of the Interstate Commerce Commission, was named Coordinator.

In his message to Congress in June, 1935, President Roosevelt said: "For many years in the past, transportation meant mainly railroads. But the rise of new forms of transportation, great expenditures of government funds for the development of waterways and for the building of great highways and the development of invention within the railroad system itself, have enlarged the problem far beyond that conception which dominated most of our past legislation on the subject." He proposed that the Interstate Commerce Commission be enlarged and broken up into departments with control over all forms of transportation, including railroads, highway, air, river and coastwise shipping.

Meanwhile, Coordinator Eastman reported against any immediate action in the direction of government ownership, though admitting it as a possibility eventually. On that point, he said: "It is at least possible that, regardless of theoretical considerations, we shall reach the state which many other countries have reached where, as a practical matter, it will be necessary to take the railroads over because they have ceased to be an attractive field for private capital and enterprise, and no other alternative will be open." His immediate program called for rate reductions and improved service to the end of meeting new competition. Railroad management countered with a demand for increased rates. The western lines, however, began experimenting with reduced fares and increased their passenger business 50 per cent with a 2 cent fare. After much delay, the Interstate Commerce Commission ordered passenger rates on all roads reduced from 3.6 cents to 2 cents a mile. Eastern roads reluctantly obeyed the ruling and the new fares went into effect on June 2, 1936. How much of the $700,000,000 lost in annual passenger receipts since 1926 would thus be regained, remained to be seen. The second step toward railroad rehabilitation was taken by technology. Light-weight Diesel engines were made available for railroads in 1933 and immediate steps were taken to introduce speed into railroad service. Elimination of grade crossings was begun in earnest through federal grants-in-aid, $300,000,000 of the public works fund being allotted to that purpose. The combination of improvements gave promise of a successful future for streamlined trains. Two other measures of extraordinary importance were undertaken. Congress provided for a Senate investigation into railroad financing by a committee consisting of Senators Burton K. Wheeler, Robert F. Wagner, James Couzens, Brown of New Hampshire, Bone of Washington and Minton of Indiana; and the Wheeler Bill, extending the jurisdiction of the Interstate Commerce Commission over trucks and busses engaged in interstate commerce, was introduced in Congress. The bill passed the Senate but was lost in the legislative jam in the summer of 1935. The final step recommended to rescue the railroads, relief from the excessive burden of taxes they had long borne, could come only by the painfully slow process of local and state tax reform.

Relief for the Unemployed

The most difficult problem with which the Roosevelt Administration had to deal was that of unemployment relief. The formulation of a program was largely the work of Secretary Perkins and Senators Wagner of New York, Costigan of Colorado, and La Follette of Wisconsin. The purpose of the Administration was to relieve distress among the unemployables until the financially embarrassed local governments could resume the burden and to avoid the dole by giving men work wherever possible on socially useful projects with sufficient pay to provide the necessities of life and to restore purchasing power until the increased demand for consumers' goods reabsorbed them into private industry. To accomplish these two things Congress created (1) the Civilian Conservation Corps on March 31, 1933, which was an independent agency and will be discussed later; (2) the Federal Emergency Relief Administration, provided for by act of May 12, 1933, and inaugurated by the appointment of Harry L. Hopkins as Administrator on May 22, 1933; and (3) the Public Works Administration, provided for in the National Industrial Recovery Act of July 16, 1933. The slowness with which the Public Works program got under way necessitated the setting up of a temporary program of quick relief on made-work projects during the winter of 1933-1934.

This was the short-lived Civil Works Administration. Contributions for the care of all not employed in public work were made jointly by the state and local governments and the Federal Emergency Relief Administration. This continued until the spring of 1935 when unemployables were turned back to the local governments, the Federal Emergency Relief Administration was abandoned, funds for the Public Works Administration were virtually stopped and all federal aid was brought together under a new agency, known as the Works Progress Administration. The funds for all of this relief work were provided by a $3,300,000,000 appropriation in 1933, $4,880,000,000 in 1935, and $1,425,000,000 in 1936, plus a separate appropriation of $308,000,000 for the Civilian Conservation Corps in 1936. Full authority was delegated to the President to allocate funds to the several projects. From the first appropriation, for instance, $400,000,000 was given as federal aid for highway construction, $238,000,000 for naval construction, $50,000,000 for road construction in the public domain, and $77,000,000 for flood control on the Mississippi River. $150,000,000 went to the Grand Coulee Dam project on the Columbia River, $12,000,000 to Boulder, and smaller amounts to the Casper-Alcove project and the All-American Canal in California.

Secretary of the Interior, Harold I. Ickes, was made Public Works Administrator. The states were grouped into ten regions, each with a regional director. Each state had a nonpartisan board of three members and an engineer administrator, all appointed by the President. The total personnel of the agency numbered 11,000, including 170 attorneys, 1,000 engineers, 80 finance examiners, 800 accountants and 225 special agents. There were legal, engineering, and financial departments of the Administrative Board at Washington, and a special Labor Board of Review and a Division of Investigations to iron out any labor troubles which might arise and prevent corruption and graft. The state boards sent their recommendations to

Washington for approval until June, 1935, when the system was decentralized.

Three problems confronted the Public Works Administration from the first: labor, types of projects and legal obstacles. It was decided that, before a project would be approved, it must be socially useful, sound from an engineering standpoint, an aid to the revival of industry, and provide immediate work for the unemployed. The difficult task was not to find projects which met these requirements but to overcome an inherent defect in the program of launching public work by providing financial aid to states and municipalities. Local governments were frequently restrained from borrowing money by charter provisions or state constitutions. In many cases, there was reluctance on the part of officials or of the voters in special elections to participate because it was felt that no further debt burdens should be incurred. Under Title II of the National Industrial Recovery Act, the Public Works Administration was permitted to make an outright contribution for non-federal public works of 30 per cent of the labor and material costs and lend, if the applicant desired, the remaining 70 per cent on reasonable security. In 1934 Congress authorized the Reconstruction Finance Corporation to purchase such securities from the PWA and the PWA to use the money from such sales to make further loans. These rules applied only to funds made available from the 1933 relief appropriation of $3,300,000,000. The Emergency Relief Appropriation of 1935 amounting to $4,488,000,000 and definitely allocating $446,000,000 to the PWA allowed administrative determination of the federal percentage, which was fixed at 45 per cent of the cost of the project. The final difficulty arose from the desire to keep wages low enough to encourage men to seek reemployment in private industry and reluctance of labor unions to consent to lower rates than those required by the rules of the craft. Title II of the National Industrial Recovery Act required a 30-hour week for all workers on PWA projects. By executive order of the President, the hours of work for all projects financed under the Emergency Relief Appropriation Act of 1935 were restricted to eight per day and 130 per month. In 1933, minimum hourly wages for skilled and unskilled labor were set at $1.20 and .50 in the Northern Zone, $1.10 and $.45 in the Central Zone, and $1.00 and $.40 in the Southern Zone. On all contracts let after October 9, 1935, rates were to be equal to the prevailing wages in the locality where the project was located. It was estimated that for every person directly employed on PWA projects, indirect employment was provided for five persons. The 8010 non-federal projects undertaken under the Administration were estimated to have provided full time direct employment for one year to 720,000 persons and indirect employment to 3,500,000, at an annual average cost for those directly employed, in labor and material, of $2470. $741 of this came from the federal government and the remainder from other sources. Before the end of the fiscal year 1935-1936, the Public Works Administration had carried out projects costing $2,410,828,000. Of this sum $711,337,000 came from the 1933 appropriation; $579,703,000 from the 1935 appropriation; $395,418,000 from the sale of collateral securities; and $723,369,000 from the contributions of local governments. To this amount was added $300,000,000 by the Emergency Relief Appropriation Act of 1936. In spite of the inherent difficulties in the program and the steady decline in its prestige among administrative agencies, the Public Works Administration accomplished an amazing amount of construction work, including 883 sewer projects, 1497 waterworks, 23 garbage disposal plants, 263 hospitals, 741 street and highway projects, 166 bridges and viaducts, 32 railroad improvements, and 70 municipal power plants. $238,000,000 went for naval construction; $25,000,000 to the Coast Guard; $3,000,000 to the Bureau of Air Commerce; $15,000,000 to the Army and Navy Air Service; $8,000,000 to Public Health Work; $241,000,000 for sewage disposal and filtration plants; $125,000,000 to the Federal Housing Administration; $463,000,000 for secondary school, college and university buildings; and $142,000,000 for slum clearance.

During the last year of Hoover's Administration the Reconstruction Finance Corporation made what amounted to a gift of $200,000,000 to the several states for relief purposes. The sums were advanced as loans but the only security was a lien by the federal government against future appropriations for highway construction. State and local funds were so completely exhausted that 89 per cent of relief funds came from this federal money during January, 1933. The first relief bill of the Roosevelt Administration was introduced in the Senate, March 27, 1933, "to provide for cooperation by the Federal Government with the states and territories and the District of Columbia in relieving hardship and suffering caused by unemployment and for other purposes." The bill authorized the Reconstruction Finance Corporation to borrow $500,000,000 which was to be made available to aid the states in carrying the relief load, but was to be dispensed through a special relief Administrator. The bill stated the principle that federal aid was to constitute "⅓ of the public money expended by state and subdivisions" but left the way open for additional amounts if necessary. Two amendments were added, providing that no one state should receive more than 15 per cent of the total amount, and requiring a monthly report from the Administrator. The Act was approved on May 12. Ten days later the Federal Emergency Relief Administration began to function under the direction of Harry L. Hopkins, former associate of Frances Perkins, Herbert Lehman and Robert Wagner in social work in New York, Chairman of the Southern Division of the Red Cross during the war, and Emergency Relief Administrator in New York State under Governor Roosevelt.

The Administrator had final power under the President to decide when state funds had been exhausted. From the first, the policy was followed of placing responsibility upon the state administrations. The Federal Emergency Relief Administration exercised no control except that of making or refusing to make grants in aid. Its authority ceased when grants were approved and within the states the funds were dispensed in various ways. To obtain funds, the governor of a state was required to make application, stating the amount of money needed, the amount of available public and private funds, how the funds were to be administered and what the standards of relief were. From first to last the federal administration insisted that relief was primarily a state and local problem and that federal funds could only be allowed when public and private resources within the state were exhausted. The case load of those unemployed or under-employed and being cared for in part by federal funds varied as follows:

April, 1933	4,475,322
September, 1933	3,000,000
January, 1934	2,485,000
April, 1934	3,864,000
December, 1934	4,459,000
April, 1935	4,464,000
December, 1935	2,079,369

The low figures for January, 1934, were due to the operation of the Civil Works Administration and for December, 1935, to the existence of the new Works Progress Administration.

Both direct relief in the form of food, shelter, clothing, light and fuel and work relief were furnished under the FERA. Much of the work relief was on government properties; much in the nature of "made" work which came to be called "boondoggling" because it seemed to lack social value. The rates paid for FERA work were determined locally, the average being 42 cents per hour, and workers were allowed a sufficient number of hours to provide the difference between the other income of the family, if any, and the amount required to provide the necessities of life. The nature of the work varied greatly. Surplus commodities were purchased, processed and distributed to the needy under the Federal Surplus Relief Corporation.

Destitute rural families were put to work under the Rural Rehabilitation Program, exchanging labor for food, tools, livestock, etc. Nursery schools, rural educational extension courses, vocational training, literary classes and adult education classes were established under the Emergency Education Program. Money was used to continue schools which would have had to close for lack of funds. A Student Aid Program, later continued as a part of the National Youth Administration, was set up in February, 1934, funds being made available to help boys and girls in schools and colleges. Two hundred families were sent from Michigan, Minnesota and Wisconsin to Matanuska, Alaska, in a unique re-settlement program. Educational camps for unemployed women, based on Civilian Conservation Corps ideas, were started in 1934. In March of 1935, 15 per cent of the persons on relief were employed in the production of goods to be distributed to the unemployed.

The original appropriation of $500,000,000 from the Reconstruction Finance Corporation was soon exhausted and further grants were made from the relief appropriations by presidential order. $3,080,595,085 had been spent by January 1, 1936. The state governments had spent $521,477,560 and the local governments $663,000,000 during the same period. There was no uniformity in the amounts contributed by the several state and local governments. From January, 1933, to June, 1934, Massachusetts provided 74 per cent of its relief load and South Carolina .6 per cent. Only twelve states were carrying more than 30 per cent of the burden when the FERA was abandoned. Many charges of partisanship in the administration of relief were made, probably with little foundation. The chief criticism was directed against projects of dubious social usefulness. The membership of the relief rolls changed constantly. Some persons who had been on relief secured employment. Their places were taken by persons whose savings had finally become exhausted, who chose aid from the government rather than from relatives as the depression continued, or who were thrown on public relief by the withdrawal of private charity. Hundred of thousands who had been giving privately between 1929 and 1933 ceased to do so when the whole system was placed on a public expense basis. Allowances necessarily increased as prices rose, and reluctance to receive relief lessened. No doubt the local dispensing agencies continued to be more liberal with federal funds than they would have been with state and local funds. More and more the relief rolls came to be made up of unemployables, those with larger than average families, the poorly educated, and the manual labor group. This fact determined the end of the Federal Emergency Relief Administration. In his message to Congress, January, 1935, President Roosevelt said: "The lessons of history confirmed by the evidence immediately before me show conclusively that continued dependence upon relief induces a spiritual and moral disintegration fundamentally destructive to the national fiber. To dole out relief in this way is to administer a narcotic, a subtle destroyer of the human spirit. . . . Local responsibility can and will be resumed for all unemployables, for common sense tells us that the wealth necessary for this task existed and still exists in the local community and the dictates of sound administration require that this responsibility be in the first instance a local one." Final grants by the FERA were made in December, 1935, and states were given back the task of providing for all unemployables.

The period of the Civil Works Administration was the critical period of unemployment. The Public Works Administration set up by the National Industrial Recovery Act was slow in getting started and the winter of 1933-1934 was approaching with local relief funds exhausted and a minimum of 11,000,000 persons unemployed. The Civil Works Administration was launched to carry some 4,000,000 men over the winter until the Public Works Administration could absorb them. The executive order creating it and naming Hopkins, already Federal Emergency Relief Administrator, Civil Works Administrator was issued on November 8, 1933. Four hundred million dollars were released by the FERA for the program and state and municipal officials were hurriedly called to Washington on November 15 to get it started. Four million men were to be put to work before December 1, one-half to be taken from the relief rolls and the remainder selected from the self-sustaining unemployed by the local employment agencies. The entire machinery for the program was set up within one week. It was completely decentralized and consisted for the most part of existing relief agencies in all of the counties. This was a part of the Public Works provided for under the Recovery Act, but all work was done by day labor and no contracts were let. Local and state Civil Works Administrators supervised the work. Money was advanced only as needed to meet payrolls through the agency of the Veterans Administration Bureau. All employees were placed on a thirty hour week and eight hour day, with the same wage scale as other Public Works projects. No projects were undertaken which could not be completed within three months. They included work on streets, roads and highways; schools and universities; parks and playgrounds; public buildings and equipment; public lands; pest control; sanitation; waterways; utilities; and clerical work. All projects were approved by state and local authorities. Hundreds of different types of work were undertaken. A partial list would include: highway work, such as clearing right of way, grading, paving, resurfacing, eliminating curves, repairing ditches and traffic signals, and building parking spaces; school buildings, such as small construction work, painting, plastering and plumbing, building athletic fields, tennis courts, grading grounds and constructing paths, landscaping, constructing roadways and fencing; bathing beaches, golf courses, skating rinks, picnic grounds, etc.; waterways, such as flood control, soil erosion, building filter plants, pumping stations, etc.; utilities, such as removing old car tracks, repairing gas lines, installing fire alarms, lighting bridges, etc. The charge that the nation was put to raking leaves was utterly ridiculous. When the final chapter is written the sum total of work done both under the Civil Works Administration and the Federal Emergency Relief Administration will be found to constitute a monumental list of socially useful work that had been neglected during the materialistic twenties and which could not possibly have been undertaken with depleted local funds during the depression. Local politics crept into the administration of the work. There were some strikes by labor, farmers and other local employees of labor objected to the high hourly wage rate; but on the whole the administration was remarkably well handled. Demobilization was begun on February 23, 1934, with the reduction of the personnel to 3,100,000. The whole program was terminated on April 1 with the exception of sufficient personnel to close accounts, etc. There was widespread regret at its abandonment. Weekly wages averaged $14.78 and the total cost amounted to $877,-882,055 of which only $811,000 went for administrative expenses.

The second phase of the relief program began with President Roosevelt's message of January, 1935. Unemployables were to be returned to the care of state and local governments and the federal government was to withdraw completely from direct relief. The federal government assumed the responsibility of supplying work to all employables who wanted to work. In deciding whether to make the 1935 appropriation for $2,-880,000,000 or for $4,880,000,000, Congress chose the latter to make possible work relief instead of the dole. In deciding whether to give the money to Public Works Administrator Ickes or to Federal Emergency Relief Administrator Hopkins, President Roosevelt chose the latter because the type of projects carried on by the FERA and the CWA provided flexibility with a maximum outlay for wages and a minimum for materials. They might be considered less useful projects over the long view, but they were better suited to the period of final recovery.

The Works Progress Administration was created by Executive Order on May 6, 1935, with Hopkins as Administrator to provide for "coordinated execution of the work relief program as a whole and for the execution of that program in such manner as to move from the relief rolls to work on such projects or in private employment the maximum number of persons in the shortest time possible." All existing work relief agencies were brought under his control. Local governments units were to initiate plans for projects and these passed through the hands of Works Progress Administrator and the Bureau of the Budget to the President. Projects were to be of two kinds: construction and non-construction. Construction projects, including highways, roads, streets, public buildings, parks, playgrounds, sewer systems and airports received 80 per cent of the funds allotted before January 1, 1936. The remaining 20 per cent went to non-construction projects including forestation, erosion control, sanitation, education, etc. All workers were required to be sixteen years of age, in good health and on relief during May, 1935. Placement of all workers was made by the United States Employment Service. Ninety per cent of all workers had to be taken from the relief rolls and only one member of a family was to be employed. The maximum hours of work were eight per day and forty per week. The country was divided into four regions and within those regions wage scales were fixed for unskilled work, intermediate work, skilled work and professional work and according to population centers.

By January 1, 1936, 69,152 projects had been approved at a cost of $947,732,727 to the federal government and $221,918,153 to local governments. Twenty-three thousand one hundred and five of these projects were for highways, roads and streets; 10,109 for educational work; 9,508 for public buildings; 6,256 for water supply and sewer systems; 4,892 for parks and playgrounds; 2,989 for conservation and flood control; 2,309 for sanitation and health; and 130 for electric utilities.

Relief for Youth

Among the first agencies for public works established by the Roosevelt Administration was the Civilian Conservation Corps. The purpose of the project was to restore the nation's forests and salvage the young men of the country from the attitude of despair so widely prevalent. As has been said, one of the most discouraging aspects of the depression was the indiscriminate hordes of homeless youth wandering aimlessly about the country. Secretary Perkins and Senator Robert Wagner devised the plan for emergency conservation work and the act was passed and approved on March 31, 1933, after bitter debate. President William Green of the American Federation of Labor objected strenuously to what he called regimentation of labor in peace time, to the wages of $30 per month, to the forced allotment of a portion of the wage to dependents, and to the requirement for a physical examination. Chairman Connery of the House Committee on Labor and Education demanded a wage of $80 per month for married men and $50 for unmarried men. Unable to agree on the details of the plan, Congress omitted all controversial features and left to the Administration the task of supplying them.

Robert Fechner, Vice-President of the International Association of Machinists, was appointed Director of Emergency Conservation Work, with an advisory Council representing the Departments of War, Interior, Agriculture and Labor. Members of the Conservation Corps consisted mostly of young men between the ages of seventeen and twenty-eight. They received $30 per month, of which $22 was sent to their dependent families. Five per cent of each company were allowed $45 per month for meritorious work and an additional eight per cent $36 per month. The age requirement was waived in the case of veterans who were sent to separate camps. A representative of the Department of Labor in each state selected the men through local public welfare agencies. Enrollment was entirely voluntary and selection was made from the most needy families. As soon as men were selected, they were sent to Army stations for physical examinations and two weeks of conditioning exercises. There was neither military training nor military discipline, but the War Department was responsible in all camps for food, clothing, camp construction, sanitation, medical service, education and religious services. The educational program was essential because there were 10,000 illiterates among the 350,000 enrolled; 50 per cent had not completed the eighth grade; 46 per cent had gone to high school, but only one-third of those had graduated; and only one-fifth of one per cent had graduated from college. Participation in the educational program was optional, with 60 per cent participating in June, 1935, about 9000 of whom were learning to read and write. Courses in vocational training, dramatics, music, and debating were offered. Libraries and newspapers were provided. The Department of Interior supervised all works in national parks, Indian reservations, and reclamation projects. The Department of Agriculture was responsible for reforestation and erosion control. Among the types of work undertaken were the building of telephone lines, fire breaks, truck trails, erosion control dams, reservoirs for wild-life, diversion dams; planting of trees; fighting forest fires; controlling insect pests and rodents. During the first eighteen months, 5,000,000 acres of forest lands were added to the national forests and 67,000 acres to national parks; 15,000,000 trees were planted; 34,570 miles of truck trails, 23,000 miles of fire breaks and 609,000 soil erosion dams were constructed.

The service cost $851,009,459 before the end of the fiscal year 1934-1935 and $1,204,560,000 by March 1, 1936. Of the latter amount $266,000,000 was forwarded to dependent families and $615,000,000 went for the purchase of materials and supplies. The average annual cost for each person enrolled was $1175. The personnel costs of the administration were exceedingly low, with only fifty-eight persons engaged. One million men passed through a period of service in the camps before June 30, 1935, emerging into private employment with improved physique and new attitudes toward life. Funds for the maintenance of the camps came first from the $3,300,000,000 appropriation in 1933, no separate funds having been provided in the act establishing the corps. The Emergency Appropriation Act of 1935 ($4,880,000,000) designated $600,000,000 for the continuation of the CCC until 1937. President

Roosevelt desired to reduce the number of enrollees from 500,000 to 300,000 by July, 1936, as a part of the program to cut relief costs, but met strenuous opposition in Congress. A compromise was reached and instructions were issued to Administrator Fechner on March 23, 1936, gradually to reduce the number to 350,000 by March 31, 1937. There seemed to be little doubt at that time about the work continuing as a permanent part of the government's conservation program.

The second definite program for assistance to young people evolved out of the Student-Aid Work and Educational Camps for Unemployed Women of the original FERA program. The National Youth Administration was established by Executive Order on June 26, 1935, as a division of the Public Works Administration. Efforts to have it placed under the control of the Commissioner of Education or the Department of Labor were rejected and it was made an integral part of relief work with Aubrey Williams, former Director of the Wisconsin Conference for Social Work, as Executive Director. As in the case of FERA work for students, responsibility is placed upon state and local committees, including a personnel of 11,500 persons who serve without pay, for the administration of the work. The schools themselves are responsible for selecting students and assigning work. In May, 1936, there was a total of 605,200 young people receiving assistance: 6600 graduate students, 125,000 college students, 263,000 high school students, and 210,000 young men and women working on miscellaneous work projects. There were also 4500 young women in camps for unemployed women. Maximum rates of pay were $6 per month for high school students whose families were on relief, $15 for college students, and $25 for graduate students. Young people between the ages of sixteen and twenty-five from relief families who were not in the above groups constituted the 210,000 on work projects under the supervision of a State Director. These projects included community development, recreational leadership, public service and research. Women in camps for unemployed were receiving training for the most part in household management. In addition, 2000 young people were apprenticed in various crafts with the employer paying the wages. The organization cost $49,750,000 during its first year with an allocation of $71,250,000 for the year 1936-1937. The program, from the date of its inception under the FERA, kept thousands of young people in school, prevented idleness and competition of young people in the labor market; but its inadequacy was clearly shown by the fact that an estimated 8,000,000 young people had reached maturity during the depression with nothing to do.

CHAPTER XVII

AN EXPERIMENT IN INDUSTRIAL DEMOCRACY

Agriculture

Having considered the one really effective measure designed to rebuild the price structure and eventually to bring prices into proper balance by raising those which had not been artificially maintained, and the various measures which served to restore confidence and tide the unemployed over the period of distress, we must turn to those two measures which were designed to stabilize industry and restore the purchasing power of the farmers. The direct and immediate restoration of prices was attempted by the crop curtailment provisions of the Agricultural Adjustment Act and by certain provisions of the National Industrial Recovery Act. Both measures were intentionally limited in duration to a two year period and quotas of production were subject to revision because over-production existed only in the sense of depleted consumer purchasing power. It is from the additional reform aspects of the two acts, however, that their proper place in history must be considered.

We must remember that the depression in agriculture began immediately after the World War and that during the twenties relief was sought through the subsidy schemes of the McNary-Haugen bill. The next subsidy scheme to gain favor was the domestic allotment plan. This device originated with Walter J. Spillman of the Department of Agriculture. Professor John D. Black of Harvard University, Professor N. L. Wilson of Montana State College, Secretary Henry A. Wallace of the Department of Agriculture and Chairman Henry I. Harriman of the United States Chamber of Commerce assisted in its development. It was first introduced into Congress as the Jones Bill and enacted, May 12, 1933, as an Act to Relieve the Existing National Emergency by Increasing Agricultural Purchasing Power. It had the endorsement of more than thirty leading farmers' organizations. The purpose of the act was to restore the exchange value of farm produce to its 1914 parity with other commodities. The farmers' purchasing power had fallen so far that the Department of Agriculture estimated it was responsible for the unemployment of 4,000,000 men in the cities, a fairly conservative statement in view of the fact that the rural market normally consumed one-fourth of the goods and services in the nation. This restoration of purchasing power was to be accomplished under the direction of the Secretary of Agriculture, a distinct departure from all previous schemes for solving the agricultural problem. An Agricultural Adjustment Administration was set up within the Department of Agriculture and divided into two divisions, one for production control and the other for regulation of processing and marketing. The act provided for voluntary reduction of crop acreage of basic agricultural commodities: wheat, cotton, corn, hogs, rice, tobacco, and milk, all of which had fallen to exceptionally low prices, had large exportable surpluses, and required processing before consumption. This reduction was to be accomplished by contracts, voluntarily agreed to, between the government and the individual farmer, the farmer reducing his acreage by a specified amount for a consideration or subsidy in cash from the government. The Secretary of Agriculture was given discretionary power to specify what use was to be made of land thus taken out of production. The money for such subsidies was to be raised through processing taxes and thus passed on to the consumer. This program aimed to do for the farmer what the manufacturers had already done for themselves by reducing production 48.7 per cent in four years. The farmer meanwhile, by choice or by drought, had reduced production by less than five per cent.

Under the administration of this act, state committees were

created to assign quotas of production to the several counties and county committees to assign quotas to individual farmers, with no power except public opinion to force any farmer to join in the program. The quotas were based upon the average production over the preceding five years, and the individual farmer received from the government 42 cents per bushel of wheat to the amount of his quota, 5 cents per pound for cotton, 4 cents for tobacco and 2 cents for hogs. To meet these payments, a $1,000,000,000 processing tax—amounting to a sales tax—was imposed of 30 cents per bushel on wheat, 4.2 cents per pound on cotton, etc. The cotton agreements were entered into first with 1,000,000 growers, controlling 73 per cent of the cotton acreage. They plowed under 10,000,000 acres, thus reducing the prospective crop by an estimated 4,400,000 bales. In return, the government paid them $112,000,000 and the value of their cotton crop increased from $425,488,000 in 1932 to $857,000,000 in 1933. Five hundred and fifty thousand wheat growers, controlling 77 per cent of the acreage, signed contracts. The government paid them $95,000,000 and the value of their crop increased from $169,000,000 in 1932 to $376,000,000 in 1933. In the case of hogs, the government purchased more than 7,000,000 pigs and brood sows, had them processed and either distributed the pork for emergency relief or destroyed it. The net result of the Agricultural Adjustment Administration's activities at the end of the first year was an increase in the farmer's total income of 38 per cent and in his purchasing power of 25 per cent. Not satisfied with results achieved in the control of cotton, Congress passed the Bankhead Cotton Control Act which placed a prohibitive tax of one-half the prevailing market price upon all cotton offered for ginning by a grower in excess of his assigned quota. There was no mystery about the reason for doing this. Inspired by higher prices to return to independent production, about one-half the cotton growers evinced a determination to refrain from signing contracts for acreage reduction and to increase production. The Bankhead Act was designed to save the system from collapse.

It represented a radical departure from the principle of the original Agricultural Adjustment Act in that it introduced the element of compulsion into the system. The 1934 crop, therefore, was reduced to less than 10,000,000 bales and the price rose to 13 cents per pound, exactly double the price of 1932. This gave the farmer more money for his crop than he had previously received for 14,000,000 bales, plus $117,000,000 in benefit payments. The government also made direct loans to cotton growers, through the Commodity Credit Corporation of 10 cents per pound on the 1933-34 crop, 12 cents on the 1934-35 crop and 9 cents per pound on the 1935-36 crop. If the price advanced beyond the amount of the loan, the excess went to the farmer. If it did not rise, the government retained the cotton. This amounted to pegging the price of cotton above the world market price. The market price in 1933-34 was such that farmers were able to sell their crop and reimburse the government; but the 12 cent loan in 1934-35 left the government with a carry over of nearly 4,000,000 bales. That and the belief by many that the South could compete in world markets with ten cent cotton accounted for the reduction in 1935-36.

In spite of its widespread benefits to the agricultural producers, there was much opposition to the program and weighty arguments against its continuance. There was no question of its effectiveness with respect to crop reduction, and there was good reason for millions of acres of submarginal land being taken out of production. Moreover, it did not subsidize exports to further intensify the world trade war; and it made adequate provision for financing. But there was difficulty in effecting an equitable assignment of quotas and certain to be complications from the revision of quotas and from the increase in production by non-participating producers. It placed a heavy sales tax upon the consumer in urban communities for the benefit of the farmer. Between the tariffs on manufactured goods and the processing taxes, the consumer was in a difficult position. The reductions of crop acreage benefited some farmers, but worked untold hardship upon the men who made their living on the railways, in the warehouses, on the wharves and upon the tenant farmers and agricultural laborers. In many sections of the South, the effect upon the cotton share cropper was disastrous. There was normally a total of 1,500,000 share croppers whose position was little better than that of peons. The retirement of cotton acreage drove so many of them off the land as to add nearly 1,000,000 people to the relief rolls. The program likewise worked hardship upon those classes of agricultural producers who depended upon other crops for their raw materials. Poultry raisers and dairy men suffered most.

Moreover, as the United States reduced its acreage, particularly of wheat and cotton, other nations increased theirs to the highest levels in history. The Agricultural Adjustment program did not provide any method by which foreign markets, lost through the international tariff and currency war, could be regained. The share of the United States in world trade had decreased from 14 to 10 per cent, and Great Britain displaced the United States in 1933 as the leading nation for the first time since 1913. This decline in world trade was a major factor in the unemployment situation, Secretary Wallace estimating that 7,000,000 persons were normally engaged in export services. Pegging the price of cotton above the world market price caused Brazil alone to increase her crop from 300,000 to 1,000,000 bales, to the particular injury of Texas which had been exporting 90 per cent of her crop annually. Secretary Wallace, perfectly cognizant of that aspect of the situation, said: "Unless ways can be found to increase America's exports, the recovery of cotton exports on a permanent basis is doubtful." In his *America Must Choose*, he predicted that a program of self-containment would require the retirement from production of 50,000,000 acres of land. Finally, there existed considerable doubt, based upon scientific observation, whether there really was such a thing as over-production; whether surpluses had not accumulated because of improper distribution and a subnormal standard of living on the part of a considerable portion of the population. Certainly, the destruction of foodstuffs, including the dumping of more than $300,000 worth of pork into the Mississippi River at one time, was nothing but criminal waste; and, at a time when 15,000,000 families were dependent on public and private charity for the bare necessities of life, was not conducive to general approval of the scarcity theory.

In the midst of the trial period of the Agricultural Adjustment Administration's program, a drought of the first magnitude—the worst since 1894—occurred in the West. Millions of acres of crops were burned out completely and in some states benefit payments for acreage reduction were all the returns the farmers received for the year's income. Crop reduction and the drought combined added nearly 1,000,000 farm families to the relief rolls. The drought made the Administration's efforts at crop reduction appear feeble indeed. The hog reduction program had killed some 6,000,000 of the 82,000,000 unfattened pigs in 1933 and corn acreage was reduced 20 per cent by contract agreements. The drought reduced the corn crop to less than 50 per cent of the anticipated yield in 1934. It killed off by starvation 16 per cent of the cattle and about 20,000,000 swine, or 30 per cent of the total, reducing the number in the country to nearly 8,000,000 less than the anticipated number under the AAA control program. There was not, and probably never will be, agreement as to whether acreage reduction, the drought or inflation of currency and credit was most responsible for increasing the price of farm products. In view of the fact that the farmer's percentage of the national income had dropped from 18 in 1919 to 7 in 1932 and that the increase between 1933 and 1934 gave them an added 25 per cent purchasing power, some credit must go to the acreage reduction program.

On January 6, 1936, the Supreme Court by a six to three decision declared the Agricultural Adjustment Act invalid (*United States* v. *Butler*). It was held to be an invasion of the reserved rights of the states. The Court said further: "Congress has no power to enforce its commands on the farmer to the ends sought by the Agricultural Adjustment Act. It must follow that it may not indirectly accomplish those ends by taxing and spending to purchase compliance." The minority opinion, written by Justice Harlan F. Stone, replied to this argument by saying, "It is a contradiction in terms to say that there is power to spend for the general welfare, while rejecting any power to impose conditions reasonably adapted to the attainment of the end which alone would justify the expenditure." The decision clearly pointed the way to invalidation of the Bankhead Act and Congress repealed it shortly afterward. It immediately put an end to the collection of processing taxes, but left the government obligated to fulfill its contracts with the farmers totalling an unpaid balance of about $500,000,000. It freed the Administration and the country from an institution which was devised as an emergency measure and which never had the full endorsement even of its Administrator, Secretary Wallace; one which had already created so much of a vested interest that there was extreme doubt of the ability of Congress ever to abolish it. The processing taxes had been regarded as a subsidy to agriculture for the purpose of equalizing the injustices of the tariff subsidies to manufacturers. Neither the tax nor the subsidy, according to the provisions of the law, were to go beyond the point of raising the exchange value of farm produce to 1909-1914 levels. It had accomplished about 85 per cent of its objective before being invalidated, but only by reduction of crops and completely destroying the purchasing power of many people formerly a part of the agricultural industry. That the government would have encountered resistance to the abandonment of a measure which was clearly designed to meet an emergency was shown by the haste with which a substitute program was devised.

The action of the Court left the farm problem exactly where it was in 1933, with the choice of reverting to cutthroat competition among 6,500,000 producers or devising a new formula for collective regimentation. A new law, known as the Soil Conservation and Domestic Allotment Act, was devised within a week and passed by Congress within two months after the

Agricultural Adjustment Act was declared unconstitutional. It sought to regulate production indirectly through soil conservation. It provided for state Agricultural Adjustment Administrations to be financed by federal subsidies. Until the several states established these administrative bodies, if ever, the federal government was to continue to subsidize the farmers from the general funds of the Treasury through payments for planting soil conservation crops. It was an application to agriculture of the established principle of grants to states for roads, schools, etc. It was intended to be a permanent institution, and gave the Secretary of Agriculture wide discretionary power in the spending of an authorized $500,000,000 annually.

Industry

The National Industrial Recovery Act of June 16, 1933, may not be the most important single piece of legislation in Congressional history, but it is certainly one of the most interesting. In some respects, it was a legislative monstrosity. It combined two acts in one: (1) the Public Works program, which was a relief and recovery measure; and (2) the industrial control section, which was both a recovery measure and the most sweeping reform measure ever enacted in the nation's history. There was, and still remains, much confusion of thought about the act because the administration of the industrial control section was called incorrectly the National Recovery Administration. Neither the economic setting, the philosophy of its sponsors nor the administration of the act justify any such limited interpretation as the name implies.

The National Industrial Recovery Act intended (1) to legalize those voluntary trade associations which President Hoover had encouraged by removing the restraints of the anti-trust laws; (2) to make them effective by bringing the recalcitrants into line through compulsion; but (3) to bestow these privileges upon trade and industry in return for an acknowledgment of their social responsibility in the form of concessions to labor and the consumer. In short, the act recognized the fact that competition had neither been preserved nor restored, repudiated the idea of organized cartels without control in the public interest, and sought to compose differences within the associations, bring them into harmony with the interests of society, and thus institute permanent economic stability. In doing this, it was intended to bring to a final settlement the two most vexing problems in modern economic history: that of the right of labor to organize and bargain collectively; and the efforts of the state government under the police powers and the federal government under the interstate commerce and taxing powers to end child labor, establish minimum wages, limit hours of labor, and control in the interest of social security the exploitation of women in industry.

The act was born in the midst of confusion. Returning security makes it easy to forget, after four years, the dark pall of disaster which had settled over the country. Fifteen million people were out of work and purchasing power had all but been destroyed by price and wage cutting, part time employment, public and private economies. People who had money were hoarding it and people who had employment were living in daily fear of being discharged. Cities were facing complete bankruptcy, farms were being sold by the thousands, millions of people were being dispossessed of their homes, factories and banks were closed. Low wages, long hours, tragic waste, were the order of the day, particularly in industries like coal and oil. Steel plants, automobile factories, and innumerable other industries touched an all-time low in volume of production. Manufacturing and trade were in chaos as individual units sought to save themselves by cutthroat competition of the worst sort. Voluntary trade associations were helpless and labor was in danger of losing the gains of a half century of progress. Labor and industry both were clamoring for some sort of emergency relief and the National Industrial Recovery Act was the result.

The act was approved on June 16, 1933. The first section,

dealing with industrial control, stated in its declaration of policy:

"A national emergency productive of widespread unemployment and disorganization of industry, which burdens interstate and foreign commerce, affects the public welfare, and undermines the standards of living of the American people, is hereby declared to exist. It is hereby declared to be the policy of Congress to remove obstructions to the free flow of interstate and foreign commerce which tend to diminish the amount thereof; and to provide for the general welfare by promoting the organization of industry for the purpose of cooperative action among trade groups, to induce and maintain united action of labor and management under adequate governmental sanctions and supervision, to eliminate unfair competitive practices, to promote the fullest possible utilization of the present productive capacity of industries, to avoid undue restriction of production (except as may be temporarily required), to increase the consumption of industrial and agricultural products by increasing purchasing power, to reduce and relieve unemployment, to improve standards of labor, and otherwise to rehabilitate industry and to conserve natural resources."

It must be remembered, at the outset, that this program of a planned economy could not be accomplished in anything but a closed domestic market. The statement of purpose then, "to remove obstructions to the free flow of . . . foreign commerce which tend to diminish the amount thereof," would seem to be in contradiction with the remainder of the program. That was temporarily true, and President Roosevelt did abandon the attempt to stabilize international currency at the London Conference, and turn to the plan of economic self-sufficiency by inaugurating the NRA in July, 1933. Whether the London Conference was abandoned as inconsistent with the NRA or whether the NRA was pushed rapidly forward because the London Conference failed still awaits adequate investigation. That no one is quite certain is clearly shown by the guarded statement in the 1936 Republican platform: "We will cooperate with other countries toward stabilization of currencies as soon as we can do so with due regard for our national interests and as soon as other nations have sufficient stability to justify such action." Secretary of State, Cordell Hull, was the outstanding opponent of protective tariffs in the Administration. He had bitterly denounced the Payne-Aldrich and Hawley-Smoot Acts, and continued to negotiate one reciprocal trade agreement after another during Roosevelt's first Administration. That, coupled with the time limitation upon the National Industrial Recovery Act, indicates that self-sufficiency was never intended to be a fixed policy. The provisions relating to labor and public works will be discussed separately.

The act provided (1) that codes of fair competition were to be written for each trade or industrial association, either by the President or such agents as he might designate, or by the association itself with presidential approval; (2) that no codes were to be approved which created monopolies or which failed to comply with the labor provisions of the act; (3) that the anti-trust laws were suspended with respect to any action taken in conformity with the codes; and (4) that the President might require licenses for producers in any industry where necessity demanded. This was the device for bringing recalcitrants into line and provided $500 fines and six months' imprisonment for each violation.

The significance of the first provision lay in the fact that the making of laws intimately affecting the lives and fortunes of the people and the violation of which was a criminal offense, was delegated by Congress to the President, by the President to Administrator General Johnson, and by Johnson to private citizens sitting as members of the code authorities. The second provision was already violated before it was written. It was humanly impossible for the Administrator, any other man or single group of men, to have written the nearly 500 codes before the expiration of the act. The mere detail of assembling representatives of the several trades and industries would have been impossible had not the associations fostered by Hoover's large staff of experts during the twenties already been in existence. The codes were written by associations themselves, by their legal talent which was well versed in the art of evading the anti-trust laws, and the monopolistic practices brought to light by the codes were already practiced arts before the law was written. In most cases the codes were little more than the existing trade association agreements and, in some cases, they were exact copies of such agreements. The suspension of the anti-trust laws was equally interesting. They had been enforced during the Harding-Coolidge-Hoover regime only through the indirect force of advisory opinions from the Attorney-General's office. They were to be enforced under the NRA only by the opinion of the NRA Administrator as evidenced by his willingness to approve the provisions of a particular code. Nothing in the act, however, forbade appeals to the Federal Trade Commission by aggrieved individuals and numerous appeals were made. The licensing provision provided the teeth of the act. In practice, the government exercised as little compulsion as possible. Administrator Johnson conceived the idea of issuing to all firms complying with the provisions of the codes an insignia consisting of a blue eagle which they might display in their places of business and on their products as evidence of cooperation. It had no legal significance, but its absence was an invitation to the public to boycott the producer's goods. Public opinion never rallied to its support and Henry Ford's refusal to display it led to its early disuse. In addition to the right of prosecution under the licensing provisions of the act and the power to deprive violators of their blue eagles, the government might seek the assistance of the courts by applying for injunctions and it might institute proceedings through the agency of the Federal Trade Commission.

To administer the law, President Roosevelt established the National Recovery Administration with General Hugh S. Johnson the first Administrator and Donald Richberg his successor. He was provided with an assistant for industry, one for labor, a General Counsel and an Economic Advisor. There were eight divisional Administrators for preparing and administering the codes: (1) mining, utilities, automobiles, rubber and shipping; (2) lumber and machinery; (3) chemicals, leather and construction; (4) textiles; (5) amusements and services; (6) foodstuffs and agricultural products; (7) publishing and graphic arts; and (8) miscellaneous. There was an Industrial Advisory Board, a Consumer Advisory Board, a Labor Advisory Board, and a National Compliance Board. There were deputy administrators and code authorities for each trade and industry under the Divisional Administrators. There were state and local compliance boards, public relations boards and code review boards. Finally, the National Labor Board was created to enforce the right of collective bargaining. The system was made to function within a few months, partly because of the indefatigable labors of Johnson, partly because too little time was allowed for hearings on the codes before they were put into force, but largely because associations already in existence drew up their own codes and merely submitted them for approval.

The original purpose of the act was to establish a tripartite administration of the industrial system by management, labor and the government. The anti-trust laws were suspended to enable cooperation, industrial coordination and unified planning. Management, in return, was to recognize labor's right of collective bargaining, agree to certain minimum standards of wages, hours and working conditions. Government, in turn, was to force compliance by all the units of industry and trade. Many Congressmen of both parties, who still professed belief in the ideal of competition under the anti-trust laws, denounced their suspension. Senator Borah said: "We will have the steel industry, the drug industry and the different industries of the United States meeting and combining for the purpose of formulating a code, the great objective of which will be to fix prices." When President Roosevelt approved the act, he said: "The aim of this whole effort is to restore our rich domestic market by raising its vast consuming capacity. If we now inflate prices as fast and as far as we increase wages, the whole project will be set at naught. We cannot hope for the full effect of this plan unless, in these first critical months, and even at the expense of full initial profits, we defer price increases as long as possible."

It soon became apparent that the fears of Borah, President Roosevelt and other were well-founded. Congress, which had never been able to frame laws for the regulation of transportation and utilities in the interest of consumers, presumed too much on the sweet reasonableness of management and the strength of a liberal administration when it expected the whole of industry to sacrifice profits to a better balance between prices and wages. Industry was perfectly willing to shorten hours and increase wages, but it insisted upon raising prices too and faster than it raised wages. It succeeded in doing so in writing the codes in spite of the fact that a Consumers Advisory Board was appointed, consisting of Mrs. Mary Rumsey of New York, President Frank Graham of the University of North Carolina, Mrs. Joseph J. Daniels of Indianapolis, and Mrs. Belle Sherwins, President of the National League of Women Voters. In many cases, too, labor was as intransigent as management. There were too many instances such as Harvey C. Fremming of the Oil Workers Union refusing to serve on the Labor Advisory Board for the oil industry unless the American Federation of Labor were empowered to name the other two labor representatives. Finally, the government not only went too far in attempting to place all industry under code authorities and in permitting price-fixing provisions to be written into the codes, but Administrator Johnson made the mistake of attempting to inspire boycotts against industrialists like Henry Ford who, for one reason or another, refused to display the blue eagle insignia.

The original intention of a tripartite administration was violated in the most important part of the program: the drawing up of the codes. Most of the code authorities consisted solely of representatives of the trade associations. They did agree to the establishment of a forty hour week, to minimum wages of between 12 and 15 dollars per week and to the elimination of child labor. Those provisions were written into virtually all codes. They straightway violated the spirit of the law's collective bargaining provision, however, and sought to turn it to their own advantage by organizing company unions. The law specifically forbade "monopolies and monopolistic practices," but existing monopolies were retained and others were created. This was partly due to the physical impossibility of directing the mass of detail involved in organizing the codes; to the complex problems of policy involving an interpretation of the law; and to the existence of the system during such a short emergency period that decentralization of responsibility and of the several administrative functions was never carried out. It was due largely, however, to giving voting control in the code authorities to the large producers, who concealed their war against independents behind fixed prices, wages and production quotas. The steel industry, for instance, re-established in its code the basing point system by which shipping costs from distant factories were added to the price of steel produced and sold locally. This practice had been outlawed by the Federal Trade Commission in 1924. The Commission, after examining the code, reported that a complete monopoly had been re-established in violation of the Sherman Act, the Clayton Act, and previous orders of the Commission. Much difficulty was encountered from provisions prohibiting sales below cost. In determining costs, efficient and inefficient producers were lumped together to strike an average. It was impossible to average overhead costs at a time of depression or to determine a fair price for raw materials purchased at different times. In spite of these facts, open price-fixing provisions were written into more than one-half of the codes. Prices of commodities produced in these industries rose, in 1934, to 23 per cent above 1929 levels. Many codes curtailed output by limiting the hours per week during which machinery could be kept in operation and by assigning quotas of production to particular plants. Others forbade the purchase of new machinery or the expansion of plant facilities.

The rayon, hosiery and textile codes limited the working hours of machinery. The rayon, cement and ice codes forbade machine replacements. The oil and lumber codes assigned production quotas. All of these provisions gave new life to the old monopolies, increased living costs and retarded consumption. Violations of the codes soon became so frequent that enforcement was not even attempted.

Before the end of 1933, it became apparent that the National Recovery Administration was a failure. An open forum was held in Washington to which any one was welcome who had a grievance. Price-fixing was denounced at these hearings by representatives of the chain stores and mail order houses, government purchasing agents, the Farm Bureau Federation and the League of Women Voters. Trade association executives favored its retention; but, even among business men, price-fixing of products in other industries than their own was frowned upon. Reports by the Consumers Advisory Board, by the Federal Trade Commission and by the Brookings Institution further convinced the country that the system was a failure. The purpose of the act, as stated in the preamble, "to promote the fullest possible utilization of the present productive capacity of industries, to avoid undue restriction of production, to increase the consumption of industrial and agricultural products," had been defeated by price-fixing, the protection of monopolies and restrictions upon production. The Brookings Institution report placed emphasis upon under-consumption rather than over-production as the cause of the country's ills. A report by a committee headed by Clarence Darrow blamed the repeal of the anti-trust laws for the creation of monopolies and advocated a system of state socialism. The other reports placed emphasis upon the evils of price-fixing.

Liquidation of the NRA began in less than one year after the passage of the act. Its most complete failure had been in the service trades such as barbers, cleaners and automobiles. President Roosevelt ordered abandonment of the codes in these trades in May, 1934. These industries were almost entirely local in nature and not a part of interstate commerce. They were given permission to establish local codes by retaining the provisions of their former codes relating to hours and wages. These local agreements could be arranged by 85 per cent of the members of a particular industry. Those who refused to join in the agreement were to be turned over to the mercies of an outraged public opinion by being deprived of their blue eagles. The next step in the liquidation process was taken by the Supreme Court. In the case of *Panama Refining Co.* v. *Ryan* (1933), it invalidated Section 9c of the National Industrial Recovery Act. This was a separate and distinct part of the act which gave the President, among other things, the power "to prohibit the transportation in interstate and foreign commerce of petroleum and the products thereof produced or withdrawn from storage in excess of the amount permitted to be produced or withdrawn from storage by any state law. . . ." The Court did not raise the fundamental question of whether Congress could regulate production under the Commerce Clause, but it denied the right of Congress to delegate unlimited legislative power to the Executive branch of the government. It condemned both branches of the government for failure to make declarations of policy and establish rules. On that point, it said: "Both Section 9c and the executive orders are in notable contrast with historic practice by which declarations of policy are made by the Congress and delegations are within the framework of that policy and have relation to facts and conditions to be formed and stated by the President in the appropriate exercise of the delegated authority." The third step was the resignation of Administrator Johnson and the elevation to that post of Donald Richberg from the position of General Counsel.

Meanwhile a sharp attack was made upon the system by the liberal forces in the 1934 Congress. Senators Borah and Nye led in denouncing it as having retarded recovery, embittered relations between capital and labor, raised prices to the consumer, and failed to solve the problem of unemployment. They demanded that it be completely abandoned or drastically modified. The attack was not a partisan one, but came from liberals throughout the nation who recognized some virtue in the experiment. They believed that such achievements as minimum wages, abolition of child labor, etc., could be retained in some other way. This school of thought was that of Theodore Roosevelt, of Woodrow Wilson, and of Justice Brandeis. It believed that business and industry should be decentralized and kept that way by strict regulation; that competition could be restored. It was opposed to the new theory of a planned economy.

Administrator Richberg immediately declared for a radical change in policy which, if it had been carried through, would have eliminated price-fixing devices from all codes and placed codes on an entirely voluntary basis. It would have segregated the extractive industries into a special group and permitted cooperative planning to prevent waste of natural resources. All others would have been returned to a competitive basis under the anti-trust laws. It would have withdrawn the government from all participation in labor disputes. Finally, it would have sought some new way to prevent unsocial practices in business. President Roosevelt asked Congress, in February, 1935, to extend the National Industrial Recovery Act for another two years. His message contained a frank admission of its many failures and claimed for it many accomplishments. He admitted that it had fostered monopoly practices and sometimes worked hardships upon small producers; but insisted that these were more than outweighed by the elimination of child labor, of unethical practices in competition and by gains in wages, collective bargaining and re-employment. He suggested that the system be placed on a voluntary basis and that price-fixing be abolished. His statement that "incorrigible minorities within an industry should not be allowed to write the rules of unfair play and compel all others to compete upon their low level" was a concise explanation of why trade and industrial associations had been formed originally. His further statement that "we must make certain that the privilege of cooperating to prevent unfair competition will not be transformed into license to strangle fair competition under the apparent sanction of law, or work to the oppression of small industries" explained equally well why the trade associations of the twenties were intolerable without government regulation.

In Congress, and in the nation at large, there was strong opposition to continuing even a revamped law. Sentiment in favor of its extension was equally strong. Business and industrial groups, of course, were heartily in favor of preserving the code authorities rather than returning to the enforcement of the anti-trust laws by the Federal Trade Commission. Self-regulation had been their own idea and the Chamber of Commerce reported 1508 of its members favored its continuation with only 420 opposed. The coal, oil and textile industries had benefited so greatly that they viewed a return to competition with genuine alarm. The durable goods industries, hard-boiled to the last, wanted to continue price-fixing by code authorities with a minimum of representation for labor and consumer groups. In short, they clung to the theory of high prices and low wages which had been the country's undoing. Those liberals who supported the extension of the law had ample justification for their position. They felt that it had served a useful purpose as an emergency measure. Restriction of production had prevented those industries able to do so from piling up huge surpluses at depression wage and price levels and thus served to stabilize recovery when the banking and hoarding crisis had passed. It had given employment to at least 3,000,000 people. President Roosevelt placed the number at 4,000,000. It had increased the total annual returns to wage-earners by $3,000,000,000. The psychological effect of the inauguration of the system had been good. The country at large was certainly better informed on social and economic questions than it had been previously; and people were more cognizant of economic ills which needed to be corrected. Child labor and sweat shops had been eradicated. Labor had made great gains in organization. Others denied that these things were true. They claimed that more than 40 per cent of all employees in coded industries were working more than 40 hours per week and that 10 per cent were working more than 48 hours. They denied that child labor had been eradicated and pointed to continued exploitation by newspapers and in agriculture as evidence. The Brookings Institution report went so far as to deny that the code had stimulated employment or raised wages; that, on the contrary, it had retarded re-employment and lowered the aggregate returns of labor. About all that can be said, as between the two assumptions, is that the millions of statistics can be used to prove anything.

The two questions before Congress were (1) whether the system could be simplified in such a way as to correct its weaknesses, and (2) whether any action should be taken before the Supreme Court had passed upon the disputed constitutionality of the original act. Meanwhile, the Schechter Case was on its way through the courts. Those constitutional lawyers who believed in the letter of the law and the inflexibility of the Constitution, led by Congressman James M. Beck of Philadelphia, had denounced the act as contrary both to the letter and the spirit of the Constitution from the day of its enactment. This group held the theory of emergency to be, as Beck expressed it, "the most dangerous legal heresy that could be invented." On the other hand, there was a not inconsiderable school of thought, which regarded the Constitution as a living charter and sufficiently flexible to permit emergency action. How far the Supreme Court would go in the direction of constitutional elasticity, no one knew. The lower courts were divided. When Secretary Ickes' control of oil shipments under Section 9c had been challenged in the courts by F. W. Fischer of Tyler, Texas, and the case had gone to District of Columbia Courts, Justice Joseph Cox upheld the law with these words:

"In the law, it is recognized that necessity confers many rights and privileges that without the necessity might not be conferred. It is said that self-preservation is the first law, and this principle, in some degree at least, seems to extend to governments. . . . All laws, including the Constitution, should be read in emergencies in the light of the law of necessity."

The philosophy back of this decision was that legislative bodies should be allowed wide latitude for experimentation in the solution of social and economic questions; that judicial bodies could act only in a negative capacity without power to make substitutions for any legislative action they might invalidate; and that upon the executive and legislative departments of government, both subject to political control, should rest the responsibility for determining economic policies. The Supreme Court, however, invalidated Section 9c of the act; and, then in the case of *Schechter Poultry Corporation* v. *United States* (June 3, 1935) overthrew the whole network of 750 code authorities by declaring the act to be an unconstitutional delegation of legislative power and an attempt to invade intra-state commerce. It denied the theory that an emergency justified an invasion by Congress of the jurisdiction of the states. The decision was by an unanimous Court. There can be no question about the sentiment of the country. It endorsed the decision. The system had failed and was already moribund before the Court's decision was rendered. Other recovery measures had taken effect, the emergency had passed and the issue had lost its appeal. The decision of the Court had come mid-way between presidential elections, which made it impossible to present the questions of judicial review or constitutional amendment as campaign issues. There is no evidence that the people would have supported, even at that time, an amendment giving the federal government control over wages, hours, trade practices or prices. President Roosevelt announced and Congress authorized continuation of a skeleton organization as a fact-finding agency. James L. O'Neill was appointed Administrator, and Leon C. Marshall was assigned to the task of compiling the organization's records. Their task was in reality that of writing a history of the organization and determining the results of its invalidation.

There were many offers of voluntary cooperation from industrialists, but there was much evidence, too, of immediate wage and price reductions and increases in the hours of labor. The

National Association of Manufacturers urged its members "to take immediate steps to stabilize wages, hours, working conditions and competitive practices on a voluntary basis" through their trade associations. President Harper Sibley of the Chamber of Commerce of the United States took the same attitude, and recommended continuation of the cartels on a voluntary basis. Industry's chief concern was that the ten per cent of business and industry not under the codes would introduce cutthroat competitive practices and thus destroy whatever gains had been made. Conservative newspapers and, particularly, political opponents of the Roosevelt Administration hailed the Supreme Court as the Savior of the Constitution and the decision as returning the country to sound fundamentals. Few people realized the complete significance of what had happened. Most people believed that their ideal of free competition in trade and industry was a fact. Actually, the invalidation of the National Industrial Recovery Act, like all Supreme Court decisions, took the country back to where it started from when the act was passed. The only difference in this case was that free competition was less a fact than before and the government was in possession of a vast amount of information for use in finding some other solution to the problem. Responsibility was placed once more upon the Federal Trade Commission, the Department of Justice and Congress to restore and preserve competition by reframing and effectually enforcing the antitrust laws. It was not enough to say, as Senator Borah did, that there was power under the existing Constitution to do the things which needed to be done. That remained to be demonstrated. Congress still had its taxing and spending powers and its control over the tariff, all of which were regarded as effective weapons for the control of industry and trade if properly used. Meanwhile, President Roosevelt adopted the practice of pressing through Congress acts of doubtful constitutionality. He was denounced most bitterly by partisan opponents for so doing. The problem of social and economic control, however, had become so insistent that the limits of the powers of Congress and of the state legislatures under the Constitution needed to be fully explored before the question of a constitutional amendment could be intelligently considered. Whether that idea was behind the Administration's action or political expediency as claimed by its critics, can be determined only from the perspective of time. The result will not be materially different whatever the motive may have been.

The first of these acts was the Bituminous Coal Conservation Act of 1935, generally known as the Guffey Coal Act. It was designed to take the place of the NRA code in the bituminous coal industry. The act established a national Bituminous Coal Commission in the Department of Interior, provided for limited amounts of production, and placed a 15 per cent tax on the price at the mine, 90 per cent of which was to be returned to producers who complied with the code. Minimum and maximum prices were to be established and a Labor Board was to settle all disputes between employers and employees. This was the first attempt to set up little NRA's in each of the basic industries. The act was quickly contested in the courts and, in *Carter* v. *Carter Coal Company* (May 19, 1936) the Supreme Court invalidated the act on the grounds (1) that the tax was not a revenue measure but a penalty to obtain compliance with regulatory provisions; (2) that Congress can regulate commerce but not production; (3) the federal government possesses no inherent powers.

Labor

The labor provisions of the National Industrial Recovery Act embodied a sweeping repudiation of all that had gone before. The first and, in some ways, the most important part of the act with respect to labor was that which provided for codes in each industry. The long, unsuccessful battle against child labor by state legislation, required school attendance and an unratified constitutional amendment was brushed aside. A provision was written into all codes, at the insistence of Secretary Perkins, banning the labor of children under sixteen years of age. Minimum wages and maximum hours for labor were also established for the whole of every industry on the principle of protecting the efficient and well-intentioned producer against any who sought to profit by unrestrained exploitation. Nearly all codes limited the working week to 40 hours, with many exceptions for seasonal and unusual periods of production. Minimum wages were set at not less than $12 a week and, in some cases, were slightly above that amount.

Section 7a of the act dealt specifically with the question of collective bargaining. It said:

"That employees shall have the right to organize and bargain collectively through representatives of their own choosing, and shall be free from the interference, restraint, or coercion of employers of labor, or their agents, in the designation of such representatives or in self-organization or in other concerted activities for the purpose of collective bargaining, or other mutual aid or protection; that no employee and no one seeking employment shall be required as a condition of employment to join any company union or to refrain from joining, organizing, or assisting a labor organization of his own choosing; and that employers shall comply with the maximum hours of labor, minimum rates of pay, and other conditions of employment approved or prescribed by the President."

The long controversy over the closed or open shop was thus thought to have been settled. The principle of cooperation was substituted for that of industrial warfare. The application of that principle, however, proved far more difficult than was anticipated. The history of the attempt includes the setting up of machinery for administering the labor provisions of the act; the interpretation placed upon the act by the government through its administrators; the inability of the government to secure acceptance of this interpretation from either capital or labor; and, finally, the return to open warfare when the government proved powerless to enforce its mandates.

General Hugh S. Johnson—and later Donald Richberg—was Chief Administrator of the National Recovery Administration. Under the Chief Administrator, as one member of his personnel staff, was an Assistant Administrator for Labor, and one of the three Advisory Boards was that of labor. Finally, August 5, 1933, the President created a National Labor Board under the chairmanship of Senator Robert F. Wagner of New York. The National Labor Board established regional boards to supervise all relations between employers and employees.

The first interpretation of Section 7a by the National Labor Board, the Regional Boards and General Johnson established the following principles: (1) All provisions in the codes with respect to hours, wages, etc., were the minimum the government would recognize in any case. To that extent, the government dictated to both capital and labor; (2) employers and employees were at liberty to agree upon shorter hours, higher wages, etc., and to make any other arrangements which did not contravene code provisions; (3) employees might organize without interference from employers, but the government assumed no responsibility to promote labor organizations. Employers must recognize and bargain collectively with their employees through their chosen representatives; (4) workers might continue to deal individually with their employers if they chose to do so; (5) employers must not interfere with any employee's freedom to join any labor organization, and labor unions must not coerce a non-union employee. This effort of the government to compel each side to respect the rights of the other met difficulty from the first. The dead weight of the past militated strongly against abandonment of the lockout, the blacklist, the strike, the fight for the open and closed shop. The American Federation of Labor, having its local crafts already widely established, moved immediately to strengthen its position. Its membership rose to 4,500,000 within a few months, much of the increase being in new vertical unions chartered directly by the A. F. of L. and not a part of the craft organizations. The large industrialists, reluctant to abandon the principle of the open shop, met the challenge of the A. F. of L. by organizing company unions. The spirit of warfare, which was supposed to have been rendered obsolete by the new scheme, flared anew;

and the conflict revealed several fundamental weaknesses in the new order. The steel industry, with its many subsidiaries, always had led the fight against new principles such as the eight hour day, collective bargaining, etc., and did not depart from its traditional rôle in this instance. The Wierton Steel plants at Clarksburg, West Virginia, and Steubenville, Ohio, were closed. The automobile accessory plants of the Budd Manufacturing Company at Philadelphia were purged of all striking employees. The organization of a company union by the H. C. Frick Coke Co. of Pennsylvania precipitated a strike of 15,000 coal miners. In a hundred localities, furious industrial strife threatened, and compelled the government to take its second step in the new program.

The National Recovery Administration, in line with its pronounced policy, requested strikers to resume operations during a period of settlement by negotiation. President Roosevelt made a personal appeal for peace, and then appointed Senator Robert F. Wagner head of a nation-wide system of arbitration boards. The task undertaken by the National Labor Board was extremely difficult. It had no legal status other than Presidential fiat. The liberal press, including the *Nation* and the *New Republic*, was roundly criticizing the government for asking labor to forgo the use of the strike before it had outlawed the company union. The American Federation of Labor was striving for a dominant position in each industry in order to control the representatives for collective bargaining. The industrialists were contending for the open shop or, at most, company unions. The government was insisting that all laborers were free under the law to join any description of union or none at all as they saw fit, but that coercion of all kinds was forbidden. The workers of the Wierton Steel Company appealed directly to President Roosevelt against the company union, and he ordered a survey by the National Labor Board to determine whether workers in that company were being coerced into joining the company union. More important, however, was his direction to the Board to hold elections under its own auspices, where necessary, to determine the wishes of the majority of the workers, which majority was then to speak for the whole. This principle of majority rule, a distinct departure from the first position of the government, played directly into the hands of the American Federation of Labor, and destroyed all rights of minority groups. It was specifically enunciated in the Denver Tramways Case (March 2, 1934) where the majority vote went to the Amalgamated Association of Street and Electric Railway Employees union.

This principle of elections under government supervision with the majority authorized to make agreements with the employers which would be binding upon all workers in the industry had a short life. It was incorporated in a bill introduced into Congress by Senator Wagner in February, 1934. The industrialists opposed the bill, of course, but so did the Civil Liberties Union and a large section of laboring men. It was directly contrary to the philosophy of Samuel Gompers who had repeatedly warned the workers against permitting government to interfere by compulsory arbitration, compulsory unemployment insurance, etc. Here was a time when the national administration was distinctly friendly to labor. President Roosevelt himself, Secretary Frances Perkins, General Council of the NRA Donald Richberg, the members of the Labor Advisory Board: Leo Wolman, Sidney Hillman, William Green, John Frey and George L. Berry, made the Administration the most sympathetic to labor in history. Once the element of compulsion had been introduced, however, and organized labor became the creature of the government a struggle for its control was inevitable. Labor courts were the certain road to Fascism, when government fell into the hands of a less friendly administration. Farsighted friends of labor saw it and opposed the Wagner bill.

More important, however, from the standpoint of the individual laborer, was the provision which would have given to representatives of the majority the exclusive power to make agreements with their employers. Chairman Francis Biddle of the National Labor Relations Board defended it as an application of the democratic principle of majority rule which, of course, it was not because practically applied it would deny to all minorities in industry a voice in the determination of wages, hours, etc. It was a grave distortion of the principle of collective bargaining.

Meanwhile, a strike in the automobile industry which was leading the way to recovery again brought President Roosevelt's personal intervention. The settlement of March 25, 1934, repudiated this principle of majority rule and set up an industrial parliament established on the basis of proportional representation of all important groups of workers. Theoretically, it was the only correct application of the government's first interpretation of Section 7a. It thwarted the plans both of the American Federation of Labor to dictate the working agreements of all labor and of the employers to compel membership in company-dictated unions. It laid the basis for the evolution of industrial unions. It abandoned the dangerous trend toward government-supported unions inherent in supervised elections and majority rule. It restored the government to its former position of neutral arbiter for voluntary mediation. It weakened the prestige of the National Labor Board, however, as it did that of the American Federation of Labor. That Board, meanwhile, had been refused permission to supervise an election in the Wierton Steel Company case. An appeal to the courts for an injunction was made and refused. Thus was the Norris-La Guardia Act turned against a government agency in its first test in the courts. Finally, the Wagner bill was drastically revised and emerged as the Labor Disputes Joint Resolution of June 19, 1934. The National Labor Board was abandoned, but the act empowered the President to appoint boards for investigation and voluntary arbitration upon request by both sides to a dispute. These boards were to supervise elections for collective bargaining, and fines and imprisonment were to follow refusal to obey their orders. Their life was limited to the one year period remaining of the National Recovery Act.

The enactment of the Joint Resolution marked the end of the most significant year in all labor history. It began with an attempt by the government to induce capital and labor to voluntarily respect each other's rights and substitute cooperation for industrial warfare. The American Federation of Labor and employers each moved to secure a dominant position in the new program. The employers violated the spirit of the act by organizing company unions and labor retaliated with strikes. The government then moved to compel compliance and failed. Finally, it abandoned compulsion and set up machinery for voluntary arbitration at the moment when capital and labor were marshalling forces for a supreme test of strength all over the country.

This abandonment of compulsion can not be over emphasized. It meant that henceforth wages would be determined by the relative strength and skill of employer and employee and that labor would seek that form of organization best calculated to put its maximum strength and bargaining power into the contest. It meant, also, that in the test, government would offer its services for arbitration with both sides free to accept its findings or not as they chose, and with government free from suspicion of bias in the performance of its primary function of protecting the lives, property, and health of the people.

A strike occurred in the Electric Auto-Lite Company of Toledo in February, was temporarily halted in March, and resumed in April. Wages and recognition of the United Automobile Workers Federal Union were involved. Injunctions, company-paid deputies and, finally, state militia were brought into the struggle against the strikers. There was much destruction of property and several deaths. The strikers won their demands through threat of a general strike and the mediation efforts of the government, and the strike ended on June 5. A strike was threatened in the steel industry ten days later and was averted only through the influence of William Green, president of the American Federation of Labor. Late in June, President Roosevelt created the National Steel Relations Labor Board under authority of the Joint Resolution of Congress with power to investigate and settle the dispute. On July 16, the first general strike was finally called in San Francisco. It began with a strike of 12,000 members of the International Longshoremen's Association and soon involved all marine workers. The American Federation of Labor was drawn in to protect its craft structure against the threat of industrial unions and, on July 16, all the San Francisco district was tied up. Again troops were brought into the contest, violent propaganda charging subversive communist activities was disseminated, and a wave of terrorism was begun by the employers with the active support of state and municipal administrations and the tacit support of General Johnson. More important than the injection of communistic charges into the dispute, however, was the general attitude of the public. The two can not be entirely separated; but, however sympathetic people might have been to the cause of the union labor, they were unquestionably hostile to the principle of the general strike. A general strike is not an economic weapon but a revolutionary political weapon. It is not a strike against particular employers but against society and the state itself. It is so directly contrary to traditional public policy in the United States that it was the most impolitic and inexpedient action labor could have taken. Sensing the situation and seeking to save the face of the American Federation of Labor at the expense of the San Francisco laborers, President William Green disavowed any responsibility for it on behalf of his organization. The craft unionists went back to work and the longshoremen were forced to submit their grievances to arbitration.

The American Federation of Labor had failed to do more than increase its membership by 2,000,000 in the early days of a frankly friendly national administration. It failed to take advantage of its opportunity to organize along industrial lines and thus fortify itself against the day of a hostile administration. Instead, it supported the Wagner bill and the National Labor Board, thus actually seeking to make itself the ward of the government, surrendering its freedom of action at times of industrial strife, and laying itself open to destruction in event of hostile control. It had been frustrated in its attempt to establish a labor dictatorship (which was so nearly within its grasp after the Denver Tramways Case) by the automobile code and the abandoment of the original Wagner bill. Its prestige was further weakened by the action of President Green in the San Francisco strike. Meanwhile, the solidarity of labor was proved in the Toledo strike. It was apparent that the next chapter in labor history would involve the question of who was to speak for labor in its controversies with capital, of the form of labor organization, rather than of contests between capital and labor.

The two principals in this contest were President Green of the American Federation of Labor and President John L. Lewis of the United Mine Workers of America. Miner's unions are essentially industrial unions, sometimes called vertical unions. The new federal unions chartered by the A. F. of L. in such industries as automobile, steel and rubber, were vertical unions within a single plant, but with the important exception that members of crafts (17 in the automobile industry) remained with their former organizations. Lewis contended that to deprive new unions of these skilled workers in an industry was to rob them of their skilled leadership and limit them to easily replaced, unskilled mass production workers. The issue was joined at the San Francisco convention of 1933 where Lewis secured indorsement of the principle of industrial unions. The question of permitting them to have the skilled craftsmen was fought out at the Atlantic City convention in 1935 and, because federal unions were denied full voting strength, Lewis was defeated. A few weeks later the supporters of the industrial program met at Washington, D. C., and formed a Committee on Industrial Organization. President Green ordered the Committee disbanded. Lewis defied the order, resigned from the

Executive Council of the A. F. of L. and was given authority to withhold his union's dues from that organization. The contest was no mere struggle for power. It was as broad as the labor movement itself. It was the difference between craft and industrial organization which meant a static labor movement or a vigorous labor movement in conformity with modern industrial conditions.

CHAPTER XVIII

SECURITY AS A SOCIAL IDEAL

Protecting Investors and Consumers

The year 1933 marked the resumption of the reform movement arrested by the World War. It differed from the reform period of Theodore Roosevelt and Woodrow Wilson only because reform measures were enacted almost before recovery had begun, whereas the reform legislation of the earlier period was passed after recovery had been completed. The country was passing through a social readjustment as well as a depression. The Roosevelt philosophy embraced the idea that people must somehow be sustained until they were able to find work and, afterward, should enjoy a decent standard of living. Men and women were seeking, not economic opportunity, but economic security. The reform measures enacted by Congress represent the demands of the people for new controls and adjustments for a greater degree of economic equality. It is not a question of their having emanated from the White House. The question is whether the measures sponsored by Roosevelt were more liberal or more conservative than Congress would have enacted had it been free from administrative restraint. Evidence indicates that they were more conservative; that the Roosevelt influence was a restraining influence at a time of social disintegration. Roosevelt was a conservative but his great popularity was due to his independence of vested interests and his sincere desire to restore recovery by bettering the condition of the average man. He restored the morale of the nation by the way in which he handled the monetary and banking situation. He boldly faced the relief problem; eased the farmers' debts in the AAA; attacked child labor and the sweat shops in the NRA; and extended a helping hand to labor; but his program also included the regulation of utility rates, security sales and the stock exchange; home building; old age and unemployment insurance; reciprocal tariffs; crime control and neutrality legislation.

The regulation of stock exchanges and the marketing of securities grew out of the orgy of speculation after the World War, in which unscrupulous manipulators of the stock exchanges fleeced no less than a million investors out of an estimated $25,000,000,000. No one, probably, will ever know the complete details of what happened; but there can be no question as to some of the contributing factors. Securities were sold to unsuspecting purchasers by false and incomplete statements of fact as to their real value. Many people bought securities for speculative purposes who were ignorant of everything except vague rumors of sudden wealth to be acquired by so doing; or who would have been incapable of sound investment or unwilling to heed sound advice even had all the facts been laid before them. Banks and investment trusts, which should have used scrupulous care in investing their clients' money and exerted every effort to advise their depositors against their own folly, too often did neither. Hundreds of men of prominence in business and public life, in whom the people had confidence, were engaged in promoting speculative pools, accepted gratuities in the form of stocks at less than market price, and assisted in erecting nefarious holding companies which could accomplish no other purpose than increase consumers' costs, rob operating companies of legitimate revenues and further the ends of financial chicanery. Officers of investment trusts, who were also directors of industrial corporations, used their dual position to unload worthless foreign and domestic stocks and bonds upon their investors. These things were possible because of the complete lack of regulation of the stock exchanges, the loose incorporation laws of the several states under which charters were secured, the interlocking directorates between commercial banks, investment banks and industrial corporations, and the freedom from penalties under the law of the sellers of securities.

Concerning these things, Roosevelt said, in his inaugural address: "Practices of the unscrupulous money changers stand indicted in the court of public opinion, rejected in the hearts and minds of men. We require two safeguards against the return of the evils of the old order; there must be a strict supervision of all banking and credits and investments; there must be an end to speculation with other people's money." Reform along these lines carried a wider appeal and the endorsement of more people, liberal and conservative alike, in the country than any other suggested by the Administration. Many economists agreed with the great British economist, John Maynard Keynes, that stock market speculation in the United States had robbed normal business all over the world of its legitimate capital and contributed heavily to the world depression. Some, no doubt, would have endorsed the statement of the iconoclastic John T. Flynn that not more than ten per cent of the stock market transactions were made by legitimate investors or served any useful purpose to society. It was Professors Felix Frankfurter and James M. Landis, both of the Harvard Law School, who were responsible for the Truth-in-Securities Act. Chairman Richard Whitney of the New York Stock Exchange was in favor of reform. On the other hand, its opponents were the most powerful minority in the country.

Several types of legislation were proposed: (1) federal regulation of the stock markets; (2) the limitation of stock issues to equivalent capital investment and their sale to investors; (3) the fixing of responsibility upon the vendor of stocks and bonds; (4) prohibition of bonuses and management fees to directors of holding companies; and (5) federal charters for all corporations engaged in interstate commerce. One of the first acts of the special session of Congress in the spring of 1933 was passage of the Federal Securities Act, which was approved by President Roosevelt on May 27. This act required that all security issues offered for sale must first be registered with and approved by the Federal Trade Commission, to which President Roosevelt appointed James M. Landis, one of the authors of the act. It also gave to the purchaser of a security the right to recover any losses incurred by misrepresentation and subjected the seller to a fine of $5,000 and five years' imprisonment.

The following twelve months witnessed one of the historic dramas in the political history of the country. Wall Street, La Salle Street and all the lesser stock and brokerage communities throughout the country united forces to bring about a modification of the law at the next regular session of Congress. The same general indictment raised against all the reform measures of these years was again invoked: that it was delaying recovery—in this case, by retarding the re-financing essential to industrial expansion. The Investment Bankers Association of America adopted a resolution demanding a re-definition of "the indefinite liabilities imposed by the Securities Act, so as to make it possible for responsible enterprises to meet their requirements for new capital and to cooperate with the Recovery Program." For the most part, it was those financiers who had been responsible for the stock and bond swindles and those corporation directors and lawyers who had always opposed social legislation who led the attack and who, there is some reason to believe, delayed re-financing with the fixed purpose of bringing pressure to bear upon Congress for modification of the act. Meanwhile, the Federal Trade Commission disavowed any intention to hamper legitimate refinancing, the Senate invited the presentation of all grievances substantiated with facts, and Ferdinand Pecora was instructed to close up his investigation of banking practices and proceed with that of the stock exchanges.

Early in the year, President Roosevelt appointed a committee, under the chairmanship of Secretary of Commerce Roper, to investigate the practices of the stock exchanges. This committee made its report in January, 1934. This report recommended (1) that every exchange should be denied the use of the mails and other channels of interstate commerce unless licensed by the federal government; (2) that a federal administrative board be established to regulate the exchanges to the end of fair business practices; and (3) that definite rules be established by law, the violation of which would subject an exchange to severe penalties. President Roosevelt transmitted this report to Congress together with recommendations for a regulatory law "for the protection of investors, for the safe-guarding of values, and so far as it may be possible, for the elimination of unnecessary, unwise and destructive speculation." The Fletcher-Rayburn bill was introduced the following day. This bill was originally drawn up by Benjamin Cohen, associate counsel for the Public Works Administration, and Thomas Corcoran, associate counsel for the Reconstruction Finance Corporation. Both were graduates of the Harvard Law School and disciples of Felix Frankfurter. The bill was then revised by Ferdinand Pecora's staff of experts and James M. Landis. It placed all stock exchanges under the control of the Federal Trade Commission; required a 60 per cent margin on stock exchange transactions; gave the Commission access to all records of the brokerage houses; and prohibited short selling and pools. It carried a fine of $25,000 and ten years' imprisonment for violations by individuals and a fine of $500,000 for exchanges.

Opponents of the bill deluged the country with propaganda to defeat it. It was charged that the margin required on brokers' transactions would extend to bankers' loans; that these same requirements would force banks to flood the market with securities; that business would languish and recovery stop. In Congress, every effort was made to keep regulation out of the hands of the Federal Trade Commission.

As finally passed in June, 1934, the act, variously known as the Securities Exchange Act and Stock Exchange Act, placed a limitation on bank credit for speculative purposes, established safeguards against the manipulation of the market and insured full information to the buyer of securities. Specifically, it established the Securities and Exchange Commission and transferred to it the power over security sales formerly vested in the Federal Trade Commission. It gave the Federal Reserve

Board discretionary power over credit facilities available for stock transactions. It prohibited pools, options and other devices for the manipulation of prices, active trading by members of the exchange, and false information to purchasers. Shortly thereafter President Roosevelt appointed as the five members of the new commission: Joseph P. Kennedy, a financier and distinct friend of Wall Street who had rendered valuable service to the Roosevelt campaign; George C. Matthews, a former member of the Wisconsin Public Utilities Commission; Robert E. Healy, Counsel of the Federal Trade Commission; Ferdinand Pecora; and James Landis.

On May 18, 1933, the Tennessee Valley Authority was created and the great power plant at Muscle Shoals once more became something more than a political football. The Tennessee Valley Authority was the largest and most comprehensive agency ever created in the United States for social service. It was to serve seven states—Tennessee, Virginia, North Carolina, Georgia, Alabama, Mississippi, and Kentucky—with electric power and agricultural fertilizers. Its work was to include reforestation, control of floods and soil erosion; and it had authority to resettle the population, establish subsistence homesteads and provide vocational education facilities. The funds were provided from the PWA. The power companies which had fought against the operation of the government-owned plant at Muscle Shoals for nearly two decades, once more threw their full strength against the whole adventure but without success. The right of the government to manufacture and dispose of power was upheld by the Supreme Court on February 17, 1936.

The second act of the Administration which aroused bitter opposition from the utilities companies was the creation of the Public Works Administration with an immense sum of money to offer municipalities a 30 per cent outright gift for the construction of water, gas, electric and transportation projects. The utilities opposed it, as they had always opposed such public projects, on the ground that they destroyed private investments;

but their strongest attack was an indirect one against the delegation of power to the Executive Department of the government. Here was a case where the allotment of funds was left to the discretion of the Administrators of the Public Works Administration and the powerful lobby of the power interests was as helpless against them as it was effective against Congressional action. The significance of the government action lay in its encouragement by publicly owned utilities designed to force private companies to reduce their rates to the basis of the fair return on an honest investment.

The third step was the creation by executive order of a subsidiary to the Tennessee Valley Authority known as the Electric Home and Farm Authority. Its purpose was to extend the use of electricity to the 220,000 farms in the Tennessee Valley. Producers of electric power had always defended high rates with the argument that they could not be reduced until consumption was increased and blamed the excessive cost of electrical appliances for its non-popularity. Manufacturers of electrical appliances, on the other hand, blamed high rates for the fact that so few people used the labor-saving devices they produced. The Tennessee Valley Authority was designed to test the validity of existing electric rates, and the Electric Farm and Home Authority to provide appliances of standard quality to the surrounding communities. Morris Llewellyn Cooke, distinguished authority on public utilities, was appointed Administrator of another agency known as the Rural Electrification Administration, with $100,000,000 to promote the building of transmission lines into rural areas as a beginning toward putting electricity into the 6,000,000 farm homes without it.

Finally, reform by regulation was added to reform by experimentation and competition. This was accomplished by the Wheeler-Rayburn Act of August, 1935. Every resource of the utility industry was marshaled against its passage, and, in the end, some important modifications were made in the bill as originally passed by the Senate. The act as passed gave to the Federal Power Commission the power to regulate interstate power and to the Federal Trade Commission the power to regulate interstate gas. It compelled utility lobbyists to register with the Securities and Exchange Commission; forbade any officer of a bank, brokerage or investment house to serve as an officer or director of a utility company; and gave to the Securities and Exchange Commission authority to determine for utility companies the amounts which might be written off their books as depreciation and whether or not dividends might be allowed. The contest in Congress came over Section 11, the famous "death sentence" clause of the Senate bill, which had been added by an amendment sponsored by Senator Borah. This provision, compelling the Securities and Exchange Commission to dissolve all public utility holding companies except those directly above the operating companies within seven years, was rejected by the House. The act, as finally passed, gave the Commission authority to liquidate all such holding companies which it believed to be contrary to the public interest; but, meanwhile, forbade holding companies to profit from transactions with their operating constituents.

Housing Program

Not only did the Roosevelt Administration seek to save homes to their owners by the Frazier-Lemke Farm Bankruptcy Act and the Home Owners Refinancing Act, but it undertook to revive the building industry by making funds available for building and repairs and to provide low-cost housing for the low income groups.

The construction industry had suffered an almost total collapse during the depression. Expenditures for all construction purposes had shrunk from $11,000,000,000 in 1928 to $3,000,000,000 in 1933. The construction of residential property declined 95 per cent. Normally, two and one-half million men were engaged in construction work and as many more fabricating materials for construction projects. Recovery was impossible until the building industry revived. Houses had fallen into dis-repair, with $500,000,000 spent for such purposes in 1928 and less than $50,000,000 in 1933.

The National Housing Act of June 28, 1934, created a Federal Housing Administration which, under the direction of James A. Moffett, operated along conservative lines in assisting private agencies to finance building, repairs and improvements. It enabled home owners to borrow from banks, trust companies, building and loan associations and finance companies, as much as $2000 for the improvement of homes, apartment buildings, stores, offices, factories, and farm buildings. A Home Credit Insurance Corporation was established to enable an individual to borrow 80 per cent of the cost of building a new home from such companies at 5 per cent for twenty years. The purpose of the plan was to loosen credit and to aid the builder by eliminating all mortgage fees and service charges for periodical re-financing. If payments were not made, the lending agency was authorized to take over the property and be guaranteed against loss by the government to 80 per cent of its value. The act also created a Federal Savings and Loan Insurance Corporation to guarantee the deposits of Building and Loan Associations and authorized national mortgage associations under the supervision of the Federal Home Loan Bank Board. This attempt to attract private capital into the building industry and to lower the cost of credit to home builders was offset by the increased cost of building under the NRA codes and by the government's experimental housing program.

That part of the federal housing program which aroused the most heated controversy was under the direction of the Public Works Administration, and included projects (1) for the building of model homes with low rental value in the cities, and (2) the re-settling of farmers from sub-marginal lands in semi-rural villages known as subsistence homestead centers. In cities, money was made available to seven limited dividend corporations for the construction of low-rent apartment buildings. The Public Works Administration then undertook directly to eliminate twenty-seven slum districts; to construct model homes in these districts; and to build low rent houses in twenty-three semi-urban districts. Only one of these fifty projects, Techwood Homes at Atlanta, had been completed by the summer of 1936, but all were in process of construction. They were located in thirty-five different cities. In all cases, the management of these new housing centers was to be placed in the hands of city housing authorities wherever they existed or were created. The sole interest of the Public Works Administration in the completed projects, representing an estimated investment of $208,000,000, was to be financial. Seventy-five per cent of the cost of construction went into payrolls of men engaged in building or producing materials.

The purpose of providing low cost housing can not be said to have been entirely successful. One hundred and thirty million dollars had been spent to provide 25,000 dwellings for approximately 130,000 persons, making the rental values excessive for the lowest income groups. The high cost was due in part to the necessity of purchasing slum property directly from the 11,000 owners, ofttimes at excessive values. The type of construction, however, was modern in every detail, with fireproof materials, plumbing and sanitation, fresh air and sunlight.

The Resettlement Administration undertook to construct four modern towns near industrial centers: Washington, Milwaukee, Cincinnati and Bound Brook, N. J. They cover hundreds of acres and include homes, garden plots, small farms and recreation centers.

The work of the Resettlement Administration was severely criticized as being an excessive expenditure of public funds in a field which belonged exclusively to private enterprise without going very far toward relieving the need for an estimated 16,000,000 new home units. It was said to be an experiment in state socialism which caused private construction companies to hesitate to embark upon new building programs. Both observations were probably correct. The housing program must be regarded as an experimental reform, much the same as the Tennessee Valley Authority. Its purpose was to prove that the enormous slum areas of the industrial centers, with their unhealthful, immoral and depressing atmosphere, could be eliminated; that they could be supplanted by community centers embracing all the conveniences and conditions of life made possible by technology and boundless natural resources; and that exploitation of the urban masses by real estate speculators must give way, if necessary, before government competition in the housing industry.

Social Insurance

The Social Security Act was, after the National Industrial Recovery Act, the most interesting legislative experiment of the Roosevelt Administration. Most states already had provided against the hazards of industrial accidents with Workmen's Compensation laws, most of them had widows' and children's pension plans and about half of them old age pensions. Only Wisconsin, however, had ventured into the field of unemployment insurance. Society was no longer in a mood to tolerate an industrial system which reaped huge profits in good times and then cast the burden of supporting its laboring men upon society during depressions. This was the period of the Townsend Old Age Pension faith and an equally strong agitation for unemployment insurance, though the sentiment for either program was not universal. On July 8, 1934, President Roosevelt sent a social security message to Congress in which he stated his intention to appoint a Committee on Social Security to draw up a program for the consideration of the next Congress. He appointed the committee, consisting of Secretaries Perkins, Morgenthau and Wallace, Attorney-General Cummings and Relief Administrator Hopkins; and it, in turn, called together one of the most able groups of technical advisors ever assembled to advise the government on a special problem, headed by Professor Edwin E. Witte of the University of Wisconsin. The report of this Commission was submitted to the President January 15, 1935. The Commission rejected health insurance from its recommendations and emphasized old age annuities, benefit and unemployment insurance. The major problems in these were the relationship which should exist between the state and federal governments and who should pay the costs. The Commission suggested three possibilities: (1) a national system to be financed from the regular revenues of the Treasury; (2) a system of federal contributions to state devised programs; (3) a tax system previously presented in the Wagner-Lewis bill, of federal levies on payrolls, from which would be deducted any taxes to state unemployment insurance programs.

The recommendations of the Committee were incorporated into a bill and introduced into Congress by Senator Robert F. Wagner and Representative Davis L. Lewis on January 17. Hearings on the bill by committees in the two houses continued over a period of several months and it did not become a law until August 18. It provided for pensions to the aged, the blind and dependent children; insurance annuities to the aged and unemployed; and services for maternity and child welfare, the physically infirm and delinquents. The first provision of the act was so designed as to encourage state governments to enact old-age pension laws by providing federal contributions up to $15 per month for those over sixty-five years of age providing that the state (1) contributed at least an equal amount; (2) established state supervision of a statewide system; (3) complied with the administrative requirements of the Federal Security Board; (4) set an age limit of not over sixty-five; (5) admitted to benefits all who had resided in the state five of the preceding nine years. This part of the act carried an appropriation of $24,660,000 to finance the program until June 30, 1936.

The second provision, designed to lighten the burden upon the Treasury after January 1, 1942, provided for old age annuities after that date, for employees working some part of each of the five preceding years and earning a total during that time of not less than $2000. This did not apply to agricultural laborers, domestic servants, casual employees, public servants, nor employees of non-profit, religious, charitable, scientific, literary and educational institutions. The amount of the benefit payments each month was to be one-half per cent of the first $3000 total wages received between 1936 and the date of eligibility, one-twelfth per cent of all between $3000 and $45,000 and one-twenty-fourth of all over that amount. The maximum monthly benefit payment was to be $82.50 and the minimum $10. These benefits were to be paid from an Old Age Reserve Account in the United States Treasury; but the money was to be derived from an income tax on employees and an excise tax on employers. All employees coming under the annuity benefit plan were to pay 1 per cent on their annual wage under $3000 during 1937-1939; 1½ per cent during 1940-1942; 2 per cent during 1943-1945; 2½ per cent during 1946-1948 and 3 per cent after January 1, 1949. Employers were to pay an equal amount on their total payrolls.

The third provision was for unemployment insurance. All employers of eight or more persons, except in agriculture, domestic service, merchant marine, and non-profit institutions, must pay a tax on total payrolls of 1 per cent in 1936, 2 per cent in 1937 and 3 per cent thereafter. All funds paid into a state unemployment insurance fund were to be credited up to 90 per cent of the federal tax providing the Social Security Board had approved the state system. Among the requirements were that compensation could not be denied any eligible individual for refusing to accept work (1) during a strike, lockout or labor dispute; (2) if the wages and hours were substantially less favorable than those prevailing in the community; (3) if the individual by accepting work would be required to join a company union or refrain from belonging to another labor organization. Otherwise, the states had considerable leeway although it was hoped that state plans would allow concessions to employers guaranteeing a minimum number of weeks' work to their employees during the year. The ten per cent non-deductible from the federal tax was to be returned to the states on the basis of need for administrative purposes.

The act further provided that each state was to be given $20,000 annually for maternal and child health services in rural areas, with $1,800,000 more to be distributed on the basis of need; each state to receive $20,000 annually for medical, surgical and corrective services to crippled children, with $1,830,000 more to be distributed on basis of need; $1,500,000 to be distributed annually for child welfare among delinquent, homeless and dependent children in rural areas, no state to receive less than $10,000; and $15 per month federal grant to blind persons not in institutions or receiving old age pensions. Eight million dollars was to be available each year for public health work. The administration of the act was to be in the hands of a Social Security Board consisting of three members.

President Roosevelt spoke of the act, when he signed it, as being "a corner-stone in a structure which is being built which is by no means complete." It was certain that efforts would be made to repeal the act, that it would eventually be drastically revised, and that a test of its constitutionality would be made. It was variously criticized as being an incentive to further technological replacements, a hindrance to recovery and wholly inadequate. The most serious indictments were (1) that the huge accumulations of reserves in the Treasury and the passing along of the costs to employees and consumers would decrease purchasing power; (2) that, at times of serious depression, funds would soon be exhausted and the system become a federal dole; (3) that not more than one-half of the wage-earners of the nation would benefit; and (4) that the large fund in the Treasury for investment would give that department tremendous additional powers for the stabilization of credit. Many men held that a well-planned public works program would be more adaptable to the needs of a depression. The act was not designed as a recovery measure, but for the purpose of easing employees over future short periods of unemployment and as an incentive to the establishment of an annual wage system in industry. By February 1, 1936, 32 states had set up old age pension systems to share in the program and seven others already had laws that needed no change. Thirty-three states had complied with the requirement for benefits to the blind; 46 for dependent children; and 11 for unemployment insurance.

Meanwhile, Congress had passed and the President approved on June 27, 1934, the Railway Pension Act, providing for retirement annuities for railway employees. The funds for these annuities were to be contributed by the employer and employee and administered by a new agency known as the Railroad Retirement Board. Less than one year later (May 6, 1935) the act was invalidated by the Supreme Court in another five to four decision with Justices Hughes, Brandeis, Stone and Cardozo dissenting. The majority held once more that Congress had no power to regulate hours and wages in industry under the commerce clause.

Tariffs and Neutrality

Shortly after his inauguration President Roosevelt arranged through conversations with the representatives of the leading powers for an International Economic Conference at London. This conference opened on June 12 and did not adjourn until July 27. Its purpose was to revive world trade by the stabilization of currencies on a bimetallic basis, elimination of tariff barriers and, perhaps, some agreements with respect to the control of production. For some reason, though no one can say definitely as yet, the conference failed to accomplish anything with respect to currencies and tariffs. That Roosevelt's decision to attempt the experiment of a commodity dollar and the self-containment program embodied in the NRA and AAA contributed to the failure is certain; but it was not necessarily the determining factor. The people of the United States had fallen back into an attitude of isolation following the failure of Wilson's Peace Program and that attitude had been strengthened by the controversy over the League of Nations and the threat of a new war in Europe. The NRA and AAA program was no more economically nationalistic than the tariff policy of the twenties had been. Until the attitude of the people changed, neither the Roosevelt Administration nor any which might succeed it could boldly take the lead for international cooperation, economic or political, and hope to remain in power unless the moment were propitious for quick success. The one real promise for future world recovery and political security, even security from war, lay in the abandonment of trade barriers. Economic nationalism and isolation stood in the way of recovery in the United States and throughout the world. Following the collapse of the London Conference, the Administration moved quickly in that direction by the negotiation of reciprocal trade pacts. That it was politically dangerous is shown by the haste with which ex-President Hoover, Alfred E. Smith, and Chairman Fletcher of the Republican National Committee denounced the Canadian agreement. Further evidence will be found in the party platform of 1936. It is probable that any effort to move more rapidly would have brought the same fate that befell Woodrow Wilson. The people of the United States needed a new attitude with respect to foreign policies; and they were not likely to acquire it until they finally discovered that men could not be re-employed and industrial recovery accomplished until world trade was restored. Either Roosevelt's own amazing political acumen or trusted advisors may have had something to do with the sudden change in attitude in the summer of 1933.

Cordell Hull, Secretary of State, had long been an advocate of tariff reciprocity if not a free trader. He was one of the most bitter opponents in Congress of high protective tariffs from the Payne-Aldrich Act to the Hawley-Smoot Act. He strongly urged reduction of tariffs at the Pan-American Conference in the winter of 1933-1934 and followed that action with a bilateral trade agreement with Colombia. In the spring of 1934, two export-import banks were established by the government to extend credits for trade with Cuba and Russia and, in June, a Trade Agreements Act was passed by Congress giving the President power to raise or lower 1930 tariff rates by as much as 50 per cent to encourage exports. It was understood, of course, that exports could only be encouraged by an exchange of goods which necessitated lowering our own tariff barriers. Being a creditor nation, it was inevitable that trade revival would show an excess of imports over exports. This was true, beginning in 1933, but was seized upon by opponents of the Administration as damaging evidence of the injury the new trade pacts were doing to American producers. The American Manufacturers Export Association, however, strongly supported the Administration's policy with the claim that one-third of the 45,000,000 wage-earners of the nation were in some way dependent upon export-import business. On the other hand, ex-President Hoover denounced the Canadian pact as "hasty economic planning." The effect of the Hawley-Smoot tariff so far as it effected Canadian trade may be seen from the fact that between 1929 and 1933 exports to that country dropped from $949,446,000 to $210,651,000 and imports from $503,496,000 to $185,-408,000. In 1929 we exported to Canada $11,997,000 worth of structural steel, $13,808,000 worth of tractors, and $33,-353,000 worth of automobiles. Four years later the value of these three items exported amounted to $345,000, $119,000, and $574,000 respectively. The value of our trade with Canada increased more than 10 per cent within a year after the reciprocal trade agreement was negotiated. Fourteen such pacts were signed before 1936, but the work was painfully slow and our exports in 1935 amounted to only $2,242,000,000—less than in 1912. Meanwhile the steady flow of gold to the United States further compounded the difficulty of establishing world currency stabilization. Between 1913 and 1931, 104,000,000 ounces were imported into the United States. In 1932 and 1933, there was a loss by export of 22,000,000 ounces; but between 1933 and 1936 gold returned at such a rapid rate that it raised the total imports since 1913 to 164,000,000 ounces.

The second important step in foreign relations was the abandonment of the policy of armed intervention in Latin American nations already mentioned, the abrogation of the Platt Amendment, and the announcement of a "good neighbor" policy in Roosevelt's inaugural. On December 28, 1933, he definitely committed the United States never again to resort to armed intervention and went on to say: "The maintenance of law and the orderly processes of government in this hemisphere is the concern of each individual nation within its own borders first of all. It is only if and when the failure of orderly processes of government affects the other nations of the continent that it becomes their concern; and the point to stress is that in such event it becomes the joint concern of a whole continent in which we are all neighbors." The effect of this changed policy was very evident in the replies of seventeen Latin American nations to President Roosevelt's proposal, three years later, for an inter-American peace conference. There were to be found in those replies the germs of a possible League of Nations for the American continents. The same attitude of willingness to abandon the isolationist attitude which followed the collapse of Wilsonianism and assume the leadership toward peace and economic stability throughout the world was evident in Roosevelt's message to the governments of the world and in Ambassador Norman H. Davis's address during the International Arms Conference at Geneva. The delegates of the United States to the International Institute of Agriculture at Rome likewise suggested a re-examination of the international effects of trade barriers and monetary policies. Meanwhile, the Senate ratified on June 15, 1934, a Treaty of Non-Aggression and a Convention on Rights and Duties of States, binding the nations of the Western Hemisphere not to resort to war over boundary disputes, not to recognize any re-arrangement of boundaries brought about by war, and not to interfere in the internal affairs of each other.

The fifteen year interlude in friendly relations with Russia came to an end with the resumption of diplomatic relations on November 17, 1933. Each nation agreed to respect the territorial integrity of the other and to countenance no activity for the violent overthrow of the other's political and social order. Recognition was the result of the express promise of the

U.S.S.R. in a letter of Maxim Litvinoff, November 16, 1933, "not to permit the formation or residence on its territory of any organization or group . . . which has as its aim the overthrow of . . . the political or social order of the whole or any part of the United States." Secretary Hull promptly protested, in August, 1935, against the action of the Third International Congress at Moscow in instructing Communist parties everywhere to encourage "revolutionary assumption of power" by the proletariat. Russia refused to admit that she had broken her pledge or to assume any responsibility for the action of the Communist International; but diplomatic relations were not broken off because of the incident.

The one failure of the Administration to bring about more friendly relations with foreign powers was in the case of Japan. The United States refused to recognize the conquest of Manchoukuo, or to give Japan a larger naval ratio at the London Naval Conference; launched a huge naval building program; recognized Russia; and remained the good friend of China. In April, 1934, Japan announced to the world that China was her own special province for exploitation, and that she would not permit even financial assistance to China against Japanese domination. The United States protested against this pronouncement as a violation of the Open Door policy and the Kellogg-Briand anti-war pacts, but without success. Relations between the two nations continued to rest upon mutual suspicion. Japan renounced the Washington and London naval ratios of 5-5-3 and the London Naval Conference of 1936 left all nations free to build to the limit of their capacity. This was a blow and a distinct diplomatic defeat for Japan, which wanted naval parity. It removed the restraints upon Great Britain and the United States and placed Japan at a tremendous disadvantage in any race of naval building because of her relatively weak economic position. On March 27, 1934, the Vinson Naval Parity Act was approved providing for the building over a five year period of 102 new warships at a cost of one billion dollars. Both the army and navy were strengthened with a combined appropriation of $1,100,000,000 for the fiscal year 1936-1937.

It is difficult to see what the Administration could have done that it did not do to bring about disarmament. The world was in an extraordinarily belligerent mood and approaching closer to a new catastrophe month by month. It became the settled conviction of nearly all competent observers that another world war was inevitable. That conclusion awakened the isolationists to a realization that perhaps their policy was, after all, not the sure road to security. Wilson's theory that the United States could not long remain neutral in event of a major conflict and that our only hope lay in active cooperation with other nations to prevent war was utterly repudiated in the election of 1920 and, for fifteen years, the isolationist or Republican theory had prevailed—that any cooperative action with other nations was certain to thrust us into war. For fifteen years, also, that party in power neglected to consider the question of how to make our neutrality policy really effective. A Senate investigation of the munitions racket, the threatened naval building race with Japan, and the Italian-Ethiopian conflict, revealed in the United States an intense desire to keep the nation out of war and widespread confusion as to how neutrality might be attained. Out of the discussion emerged a Neutrality Act and a Presidential proclamation, October 5, 1935, placing an embargo on the sale of arms, munitions and implements of war to belligerent nations, setting up a National Munitions Control Board to administer the act and warning citizens that, if they travelled on the ships of belligerent nations, it must be at their own risk. The act, which expired February 29, 1936, was extended to May 1, 1937, with the added provision that there were to be no loans or credits to any belligerent by the government or private agencies. Any nation under the protection of the Monroe Doctrine and attacked by an aggressor was not subject to the embargo. By this act, the United States abandoned her traditional attitude of insisting upon neutral rights of trade and freedom of the seas. Coupled with the Johnson Act of April 13, 1934, forbidding any loans or sales of securities by nations in default on war debts, it was at least a temporary safeguard against a repetition of the events from 1914 to 1917.

Meanwhile, however, there was a determined but ill-considered move in Congress to further safeguard the nation from being drawn into war. Senator Nye, who sponsored the munitions investigation, was insistent upon writing into law the principle that all resources of the nation as well as man power should be immediately subject to conscription at the outbreak of war. The purpose, of course, was to bring financial and commercial interests to a realization that they had everything to lose and nothing to gain by war; but the practical effect would have been to build up a powerful war machine ready for use at a moment's notice and to have relieved an administration of the restraining influence of public opinion. There would no longer be a question of whether Congress would support a war with the necessary legislation for men and supplies. The second attempt to fortify peace was by strict legislation providing for automatic embargoes against all warring nations. There was a settled conviction on the part of the Roosevelt Administration that rigid neutrality legislation might bring the result it was designed to prevent, and that discretionary power to lay embargoes might better be placed in the hands of the President. Realizing that embargoes might provoke war, many were opposed to giving the Chief Executive such discretionary power. On the other hand, it was pointed out that the power to impose or withhold an embargo was a reliable diplomatic weapon and that Presidential power to distinguish between aggressors and non-aggressors might well serve to prevent our being drawn into a conflict. Those who believed in cooperative action, as by the League of Nations, to prevent aggression were opposed to legislation which would place aggressor nations on the same level with those striving to preserve peace. Competent observers insisted upon the inability of any one to determine in advance what action the interests of the United States might require. There was a general feeling of the futility of any neutrality legislation because the emotions of the people were, in the final test, the determining factor in a given situation. Few men were willing to further damage our foreign trade by serving notice upon other nations that the things they bought from us in peace time would be denied them in time of dire necessity, or to predict that the people of the United States would choose depression, unemployment and complete loss of foreign markets rather than run the risk of becoming involved in war by trading.

Prohibition and Crime Control

In some respects the most important reform measures of the Roosevelt Administration were those dealing with the liquor traffic and the control of crime. There was, all through the twenties, a constant lowering of moral standards, increasing disrespect for law, and the growth of great crime syndicates in the cities with their activities reaching to all parts of the country. It was a period of widespread demoralization and lawlessness. The World War and prohibition were equally blamed. Home environment, education, and the churches were charged with responsibility. Whatever the cause, the age of criminals became steadily lower, particularly of those committing serious offenses, and it became increasingly apparent that the whole structure of society needed re-examination. It was equally apparent that national prohibition had failed to solve the problems of modern youth. Illicit liquor flowed as copiously as legal liquor ever had flowed. The hazards of getting a drink appealed to the craving for excitement of adventurous young people, and the liquor problem became an ever present concern to parents and teachers. Slowly people rallied to the cause of repeal, reluctant to admit that the experiment had failed. The contest began in 1924 when the Smith and McAdoo forces waged a bitter battle in the Democratic National Convention. Smith was the Democratic candidate in 1928 and openly favored repeal. In 1931, the Wickersham Commission reported that prohibition enforcement had completely broken down. In the spring of 1932, a *Literary Digest* poll showed widespread sentiment for repeal. The prohibition forces sought to discredit the poll by charging that it was being subsidized by anti-prohibitionists and that ballots were being improperly distributed. Actually, when the first half of the states had later voted, the *Digest* was shown to have been wrong by less than one-half of one per cent. The poll was taken just previous to the party convention and the question could not be ignored. The Republican platform read:

"We do not favor a submission limited to the issue of retention or repeal. We, therefore, believe that the people should have an opportunity to pass upon a proposed amendment, the provision of which, while retaining in the Federal Government power to preserve the gains already made in dealing with the evils inherent in the liquor traffic, shall allow the state to deal with the problem as their citizens may determine, but subject always to the power of the Federal Government to protect those states where prohibition may exist and safeguard our citizens everywhere from the return of the saloon and attendant abuses."

The Democratic platform declared: "We advocate the repeal of the Eighteenth Amendment. To effect such repeal we demand that Congress immediately propose a constitutional amendment to truly representative conventions in the states called to act solely on that proposal. We urge the enactment of such measures by the several states as will actually promote temperance, effectively prevent the return of the saloon, and bring liquor traffic into the open under complete supervision by the states."

Popular interest in the conventions centered on the prohibition question. There was a thorough discussion of the issue throughout the campaign, and the Democratic landslide was in part at least due to the desire for repeal. The short session of Congress passed, February 20, 1933, the Twenty-first Amendment to the Constitution and submitted it to conventions in the several states. The states themselves were allowed to arrange the time and method of holding the conventions and, although there was much diversity in methods chosen, the process marked the first popular referendum on a national issue. The amendment was ratified within a year and state legislatures faced the task of devising effective methods for the control of the liquor traffic, a task that was likely to cover many years. The desperate need for public revenues at the time led to heavy liquor taxes by state legislatures and Congress, and heavy taxation kept the price of beer, wines and liquors at such a high level that bootlegging gave promise of continuing to complicate the problem of law enforcement. On March 22, 1933, before the ratification of the Twenty-first Amendment, Congress legalized the sale of all beverages containing not more than 3.2 per cent alcohol wherever state laws did not prohibit; levied a manufacturers' tax of five dollars a barrel on beer and wine; and rewrote the Webb-Kenyon Act for the protection of dry states.

Reform of the nation's criminal codes followed almost immediately after the disposal of the prohibition question. The cities of the United States had a homicide rate of 5.1 per 100,000 in 1900. The rate more than doubled by 1933. In the nation as a whole, it was 9.6 per 100,000 in that year with the total number of homicides exceeding 12,000. The annual property loss was estimated at 13 billion dollars. The consensus of opinion was that defective criminal laws were largely responsible. Ex-President Taft, in 1928, maintained that the laws and not the courts were to blame. Specifically, he recommended (1) the improvement of jury personnel by making it impossible for criminal defense lawyers to challenge those best fitted for service; (2) that judges in state courts be given the right to comment on evidence; (3) that criminal procedure be expedited. To these may be added indictments of prevailing conditions by other observers, including (1) the influence of politics in local and state law enforcement; (2) the unethical practices of criminal lawyers; and (3) the sensationalism of the yellow press. The national emergency created by the growth of bootlegging, kidnapping and racketeering during the early years of the depression, accentuated as it was by poverty and unemployment and the almost complete collapse of public morality, forced the federal government to intervene. President Roosevelt had long been a member of the National Crime Commission and his private secretary, Colonel Louis M. Howe, had been Secretary to the Commission for many years. The President took the lead in a movement to strengthen the federal Criminal Code and encourage more active participation by the Department of Justice in curbing crime which had interstate ramifications. Raymond Moley, Assistant Secretary of State, was assigned the task of making a special study of criminal law and its relation to the federal government. A special division of the Department was created to deal with racketeering and kidnapping and seventeen new laws were placed on the statute books. These laws passed in May and June, 1934, were designed (1) to prevent extortion and kidnapping by making it a federal offense to use telephones, telegraph or radio to extort and imposing a maximum penalty of death for transporting the victim of kidnapping across state lines; (2) to prevent any person from fleeing across state boundaries to escape from prosecution or from giving testimony in cases of murder, kidnapping, burglary, or robbery; (3) to simplify criminal procedure in federal courts; (4) to regulate the manufacture and sale of firearms; (5) to punish under federal law any offense against banks belonging to the Federal Reserve System; and (6) to permit the several states to enter into compacts for the suppression of crime.

The Supreme Court

The repercussions from Supreme Court rulings on the several recovery and reform acts may well alter the course of American history. Those decisions, following clearly defined precedents, re-affirmed the following principles:

1. That Congress can not delegate its law making powers to any other department of the government, nor to any administrative agency, nor to private individuals. It must formulate the nation's policies on a given subject and it must establish standards, although it may leave to "selected instrumentalities the making of subordinate rules within prescribed limits" for

the purpose of executing the law. Concerning Section 9c of the National Industrial Recovery Act, the Court said, in an unanimous decision: "[Congress] has declared no policy, has established no standard, has laid down no rule. There is no requirement, no definition of circumstances and conditions in which the transportation is to be allowed or prohibited."

2. Congress has no power to regulate conditions in industry under the Commerce Clause. Commerce does not begin until goods are placed in transit or in the hands of the agents who are to transport them, and manufacture for interstate commerce is not interstate commerce. Congress, therefore, may not exclude any article from interstate commerce because it disapproves of the manner of manufacture. Control over interstate commerce can not be used to effect social reforms (Railway Pensions case, with Hughes, Stone, Cardozo and Brandeis dissenting).

3. Congress has no general powers "apart from the specific grants of the Constitution." Said Chief Justice Hughes: "If the people desire to give Congress the power to regulate industries within the states, and the relations of employers and employees in those industries, they are at liberty to declare their will in the appropriate manner, but it is not for the Court to amend the Constitution by judicial decision."

4. The power of Congress to tax does not include the power to accomplish indirectly by taxation a social reform which Congress has no constitutional power to accomplish directly. Nor may Congress levy taxes for the regulation of production.

5. Emergency conditions permit state governments to call upon reserved powers, but do not create or enlarge the Constitutional powers of the federal government. New York State was allowed to fix the price of milk, because "neither property rights nor contract rights are absolute; for government cannot exist if the citizen may at will use his property to the detriment of his fellows, or exercise his freedom of contract to work them harm." Minnesota was allowed to modify the obligations of contracts because "the question is no longer merely that of one party to a contract as against another, but of the

use of reasonable means to safeguard the economic structure upon which the good of all depends." Both decisions, however, were by a bare majority, with Justices Sutherland, Van Devanter, McReynolds, and Butler contending that an emergency does not overthrow the provisions of the Constitution designed to protect creditors from debtors relief laws. Finally, under no circumstances may either the federal government or the state governments impair the constitutional right of the individual to work for whatever wages he may desire. This principle was established in the New York Minimum Wage Case and, historically, may become one of the celebrated cases of the Court. The decision of the New York Court of Appeals was a 4 to 3 decision and based upon the Supreme Court's ruling in *Adkins* v. *Children's Hospital* (1923). Chief Justice Taft and Justice Holmes had dissented vigorously in this case and Justice Brandeis had taken no part in the decision. The Supreme Court's acceptance of the New York Court's decision was without a hearing of the case on its merits, with Chief Justice Hughes and Justices Stone, Cardozo and Brandeis contending that the Adkins Case was not applicable. Chief Justice Hughes said: "We have here a question of constitutional law of grave importance, applying to the statutes of several states in a matter of profound public interest. I think we should deal with that question upon its merits, without feeling that we are bound by a decision which on its facts is not strictly in point."

The legislation which these several decisions of the Court invalidated was passed at a time of grave economic emergency. It was customary, at the time, to speak of the legislation as constituting a program of economic planning. Nothing could be farther from the truth. It was true that the decade of the twenties had been a period of general governmental incompetence; that altered economic conditions had caused many to regard further concentration of power in the federal government as inevitable; and that the invalidation of many congressional acts by the Supreme Court caused many to believe that our constitutional form of government did not permit the measure of government control essential to an ordered economic life under the new industrial scheme; but Congress had no plan, no policies; President Roosevelt had none; and the nation had none. The greatest achievement of the Roosevelt Administration was that it took a bewildered nation and, in a few short weeks, restored its morale and gave it renewed confidence. The Administration recognized the need for economic control, even though its methods failed; but its methods did not constitute a policy. If there was one single fact which reduced the charges of fascist or communistic tendencies to an absurdity, it was the conflict of purposes and division of counsels within the Administration from the first. What actually happened was that Congress, faced with the difficult task of legislating on modern social and economic questions in the crisis, and under extreme pressure from organized minorities, abandoned its legislative functions to the Administration. The decision of the Supreme Court invalidating the National Industrial Recovery Act may be considered, in one respect and in one only, one of the greatest decisions ever rendered. Here was a case where the sovereign powers of self-government were handed over to private business men, whose trade and industrial association regulations were clothed with the authority of federal statutes and, although they were written for private gain, without thought for the welfare of society as a whole, they were presented to the people as economic planning—the policies of the nation as determined by the considered judgment of Congress. There can be no question but that the Court's decision was in line with public sentiment. The enforcement of the law had completely broken down before the Court passed upon the question of its constitutionality. The public had awakened to the fact that it condoned price fixing, fostered monopolies, and led to rigidity in wages, hours, and prices. Why, then, did they criticize the Court's decision? Why did President Roosevelt speak impetuously of its having taken us back to horse and buggy days? First, because of the feeling that there must be social planning; that it must be translated into law for the control of economic life; and that legislative bodies, as constituted, were unfitted for the task. Second, because the several decisions of the Court eliminated all hope of controlling the conditions of production except by constitutional amendment. Third, because of the doubt that social-economic planning could be accomplished through the agencies of the forty-eight state governments.

There were circumstances connected with the constitutional test of the New Deal legislation which were of importance, but might well be overlooked. Opponents of the Administration denounced the whole of the legislative program as unconstitutional and adopted a settled policy of overwhelming the Justice Department with appeals in the lower courts. The situation was such as to recall the words of former Chief Justice White: "There is great danger, it seems to me, to arise from the constant habit which prevails where anything is opposed or objected to, of referring without rhyme or reason to the Constitution as a means of preventing its accomplishment, thus creating the general impression that the Constitution is but a barrier to progress, instead of being the broad highway through which alone true progress may be enjoyed." Added to this was the extraordinary spectacle of Chief Justice Hughes' denunciation of the majority opinion in the Railway Pension Case as reactionary; of Justice McReynolds' bitter words in the Gold Clause decision; and of the President's remarks following the NRA decision. The Court was divided on many cases, with Justice Cardozo representing the extreme liberal viewpoint, Justice McReynolds the extreme fundamentalist or State Rights viewpoint, and Justice Roberts holding the balance of power. These things being true, it was inevitable that the public should have thought in terms of what the Administration was seeking to accomplish (re-employment, increased purchasing power, elimination of child labor and vicious business practices), rather than in terms of methods; or that it should have regarded with some scepticism the statement of Justice Roberts in the AAA decision that "when an act of Congress is appropriately challenged in the Courts as not conforming to the Constitutional mandate, the judicial branch of the government has only one duty—to lay the Article of the Constitution which is invaded beside the statute which is challenged and to decide whether it squares with the former." On the other hand, there was remarkable unanimity in the Court on the important cases. A different decision in the Humphrey Case would have opened the way to executive raids on the personnel of the several administrative agencies. The Frazier-Lemke Act would eventually have destroyed the credit market of the farmers. The National Industrial Recovery Act would have given the President the power of life and death over all business and industry, with control of wages, hours of labor and prices, would have legalized cartels and trusts, and would have destroyed small business. All of these decisions, handed down on the same day, were by a unanimous Court. Section 7c of the NRA was held unconstitutional by an 8 to 1 decision; the Agricultural Adjustment Act by 6 to 3; and the Tennessee Valley Authority Act was upheld by 8 to 1. The Railway Pension Act and the New York Minimum Wage law were invalidated by 5 to 4 decisions and these were the cases which promised to be of more than ordinary political significance. In the latter case, President Roosevelt criticized the decision because it created a sphere in which neither the state governments nor federal government could legislate. The question was, Did the Court correctly place statutory regulation of wages along with *ex post facto* laws, etc., as powers forbidden to both governments?

Several courses of action were suggested by those who felt that some way must be found to control modern social and economic conditions. The first impulse of many was either to deprive the Court of the power of review or to wait for an opportunity to appoint new and more liberal judges to the bench. These proposals were not new in American history, having been made many times in the past. One of the major items on the agenda of the Republican party when it came into power in 1861 was to secure a reversal of the Court's attitude toward slavery and both of the above methods were advocated on many occasions. The second suggestion was to secure the adoption of a constitutional amendment giving both the states and the federal government control over production, or for an amendment giving the states power to regulate wages, hours, and conditions of work in industry. The difficulty was that, while many people wanted a changed Constitution, no one could suggest the exact nature of the amendment desired. Neither party was willing to risk advocating such an amendment on the eve of a presidential election, but the issue was certain to be raised again after the election. The third course of procedure, and the one immediately adopted, was to attempt to do by means of interstate compacts what Congress had not been allowed to do by the Court. Finally, it was felt by some that the power of Congress over production was almost unlimited by a judicious use of the tariff and internal taxing powers.

The first of these courses of procedure was embodied in a Constitutional amendment introduced into Congress by Senator Norris. It read:

"The Supreme Court shall have original and exclusive jurisdiction to render judgment declaring that any law enacted by Congress in whole or in part is invalid because it conflicts with some provision of the Constitution; but no such judgment shall be rendered unless concurred in by more than two-thirds of the members of the Court, and unless the action praying for such judgment shall have been commenced within six months after the enactment of the law."

This amendment, if adopted, would prevent the opponents of legislation from swamping the Justice Department with cases in the lower courts as was done in the case of certain legislation, but would deprive the Supreme Court of the valuable opinions of the 142 Federal District Judges and 41 Circuit Judges and over-burden it with work. It would require the concurrence of seven members of the Court to invalidate an act of Congress and thus lessen the number of dissenting opinions. Finally, it would permit the executive department to delay putting a law into effect until after six months had elapsed, and thus forestall any test whatever of an act's constitutionality. Josephus Daniels advocated a national convention to revise the Constitution to meet modern conditions. Governor Harold G. Hoffman of New Jersey favored a constitutional amendment requiring the Supreme Court to pass upon the constitutionality of acts of Congress before they go into effect. This, of course, would make the Court a third house of Congress and deprive them of the benefit of facts in the operation of the law before passing upon its constitutionality. Various measures of one kind or another were proposed by Representatives Dobbins of Illinois, Monaghan of Montana, Marcantonio of New York, Maverick of Texas, and Senator Pope of Idaho.

The inauguration of interstate compacts was well under way before much of the federal legislation was invalidated. The several states had joined with the Department of Justice in supporting these laws before the Supreme Court. Illinois, Indiana, Ohio, Pennsylvania, Kentucky, Washington, and New Mexico were represented in the discussion of the Guffey Coal Act. Illinois, Massachusetts, Ohio, Connecticut, New Hampshire, New Jersey, and Rhode Island supported the New York Minimum Wage law. Massachusetts created an Interstate Labor Compact Commission in 1933. New York called a six state conference on milk control. Virginia originated an Interstate Compact to limit the production of tobacco which was validated by Congress and embraced Pennsylvania, Ohio, Connecticut, and Wisconsin. Texas and Oklahoma took the lead in setting up control of oil production in the Southwest by Interstate Compact. Twenty-two states sent delegates to Chicago for a discussion of the whole range of activities in June, 1935, and definite movements were launched for agreements along the lines of crime control, traffic on highways, corporate taxation, marriage and divorce, hours of labor, health regulations, flood control, relief, and liquor licensing.

CHAPTER XIX

THE ELECTION OF 1936

THE adjournment of the Seventy-fourth Congress in the summer of 1936 brought to a close another epoch in American history. The social revolution, so imminent in 1933, had been thrust aside by the relief measures of an administration which was far more conservative than the temper of the people. The adjustment of parties to social and economic realities had failed to materialize, reaction was in the saddle, and a more conservative government during the ensuing four years was inevitable.

It had appeared for a time that production for profit was giving way to production for consumption, with capital and not labor destined to work for wages, with economic security replacing economic opportunity as the great *desideratum*, and with the accumulation of wealth losing ground as a social ideal. The Roosevelt Administration had sought to encourage this evolutionary process. The prostitution of the National Industrial Recovery Act to the selfish desires of the monopolists should not obscure the spirit in which it was conceived. Cartels were the product of the twenties. Hoover had fostered them and they were firmly established with stabilized production and prices at the beginning of the depression. Stabilization was only another name for restraint of trade and directly contrary to low prices, high values, and high wages. Directly opposed to the artificial maintenance of high price levels by monopolies and cartels was a large group of forward-looking industrialists and business men like Ford, Filene, Kellogg and Procter who were convinced of the need to lower prices and raise wages; to reduce the margin of profit by mass production in order to maintain mass consumption. Whatever differences there were between their methods and the experiment in industrial democracy in the NRA, the objectives were the same. Cartels were hostile to those objectives; hostile, and strong enough to dominate both the minority and the government in writing the codes. They emerged from the experience stronger than they were before. It was the revolt of the consumers and the devastating criticisms of the liberals, not of the industrialists, which caused the NRA system to break down long before it was invalidated by the courts. The Chamber of Commerce openly advised its members to continue the code agreements following their invalidation by the Supreme Court; and on August 29, 1936, it denounced government control of production as "indefensible" but urged that industries be allowed to formulate their own agreements. In short, it wanted a return to the conditions of the twenties, without government regulation along the lines intended in the National Industrial Recovery Act and without regulation by the Federal Trade Commission and the anti-trust laws.

The unanimity with which the Supreme Court declared the NIRA unconstitutional precluded its revival without the adoption of a constitutional amendment. The Roosevelt Administration left no doubt as to its attitude. It favored an enlargement of federal power for the control of wages, child labor, and industrial relations. Roosevelt's philosophy regarded unemployment relief, child labor, minimum wages, hours of labor, soil conservation, agricultural production, flood control, etc., as national in scope and requiring the definition of policies by Congress. The Democratic platform was a frank endorsement of the Roosevelt Administration and it said that such questions could not be "adequately handled exclusively by 48 separate state legislatures, 48 separate state administrations, and 48 separate state courts." At the same time, it said: "We have sought and will continue to seek to meet these problems through legislation within the Constitution." It did not mention specifically the need for constitutional amendment, but Senator Barkley, in his keynote address, assured the country that "if, in the future, further amendment should become necessary to enable the people to work out their destiny and protect their fundamental rights or to govern some archaic interpretation never intended by its framers, I doubt not that the people will face that duty with the same calm intelligence which has guided them in the past." Meanwhile, men continued to denounce the NRA for what it was, forgetful of what it was intended to be and of the drastic liquidation undertaken by the government before its demise. Newton D. Baker, L. W. Douglas, and Leo Wolman published a joint letter condemning the Harding, Coolidge, Hoover and Roosevelt Administrations as economically reactionary. On this point, they said: "We believe that the New Era and the New Deal are two streams from the same source. The one fostered private monopoly in the name of national prosperity. The other has fostered state controlled monopolies in the name of national welfare." The Republicans made every effort to help the country forget, or rather keep them from understanding, the trade association movement of the Hoover regime. Their platform declared that "regulated monopoly has displaced free enterprise." It included the Democratic plank of 1912: "We favor the vigorous enforcement of the criminal laws, as well as the civil laws, against monopolies and trusts and their officials, and we demand the enactment of such additional legislation as is necessary to make it impossible for private monopoly to exist in the United States." The Republican candidate, Governor Landon, in his Portland speech, September 12, said: "What the NRA really undertook to do in this country was to terminate our system of free competition, and to substitute for it a system of Government created and Government protected monopolies. . . . We pledge ourselves to maintain a free competitive system, with a strict, impartial enforcement of Federal laws."

The issue here would seem to have been clearly drawn for and against the traditional American belief in the efficacy of free competition as written into the anti-trust laws and exemplified in the careers of Wilson and Brandeis. But the issue was not so clear. The two outstanding factors in the strangulation of the free competitive system were the protective tariff and the cartels. The Republican platform openly endorsed the high tariff policy, condemned the reciprocity tariff agreements of the Roosevelt Administration and promised to repeal straightway the reciprocity trade agreement law "as futile and dangerous." Landon denounced these agreements as having "sold the farmer down the river," yet they were probably the soundest and least open to criticism of any of the Roosevelt policies. In the second place, the "stabilizers" among the manufacturing and financial interests were throwing their full support behind the Landon candidacy. With respect to the question of constitutional amendment, the Republicans generally opposed any delegation of power over production to the federal government and endorsed the idea of state compacts as a solution to the problem, with Landon himself favoring an amendment giving the states additional legislative powers, if necessary. Many men of both parties believed that government should be kept decentralized to avoid bureaucracy, to protect minority social and economic interests, and to preserve the experimental possibilities of state governments. But bankers and utility interests and the managers of transportation and industry were notorious champions of state rights or centralization, according as they believed one or the other department of government less likely to overcome the difficulty of bringing them under regulation. For all these interests suddenly to join forces in extolling the virtues of state rights raised some doubts as to their disinterestedness. President Hoover was a great centralizer of power. He championed prohibition to the last. He fostered industrial and trade cartels. He travelled far toward socialism by giving the federal government a tremendous financial stake in banks, railroads and insurance companies, and with his Farm Board program. But after Roosevelt's election, he suddenly emerged as the apostle of rugged individualism in economic life and state rights in constitutional theory. President Roosevelt, who had so fervently denounced boards and bureaus in 1932, and who had the solid support of the Bourbon, state-rights democracy of the South, had built up the greatest system of bureaucracy in the history of the nation and stood for an expansion of federal powers. The thing simply did not make sense to the independent voter.

There were forces at work, however, which gave promise of modifying the future political significance of the problem. Not only was the philosophy of Filene and others gaining new adherents among industrialists, but a new movement—the cooperative—was forcing business men to give serious thought to the problem. Farm marketing and purchasing cooperatives numbered 8800 and handled $1,343,000,000 worth of produce in 1933. The Clayton Anti-Trust Act had excepted agricultural cooperatives from prosecution for restraint of trade; and the Federal Farm Board Act of Hoover's Administration lent government support to their organization. Consumers' cooperatives, 2000 in number, bought $200,000,000 worth of products in that year. These combinations were striking at the very vitals of old-type business organization and, if carried to the point of efficiency already attained in Great Britain and the Scandinavian countries, were destined completely to alter community life and dislocate many people from their mode of living. They were fostering production and distribution for consumption at the expense of production and distribution for profit. Cooperative credit organizations, usually organized on the basis of an occupational or community group, to free people from the usurious loan companies, were given a strong impetus by Edward A. Filene who financed the Credit Union National Extension Bureau in 1921, and by the formation of the Farm Credit Administration of the federal government in 1934. Credit unions were authorized anywhere in the United States by the Sheppard Act of that year and by law in thirty-eight states. By 1936, they had one million members. Convinced of the importance of the movement, already supported by the churches and federal government and widely discussed in the schools, President Roosevelt sent a commission to Europe to study it. The members of the commission were Jacob Baker, Assistant Works Progress Administrator; Leland Olds, Secretary of the New York Power Association; and Charles E. Stuart, a New York engineer. They spent two weeks in Sweden where more than one-third of the population belongs to retail cooperatives, owning 4100 stores and doing an annual business of $100,000,000 and where monopolies and trusts are on the wane. They went to Great Britain where a Cooperative Wholesale Society does a $500,000,000 business annually; where cooperatives manufacture a wide variety of consumers' goods in 156 factories, own their own coal mines, conduct a $3,500,000 banking institution, and operate an insurance company with total assets of $70,800,000. The Committee returned to the United States during the presidential campaign, but their report was not made public at the time. The attack upon the Administration for its socialistic and communistic tendencies had developed into a major campaign issue, and there was every reason for the report, whatever it contained, to be withheld until after the election.

Closely allied with this whole movement of industrial democracy and economic cooperation, which the Roosevelt Administration could confidently be expected to encourage if returned to power, was the program of subsistence homesteads, the Tennessee Valley Authority, government generation and sale of power, and the program of work relief. Here was one of the most important issues facing the country. Flood control had passed the stage of debate. It was certain to occupy a prominent place in public works as road-building had in the past. Flood control, reforestation and checking of soil erosion were all part of a single problem. Engineers had already abandoned the old methods of operation for the newer system of controlling headwaters by drainage basins, reforestation, maintenance of grass lands, and small reservoirs. These things involved the erection of thousands of small power plants, recreation centers, the pollution of streams, internal navigation, and rural resettlement. The Tennessee Valley Authority, embracing the manufacture of fertilizers and electric power, soil erosion, reforestation, and flood control, was the largest single project along these lines. A shelter belt of trees one hundred miles wide and extending 1000 miles from Canada to the Texas Panhandle, embracing 64,000,000 acres, was the second largest. Land was being secured by cooperation with the farmers, through purchase or lease. The project was estimated to cost $75,000,000 and extend over a period of ten years. It was being carried out by the forestry service of the Department of Agriculture, which planned to plant a total of 2,000,000,000 trees. Construction projects were under way on the upper Mississippi and Missouri, the former including thirty-six projects; and similar work on the headwaters of the Ohio was contemplated. The Republicans were silent as to what they intended with respect to this whole program. Nor did they differ radically from the Democrats with regard to continued subsidies to the farmers. The Republican platform promised to "protect and foster the family type of farm, traditional in American life"; to retire submarginal land; to balance "soil-building and soil-depleting"; and "to provide in the case of agricultural products of which there are exportable surpluses, the payment of reasonable benefits upon the domestically consumed portion of such crops in order to make the tariff effective." This meant an endorsement of the old McNary-Haugen equalization fee scheme, or of AAA benefit payments; and the continuation of the program by which the Roosevelt Administration had retired 3,000,000 acres of land at a cost of $100,000,000. The idea of family type farms meant nothing. One of the chief indictments brought by Senator Vandenberg against the AAA benefit payments was that too much money was going to large industrial agricultural firms, and Congress placed restrictions on large payments under the new soil conservation program. The entire procedure was political. The disheartening thing about the revelations was the degree to which agriculture was being commercialized. Elimination of large farms from the conservation program simply fostered the process. A subsequent report of the Agricultural Department revealed that 100,000 farms were owned by 300 banks and insurance companies, one insurance company owning 2158 farms and another 4500 farms. Midwestern lands had fallen into the hands of the eastern financial interests through foreclosures during the depression. The consequence was an increase in the number of renters. It was this that the Frazier-Lemke Act had sought to prevent. Any attempt to subsidize with government funds the re-purchase of these lands would simply bail out the financial interests and shoulder a debt burden upon the taxpayer beside which the AAA benefit payments would appear small indeed. Yet so important was the farm vote in the election, and so eager were both parties to promise the farmers everything, that there was danger of one party or the other promising to do just that. Meanwhile, a new complication was developing in the South.

One of the principal objectives of the National Recovery Administration had been to eliminate child labor from industry; but 80 per cent of the child labor of the nation was in agriculture. The cotton-growing states of the Black Belt remained the most backward section of the United States with respect to the labor of women and children. The bottle-neck of the cotton industry is cotton picking. The South lost its world markets under the Agricultural Adjustment Administration because the price of cotton was pegged above the price at which it could be grown in Brazil. This reduction in cotton acreage brought misery to hundreds of thousands of share-croppers and agricultural laborers. It was true, however, that they were little worse off without work than they had been when cotton was selling for five cents per pound, and the government promptly offered them relief through the PWA and FERA. High protective tariffs and abandonment of government relief offered little hope to these millions. Abandonment of cotton growing and utilization of land for diversified farming would compound the difficulties of the farmers in the West Central states. Meanwhile, two brothers, John and Mack Rust of Texas, had perfected a cotton-picking machine which, it was said, would make possible the production of cotton for five cents per pound. But what of the consequences for the additional families who would be displaced? Would the new machine foster further centralization at the expense of hundreds of thousands of share-croppers? Would the answer be found in strong labor unions, in the cooperative movement, in the rehabilitation program of the Tennessee Valley Authority, in regimentation by the Department of Agriculture, or in the encouragement of diversified farming? Here was a question for discussion in the campaign worthy of statesmen. It gave added interest to the views which the candidates might express in the October campaign, and dismay to the intelligent voter who attempted to weigh the merits of Republican promises of "adequate credit at reasonable rates" against Democratic promises of refinancing "at the lowest possible rates," the Landon plan of grain storage on farms against Secretary Wallace's "ever-normal granary" plan, or either party's flirtations with the idea of crop insurance against the other's.

The third issue before the country was that of labor organization and labor security. It is not necessary here to review the history of the labor movement. Industrial unionism was an established fact in 1933; but the industrial unionists were outside the ranks of the American Federation of Labor and leaning in the direction of communism. The NRA experiment swept them back into the American Federation of Labor and then out again, and resulted in the formation of many company unions. A three-cornered fight for domination of the ranks of labor loomed on the horizon. The Roosevelt Administration was favorable to industrial unions, which appeared to be labor's strongest form of organization. In many ways, the NRA had fostered industrial unions. The American Federation of Labor had long been friendly to the Republican party's principles, particularly to the protective tariff. William Hutcheson, President of the Carpenters and Joiners Union, was largely responsible for the expulsion of the Lewis group from the American Federation of Labor; and he became chairman of the Labor

Campaign Committee for Landon. The United Mine Workers agreed to throw all their resources back of Roosevelt's re-election, a very significant aspect of the campaign for Pennsylvania, Ohio, West Virginia and Illinois. Sidney Hillman, President of the Amalgamated Clothing Workers, abandoned the Socialists and went to work for Lehman and Roosevelt. George L. Berry of the Pressman's Union organized leagues of labor voters in all the states for Roosevelt. David Dubinsky's support of Roosevelt was in part responsible for the charge by Chairman Hamilton of the Republican National Committee and the Hearst newspapers that Roosevelt was courting the support of the communists. All of this in spite of the fact that John L. Lewis was a Republican, prominent in his support of Harding in 1920, Berry a Tennessee Democrat, and Hillman and Dubinsky right-wing socialists. Congressional investigating committees, meanwhile, conducted extensive inquiries into the use of private detective agencies to destroy labor organizations with some possibility that their findings might figure in the last stages of the campaign. Here again, however, the thoughtful voter was puzzled by the vagaries of politics, for back of the Administration's friendliness for labor—a fact recognized by friend and foe alike—loomed the dark shadow of peonage and fascist brutality in the share-cropping regions of Senator Joseph Robinson's home state.

A more important aspect of the campaign, with respect to labor, however, centered about the Social Security Act. This was one of the major items of the Roosevelt reform program. The Republican platform denounced the unemployment insurance and old age annuity provisions of the Social Security Act as unworkable, and inequitable because they made no provision for "two-thirds of our adult population." Both the platform and Landon's interpretation of it condemned the reserve fund features of the act and offered as a substitute (1) federal contributions to old age pensions, the money to be derived from direct federal taxes; and (2) encouragement for the "adoption by states and territories of honest and practical measures for meeting the problems of unemployment insurance."

The fourth issue was that of delegation of power by Congress to the President. As has been pointed out, it was not peculiar to the Roosevelt Administration. Delegation of spending power was clearly a part of President Hoover's Farm Board program and of the Reconstruction Finance Corporation's operations. Roosevelt abused the power by allocating small sums to construction projects, such as the Passamaquoddy Hydro-Electric Power project and the Florida Ship Canal, both of which were destined to require additional millions for completion and both of which had been rejected by competent public and private engineers. He sought to make permanent emergency delegations of power before the Supreme Court stopped the process. He attempted to remove William E. Humphrey from the Federal Trade Commission because "your mind and my mind do not go along together." He was accused of sending one unconstitutional law after another to the Supreme Court to arouse popular resentment for a change in the Constitution. His recommendations to the House Ways and Means Committee on the Guffey Coal Act included the admonition, "I hope your committee will not permit doubts as to constitutionality, however reasonable, to block the suggested legislation." He formulated and rushed through Congress fundamental changes in the taxation system. A re-assertion of Congressional power in the next administration was almost a certainty. It was widely endorsed by the Republican spokesmen.

The fifth issue was that of government spending, the debt and taxation. It was the delegation of fiscal policies to the President, and the use he made of his power, that caused most disagreement. The Republican indictment, beginning with Senator Steiwer's keynote address, was that they had impaired credit, weakened confidence and retarded recovery, yet he himself had voted for the AAA, the TVA, the Thomas inflation amendment, the Frazier-Lemke Act, the proposal to pay the bonus with greenbacks and to override the bonus veto. But the debt in 1930 had stood at $16,026,000,000 and in 1936 at $33,393,000,000. The deficit for the six years of the depression stood at $19,386,000,000, for the Roosevelt Administration at $13,969,000,000. Expenses in 1934-1935 were $7,375,000,000 and in 1935-1936 they were $8,809,923,000, with estimated tax receipts for 1936-1937 at $4,917,000,000 and a tax system which might raise the amount to $6,000,000,000 with full recovery. The questions in every one's mind were: How long could the deficits continue without permanent damage? Were they necessary? Had value been received for the money spent? It was said that the WPA was an unplanned and haphazard undertaking with no lasting benefits; that industry, if relieved from uncertainty by a balanced budget, would speed up expansion and re-absorb the unemployed. The Republicans were chary about promising to balance the budget immediately. An examination of the expenditures of the Seventy-fourth Congress explains the reason for their hesitancy. That Congress had appropriated $4,880,000,000 and $1,425,000,000 for emergency relief, plus $308,000,000 for the CCC. It had voted a $1,730,000,000 bonus bill; $296,185,000 for the AAA deficit; $440,000,000 for the Soil Conservation Act; $1,100,000,000 for national defense; $320,000,000 for floods in the East; $272,000,000 for flood control on the Mississippi; $50,000,000 for the first installment of a $410,000,000 rural electrification program; and $125,000,000 for road building. The estimated cost of the most important items of government expense for 1936-1937, exclusive of relief, was $992,000,000 for ordinary expenditures; $585,000,000 for farm benefits; $1,160,000,000 for veterans; and $920,000,000 for national defense. It was inevitable, therefore, that when the opposition spoke of economizing, it should speak in general terms. Nevertheless, deficits of $3,989,000,000 in 1934, $3,500,000,000 in 1935, and $4,764,000,000 in 1936 were an encouragement for voters to support that party which gave most promise of reducing expenditures. The Democratic platform of 1932 had condemned extravagance in government and expansion of government bureaus and commissions; and the same indictment of their own administration was used effectively by the opposition in 1936. The country, incidentally, had finally come to believe that the Roosevelt policies of work relief had not provided adequate relief; had wasted funds on projects which were not regarded as socially useful; and had not given society full value for its enormous debt burden.

On the matter of taxes, however, there was great confusion of thought. Landon's financial views apparently included the idea that government revenue should be derived from direct taxes on incomes of individuals and corporations; that a continued large debt might find the country unable to meet a new emergency; that the tax on corporate surpluses should be repealed; that no further change should be made in the gold content of the dollar; and that dollars should be convertible in gold. The most important issue here was that of the income tax and corporation surplus tax. The Roosevelt Administration had not lowered the income tax base as far as many people thought socially desirable; but the Republicans refrained from stating what exemptions they favored. They denounced indirect and hidden taxes, but insisted upon retaining the most offensive of all such: the tariff duties. Finally, Landon denounced the undivided-profits tax on corporations as "the most cock-eyed piece of tax legislation ever imposed in a modern country." It happened that this tax measure was designed to eliminate the most flagrant method of evading income taxes. It was passed in the last days of the Seventy-fourth Congress and provided (1) for corporation income taxes of from 8 per cent on the first $2000 to 15 per cent on everything above $40,000; and (2) for a graduated tax, with a maximum of 27 per cent on undivided profits. The purpose of the tax was to prevent men whose income was derived from corporation profits from evading large personal income taxes by allowing the profits to be ploughed back into the business without first being distributed as dividends and then re-invested. The principle of the tax was thoroughly in line with the attempt to revamp the income tax laws to prevent the evasions of the twenties, however much practical experience might prove the necessity for revision of rates. Landon denounced the tax as a measure which prevented expansion by the small business man; but others denounced it on the broader indictment that it was a measure of social reform. This once more raised the issue, currently discussed since the first income tax of 1913, of how far reform should be the objective of taxation policies. An ascendancy of the negative view boded ill for the much discussed proposal of Nelson B. Gaskill, former chairman of the Federal Trade Commission, that the objectives of lower profits and higher wages be attained by a corporation profits tax with liberal exemptions for those corporations distributing a portion of their profits in the form of bonuses to employees.

Finally, there was an important issue with respect to foreign affairs. The Roosevelt Administration had advanced as rapidly as was politically expedient in the direction of international cooperation. The Republicans revived and capitalized on the isolationist philosophy of the Middle West. They condemned reciprocity trade agreements and endorsed high tariffs; repudiated the World Court and the League of Nations; promised to collect the war debts; and raised to new heights of absurdity the charges of communism.

Viewing these things in their broad perspective, there were two great and all-pervading issues before the people: (1) the relative merits of individual freedom under a government of limited powers *versus* the hope for economic security and economic stability through expansion of federal powers; and (2) economic and political isolation *versus* cooperation toward international stability. But the minority, which had failed to rise to the status of an intelligent opposition in Congress during the preceding four years, now faltered in the shadow of the election and blundered through the most hopelessly mismanaged campaign in many decades. The Republicans had small hope of winning the election from the first; but they did have a great opportunity to rehabilitate their party on sound and enduring principles with the aid of outstanding old line Democrats, to inaugurate a re-alignment of parties along realistic lines, to give the nation an exhibition of statesmanship instead of partisanship and they failed to do so. On the contrary, they completely lost sight of principles in a desperate and, for the most part, stupid bid for votes.

The campaign entered the crucial October stage with labor, organized and unorganized, almost solidly behind Roosevelt's re-election. The Republican National Committee in conjunction with the American Manufacturers Association inaugurated, a few days before the election, an intense drive to break that support by reversion to the outmoded scheme of payroll intimidation. Workers received their pay in envelopes bearing a printed statement of the amounts to be deducted after January 1, as required by the Social Security Act which had been sponsored and approved by President Roosevelt. The effort failed to change labor's preference and reacted against the party among the millions of independent liberals who knew that men of both parties had supported the act as a non-partisan reform measure.

Again, an honest opposition to collectivism, in the name of individual liberty and opportunity, required a complete repudiation of government subsidies to special groups and whole-hearted endorsement of free trade. Landon sought to win the farm vote by denouncing the most widely approved measures of the Roosevelt Administration: the reciprocal trade agreements. The party welcomed the support of George Peek, former Director of the Agricultural Adjustment Administration, whose ideas of national self-containment were regarded as a certain road to the very regimentation embodied in the AAA. Also, every stabilizer among the manufacturing group was supporting Landon. Evidence is strong that the program of crop curtailment had been adopted by the Roosevelt Administration as a temporary emergency measure. It was certainly not endorsed as a permanent policy by Wallace. Evidence is even stronger that production curtailment was the idea of the stabilizers among the manufacturers; and that Roosevelt's experiment with the NRA was not on the basis of the scarcity theory but on the basis of industrial democracy: that is, with ultimate expansion of production through increased consumption made possible by larger returns to labor at the expense of capital. It would appear that the scarcity theory as a *Roosevelt policy* had been greatly over-emphasized. It is certain that on a clear-cut issue as stated above, the opponents of collectivism should have been supporting Hull's reciprocal tariffs instead of denouncing them; should have been offering a frank program of anti-trust legislation instead of accepting the aid of manufacturers who opposed such regulation. One of the chief indictments against Roosevelt was his failure to indicate whether he believed a constitutional amendment necessary to enable the federal government to control adequately industry and agriculture. Landon raised the issue sharply in his Detroit speech by saying that if Roosevelt believed such constitutional change necessary, he should say so, because it was a fundamental issue. He then promptly destroyed the issue by saying that if, after his election, he himself should find such an amendment necessary, he would go before the people openly and ask for it. Roosevelt did not say whether an amendment was necessary and Landon admitted he was not certain, so there was no choice. Moreover, few people believed that Congress could be persuaded to reenact an NRA, or that a Supreme Court would approve one if it were passed; and only the blindly partisan voter believed the charge that Roosevelt could or would attempt to overthrow the Court and Constitution under any circumstances. Closely allied with these things was the problem of balancing the budget and reducing expenditures. Landon promised, early in the campaign, not to curtail necessary relief and to support farm subsidies based on agricultural exports. The former was the principal reason why the budget had been out of balance, and the latter was recognized as a far more expensive program than the AAA subsidies.

A fortuitous circumstance occurred during the campaign which greatly clarified the monetary issue. France devalued the franc on September 25 and France, Great Britain and the United States promptly entered an international agreement for currency stabilization. The Treasury Department announced the action as "the culmination of a three-and-a-half year dream," which may or may not have been true, but probably was not. In any case, it was directly contrary to the principle of the commodity dollar. Its importance lay in its apparent repudiation of the latter idea and in the fact that international stabilization precluded any further alteration of the gold content of the dollar within the ten per cent range still allowed under the law.

The charge of communism, upon which the Republican party had relied so heavily in all campaigns since the World War, and which was hurled at Roosevelt from the beginning of his Administration by Dr. Wirt, the Liberty League, Alfred E. Smith and others, was finally discredited by being over-worked. It was an absurd charge in any case; but when it was leveled at such outstanding advisors of Roosevelt as Professor Felix Frankfurter of Harvard University, sometime visiting lecturer at Oxford University, it reached the heights of the ridiculous. Moreover, just as Prussianism had suddenly given way to communism in the minds of Americans as the great menace to democracy at the close of the World War, now communism had been replaced by fascism by events in Spain. Too many people felt that the Roosevelt Recovery Program had been exactly the sort of program required to save the country from radicalism of one sort or another to take the charge seriously. In short, many people believed that Roosevelt had saved both the capitalistic system of production and our democratic institutions.

Thus, potential issues were abandoned by the ineptitude and indecision of the Republican party's managers: centralization of power in the federal government; expenditures *for* and the system *of* relief; subsidies to special interests or pressure groups; balancing the budget; government-supported labor unions; the continuation of emergency powers; individual liberty *vs.* economic security. Each of these issues was worthy of wide discussion and studied debate. None of them was so considered and the independent voters were left to a choice between two personalities: one, the most amazing and commanding since the days of Thomas Jefferson; the other, colorless; one, the embodiment of culture; the other, mediocrity at best. The result was one of the most sweeping political endorsements ever given a presidential candidate. Roosevelt was returned to office by a popular majority of more than ten million and an electoral vote of 523 to 8. A hundred reasons could be given why various individuals cast their ballots as they did. Most of them probably because they, personally, and the country as a whole were economically more secure than four years before. Others, because they had seen government functioning for the welfare of the masses for the first time in their memory; because they believed the United States needed more men like Holmes, Brandeis, Stone and Cardozo in the Supreme Court and doubted if they would be appointed by those who denounced all liberals as communists; because they wanted the administration of the Securities and Exchange Acts, the Tennessee Valley Authority, and the Social Security Act to remain in the hands of their friends; because they believed the most important events of the ensuing four years would involve foreign relations and mistrusted Landon's ability to deal with such questions; because they believed that institutions survive or perish according as they meet the needs of human life, and that the government and the Constitution will live so long and only so long as they are made to function in the interests of the people. Above everything else, men refused to vote against a man who took a despairing and misgoverned nation, in one of the darkest hours of its history, and set its face toward the light, gave renewed hope and courage to its people, saved its homes and extended a helping hand to its young men and women. The talk about communism and fascism, debts and repudiation, regimentation and Farleyism, left them cold. The great endorsement given to Roosevelt in the election was not the result of bribes, or class hatreds, or yet of machine politics. It came from every class, from every economic group, from every nook and corner of the nation. It was an expression of faith, by a people who loved their institutions, in one who dared much that they might not perish. Time alone could reveal the full significance of the election. There were those who feared a dictatorship, a sweeping revival of an aggressive reform program, a new and un-American scheme of planned economy. On the other hand, certain probabilities were evident. The stage was set for the re-alignment of parties which many had been hopefully anticipating. The relegation to obscurity of the Lemke-Coughlin-Townsend-Long followers would relieve the Administration of the tremendous pressure from the Left which was such a nightmare to the Congress and the President alike for four years. The elimination of the Republican Old Guard from Congress would make it possible for conservative Democrats to oppose the Administration without being aligned with the reactionary opposition. The sweeping popular endorsement given to the President was likely to eliminate the grievous fault of shifting policies which so characterized his first Administration. All indications were for a conservative administration during the ensuing four years.

BIBLIOGRAPHY

I. The Heritage of Twentieth-century Americans

Barrett, Don Carlos, *The Greenbacks and Resumption of Specie Payments, 1862-1879* (*Harvard Economic Studies*, XXXVI). Cambridge, 1931.

Buck, Solon Justus, *The Agrarian Crusade* (*The Chronicles of America Series*, XLV). New Haven, 1921.

—— *The Granger Movement* (*Harvard Historical Studies*, XIX). Cambridge, 1913.

Cleveland, Frederick Albert and Powell, Fred Wilbur, *Railway Promotion and Capitalization in the United States*. New York, 1909.

Couch, William Terry, ed., *Culture in the South*. Chapel Hill, 1934.

Dabney, Charles W., *Universal Education in the South*. 2 vols. Chapel Hill, 1936.

Dabney, Virginius, *Liberalism in the South*. Chapel Hill, 1932.

Emerson, Guy, *The New Frontier*. New York, 1920.

Fine, Nathan, *Labor and Farmer Parties in the United States, 1828-1928*. New York, 1928.

Fleming, Walter Lynwood, *The Sequel of Appomattox* (*The Chronicles of America Series*, XXXII). New Haven, 1919.

Gildersleeve, Basil Lanneau, *The Creed of the Old South, 1865-1915*. Baltimore, 1915.

Glasson, William Henry, *Federal Military Pensions in the United States*. New York, 1918.

Harris, Julia Collier, *Joel Chandler Harris: Editor and Essayist*. Chapel Hill, 1931.

Haynes, Frederick Emory, *Third Party Movements Since the Civil War*. Iowa City, 1916.

Hendrick, Burton Jesse, *The Age of Big Business* (*The Chronicles of America Series,* XXXIX). New Haven, 1919.

Hepburn, Alonzo Barton, *A History of Currency in the United States.* New York, 1915.

Hibbard, Benjamin Horace, *History of the Public Land Policies.* New York, 1924.

Hicks, John Donald, *The Populist Revolt.* Minneapolis, 1931.

Hough, Emerson, *The Passing of the Frontier.* New Haven, 1918.

Ise, John, *The United States Forest Policy.* New Haven, 1920.

Johnson, Charles Spurgeon, *The Negro in American Civilization.* New York, 1930.

Kendrick, Benjamin Burks and Arnett, Alex Mathews, *The South Looks at Its Past.* Chapel Hill, 1935.

Lewinson, Paul, *Race, Class and Party.* London, 1932.

Moody, John, *The Railroad Builders* (*The Chronicles of America Series,* XXXVIII). New Haven, 1919.

—— *The Masters of Capital* (*The Chronicles of America Series,* XLI). New Haven, 1919.

Myers, Gustavus, *History of the Great American Fortunes.* 3 vols. Chicago, 1909-1911.

Nevins, Allan, *The Emergence of Modern America* (*A History of American Life,* VIII). New York, 1927.

—— *Grover Cleveland: A Study in Courage.* New York, 1932.

Odum, Howard Washington, *An American Epoch.* New York, 1930.

—— *Southern Regions of the United States.* Chapel Hill, 1936.

Oliver, John William, *History of Civil War Military Pensions, 1861-1885* (University of Wisconsin, *Bulletin No. 884*). Madison, 1917.

Parrington, Vernon Louis, *The Beginnings of Critical Realism in America* (*Main Currents in American Thought,* III). New York, 1930.

Paxson, Frederic Logan, *History of the American Frontier, 1763-1893*. Boston, 1924.

Riegel, Robert Edgar, *The Story of the Western Railroads*. New York, 1926.

Robertson, William Joseph, *The Changing South*. New York, 1927.

Taussig, Frank William, *The Tariff History of the United States*. New York, 1931.

Thompson, Holland, *The New South* (*The Chronicles of America Series*, XLII). New Haven, 1919.

Turner, Frederick Jackson, *The Frontier in American History*. New York, 1920.

Vance, Rupert Bayless, *Human Factors in Cotton Culture*. Chapel Hill, 1929.

—— *Human Geography of the South*. Chapel Hill, 1932.

Webb, Walter Prescott, *The Great Plains*. Boston, 1931.

Woodson, Carter Godwin, *The Negro in Our History*. Washington, 1922.

II. Survivals and Symbols

Abbott, Edith, *Women in Industry*. New York, 1910.

Barber, Herbert Lee, *The Story of the Automobile*. Chicago, 1917.

Beard, Charles Austin and Beard, Mary Ritter, *Rise of American Civilization*. New York, 1927.

Beer, Thomas, *The Mauve Decade*. New York, 1926.

Blanshard, Paul, *Labor in Southern Cotton Mills*. New York, 1927.

Byrn, Edward W., *The Progress of Invention in the Nineteenth Century*. New York, 1900.

Calhoun, Arthur Wallace, *A Social History of the American Family*. 3 vols. Cleveland, 1917-1919.

Carpenter, Niles, *Immigrants and Their Children, 1920*. Washington, 1927.

Chapin, Francis Stuart, *Cultural Change*. New York, 1928.

Commons, John Rogers, *Races and Immigrants in America.* New York, 1920.

—— *Social Reform and the Church.* New York, 1894.

Cubberly, Ellwood Patterson, *Public Education in the United States.* Boston, 1919.

Dutcher, Dean, *The Negro in Modern Industrial Society.* Lancaster, Pa., 1930.

Epstein, Ralph Cecil, *The Automobile Industry.* Chicago, 1928.

Fairchild, Henry Pratt, *Immigration.* New York, 1925.

Feldman, Herman, *Racial Factors in American Industry.* New York, 1931.

Gabriel, Ralph Henry, ed., *The Pageant of America.* 15 vols. New Haven, 1925-1929.

Garis, Roy Lawrence, *Immigration Restriction.* New York, 1929.

Hall, Thomas Cuming, *Religious Background of American Culture.* Boston, 1930.

Hourwich, Isaac Aaronvich, *Immigration and Labor.* New York, 1912.

Jenks, Jeremiah Whipple and Lauck, W. Jett, *The Immigration Problem.* New York, 1926.

Kennedy, Louise Venable, *The Negro Peasant Turns Cityward.* New York, 1930.

Lindquist, Ruth, *The Family in the Present Social Order.* Chapel Hill, 1931.

Lynd, Robert S. and Helen Merrell, *Middletown.* New York, 1929.

MacDonald, Austin Faulks, *Federal Aid: A Study of the American Subsidy System.* New York, 1928.

McGiffert, Arthur Cushman, *The Rise of Modern Religious Ideas.* New York, 1915.

Mears, Eliot Grinnell, *Resident Orientals on the American Pacific Coast.* New York, 1928.

Mitchell, Broadus and Mitchell, George Sinclair, *Industrial Revolution in the South.* Baltimore, 1930.

Moton, Robert, *What the Negro Thinks.* Garden City, 1929.

Orth, Samuel Peter, *Our Foreigners* (*The Chronicles of America Series,* XXXV). New Haven, 1921.

Peck, Harry Thurston, *Twenty Years of the Republic, 1885-1905.* New York, 1920.

Potwin, Marjorie Adella, *Cotton Mill People of the Piedmont.* New York, 1927.

President's Research Committee on Social Trends, *Recent Social Trends in the United States.* New York, 1933.

Raushenbusch, Walter, *Christianity and the Social Crisis.* New York, 1907.

Ripley, William Zebina, *Trusts, Pools and Corporations.* Boston, 1916.

Rugg, Harold Ordway, *Culture and Education in America.* New York, 1931.

Schlesinger, Arthur Meier, *The Rise of the City* (*A History of American Life,* X). New York, 1933.

Slosson, Edwin Emery, *American Spirit in Education* (*The Chronicles of America Series,* XXXIII). New Haven, 1921.

Stieglitz, Julius Oscar, *Chemistry and Recent Progress in Medicine.* Baltimore, 1926.

Sullivan, Mark, *Our Times, The Turn of the Century.* New York, 1926.

Thompson, Holland, *The Age of Inventions* (*The Chronicles of America Series,* XXXVII). New Haven, 1921.

Thompson, Walter, *Federal Centralization.* New York, 1923.

Van Vleck, William Cabell, *The Administrative Control of Aliens.* New York, 1932.

Ward, Harry Frederick, *The Social Creed and the Churches.* Cincinnati, 1914.

III. Resurgence of Jeffersonian Liberalism

Adamic, Louis, *Dynamite: The Story of Class Violence in America.* London, 1931.

Ashley, Percy Walter Llewellyn, *Modern Tariff History*. London, 1920.

Bogart, Ernest Ludlow, *An Economic History of the United States*. New York, 1929.

Browne, W. R., *Altgeld of Illinois, 1847-1902*. New York, 1924.

Chase, Stuart, *The Tragedy of Waste*. New York, 1925.

Chamberlain, John, *Farewell to Reform*. New York, 1933.

Commons, John Rogers and others, *History of Labor in the United States*. 2 vols. New York, 1921-1935.

Croly, Herbert David, *The Promise of American Life*. New York, 1909.

Faulkner, Harold Underwood, *The Quest for Social Justice, 1898-1914* (*A History of American Life*, XI). New York, 1931.

—— *American Economic History*. New York, 1924.

Fish, Carl Russell, *The Civil Service and the Patronage* (*Harvard Historical Studies*, XI). New York, 1905.

Fuller, Raymond Garfield, *Child Labor and the Constitution*. New York, 1923.

Geiger, George Raymond, *The Philosophy of Henry George*. Grand Forks, S. D., 1931.

George, Henry, Jr., *The Life of Henry George*. New York, 1905.

Gompers, Samuel, *Seventy Years of Life and Labor*. 2 vols. London, 1925.

Hockett, John Alpheus, *A Determination of the Major Social Problems*. New York, 1927.

Hoxie, Robert Franklin, *Trade Unionism in the United States*. New York, 1917.

Jones, Eliot, *Trust Problem in the United States*. New York, 1921.

King, Wellford Isbell, *Wealth and Income of the People of the United States*. New York, 1915.

Kirkland, Edward Chase, *A History of American Economic Life*. New York, 1934.

Lippincott, Isaac, *Economic Development of the United States.* New York, 1921.

Lippmann, Walter, *A Preface to Politics.* New York, 1914.

Lloyd, Henry Demarest, *Wealth Against Commonwealth.* New York, 1894.

McCarthy, Charles, *The Wisconsin Idea.* New York, 1912.

McConnell, Francis John, *Humanism and Christianity.* New York, 1928.

Mitchell, John, *Organized Labor.* Philadelphia, 1903.

Munro, William Bennett, *The Initiative, Referendum and Recall.* New York, 1912.

Perlman, Selig, *History of Trade Unionism in the United States.* New York, 1923.

Pinchot, Gifford, *The Fight for Conservation.* New York, 1910.

Powderly, Terence Vincent, *Thirty Years of Labor.* Columbus, 1889.

Regier, Cornelius C., *The Era of the Muckrakers.* Chapel Hill, 1932.

Seager, Henry Rogers and Gulick, Charles A., *Trust and Corporation Problems.* New York, 1929.

Smyth, William Ellsworth, *The Conquest of Arid America.* New York, 1900.

Steffens, Lincoln, *Autobiography of Lincoln Steffens.* 2 vols. New York, 1931.

Teele, Ray Palmer, *Irrigation in the United States.* New York, 1915.

Van Hise, Charles Richard and Havemeyer, Loomis, *The Conservation of our Natural Resources.* New York, 1930.

Ware, Norman J., *The Labor Movement in the United States, 1860-1895.* New York, 1929.

Weyl, Walter Edward, *The New Democracy.* New York, 1912.

IV. Political Philosophy—Roosevelt to Wilson

Baker, Ray Stannard, *Life and Letters of Woodrow Wilson.* 4 vols. Garden City, 1927-1931.

Bowers, Claude Gernade, *Beveridge and the Progressive Era.* Boston, 1932.

Clark, Champ, *My Quarter Century of American Politics.* New York, 1920.

Croly, Herbert David, *Marcus Alonzo Hanna.* New York, 1912.

De Witt, Benjamin Parke, *The Progressive Movement.* New York, 1915.

Dodd, William Edward, *Woodrow Wilson and His Work.* New York, 1920.

Dreier, Thomas, *Heroes of Insurgency.* Boston, 1910.

Duffy, Herbert Smith, *William Howard Taft.* New York, 1930.

Gosnell, Harold Foote, *Boss Platt and the New York Machine.* Chicago, 1924.

Haynes, Frederick Emory, *Third Party Movements Since the Civil War.* Iowa City, 1916.

—— *Social Politics in the United States.* Boston, 1924.

Hibben, Paxton, *The Peerless Leader: William Jennings Bryan.* New York, 1929.

Hillquit, Morris, *History of Socialism in the United States.* New York, 1910.

Howe, Frederic Clemson, *Wisconsin, An Experiment in Democracy.* New York, 1912.

Kerney, James, *The Political Education of Woodrow Wilson.* New York, 1926.

Kohlsaat, Herman Henry, *From McKinley to Harding.* New York, 1923.

La Follette, Robert Marion, *Autobiography: A Personal Narrative of Political Experience.* Madison, Wis., 1913.

Long, John Cuthbert, *Bryan, The Great Commoner.* New York, 1928.

Lowry, Edward George, *Washington Close-Ups*. Boston, 1921.
McCaleb, Walter Flavius, *Theodore Roosevelt*. New York, 1931.
Macy, John Albert, *Socialism in America*. Garden City, 1916.
Merriam, Charles Edward, *American Political Ideas, 1867-1917*. New York, 1920.
—— *Four American Party Leaders*. New York, 1926.
Olcott, Charles Sumner, *The Life of William McKinley*. 2 vols. Boston, 1916.
Payne, G. H., *The Birth of the New Party*. New York, 1912.
Pringle, Henry Fowles, *Theodore Roosevelt*. New York, 1931.
Robinson, Edgar Eugene, *Evolution of American Political Parties*. New York, 1924.
Roosevelt, Theodore, *The New Nationalism*. New York, 1910.
Rosewater, Victor, *Backstage in 1912*. Philadelphia, 1932.
Stanwood, Edward, *A History of the Presidency*. 2 vols. Boston, 1916-1924.
Stephenson, Nathaniel Wright, *Nelson W. Aldrich: A Leader in American Politics*. New York, 1930.
Tumulty, Joseph Patrick, *Woodrow Wilson as I Knew Him*. Garden City, 1921.
White, William Allen, *Masks in a Pageant*. New York, 1928.
Wilson, Woodrow, *The New Democracy*. New York, 1916.
—— *The New Freedom*. New York, 1913.

V. In Defense of Economic Freedom

Berman, Edward, *Labor and the Sherman Act*. New York, 1930.
Brandeis, Louis Dembitz, *Other People's Money*. New York, 1914.
Clark, J. D., *The Federal Trust Policy*. Baltimore, 1931.
Commons, John R. and Andrews, John B., *Principles of Labor Legislation*. New York, 1920.
Dewey, Davis Rich, *Financial History of the United States*. New York, 1934.

Frankfurter, Felix and Greene, Nathan, *The Labor Injunction.* New York, 1930.

Glass, Carter, *An Adventure in Constructive Finance.* Garden City, 1927.

Groat, George Gorham, *Attitude of American Courts in Labor Cases* (Columbia University, *Studies in History, Economics and Public Law,* XLII). New York, 1911.

Henderson, Gerard Carl, *The Federal Trade Commission.* New Haven, 1924.

Hepburn, Alonzo Barton, *History of Coinage and Currency in the United States.* New York, 1924.

Holt, William Stull, *Federal Farm Loan Bureau.* Baltimore, 1924.

Keezer, Dexter Merriam and May, Stacy, *The Public Control of Business.* New York, 1930.

Laidler, Harry Wellington, *Concentration of Control in American Industry.* New York, 1931.

Lorwin, Lewis Levitzki, *The American Federation of Labor; History, Policies and Prospects.* Washington, 1933.

Moody, John, *The Truth About the Trusts.* New York, 1904.

Ripley, William Zebina, *Railroads: Rates and Regulation.* New York, 1912.

Seager, Henry Rogers and Gulick, Charles A., *Trust and Corporation Problems.* New York, 1929.

Seligman, Edwin Robert Anderson, *Economics of Farm Relief.* New York, 1929.

Sharfman, Isaiah Leo, *The Interstate Commerce Commission: A Study in Administrative Law and Procedure.* 4 vols. New York, 1931-1935.

Spahr, E. S., *History and Theory of Agricultural Credit in the United States.* New York, 1932.

Tarbell, Ida Minerva, *The Tariff in Our Times.* New York, 1931.

Taussig, Frank William, *The Tariff History of the United States.* New York, 1931.

Walker, Albert Henry, *History of the Sherman Law.* New York, 1910.

Warburg, Paul Moritz, *The Federal Reserve System.* 2 vols., New York, 1930.

Willis, Henry Parker, *The Federal Reserve System.* New York, 1923.

VI. LAW ADMINISTRATION AND THE COURTS

Beard, Charles Austin, *The Supreme Court and the Constitution.* New York, 1931.

Boudin, Louis Boudianoff, *Government by Judiciary.* New York, 1932.

Bryce, James, *The American Commonwealth.* 2 vols. New York, 1922-23.

Cardozo, Benjamin Nathan, *The Nature of the Judicial Process.* New Haven, 1925.

Chadbourn, James Harmon, *Lynching and the Law.* Chapel Hill, 1933.

Clark, Floyd Barzilia, *The Constitutional Doctrines of Justice Harlan.* Baltimore, 1915.

Colvin, David Leigh, *Prohibition in the United States.* New York, 1926.

Comer, John Preston, *Legislative Functions of National Administrative Authorities.* New York, 1927.

Corwin, Edward Samuel, *The Twilight of the Supreme Court.* New Haven, 1934.

Dickinson, John, *Administrative Justice and the Supremacy of the Law in the United States.* Cambridge, 1927.

Elliott, William Yandell, *The Need for Constitutional Reform.* New York, 1935.

Fisher, Irving, *Prohibition at Its Worst.* New York, 1926.

Frankfurter, Felix, ed., *Mr. Justice Brandeis.* New Haven, 1932.

—— *Mr. Justice Holmes and the Constitution.* Cambridge, 1927.

Frankfurter, Felix and Landis, James M., *The Business of the Supreme Court*. New York, 1928.

Freund, Ernst, *Administrative Powers over Persons and Property*. Chicago, 1928.

Haines, Charles Grove, *The American Doctrine of Judicial Supremacy*. Berkeley, Cal., 1932.

Herring, Edward Pendleton, *Group Representation Before Congress*. Baltimore, 1929.

Hughes, Charles Evans, *The Supreme Court of the United States*. New York, 1928.

Lief, Alfred, ed., *The Dissenting Opinions of Mr. Justice Holmes*. New York, 1929.

—— *The Social and Economic Views of Mr. Justice Brandeis*. New York, 1930.

McBain, Howard Lee, *The Living Constitution*. New York, 1927.

Mason, Alpheus Thomas, *Brandeis, Lawyer and Judge in the Modern State*. Princeton, 1933.

Merriam, Charles Edward, *The Written Constitution and the Unwritten Attitude*. New York, 1931.

Merz, Charles, *The Dry Decade*. Garden City, 1931.

Moore, Blaine Free, *The Supreme Court and Unconstitutional Legislation*. New York, 1913.

Myers, Gustavus, *History of the Supreme Court of the United States*. Chicago, 1912.

Odegard, Peter H., *Pressure Politics: The Story of the Anti-Saloon League*. New York, 1928.

Pollard, Joseph Percival, *Mr. Justice Cardozo*. New York, 1935.

Powell, Thomas Reed, *The Supreme Court and State Police Power, 1922-1930*. Charlottesville, Va., 1932.

Ransom, William Lynn, *Majority Rule and the Judiciary*. New York, 1912.

Raper, Arthur Franklin, *The Tragedy of Lynching*. Chapel Hill, 1933.

Richardson, Dorsey, *Constitutional Doctrines of Justice Holmes.* Baltimore, 1924.

Taft, William Howard, *The Anti-Trust Act and the Supreme Court.* New York, 1914.

Thorpe, George Cyrus, *Federal Departmental Organization and Practice.* Kansas City, 1925.

Warren, Charles, *Congress, the Constitution, and the Supreme Court.* Boston, 1930.

—— *The Supreme Court in United States History.* 2 vols. Boston, 1932.

Willoughby, Westel Woodbury, *Principles of the Constitutional Law of the United States.* New York, 1930.

Willoughby, William Franklin, *Principles of Judicial Administration.* Washington, 1929.

VII. National Expansion

Bau, Minchien Joshua, *The Open Door Doctrine in Relation to China.* New York, 1923.

Bemis, Samuel Flagg, ed., *The American Secretaries of States and Their Diplomacy.* 10 vols. New York, 1927-1929.

Blakeslee, George Hubbard, *The Recent Foreign Policy of the United States.* New York, 1925.

Buell, Raymond Leslie, *International Relations.* New York, 1929.

Callahan, James Morton, *American Foreign Policy in Mexican Relations.* New York, 1932.

—— *American Relations in the Pacific.* Baltimore, 1901.

Carpenter, Edmund Janes, *America in Hawaii.* Boston, 1899.

Chadwick, French Ensor, *Relations of the United States and Spain.* 3 vols. New York, 1909-1911.

Chapman, Charles Edward, *A History of the Cuban Republic.* New York, 1927.

Clark, Henry W., *History of Alaska.* New York, 1930.

Clark, Victor Selden, *Porto Rico and Its Problems.* Washington, 1930.

Coolidge, Archibald Cary, *The United States as a World Power*. New York, 1908.

Cox, Isaac Joslin, *Nicaragua and the United States, 1909-1927* (World Peace Foundation, *Pamphlet X, No. 7*). Boston, 1927.

Davis, Harold Palmer, *Black Democracy*. New York, 1928.

Dennett, Tyler, *Americans in Eastern Asia*. New York, 1922.

—— *John Hay*. New York, 1933.

—— *Theodore Roosevelt and the Russo-Japanese War*. Garden City, 1925.

Diffie, Bailey W. and Diffie, Justine Whitfield, *Porto Rico: A Broken Pledge*. New York, 1931.

Dunn, Robert Williams, *American Foreign Investments*. New York, 1926.

Forbes, William Cameron, *The Philippine Islands*. 2 vols. Boston, 1928.

Garner, James Wilford, *American Foreign Policies*. New York, 1928.

Gulick, Sidney Lewis, *The American Japanese Problem*. New York, 1914.

Hagedorn, Hermann, *Leonard Wood*. 2 vols. New York, 1931.

Hill, Howard Copeland, *Roosevelt and the Caribbean*. Chicago, 1927.

Hockett, Charles Wilson, *The Mexican Revolution and the United States, 1910-1926* (World Peace Foundation, *Pamphlet IX, No. 5*). Boston, 1926.

Holt, William Stull, *Treaties Defeated by the Senate*. Baltimore, 1933.

Howland, Charles Prentice, ed., *Survey of American Foreign Relations*. 4 vols. New Haven, 1928-1931.

Jenks, Leland Hamilton, *Our Cuban Colony: A Study in Sugar*. New York, 1928.

Jones, Chester Lloyd, *Caribbean Backgrounds and Prospects*. New York, 1931.

Keasbey, Lindley Miller, *The Nicaragua Canal and the Monroe Doctrine.* New York, 1896.

Knight, Melvin Moses, *The Americans in Santo Domingo.* New York, 1928.

Kuykendall, Ralph S., *A History of Hawaii.* New York, 1926.

Latanè, John Holladay, *America As a World Power, 1897-1907* (American Nation Series.) New York, 1907.

—— *A History of American Foreign Policy.* Garden City, 1927.

Magoon, Charles Edward, *Report on the Legal Status of the Territory and Inhabitants of the Islands Acquired by the United States During the War with Spain.* Washington, 1900.

Miller, Hugh Gordon, *The Isthmian Highway.* New York, 1929.

Millis, Walter, *The Martial Spirit: A Study of our War with Spain.* Boston, 1931.

Millspaugh, Arthur Chester, *Haiti under American Control, 1915-1930.* Boston, 1931.

Nichols, Jeannette Paddock, *Alaska.* Cleveland, 1924.

Perkins, Dexter, *The Monroe Doctrine, 1826-1867.* Baltimore, 1933.

Pettigrew, Richard Franklin, *The Course of Empire.* New York, 1920.

Randolph, Carman Fitz, *Law and Policy of Annexation.* New York, 1901.

Remer, Charles Frederick, *Foreign Investments in China.* New York, 1933.

Rippy, James Fred, *The Capitalists and Colombia.* New York, 1931.

—— *The United States and Mexico.* New York, 1931.

Robertson, William Spence, *Hispanic-American Relations with the United States.* New York, 1923.

Robinson, Albert Gardner, *Cuba and the Intervention.* New York, 1905.

Robinson, Edgar Eugene and West, Victor J., *The Foreign Policy of Woodrow Wilson.* New York, 1917.

Root, Elihu, *Military and Colonial Policy of the United States.* Cambridge, 1916.

Ryden, George Herbert, *The Foreign Policy of the United States in Relation to Samoa.* New Haven, 1933.

Scott, James Brown, *The Hague Conferences of 1899 and 1907.* 2 vols. Baltimore, 1909.

Stanton, Stephen Berrien, *The Behring Sea Controversy.* New York, 1892.

Stimson, Henry Lewis, *American Policy in Nicaragua.* New York, 1927.

Storey, Moorfield and Lichauco, Marcial P., *Conquest of the Philippines by the United States, 1898-1925.* New York, 1926.

Tansill, Charles Callan, *The Purchase of the Danish West Indies.* Baltimore, 1932.

Treat, Payson Jackson, *Japan and the United States, 1853-1921.* Boston, 1921.

Wilkerson, Marcus Manley, *Public Opinion and the Spanish-American War.* Baton Rouge, 1932.

Williams, Benjamin Harrison, *Economic Foreign Policy of the United States.* New York, 1929.

Williams, Mary Wilhelmine, *Anglo-American Isthmian Diplomacy, 1815-1915.* Baltimore, 1916.

Willoughby, Westel Woodbury, *The Constitutional Law of the United States.* New York, 1910.

—— *Foreign Rights and Interests in China.* 2 vols. Baltimore, 1920.

Willoughby, William Franklin, *Territories and Dependencies of the United States.* New York, 1905.

Winkler, Max, *Investments of United States Capital in Latin America* (World Peace Foundation, *Pamphlet XII, No. 6*). Boston, 1928.

Wright, Quincey, ed., *Interpretations of American Foreign Policy.* Chicago, 1930.

VIII. War to End Wars

Allen, Devere, *The Fight for Peace.* New York, 1930.

Anonymous, *Arbitration and the United States* (World Peace Foundation, *Pamphlet IX, Nos. 6-7*). Boston, 1926.

Bassett, John Spencer, *Our War with Germany.* New York, 1919.

Beales, Arthur Charles Frederick, *The History of Peace.* New York, 1931.

Berman, Edward, *Labor Disputes and the President of the United States* (Columbia University, *Studies in History, Economics and Public Law,* CXI, No. 2). New York, 1924.

Bing, Alexander M., *War-time Strikes and Their Adjustment.* New York, 1921.

Bogart, Ernest Ludlow, *War Costs and Their Financing.* New York, 1921.

Chafee, Zechariah, Jr., *Freedom of Speech.* New York, 1920.

Chambrun, Colonel de and Marenches, Captain de, *The American Army in the European Conflict.* New York, 1919.

Clarkson, Grosvenor B., *Industrial America in the World War.* Boston, 1923.

Creel, George, *How We Advertised America.* New York, 1920.

Curti, Merle Eugene, *The American Peace Crusade.* Durham, 1929.

—— *Bryan and World Peace* (Smith College, *Studies in History, Nos. 3-4*). Northampton, 1931.

—— *Peace or War: The American Struggle, 1636-1936.* New York, 1936.

Ellingwood, Albert Russell and Coombs, Whitney, *The Government and Railroad Transportation.* Boston, 1930.

Fay, S. B., *The Origins of the World War.* 2 vols. New York, 1928.

Gibson, R. H. and Prendergast, M., *German Submarine War, 1914-1918.* New York, 1931.

Grattan, Clinton Hartley, *Why We Fought.* New York, 1929.

Harbord, James Guthrie, *America in the World War.* Boston, 1933.

Hayes, Carlton Joseph Huntley, *A Brief History of the Great War.* New York, 1920.

Huidekoper, Frederic Louis, *The Military Unpreparedness of the United States.* New York, 1915.

Kenworthy, Joseph Montague and Young, G., *Freedom of the Seas.* New York, 1928.

Lasswell, Harold Dwight, *Propaganda Technique in the World War.* London, 1927.

Noyes, Alexander Dana, *The War Period in American Finance, 1908-1925.* New York, 1926.

Ponsonby, Arthur, *Falsehood in War Time.* London, 1928.

Powell, Edward Alexander, *The Army behind the Army.* New York, 1919.

Schmitt, Bernadotte Everly, *The Coming of the War.* 2 vols. New York, 1930.

Scott, James Brown, *A Survey of International Relations Between the United States and Germany, 1914-1917.* New York, 1917.

Seldes, George, *Iron, Blood and Profits.* New York, 1934.

Seymour, Charles, *Woodrow Wilson and the World War* (*Chronicles of America Series*, XLVIII). New Haven, 1921.

—— ed., *The Intimate Papers of Colonel House.* 4 vols. Boston, 1928.

Surface, Frank M., *The Grain Trade during the World War.* New York, 1928.

Tuttle, Florence Guertin, *Alternatives to War.* New York, 1931.

Van Hise, Charles Richard, *Conservation and Regulation in the United States during the World War.* Washington, 1917.

Viereck, George Sylvester, *Spreading Germs of Hate.* New York, 1930.

Whitney, Edson Leone, *The American Peace Society: A Centennial History*. Washington, 1928.

Willoughby, William Franklin, *Government Organization in War Time and After*. New York, 1919.

IX. What Price Victory?

Baker, Ray Stannard, *What Wilson Did at Paris*. New York, 1919.

Bassett, John Spencer, *The League of Nations*. New York, 1928.

Bergmann, Karl, *The History of Reparations*. London, 1927.

Baruch, Bernard Mannes, *The Making of the Reparation and Economic Sections of the Treaty*. New York, 1920.

Brookings Institution, *United States Shipping Board*. Washington, 1931.

Davis, Jerome, *Contemporary Social Movements*. New York, 1930.

Fleming, Denna Frank, *The Treaty Veto of the American Senate*. New York, 1930.

—— *The United States and the League of Nations, 1918-1920*. New York, 1932.

Hines, Walker Downer, *War History of American Railroads* (Economic and Social History of the World War, J. T. Shotwell, ed.). New Haven, 1928.

Holt, William Stull, *Treaties Defeated by the Senate*. Baltimore, 1933.

House, Edward Mandell and Seymour, Charles, eds., *What Really Happened at Paris*. New York, 1921.

Hudson, Manley Ottmer, *Permanent Court of International Justice, and the Question of American Participation*. Cambridge, 1925.

Jessup, Philip Caryl, *The United States and the World Court* (World Peace Foundation, *Pamphlet XII, No. 4*). Boston, 1929.

Keynes, John Maynard, *Economic Consequences of the Peace*. London, 1919.

Lansing, Robert, *The Big Four and Others of the Peace Conference.* Boston, 1921.

Lodge, Henry Cabot, *Senate and the League of Nations.* New York, 1925.

Mayo, Katherine, *Soldiers What Next!* Boston, 1934.

Moulton, Harold Glenn and Pasvolsky, Leo, *War Debts and World Prosperity.* New York, 1932.

National Industrial Conference Board, *The American Merchant Marine Problem.* New York, 1929.

—— *The Inter-Ally Debts and the United States.* New York, 1925.

Noble, George Bernard, *Policies and Opinions at Paris, 1919.* New York, 1935.

Shotwell, James Thomson, *War as an Instrument of National Policy.* New York, 1929.

Temperley, Henry William Vazielle, ed., *A History of the Peace Conference of Paris.* 6 vols. London, 1920-1924.

Tuttle, Florence Guertin, *Alternatives to War.* New York, 1931.

X. Post-war Reaction

American Civil Liberties Union, *The Attempted Deportation of John Strachey* (1935); *Bills in Congress for Freedom of the Air* (1936); *Civil Liberties in American Colonies* (1933); *Free Speech in 1924* (1924); *Free Speech, 1926: The Work of the Union* (1926); *Fight for Civil Liberty, 1930-1931* (1931); *Gags on Teaching New York* (1933); *How Goes the Bill of Rights?* (1936); *Land of the Free* (1935); *Land of Pilgrims Pride, 1932-1933* (1933); *Liberty Under the New Deal* (1934); *So This is Free Speech!* (1935); *So This is Liberty!* (1924); *State Laws Against Free Speech* (1926); *State Police in Relation to Labor and Civil Liberties* (1924); *Strike is Criminal Syndicalism—in California* (1932); *Sweet Land of Liberty* (1932); *War-Time Prosecution and Mob Violence* (1920); *What Shocked the Censors* (1933); *Who's Un-American? An Answer to the "Patriots"* (1935).

Bates, Ernest Sutherland, *This Land of Liberty*. New York, 1930.

Chafee, Zechariah, Jr., *Freedom of Speech*. New York, 1920.

Chafee, Zechariah, *The Inquiring Mind*. New York, 1928.

Cole, Stewart Grant, *The History of Fundamentalism*. New York, 1931.

Coleman, McAlister, *Eugene V. Debs: A Man Unafraid*. New York, 1930.

Counts, George Sylvester, *Soviet Challenge to America*. New York, 1931.

Frank, Waldo David, *The Rediscovery of America*. New York, 1929.

Frankfurter, Felix, *The Case of Sacco and Vanzetti*. Boston, 1927.

Garrison, Winfred Ernest, *Intolerance*. New York, 1934.

Haynes, Frederick Emory, *Social Politics in the United States*. Boston, 1924.

Hapgood, Norman, *Professional Patriots*. New York, 1927.

Hayes, Arthur Garfield, *Let Freedom Ring*. New York, 1928.

—— *Trial by Prejudice*. New York, 1933.

Hillquit, Morris, *History of Socialism in the United States*. New York, 1910.

Irwin, William Henry, *How Red is America?*. New York, 1927.

Joad, Cyril Edwin Mitchenson, *Liberty Today*. New York, 1935.

Kirkpatrick, Clifford, *Religion in Human Affairs*. New York, 1929.

Lippmann, Walter, *American Inquisitors*. New York, 1928.

Mecklin, John Moffatt, *The Ku Klux Klan: A Study of the American Mind*. New York, 1924.

Pierce, Bessie Louise, *Citizens Organizations and the Civic Training of Youth*. New York, 1933.

Raup, Bruce, *Education and Organized Interests in America*. New York, 1936.

Seldes, George, *Freedom of the Press*. New York, 1935.

Shipley, Maynard, *The War on Modern Science*. New York, 1927.

Siegfried, André, *America Comes of Age*. New York, 1927.

Thomas, Norman Mattoon, *The Conscientious Objector in America*. New York, 1923.

—— *Is Conscience a Crime?* New York, 1927.

Whipple, Leon, *The Story of Civil Liberty in the United States*. New York, 1927.

XI. The Age of the Golden Calf

Adams, James Truslow, *Our Business Civilization*. New York, 1929.

Allen, Frederick Lewis, *Only Yesterday, an Informal History of the 1920's*. New York, 1931.

Beard, Charles Austin, ed., *Whither Mankind*. New York, 1928.

Berle, Adolf Augustus and Means, G. C., *The Modern Corporation and Private Property*. New York, 1932.

Borsodi, Ralph, *This Ugly Civilization*. New York, 1929.

Carver, Thomas Nixon, *The Present Economic Revolution in the United States*. Boston, 1925.

Chase, Stuart, *Men and Machines*. New York, 1929.

—— *Prosperity: Fact or Myth*. New York, 1929.

Committee on Recent Economic Changes, *Recent Economic Changes in the United States*. 2 vols. New York, 1929.

Douglas, Paul Howard, *Real Wages in the United States, 1890-1926*. Boston, 1930.

Fetter, Frank Albert, *The Masquerade of Monopoly*. New York, 1931.

Gamio, Manuel, *Mexican Immigration to the United States*. Chicago, 1930.

Heer, Clarence, *The Post-war Expansion of State Expenditures*. New York, 1926.

Hexter, Maurice Beck, *Social Consequences of Business Cycles*. Boston, 1925.

King, Willford Isbell, *The National Income and Its Purchasing Power*. New York, 1930.

Kuznets, Simon Smith, *Seasonal Variations in Industry and Trade*. New York, 1933.

Laidler, Harry Wellington, *Concentration of Control in American Industry*. New York, 1931.

Malin, James Claude, *The United States after the World War*. Boston, 1930.

Mazur, Paul Myer, *American Prosperity*. New York, 1928.

Merz, Charles, *The Great American Band Wagon*. New York, 1928.

National Industrial Conference Board, *Cost of Government in the United States, 1928-1929*. New York, 1931.

Ripley, William Zebina, *Main Street and Wall Street*. Boston, 1927.

Slosson, Preston William, *Great Crusade and After, 1914-1928* (*A History of American Life*, XII). New York, 1930.

Twelve Southerners, *I'll Take My Stand*. New York, 1930.

Tugwell, Rexford Guy, *Industry's Coming of Age*. New York, 1927.

XII. Industry and Transportation

Black, John Donald, *Agricultural Reform in the United States*. New York, 1929.

Bonbright, James Cummings and Means, Gardiner C., *The Holding Company*. New York, 1932.

Capper, Arthur, *The Agricultural Bloc*. New York, 1922.

Clark, John Maurice, *Social Control of Business*. Chicago, 1926.

Committee on Recent Economic Changes, *Recent Economic Changes in the United States*. 2 vols. New York, 1929.

Crecraft, Earl Willis, *Government and Business*. Yonkers-on-Hudson, 1928.

Dixon, Frank Haigh, *Railroads and Government, 1910-1921*. New York, 1922.

Donald, William John Alexander, *Trade Associations.* New York, 1933.

Elsbree, Hugh Langdon, *Interstate Transmission of Electric Power.* Cambridge, 1931.

Forrester, Robert Blair, *Report on Large Scale Cooperative Marketing in the United States.* London, 1925.

Foth, Joseph Henry, *Trade Associations, Their Services to Industry.* New York, 1930.

Gee, Wilson, *The Place of Agriculture in American Life.* New York, 1930.

Hadley, Arthur Twining, *Railroad Transportation, Its History and Its Law.* New York, 1903.

Hardy, Charles Oscar, *Recent Growth of the Electric Light and Power Industry.* Washington, 1929.

Heermance, Edgar Laing, *The Ethics of Business: A Study of Current Methods.* New York, 1926.

Hoover, Herbert Clark, *American Individualism.* New York, 1923.

Jones, Eliot, *The Anthracite Coal Combination in the United States* (*Harvard Economic Studies,* XI). Cambridge, 1914.

Kirsh, Benjamin Sollow, *Trade Associations: The Legal Aspects.* New York, 1928.

Laidler, Harry Wellington, *Concentration of Control in American Industry.* New York, 1931.

Lippincott, Isaac, *What the Farmer Needs.* New York, 1928.

MacVeagh, Rogers, *The Transportation Act, 1920: Its Sources, History and Text.* New York, 1923.

Marquand, Hilary Adair, *Dynamics of Industrial Combination.* New York, 1931.

Meyer, Balthaser Henry, *Railway Legislation in the United States.* New York, 1903.

Myers, James, *Representative Government in Industry.* New York, 1924.

National Industrial Conference Board, *The Agricultural Problem in the United States.* New York, 1926.

National Industrial Conference Board, *Mergers and the Law.* New York, 1929.

—— *Trade Associations: Their Economic Significance and Legal Status.* New York, 1925.

Nourse, Edwin Griswold, *American Agriculture and the European Market.* New York, 1924.

Raushenbush, Hilman Stephen and Laidler, Harry Wellington, *Power Control.* New York, 1928.

Seager, Henry Rogers and Gulick, Charles A., *Trust and Corporation Problems.* New York, 1929.

Shannon, Fred Albert, *Economic History of the People of the United States.* New York, 1934.

Tippetts, Charles Sanford and Livermore, Shaw, *Business Organization and Control.* New York, 1932.

United States Federal Trade Commission, *Open-Price Trade Associations.* Washington, 1929.

XIII. Militant Labor

American Academy of Political and Social Science, Nov., 1928, *The American Negro.* Philadelphia, 1928.

Beard, Mary Ritter, *A Short History of the American Labor Movement.* New York, 1925.

Brissenden, Paul Frederick, *The I.W.W.: A Study of American Syndicalism* (Columbia University Studies, LXXXIII). New York, 1919.

Carlton, Frank Tracy, *The History and Problems of Organized Labor.* Boston, 1920.

Dunn, Robert Williams, *Company Unions.* New York, 1927.

Fine, Nathan, *Labor and Farmer Parties in the United States, 1828-1928.* New York, 1928.

Frankfurter, Felix and Greene, N., *The Labor Injunction.* New York, 1930.

Gambs, John Saké, *The Decline of the I.W.W.* New York, 1932.

Gompers, Samuel, *Seventy Years of Life and Labor.* 2 vols. New York, 1925.

Hallgren, Mauritz Alfred, *Seeds of Revolt*. New York, 1933.
Harris, Abram L. and Spero, Sterling Denhard, *Black Worker: The Negro and the Labor Movement*. New York, 1931.
Hoxie, Robert Franklin, *Trade Unionism in the United States*. New York, 1920.
Mason, Alpheus Thomas, *Organized Labor and the Law*. Durham, 1925.
Oneal, James, *American Communism*. New York, 1927.
Perlman, Selig, *A History of Trade Unionism in the United States*. New York, 1922.
Saposs, David Joseph, *Left-Wing Unionism*. New York, 1926.
Ware, Norman, *The Labor Movement in the United States, 1860-1895*. New York, 1929.
Wesley, C. H., *Negro Labor in the United States, 1850-1925*. New York, 1927.
Witte, Edwin Emil, *The Government in Labor Disputes*. New York, 1932.
Wolf, Harry D., *The Railroad Labor Board*. Chicago, 1927.
Wolman, Leo, *The Growth of American Trade Unions*. New York, 1924.

XIV. An Epoch of Political Decadence

Allen, Robert S., *Washington Merry-Go-Round*. New York, 1931.
Chase, Stuart, *A New Deal*. New York, 1932.
Childs, Harwood Lawrence, *Labor and Capital in National Politics*. Columbus, 1930.
Clark, Evans, ed., *The Internal Debts of the United States*. New York, 1933.
Coolidge, Calvin, *Autobiography*. New York, 1929.
Corey, Lewis, *The Decline of American Capitalism*. New York, 1934.
Donham, Wallace Brett, *Business Adrift*. New York, 1931.
Douglas, Paul Howard and Director, Aaron, *The Problem of Unemployment*. New York, 1931.
Hallgren, Mauritz Alfred, *Seeds of Revolt*. New York, 1933.

Hill, Edwin Charles, *The American Scene*. New York, 1933.

Hoover, Herbert Clark, *The Challenge to Liberty*. New York, 1934.

—— *The New Day*. Stanford University, 1929.

Jones, Joseph Marion, *Tariff Retaliation*. Philadelphia, 1934.

Looker, Earle, *This Man Roosevelt*. New York, 1932.

Peel, Roy Victor and Donnelly, Thomas C., *The 1928 Campaign*. New York, 1931.

Pollock, James Kerr, *Party Campaign Funds*. New York, 1926.

Pringle, Henry Fowles, *Alfred E. Smith: A Critical Study*. New York, 1927.

Ravage, Marcus Eli, *The Story of Teapot Dome*. New York, 1924.

Roosevelt, Franklin Delano, *Looking Forward*. New York, 1933.

Seldes, Gilbert Vivian, *The Years of the Locust* (*America, 1929-1932*). Boston, 1933.

Slosson, Preston William, *The Great Crusade and After, 1914-1928* (*A History of American Life*, XII). New York, 1931.

Smith, Alfred Emanuel, *Progressive Democracy*. New York, 1928.

Soulé, George Henry, *The Coming American Revolution*. New York, 1934.

—— *A Planned Society*. New York, 1932.

Tugwell, Rexford Guy, *Industrial Discipline and the Governmental Acts*. New York, 1933.

Waters, Walter W., *B.E.F.: The Whole Story of the Bonus Army*. New York, 1933.

White, William Allen, *Calvin Coolidge*. New York, 1925.

—— *Masks in a Pageant*. New York, 1928.

XV. Bourbons to Crack-Pots: A Medley of Ideas

Arkright, Frank, *The ABC of Technocracy*. New York, 1933.

Ayres, Leonard Porter, *Economics of Recovery*. New York, 1934.

Beard, Charles Austin, *The Future Comes*. New York, 1933.

Berle, Adolf Augustus, *America's Recovery Program*. London, 1934.

Chase, Stuart, *The Economy of Abundance*. New York, 1934.

—— *Technocracy: An Interpretation*. New York, 1933.

Coughlin, Charles Edward, *A Series of Lectures on Social Justice*. Royal Oak, Mich., 1935.

Crowell, Chester T., "The Townsend Plan: a Challenge to Congress," in *American Mercury*, XXXIV, 456-460.

Daniell, F. Raymond, "Gentleman from Louisiana," in *Current History*, XLI, 172-178.

Deane, Albert, *The Deane Plan for Mutual Security*. New York, 1936.

Ezekiel, Mordecai, *$2500 a Year, from Scarcity to Abundance*. New York, 1936.

Filene, Edward Albert, *The Way Out*. Garden City, 1924.

Hall, John Raymond, *Tomorrow's Route*. New York, 1932.

Lambert, A. B., *In Reply to Technocracy, a 100% Profit Tax*. St. Louis, 1933.

Lindley, Ernest Kidder, *The Roosevelt Revolution, First Phase*. New York, 1933.

Lippmann, Walter, "Is the Townsend Plan for Old-Age Revolving Pensions Sound?", in *The Congressional Digest*, XIV, 92-94.

Long, Huey Pierce, *My First Days in the White House*. Harrisburg, 1935.

MacDonald, William, *The Menace of Recovery*. New York, 1934.

Ogburn, William Fielding, ed., *Social Change and the New Deal*. Chicago, 1934.

Peterson, Frank, "Concerning the Townsend Plan," in *The New Republic*, LXXXI, 305-306.

Pritchett, Henry S., "The Old Age Pension as Related to American Life," in Carnegie Foundation for the Advancement of Teaching, *Annual Report, 1935*, 15-26.

Ryan, John Augustine, *A Better Economic Order*. New York, 1935.

——*Distributive Justice*. New York, 1916.

——*A Living Wage*. New York, 1906.

Samson, Leon, *The American Mind; A Study in Socio-Analysis*. New York, 1932.

Scott, Howard, *An Introduction to Technocracy*. New York, 1933.

Sinclair, Upton Beall, *The Way Out, What Lies Ahead for America*. New York, 1933.

Smith, Webster, *The Kingfish*. New York, 1933.

Strachey, John, *The Coming Struggle for Power*. New York, 1934.

Swing, Raymond G., "Dr. Townsend Solves It All," in *The Nation*, CXL, 268-270.

Swope, Gerard, *The Swope Plan: Details, Criticisms, Analysis*. New York, 1931.

Thomas, Norman Mattoon, *The Choice Before Us*. New York, 1934.

Tugwell, Rexford Guy, *Mr. Hoover's Economic Policy*. New York, 1932.

University of Chicago, "The Economic Meaning of the Townsend Plan" (Public Policy, *Pamphlet No. 20*). Chicago, 1936.

Wallace, Henry Agard, *New Frontiers*. New York, 1934.

XVI. Restoring the Nation's Morale

Beard, Charles Austin, *America Faces the Future*. Boston, 1932.

Fechner, Robert, *Report of the Director of Emergency Conser-*

vation Work, April 5, 1933-June 30, 1935. Washington, 1936.

Federal Emergency Relief Administration, *Report on Education Camps for Unemployed Women, 1934-1935*. Washington, 1936.

Holcombe, Arthur Norman, *The New Party Politics*. New York, 1933.

Hopkins, Harry L., United States Federal Emergency Relief Administration, *Monthly Reports, May, 1933-December, 1935*. Washington, 1936.

Ickes, Harold L., *Accomplishments of the Federal Emergency Administration of Public Works, July 8, 1933-May 18, 1936*. Washington, 1936.

Kelly, Fred J. and McNeely, John H., *Federal Student Aid Program* (United States Department of Interior, *Bulletin No. 14*, 1935). Washington, 1935.

Lindley, Ernest Kidder, *The Roosevelt Revolution, First Phase*. New York, 1933.

MacDonald, Austin Faulks, *Federal Aid, A Study of the American Subsidy System*. New York, 1928.

Oxley, Howard W., *Education in Civilian Conservation Corps Camps* (Civilian Conservation Corps). Washington, 1936.

Roosevelt, Franklin Delano, *On Our Way*. New York, 1934.

Schmeckebier, Laurence Frederick, *New Federal Organizations* (Brookings Institution). Washington, 1934.

United States Bureau of the Census, *Relief Expenditures by Governmental and Private Organizations*. Washington, 1932.

United States Superintendent of Documents, *Catalogue of the Public Documents of Congress and of All Departments of the Government, 1933-1935*.

Unofficial Observer, *The New Dealers*. New York, 1934.

XVII. An Experiment in Industrial Democracy

Adamic, Louis, *Dynamite*. Revised edition, New York, 1934.

Beard, Charles Austin, *The Future Comes*. New York, 1933.

Brown, Douglass Vincent and others, *The Economics of the Recovery Program.* New York, 1934.

Cahill, Marion Cotter, *Shorter Hours: A Study of the Movement Since the Civil War.* New York, 1932.

Daugherty, Carroll Roop, *Labor Under the NRA.* Boston, 1934.

Dearing, Charles Lee, *The ABC of the NRA.* Washington, 1934.

Gee, Wilson, *American Farm Policy.* New York, 1934.

Kirsh, Benjamin Sollow and Shapiro, Harold Roland, *The National Industrial Recovery Act.* New York, 1933.

Ogburn, William Fielding, ed., *Social Change and the New Deal.* Chicago, 1934.

Stein, Emanuel, *Labor and the New Deal.* New York, 1934.

Strachey, John, *The Coming Struggle for Power.* New York, 1934.

Terborgh, George Willard, *Price Control Devices in NRA Codes.* Washington, 1934.

Thomas, Norman Mattoon, *The Choice Before Us.* New York, 1934.

Valenstein, Lawrence and Weiss, E. B., *Business under the Recovery Act.* New York, 1933.

Wallace, Henry Agard, *America Must Choose.* New York, 1934.

—— *New Frontiers.* New York, 1934.

Whitney, Simon Newcomb, *Trade Associations and Industrial Control; A Critique of the NRA.* New York, 1934.

XVIII. Security as a Social Ideal

Burns, Eveline Mabel, *Toward Social Security.* New York, 1936.

Douglas, Paul Howard, *Social Security in the United States.* New York, 1936.

Epstein, Abraham, *The Challenge of the Aged.* New York, 1928.

Faÿ, Bernard, *Roosevelt and His America.* Boston, 1933.

Feldman, Herman, *Prohibition, Its Economic and Industrial Aspects.* New York, 1930.

Lief, Alfred, ed., *Dissenting Opinions of Mr. Justice Holmes.* New York, 1929.

—— *Social and Economic Views of Mr. Justice Brandeis.* New York, 1930.

Odum, Howard Washington and Willard, D. W., *Systems of Public Welfare.* Chapel Hill, 1925.

Schuman, Frederick Lewis, *American Policy Toward Russia since 1917.* New York, 1928.

Stevenson, Marietta and Spear, Ralph E., *The Social Security Program.* Chicago, 1936.

INDEX